MW00772914

TEACHINGS OF CHUANG TZU

ATTAINING

unlimited LIFE

TEACHINGS OF CHUANG TZU

ATTAINING
unlimited LIFE

HUA-CHING NI

TAO OF
WELLNESS
PRESS

Thanks and appreciation to Janet DeCourtney, Andrea
Giambrone, Liza Hughes, George Robinson and all others who
offered their time and effort to create this book.

Published by Tao of Wellness Press
An Imprint of SevenStar Communications
13315 Washington Blvd., Suite 200
Los Angeles, California 90066
www.taostar.com

Copyright © 1989 by Ni, Hua-Ching.
All rights reserved

First Printing: September 1989
Second Printing: July 2009

Library of Congress Catalog Card Number 88-63990
ISBN 0-937064-18-1
ISBN 978-0-937064-18-4

*Dedicated to those
who are aware of what the world
has become and where it should go,
and wish to live their own life
with the natural truth.*

CONTENTS

Preface ix

PART ONE: HOW THE WORLD HAS BECOME

PART TWO: WHERE THE WORLD SHOULD GO

PREFACE

Tao, generally interpreted as the wisdom of natural life, was a cultural achievement of ancient wise leaders and teachers around 2,500 years ago. Such people directed the current of their lives away from the values of mainstream society. By the end of the Chou Dynasty (1122-256 B.C.), competition had arisen between small rulers and princes. The virtuous models of leadership were weakened by this disturbing competitive ethic. Cultural leaders, such as Lao Tzu, Confucius, Mo Tzu and others attempted to rescue society from the new disorder. Each of them concentrated on a particular aspect of the ancient teaching, and through personal effort, promoted it with the intention of restoring a confused society to its natural and healthy condition. All of them had the same intention, but they wrote different prescriptions to cure the illness.

Four main schools of thought were formed.

(1) Lao Tzu presented the picture of society before the time of the Yellow Emperor, about 2,500 years earlier. This was his prescription to ease the sick person - the growing confused world.

(2) Confucius presented the picture of society from the reign of the Yellow Emperor until the early part of the Chou Dynasty. He focused on re-establishing the guidelines generated by the forefathers of the Chou Dynasty. His ambition was to revive the moral standard which was established by Yao and Shun in order to cure the moral disease of his time.

(3) Mo Tzu focused on refreshing the faith in an impersonal Heaven and presenting the virtue of universal love as his goal of life and his practical contribution in an attempt to cure the troubled world. He learned this from the Great Yu (2305-2197 B.C.), who was a selfless leader who had led his people in a fight against the big flood that lasted over a hundred years.

(4) Other minor scholars: Their efforts were to establish a method of clear thinking and communication

to help clarify the ideological confusion of all ordinary people. With this help, they hoped people might find the alternative to the unhealthy values of society. Unfortunately, they did not reach any positive conclusion or contribution, except offer some discussion.

Among all these leaders, no one denied the wisdom of the natural order of life and society. Thus, within a broader perspective, all points of view can be recognized as the voice of Tao responding to a new, accelerated world trend that is now beyond the control of any one person.

All the above mentioned schools of thought were established at that time, yet the world trend has not changed. The world has been like a person sick with malaria, sometimes better and sometimes worse. Yet attempts continue to be made by followers of these schools to save the world.

Chuang Tzu's position in relation to the teaching of Lao Tzu is like the relationship of Mencius to Confucius; Plato to Socrates; or Paul to Jesus. Without the work of Chuang Tzu, people of later generations would hardly be able to recognize the value of Lao Tzu's teaching in practical, everyday life; a teaching which touches the organic nature of human life more deeply and directly than that of all the other great teachers. I have worked in the west since 1976, and produced a number of works on the subject after examining existent translations of the Taoist classics. However, these translations represented a scholarly understanding of Taoist culture, and certainly they have had impact in the west, superficially or profoundly. I admire these translators who have both a very high level of skill and intellectual development, but there is a serious need for a deeper understanding of Taoist work, especially that of Chuang Tzu. Many visitors and students have expressed the wish that I might produce my own interpretation; particularly the work of Chuang Tzu, even though there are already a number of translations of Chuang Tzu in public libraries and bookstores. Given the advantage of my specific training, I have the responsibility from my spiritual and cultural tradition to respond to this demand. I felt I could not excuse my-self from the task of offering my interpretation.

For this reason, I have adopted the book of Chuang Tzu. It was written about 2,300 years ago; most scholars agree that he lived from approximately 369-286 B.C. In it is reflected Chuang Tzu's deepest thoughts and the greatest literature that Chinese history has to offer. I feel it has great significance to people today who wish to understand the nature of their life and improve it in a natural way. The social context of Chuang Tzu's time was quite different than it is today, so the psychological responses and orientation of the people may seem foreign at first. Chuang Tzu ex-presses his concern for a society that is developing un-naturally or, to use the term of later students of Tao, he is expressing his concern for the reversed current of the human spirit. Chuang Tzu's words do not always seem positive because he did not agree with the society he lived in. Like today's society, it deprives one of the natural right to the wholeness of human life. He real-ized that any artifice damages the wholeness of human nature. Thus he followed Lao Tzu and expanded Lao Tzu's teaching with his own spiritual depth.

Some people may think Chuang Tzu's teaching is anti-social and individualistic to an extreme. If, how-ever, you study his work carefully you can see that al-though he does sing an antisocial tune, he is not against an organic society. He simply disapproved of overly-ambitious and dominant leaders who wished to put society under their personal domain.

Ni, Hua-Ching
June, 1988

PART ONE

HOW THE WORLD HAS BECOME

CHAPTER ONE

WEBBED TOES

TWO TOES that are webbed together or the out-growth of a sixth finger may be a natural growth on the body, but they are unnecessary for completion of natural action. Warts or tumors may grow from the body, but they are an excessive growth of life. Men become attached to social customs, conventional habits, out-of-date manners, bad ideas, useless superstitions, empty rituals and harmful beliefs; whether this 'social luggage' is new or old, learned easily or with coercion or threat, it is enforced in people's lives. As it is applied and prac-ticed, the entire growth of the individual is neglected. This is antithetical to the true nature of Tao and its essence of the original virtue of life.

A person with two toes webbed together has only grown a useless bit of flesh. One with a sixth finger extending from his hand has grown a useless appendage. And he who imposes dogmatic ways and is overindul-gent in discipline and etiquette will become deluded and inflexible in the practice of social obligation. Not correct-ly developing an individual is like taking the flowers from a plant and cutting off its root. To abuse life is to empty it of its essence.

He who abuses his eyesight will be confused by life's many colors, deceived by patterns and designs, over-whelmed by hues of green and yellow, and distracted by embroidery and brocade. He will not achieve like Li Chu, who was noted for his exceptionally keen eyesight.

He who abuses his hearing will be confused by life's many notes, beguiled by the six tones, overwhelmed by the sounds of metal and stone, and distracted by strings and woodwinds. He will not reach the achievement of

Music Master K'uang, the famous musician who was keen in all musical tones and instruments.

He who is web-toed and six-fingered, filled with unnatural ideas and certain externally-imposed, superficial social obligations will destroy the wholeness of his healthy essence of life and stifle his inborn nature.

In order to gain recognition and support from their followers, leaders will erect false models riding on tall, beautiful horses in a parade, accompanied with pipes and drums, using pomp to misguide people into the service of their artificial, dogmatic ideals. What happens is that most people no longer have true models of what a virtuous, natural life should be.

He who is web-toed in his conceptual development will create intricate knots in his thoughts, with empty phrases that encourage the heart and mind to dwell on truthless political, social and religious ideology. He incites conflict by fostering a narrow vision, engendering jealousy and prejudice. He uses speech to madden people's minds. So we have ill-minded philosophers and social leaders full of extreme ideas.

All these people follow what is overly nice, web-toed, wide of the mark, sixth-fingered, not that which is true and right. The high truth never loses its naturalness, so its manifestations are not disorderly, nor its representations like the growth of extra toes. Its long manifestations it is not excessive, and, the short are not lacking. That it why it would cause misery to lengthen a duck's short legs and it would cause pain to shorten a crane's long legs. What is naturally long shall not be shortened; what is naturally short shall not be lengthened. There is no need to be distressed about the natural way of life.

The person with two webbed toes would moan if he tried to separate them; the person with a sixth finger would scream if he tried to remove it. In these two examples, one person has something extra and the other has something lacking, but they are identical in their concern over it. Presently, people of true spiritual awakening lift up weary eyes, worried over the ills of the world while the prejudiced tear their original, inborn nature to pieces because of their lust for power and

3 ATTAINING UNLIMITED LIFE

control. People have become confused by so many different dogmas, as if they were really part of man's true form. From the great time prior to the Three Dynasties[1] what a set-back dogmas and prejudiced people have caused in the world! If it is necessary to use a curve or plumb line, compass or square to make a plant grow or raise children, we undercut the inborn nature of the life we try to nurture. If we must use cords and knots, glue and paint to make a relationship or any agreement strong, we violate its natural virtue. So the distortions of social and religious ceremonies, promoted by smiles and beaming looks, soft or exciting words, phrases and speeches which are intended to guide people's hearts into accepting external control, in fact destroy their natural constancy.

In the world there must be constancy, naturalness and normalcy. When life is normal, things do not need to be made straight by using a plumb line, rounded by compasses, fastened by glue or decorated by paint. All things live and do not know how they are able to live. Simple and compliant, they get what they need and never know how they happen to receive it. All things achieve their goal, without knowing how. Nothing can injure this principle. However, when artificial social and religious institutions - those tangles and processions of glue and lacquer, ropes and lines - appear, how can the world reach truth and virtue? It cannot help but be confused!

A little confusion can change a person's sense of direction in life; confusion on a large scale can change or damage one's inborn nature. How do we find proof of this? Ever since the leaders of worldly religions began applying their spiritual cosmetics to life, people have plunged themselves into religious salvation or responded with the opposite extreme of excessive governmental control based on unnatural equality. Results have ranged from the fanatical to the demoralized. Ways that are not straight or correct alter or change inborn nature.

---

[1]Yao 2357-2258 B.C., Shun 2257-2208 B.C. and Yu 2207-1767 B.C.

From before the Three Dynasties down to the present, everyone in the world has altered his inborn nature for something external. The petty man will risk his life for wealth. The gentleman will risk it for fame and power. The high governmental official will risk it for political support. The leader will risk it for his personal ambition. These men all manage their concerns in different ways and are labeled differently with regard to fame, reputation, profit and power. But in altering their original nature and risking their lives for something external, they are all alike in their spiritual blindness.

The shepherd and the shepherdess were out herding their sheep, and both lost the flocks they were tending. Ask the shepherd what happened: well, he was reading stories. Ask the shepherdess what happened: well, she was playing cards. They managed their concerns differently, but equally suffered loss.

Po Yi, known as a model of righteous behavior[2], died to preserve his reputation at the base of Shou-yang mountain. Robber Chih died on top of Mt. Tung Ling for the sake of profit. The two died differently, but in sacrificing their lives and damaging their original nature, they were the same. Who can say that Po Yi was right and Robber Chih was wrong? When people do something that endangers their true nature it becomes even more difficult for later generations, who continue the struggle for profit and fame, reputation, power and control.

All people in the world risk their life for something external. If one risks it for political benefit and succeeds, then he is named a leader. If he risks it for profit and succeeds, then custom names him a rich and petty man. The risk is the same, and yet here we have a leader, there a petty man, each according to his success.

In sacrificing their lives and damaging their original nature, Robber Chih and the self-disciplining Po Yi were

---

[2]He relinquished his kingdom to his brother who he considered as having more ability than himself, and later choose to die of starvation rather than serve an emperor who had taken the throne in a way he did not approve.

the same. We can pick out the man of depth from the one of pettiness in such a case, but like most people, their personalities are confused.

He who applies himself to examining and experiencing the flavors of food may go so far as to become a famous chef, but I would not necessarily call him one of integral life. He who applies his nature to different musical tones may go as far with it as to become a master of music, but I would not recognize him as a man of nature. He who applies his nature to the range of color may go as far with it as to become an artist, but I would not recognize this as true natural growth.

Taking the senses as a gauge of the health of the subtle true nature, when I speak of good hearing, I mean simply attaining the natural capability itself. I do not mean the excitement of music or anything else. When I speak of good eyesight, I mean simply the wholeness of the eyes.

My definition of natural unfoldment has nothing to do with anything artificial in one's spiritual development; it means being a truthful person in regard to your true nature, that is all. My definition of a balanced nature has nothing to do with many flavors, with many notes or with many colors. It means simply following the true form of your inborn nature.

He who does not find or understand himself but accepts what others want for him, is only getting what other people have gotten for him and thus he fails to get what he already has. He finds his happiness in what comes to him from the exterior, not from life itself. Similarly, if his happiness comes from what brings happiness to others rather than from his own interests, then whether one is a Robber Chih, a typical negative person, or a Po Yi, a typical positive person, he becomes deluded or confused.

In respect for the Way and virtue of life, I do not try to raise myself up by accomplishing deeds measured by artificial religious standards, nor do I lower myself by following false or misleading practices.

CHAPTER TWO

HORSES' HOOFS

I

Horses' hoofs are good for crossing fields covered with frost or snow, their fur is made for protecting them from wind, cold and inclement weather. To eat grass, drink water from a creek and gallop freely is their true nature. Palatial dwellings, great terraces and fine halls are of no use to horses.

One day Poh Loh, a master of horsemanship, appeared and said, "I know how to take care of horses."

Then he branded and clipped them. He trimmed their hoofs and put halters on them. He tethered them and put them in stables, and it ended up that two or three out of every ten became wounded or died. Then he trained them by hunger and thirst, trotted, galloped and jumped them, groomed and trimmed them, binding them with bridles and conditioning them with knotted whips, until more than half were injured or dead.

The potter says, "I am skilled at making things from clay! To make it round, I use a compass; to square it, I use a T square!" The carpenter says, "I'm good at making things from wood! To make it round, I use a curve; to straighten, I use a plumb line."

As far as their inborn nature is concerned, clay and wood have no desire to be altered by a compass and square or a curve and plumb line, yet generation after generation praises horse trainers, potters and carpenters. What I am talking about is not just horses or clay or wood; these serve as examples of an unnatural approach to human life. The same error of unnaturalness is made by those who manage the affairs of the world.

People have certain natural instincts: they weave so they can clothe themselves, they plant so they can feed themselves. This is common to all humanity and is an endowment of Nature. Thus, at the time when natural instinct was followed, men moved quietly and their vision was steady. At that time, there were no roads in the mountains nor bridges over water. All things were developed, each for its own proper sphere or use. Birds and beasts flourished, and trees and shrubs thrived. The beasts were so tame one was safe to be near them; you could climb the trees and peep into the nests of ravens.

At that time man lived with birds and beasts, and all creation lived as one. There was no difference such as between good men and bad men. All were the same. All were equal; none had knowledge, so they did not stray from their natural virtue. All were equal; none had evil desires, so they lived in a state of natural integrity and harmony, in a state of perfection of human existence.

When the false teachings appeared, tripping people up with the teachings and binding them with standards, then doubt, prejudice and hostility found their way into the world. Then, with everyone excited over different teachings and fussing over different ceremonies, the unity of spirits became divided against itself.

If the natural integrity of things and life were left alone, then trees would not be cut down to be made into worshipping statues and sacrificial vessels. Pieces of beautiful stone would be kept unbroken, and not made into the decoration of courts or ornamental jewelry. If Tao, the virtue of natural wholeness, were not abandoned, the emphasis on fragmented benevolence such as giving alms and doing specific good deeds and fulfilling an extensive network of social obligation would not be needed. If man's natural spiritual wholeness and integrity were his abode, ceremonies for external worship would not be needed. There is no need for the establishment of different religions and extending their grouping to fit this narrow practice.

The different original colors are not confusing, but too much decoration is. The different notes are not confusing, but poor music is. Working on good, natural raw materials in order to produce objects to fit someone's idea of beauty is the crime of the artisan. Destroying Tao and its virtue in order to emphasize an incomplete teaching is the error of sages of incomplete development.

Horses live on land, eat grass and drink the water of creeks and streams. When they are content, they rub their necks together. When they are angry, they turn around and kick their heels at one another. That is as far as their natures carry them, but with bridles, bits in their mouths and a metal plate on their foreheads, they learn to cast mean looks, turn their heads to bite and resist in order to remove the bit. They are even made to join wars and the frightful slaughter of human people. Thus their natures become distorted and they learn to resemble perfect thieves.

In the times of naturalness, people did nothing in particular while resting and went nowhere special when they moved. When they had food, they rejoiced; having satisfied their hearts, they enjoyed their life. This was their capacity. But when false teachings appeared along with ceremonies and wild music, all with the intention of rectifying the form of government, then artificial charity and extensive social obligation were also dangled before the people to satisfy their hearts, and a taste for evil knowledge began to develop. At that time, people began to struggle for self-interest to the point where they could not be stopped. This was the fault of those sages of incomplete development.

The basic need to live a good life has stayed the same up to the new age. But the means of satisfying this need has become much too complicated. In reviewing the stage of ancient natural life, we must not be confused between natural life itself and the means of making a living. We should be clear about valuing life itself, without making life a slave to its means. The substance of life itself is not variable, the means of making a living is variable. However, people today have become limited by modern conveniences, technology and high speed transportation, thinking that those are more important than life itself; they forget that those things are to serve life. If we understand that to move in the correct direction of evolution is making the proper response to all challenges of life, then internals are as important as externals. With this understanding, can we say that ancient natural life is backwards and modern life forward? The balance between the two different perspectives should be found.

II

At the beginning of human society, people of strong mental ability found ways to improve their practical life. Others happily came to them for guidance, and they became leaders out of natural recognition and appreciation from others. This great time of human history in the Chinese region lasted until approximately 2,300 years B.C., when the great minds of the time responded to problems of a new kind: growing ambition and hostility between different states. Rulers strengthened their hold over the population by constantly sending people to war to fight for them. These dictatorial rulers had become lords by inheritance or military strength, and all other people were slaves. To other strong men, the only way to rise above slavery was to find a way to obtain the throne, putting oneself in the position of ruling over other people. The alternative to this dilemma was to live according to the philosophy expressed by Lao Tzu and Chuang Tzu.

By using the teaching of Yao, Shun and Yu, Confucius and Mencius worked hard with the intention of rebuilding a society in which the conscience of the people would equal that of the time of the Three Dynasties. Mo Tzu used the teachings and spiritual attainment of Yu in his attempt to guide the confused world back to the original great unity of the time before Yu. Lao Tzu and Chuang Tzu wished to extend the spiritual achievement of all the developed ones from the time before the Yellow Emperor to the present and renew the truth in each individual life. Later rulers did not make any new contributions to the world, and the fellowship between people by this time was no longer natural. These later rulers only added strength to social systems built on military force; theirs was the power to kill anyone they wanted.

Different generations of rulers misused Confucius' doctrine of social orderliness to demand obedience from the people. The followers of Lao Tzu and Chuang Tzu were uncooperative toward rulers, who were nothing other than the masters of slaves. Achieved ones avoid having anything to do with such unnatural government, except during times of confusion, when they come back into society to help restore the minimum normalcy. Then, as soon as their task is accomplished, the achieved ones leave again, because they know that people must be allowed to grow by themselves.

The old ruling force was mainly physical force. The new slavery is enforced by money; people bend themselves in every imaginable way for it. What is important and unfortunate, however, is that once a person has acquired the habit of slavery, he no longer continues to grow. Today's social system focuses on controlling rather than serving people, and slavery has become second nature to people. It is a sign of evolution that a person is not forced by violence to be a slave to money and can make the choice to live very simply instead. There are more choices today than in the past.

Question: Master Ni, I can't help saying that living according to the standards of Chinese society and family life is like slavery by western standards. No one here would tolerate the injustice and control imposed in oriental culture and family life. It would be unthinkable for an individual to allow a husband or wife, father or mother to control them or to ever respect their right to that control.

Master Ni: This does not reflect deep understanding. It comes from an insufficient observation about the Chinese family system which in the positive sense, is maintained by natural human virtue. There are duties and functions for each of its members. However, the life situation of human society as a whole is improved functionally by one's becoming aware of his slavery to the creations of culture, personal pride, spiritual ignorance, egotistical unreasonableness and so forth. One must engage in correcting one's own inner slavery to imbalanced emotions and conceptual formations.

I would like to describe to you the Chinese family system. It is a team of mutual support, offering each member reliability in difficult times, human affection and selfless love. Each member is dutiful in making his or her maximum contribution to the family as a small, natural community. The team spirit in the creation and improvement of life is of great value in a harmoniously cooperating Chinese Family. Surely it is very different than the standards of modern individual life which allow for the isolated struggling of each person. A good family life can make a contrast to the life of an isolated individual. If the family is open, each member is of great understanding to the others, all shortcomings of a big family can be mended, and at the same time, all shortcomings of any one individual are mended by the team effort. Because of my understanding, I also adopt individualism in my family life. Each member respects and accepts the differences of others, and everyone lives and works happily together. It is a joining force in creating the future of life.

I do not think it is correct that the daughters of American families who have just reached the early twenties and are not equipped with the slightest life experience should be chased out of the family to navigate their small boat in the vast ocean of life. To some young women, it may be appropriate; to others, it is cruel. As parents, you give birth to your young ones. Have you fulfilled your obligation completely? Have you given them sufficient education and equipped them with all important life knowledge that you wish them to have? I wish that all such families do not enslave their members, but give sufficient support from their group, whether young or old. If anybody stops growing, it means the death of the mind; then it is hard to get along.

However, in many aspects of modern individual life, you can find the influence of slavery, including religion, psychology, politics, economics - even in popular fashion. Traces of slavery exist in the customs of pierced ears and noses, foot-binding[3] which has evolved into today's high-heeled shoes, powdering and coloring the face, wearing

---

[3]This custom lasted close to 800 years in China.

bracelets, anklets, necklaces and neckties. These are <u>all</u> as much a sign of slavery as the brands on the back of cattle.

Modern fashion shows are a continuation of the practice of slave auctions, but the new lord and master is money. You may think that people of ancient tribes also painted their bodies, but that was for protection and had no connection with slavery. Once money became the ruling force of the world, a new slavery was established. The natural health and unity of mankind is no longer the uppermost consideration of the world. Thus life continues to go further astray and will go on that way unless a great awakening takes place. Then slavery, both functional and conceptual, will begin to diminish, and society will improve as true, natural human life appears once again.

Q: This true, natural life sounds like we are going to go back to 'days of old when maids were fair and knights were bold,' or else you're saying, subtly, that there is going to be such a disaster in the world that all this confusion is going to be destroyed and there will be another opportunity to live peaceful-ly for a while. This theme does not bear up under deep scrutiny, but it's a nice thought.

Master Ni: You have expressed the level at which you understand the world. It is a matter of different levels of understanding. The achieved ones view the world as an integral being, as one being. They view nature and the universe as an organic entity. They also view human society itself as an entire organic entity. Physiologically, they examined the sphere that people used to think of in terms of physics; i.e., considering the newborn, healthy body and its natural growth as their standard for per-fection in the world. They saw the troublesome world as something that had grown old and stiff and sick, its personality was sour and dry, its joints were fighting with its bones, its bones were fighting against its muscles, tendons and vessels, and its organs becoming disagreeable to one another. Thus it was that they taught Immortal Medicine for rejuvenation and restoration of infancy. This is the salvation offered by the ageless tradition of Tao. Deep scrutiny can be applied to all Taoist achievement by studying, learning and testing. If one studies, learns and proves for themselves all Taoist achievement, one will be able to deeply scrutinize the world and find the problem and the cure. Most importantly, the solution or the cure is not in the attainment of abstracted learning, but in continual development, which changes one's vision and stimulates true growth.

When people awaken from the personal psychology of slavery and improve their lives, the true joy of life will be regained. The new hope for a bright future of the human world will be found in the abolition of the old thought of enslaving religions and political systems that cause people to hold to a slave nature and in changing the social system now set up for war, control and enslaving people.

Q: Master Ni, this is so easy to say. Is there even one thing that could be done that would start to accomplish this? People do not give up their fixed ideas very easily. What can be done to soften their gray matter?

Master Ni: One should not be discouraged by the worldly situation. The healthy direction starts with each individual. The best thing that a person can do for the world is to work on his own internal harmony through self-cultivation. Sages of this tradition offer their teaching distinctly, but without forcefully demanding that people follow it.   The reality that you express is what has guided some to live in seclusion.   Someone always undauntedly voices a gentle and patient call for people to come back to natural health.   This has led to two kinds of spiritual attitudes.   One is to take care of personal individual life only and seek spiritual achievement for oneself alone.   The other reaches the bottom of spiritual truth: to take care of oneself spiritually is only part of the reality of spiritual undevelopment.   In this tradition, a student of Tao practices the principle of balance and offers what he or she can, without worrying about what he or she cannot do.

If an individual's understanding is not improved, they do not know what dish to order except for the poor fare to which they are accustomed.

Q: I really don't understand all this stuff about how perfect people used to be. I understand it but I just don't believe it. Life was simpler then and there were fewer people, so it was easy to live a simple life. Since the world is more complex now and there is no turning back, except through a disaster that would eliminate all human accomplishment, what is the point of idealizing the past? Also, why should we make people feel like they are the dregs of the evolutionary process? It always sounds like we are saying that mankind has gone backward instead of forward. I think the solution must be somewhere in the direction of the flow instead of backwards.

Master Ni: Spiritually, there is no real division into past, present and future. Time is what people make it. The past can be the future; the present can be the past, etc. Troubles can be reformed and reshaped. It is a matter of fact that physically people cannot go back. You must be stuck by the idea of the old, golden days. Since we have been born, we have not had any that might be called golden days; have you?

What Chuang Tzu pointed out is a spiritual direction for the human world. Spiritual unity is the cure for all kinds of modern conflicts. The real problem is that the spirit of people cannot keep flowing because they are stuck in their confusing conceptual creations. The example of the good old days is meant to teach people to flow without insisting on the untruthful ideology of any generation. In the practical example of everyday life, blindly following some dogma only aggravates the depth of the trouble. Only one who knows the process of coming back to his natural being can refresh and re-organize himself and thus continue to grow.

Chuang Tzu used natural organic human life as the foundation for his teaching. He was against anything that damages the naturalness of life. He supported the natural health and natural growth of an individual as well as the entire human society. He was against irresponsible and forceful establishment. Your appreciation of him will grow when you have studied and reached his deep understanding, his personal spiritual broadness and profundity. He has pointed out solutions to the same problems that all of us have experienced in modern times. He was kind enough to discuss how to handle an unnaturally developed life in the rest of his book. He has my great respect and appreciation. When you carefully examine the underlying fact of the troubles in your life, you will also appreciate what he has to say.

CHAPTER THREE

SAFEBREAKING

If a person wishes to guard against thieves breaking into safes, ransacking bags and breaking open trunks or chests, one must tie things with cords and ropes and make them secure with bolts and locks. This is what is called wisdom by the ordinary world. However, if a strong thief comes along and runs off with the trunk, the safe and the bag, the thief will only worry that the cords and ropes and bolts and locks are not fastened well enough. An excess of self-protection comes from short-sightedness; the man who earlier was considered wise was in fact only accumulating goods for the benefit of a thief.[4] Thus, what the ordinary world calls a wise man is, in fact, nothing other than one who is serviceable to strong thieves; and that which the world calls wisdom is nothing other than protection for strong thieves.

How do I know this? In ancient days, in the state of Ch'i, a man could see from one town to the neighboring town and hear the barking and crowing of its dogs and roosters. The land was rich and fertile and there were no wastelands. Within the boundaries of the district no shrine was dedicated, no village governed, no action taken that was not in accordance with the rules established by the sages. However, one morning T'ien Ch'eng murdered the prince of Ch'i and stole his state. But that was not the only thing he stole; along with the state, he stole the laws that the sages had devised with their wisdom. Thus, although T'ien Ch'eng gained the reputation of a thief, he lived as well as Yao or Shun.

---

[4]This prophecy was proven for most families in China during what was called the ten-year Cultural Revolution.

The smaller states dared not speak out against him; the larger ones dared not begin an attack, and for twelve generations his family ruled the state of Ch'i. Is this not an example of the laws of wisdom resulting in guarding the person of a thief?

This confirms what was already said: what the world esteems as great wisdom is only helpful to strong thieves, and what the world calls great knowledge is only protection for strong thieves.

There are more examples. Lung Feng, a minister under Emperor Chi[5], of the Tarng Dynasty was beheaded. Pi Kan, a prince under Emperor Jui[6] of the Shuan dynasty, was disemboweled. Chuang Hung Ch'i, a minister of Emperor Ling[7] of the Chou Dynasty, was torn to pieces. Tzu Hsu, a general of the State of Wu,[8] was left in a river after being killed. All four were worthy men but did not escape their demise. Each attempted to give good advice to their erring sovereigns, and each ended up being put to death or forced to commit suicide. All four were sages, but their wisdom could not preserve them from death. In fact, it only hastened their demise and wasted their lives.

An apprentice to Robber Chih asked him, "Is there any virtue in thieving?"

Chih replied, "It is impossible to speak of something in which there is no virtue. Making shrewd guesses as to how many valuables are in a room could be considered sagacity. Being the first one in could be considered bravery. Being the last one out could be considered heroism. Knowing whether the job can be pulled off could be considered wisdom; dividing up the loot fairly, benevolence. No one in the world ever succeeded

---

[5]1818-1767 B.C.

[6]1154-1121 B.C.

[7]585-544 B.C.

[8]ca. 522 B.C.

in becoming a great thief who did not have all five of these virtues!"

So we see that the doctrine of the sages is as important to Robber Chih as it is to good men. But good men are hard to find and bad men are numerous, so the benefit brought by the good men in the world is little, while evil abounds. So be plain and simple.

Hush the sages of incomplete development and let the robbers go on their way; only then will the empire be well ordered. When the stream ceases, the valley is empty; when the hill is levelled, the canyon becomes filled up. So when people of too many clever ideas are extinct, there will be no more thieves, and the world will be in peace.

Unless the people of too many clever ideas disappear, great thieves will never cease to appear. If you bring in more people of clever ideas in the hope of establishing order to the world, you will only be piling up more profits for Robber Chih. If you create cups and bushels for people to measure by, they will steal with bushels and cups. If you make scales and balances for people to weigh by, they will steal with scales and balances. If you produce marks and seals to insure trustworthiness, people will steal with marks and seals. If you teach benevolence and righteousness to reform people, these too can be used for stealing. How do I know this is true? One man steals a wallet and is condemned, while another steals a state and becomes a king. But charity and social obligation are necessary parts of ruling; does he not, then, steal charity, social obligation and the wisdom of the sages along with the state?

Men imitate the great thieves, try to obtain the rank of feudal lord and steal benevolence and righteousness along with the profits of cups and bushels, scales and balances, marks and seals. Though you try to avert them with rewards of official vehicles and high positions, you do not divert them. Though they are threatened with the executioner's ax, they cannot be deterred. Collecting profits for Robber Chih to the point where nothing can stop him is the fault of all the sages!

It is said: "Fish should not be taken from the deep waters; the weapons that guard a nation should not be shown to men." The sage is the weapon of the world, and thus should remain unknown to it.

Even if you do away with wisdom and knowledge, great robbers will not disappear! Even if you discard jade and destroy pearls, petty thieves will not cease to exist. It is only spiritual development that makes people stop destructive behavior.

It is not necessary to break up the six pitch pipes, destroy organs and flutes, and get rid of the masters of music, but this is one way people can purify themselves. Then, for the first time, they will be able to use their native hearing again.

It is not necessary to put an end to decoration, disperse the five categories of color and glue the eyes of the artist shut, but this is one way people can heighten their appreciation. Then, for the first time, they will be able to regain their natural sense of vision.

It is not necessary to destroy curves and plumb lines, throw away the compass and square, or shackle the fingers of the perfect artisan, but this is one way people can refine themselves. Then, for the first time, they will not overuse these devices to distort natural things.

Thus there is the saying, "Great or acquired skill in truth is clumsiness." The highest craftsmanship is natural simplicity.

Restraining the actions of Tseng (the example of filial love) and Shih (the example of loyalty), and stopping the mouths of Yang (a teacher of extreme individualism) and Mo (a teacher of the sages of his times), will not get rid of artificial charity and superficial social obligation unless people cultivate their own integral nature. With cultivation, for the first time, the virtue of the world will reach the state of the most profound leveling, a state in which there is a general perception not effected through any particular sense.

If each man keeps his own sense of sight to himself, the world will no longer be deluding. If each man keeps his own sense of hearing to himself, the world will no longer be wearying. If each man keeps his own wisdom to himself, the world will no longer be confusing. If each man keeps his own virtue to himself, the world will no longer go astray.

Have you ever heard about the Golden Age in China, the days of Yung Ch'eng, Ta T'ing, Poh Huang, Chung Yang, Li Lu, Hsien Yuan, He Hsu, Tsun Lu, Chu Yung, Fu Hsi, and Shen Nung? All of them were naturally recognized leaders of ancient society who had developed their spiritual integralness. At that time people used knotted cords for records and were satisfied with the food and clothing they had. They lived simple, peaceful and contented lives. Neighboring villages were within sight, and the sound of roosters and dogs could be heard from one village to the next. The people grew old and passed on without ever traveling beyond their own borders and interfering. At such a time, there was nothing but the most perfect order.

Today, however, people have reached the point where they crane their necks and become excited, saying, "Look at how much better it is over there! Let's all get ready and go to that place!" Artificial "holy lands" have been created for people to visit and, what is worse, to fight over. People neglect the holy land of their inner nature. So they throw together some provisions and hurry off, neglecting their sick parents at home, their growing children's discipline and the unaccomplished duties of their job. They travel in unbroken lines a thousand miles long through multiple territories with carts and carriages full of their things.

This is the evil effect of an exaggerated desire for excitement by our leaders. As long as men in leadership desire excitement and are without self-discipline, the world will be in great confusion.

We have developed the knowledge that enables men to create bows, crossbows, nets, stringed arrows and similar objects. With knowledge men are also able to fashion fishhooks, lures, dragnets, trawls and weirs and, along with these, pitfalls, snares, cages and traps. With floods of rhetoric they invent crafty schemes and malevolent slander, false spiritual knowledge and religious lies that bewilder the understanding of common men. So the world has become dulled and darkened by great confusion. The blame does not lie in knowledge itself, but in extending the application of knowledge in negative directions such as inventing powerful killing tools like nuclear bombs, rockets, death rays and chemical warfare, which are digging the grave of human nature and humankind.

All people know enough to seek out what they do not know, but no one knows enough to improve and control what is already known. All people know enough to condemn what he perceives as no good, but no one knows enough to condemn what he has already taken to be good, such as his own prejudicial beliefs and practices, narrow patriotism and partisanship, etc. It is through these things that brought about the great confusion, dulling the brightness of sun and moon, blocking the vigor of hills and streams, distorting the round of the four seasons. Now, there is no insect that flies and no creature that crawls that has not lost its inborn nature, so great is the confusion that has come from desire for all evil knowledge that is beyond and against life's nature.

From the Three Dynasties of Yao, Shun and Yu on down, it has been only pushing aside the pure and plain people and delighting in attractive, hustling flatterers, abandoning the clarity and calm of inaction and taking pleasure in mixed up, contradictory ideas. This has confused the world for a very long time.

CHAPTER FOUR

RESPECT THE NATURE OF THE WORLD

I

The ancient developed ones taught that the people of the world need to be free and to develop alone; to preserve and accept things rather than control them. The need is the same today: let the world be free to develop, or else its growth may be hindered. Leave the world alone in peace, or else it may shift from its natural state of normalcy. When the world is not hindered in its growth and is at peace, what is there to control?

When Yao governed the world[9], men delighted in their nature and were joyful and happy to be alive. There was no suppression over other people's organic impetus anywhere.

When the wicked King Chieh governed the world[10], he put it into anguish, and men found bitterness and anger in their lives. There was no contentment anywhere. To be without quietude, calmness or contentment is to impair the normal nature of life.

Are people too happy? Then they will damage their active, yang energy. Are people too angry? If so, they will damage their passive, yin energy. When yin and yang are awry, the four seasons are disarranged and the proper mixture of heat and cold is lacking. The reversal of what should be ordinary, normal things damage a man's organic being.

When men displace their center of gravity through jubilation or sorrow, they lose their emotional balance and are unsuccessful in thought and action. Almost all

---

[9] 2357-2258 B.C.

[10] 1818-1767 B.C.

people spoil themselves by pursuing the artificial "good life" in a way that damages their natural goodness and health. When the wild idea of surpassing others first came into the world, Robber Chih became the model of that way. So Tseng, a model son, and Shih, an excellent minister to his kingdom, were held up as examples of another way. The result of such competition was that the world was no longer able to demonstrate the authority before men to furnish adequate and timely rewards for good nor distribute adequate punishments for evil. Since this great world has not proven equal to the gross demands of men for reward and punishment, and since from the time of the Three Dynasties men have done nothing but struggle between the extremes of external rewards and public punishments, what possible peace can there be in which to adapt oneself to natural conditions and flourish?

Deriving too much pleasure from seeing - this brought about corruption in stimulation of the production of colors. Deriving too much pleasure from hearing - this brought about corruption in the excitement of the production of sounds. Deriving too much pleasure from religious conceptual teachings - this brought confusion to perfect, natural behavior. Deriving too much pleasure from duty - this perverted natural order and reason. Deriving too much pleasure from religious ritual and ceremony - this led to artificiality. Deriving too much pleasure from bad music - this only assisted a dissolution of vitality. Deriving too much pleasure from intellectual pursuit - this led to a burdened mind. Deriving too much pleasure from evil knowledge - this only produced more treacherous behavior.

As long as the world remains true to the normalcy or natural state of inborn nature, it makes no great difference whether these eight delights exist or not; they are not the central focus of one's life. If the world does not remain centered in its inborn nature, however, then these eight delights become warped, twisted, cluttered and unbalanced, and they are certain to bring confusion.

When world leaders do not beware of worldly trends, they join the populace in loving those things that carry a person away from the normal channel of life. Then the delusion of the world becomes very huge indeed! You cannot disregard the effect of these trends, thinking they are only a fancy that will pass in time. They greatly affect the normal state of humankind.

Once worldly leaders imposed false disciplines by establishing external laws and standards, it had the effect of devitalizing the blood and breath of people's nature. Nonetheless, there were still people who would not submit to their rule. Objectors were exiled and banished. No matter how hard the leaders tried, they could not make the whole world submit to their will.

By the time of the Three Dynasties, the world was in a state of great unrest. By and by, different schools of teachings arose; then came the delight and anger of rivals, deceit between the simple and cunning, recrimination between the virtuous and evil, and slander between the honest and dishonest. This multiplied until decadence pervaded the entire world. Men fell away from their original virtue; their natures became corrupt and there was a general rush for a new kind of untested learning.

There appeared axes and saws to reduce things, ink and plumb lines to devise them, mallets and gouges to pierce them. These were used for shaping things; the same concepts were applied for shaping the world. Thus the world, dazed and deluded, moved into great confusion. The wrong lay in meddling with human nature.

Then came coercion by all kinds of physical torture, bringing even greater confusion into the world, the blame for this lies in those who disturbed the natural goodness in the human heart.

As a result, wise and virtuous men took refuge in mountain caves, while the mild rulers of States stayed trembling in their palaces. The weak found refuge in the religions they created, while the tyrants enjoyed absolute power and authority over other people's lives.

In later times, victims of the death penalty were laid together, the criminals were put together, and the sufferers from unrighteous punishment were always within sight. Then came the religious leaders, waving their arms, striding into the very midst of those misfortunate men. It is preposterous that they should go this far and be so presumptuous, being without any sense of shame! Who can persuade me that the different artificial beliefs that are far from the natural spiritual truth are not, in fact, the lock that fastens the chains; that external religious standards are not in fact the lock of the prison doors? How do I know that the nice followers of these religions are not the tools of evil leaders? This is why I hold that one must break with the false sages and abandon artificial learning, so the world may enjoy good order in all its natural sublimeness.

In the face of worldly corruption, one of integral virtue is unavoidably summoned by the conscience of his moral nature, which is linked with the universal moral nature, to help his fellows. Nothing compares to promoting spiritual normalcy, the healthy growth which comes from spiritual centeredness and inaction; in keeping as it is with the natural course of harmonious events and which is exhibited through the natural life of a spiritually developed being. By means of inaction, one will be able to adapt to the natural conditions of completeness of life. Thus, one who respects the world as if it were his own life is suitable to support it, and one who loves the world as he does his own body is suitable to govern it.

If a person can keep from damaging his internal balance and from overusing his powers of the senses, remaining in utmost stillness while his dragon-force echoes around him in his life activities with profound silence, yet simultaneously with a voice like thunder, the spirit of his life will move towards Heaven, resting gentle and easy in inaction from the extra hustle and bustle of the world. Then all things of life will be brought to maturity and thrive naturally, without need for any artificial scheming and struggling. It is not hard to see: what necessity has such a one to set about managing other people's activity of confronting the world?

II

Ts'ui Chu asked Lao Tzu, "If the world is not to be governed externally, then how are people's minds and hearts to be kept moderate?"

"Be cautious," replied Lao Tzu, "and do not interfere with the natural virtue of the mind and heart of people. A person's mind and heart may be either repressed or agitated. Either way may be fatal for the mind and heart.

"With gentleness, the hardest mind and heart may be softened, but where there is rigidity and harshness it can become as hot as a scorching fire or as bitterly cold as solid ice. When eager to do something, its speed is such that in the time it takes to raise and lower one's head, it can twice pass over the face of the earth. When inactive, it is as calm as a quiet pool. When active, it is boundless and creative. The human mind and heart, once moved, cannot be stopped!"

III

Long ago, a developed teacher asked Yao, "As a man of authority, how do you use your mind?"

"I have sympathy for the defenseless," replied Yao. "I help the poor. I grieve for those who die and comfort the widows. I have compassion for the orphans. Beyond this, nothing."

"That is good!" cried the teacher, "but it is not yet of greatness."

"In that case, what should I do?" inquired Yao.

"Be receptive" said the teacher, "like the virtue of the universe. The sun and moon shine; the four seasons change; day and night interchange; clouds come and rain falls. All follow what is nature."

"Oh my!" cried Yao, "what disarray I have been causing. You move in harmony with nature; I move in harmony with man."

It was in nature that the ancients found their greatness. The Yellow Emperor, Yao and the developed teachers are unified in their respect and exaltation of it. So how did the ancients care for the world? By acting like all of nature.

IV

When Yao ruled, Po-ch'eng Tzu-kao was an important person in the government, but after Yao ceded the throne to Shun and Shun ceded it to Yu, Po-ch'eng Tzu-kao relinquished his title and became a farmer. Yu went to see him where he was working in the fields. Yu walked over in a humble manner, stopped in front of him, and said, "When Yao was ruling, you held an important position in his government, but when Yao gave the throne to Shun and Shun to me, you relinquished your title and took up farming instead. I would like, sir, to ask you why."

Tzu-kao said, "When Yao ruled the world, he did not reward and yet people worked hard. He did not punish and yet people were cautious. I enjoyed giving my support. Now you reward and punish people, and their nature has changed. Virtue has begun to decay; penalties have begun to dominate. People will need to live up to the push of political pressure. Future generations will inherit the disorder started here. So please go on your way. Do not interrupt my honest labor any more!"

He turned and continued with his farm work, never looking back.[11]

Q: If intellectual knowledge leads to mental complication, why write books?

Master Ni: Once intellectual knowledge is developed, an individual's intellectual centeredness dominates in all matters, and their spiritual sensitivity to universal life shrinks to nothing. Pure spiritual knowledge does not teach you to add something to your natural life; it aims to take something away from your squeezing intellectual head. This book and the Tradition of Tao do not teach intellectual knowledge. They teach the wisdom of a natural life.

Q: I like this whole chapter except it leaves me feeling that

---

[11]It was not a fact that Yu's government was unvirtuous, but this description was an expression of the time of Chuang Tzu, when governmental interference first began and the normalcy of natural life started to erode.

even a virtuous government produces corrupt people and eventually fails.

Master Ni: It is the worst thing for a government to make people rely on it to be good.

Q: Why are we concerned about whether there is a good or bad government since even with a natural government people still degenerate and corruption still happens?

Master Ni: We purposely learn different kinds of government to learn how to govern our own life.

Q: When Tzu-kao says, "When Yao ruled the world, he handed out no rewards, and yet the people worked hard," does he mean they were not paid a salary, or that all government people were also farmers?

Master Ni: It is unnatural for a government to make people rely on it to be rewarded or punished. Tzu-kao is not talking about people's jobs. He is talking about crime and punishment, good deeds and artificial rewards.

CHAPTER FIVE

LET THE WORLD MOVE
IN ITS NATURAL WAY

"The sky turns and the earth follows. The sun and moon pursue one another. What brings this about? Who arranges this? Who has enough energy to make these movements continue?

"Do clouds cause rain or does rain cause clouds? Whose kind generosity or whose unkind mischief is this? Who has enough energy to bring about such a thing?

"A chilly wind comes from the north. First it blows east, then west; at times it spins about. Who exhales it outward? Who has suficient energy to send it this way or that?

"I would like to know the cause of all this. Is it a mechanical arrangement which makes these bodies move as they do? Or do they revolve without being able to stop, by mutual attraction and resistance?" asked the ancient students who were in quest of an answer.

The spiritual man, Han Chao, said, "Come sit down and I will explain it to you.

"Physical nature has knowable limits and formality to its movements. The developed one goes deeply from the mechanical surface into the subtle sphere of the universe.

"The mystic diagrams which were revealed to Fu Hsi and Yu by the high spiritual realm of the universe are the greatest guidance for all generations of human life.

"Nature unfolds itself in ⸻ and ⸻ ⸻ , and continues further into ⚏, ⚍ , ⚎ and ⚌ . They represent the strong and the less strong; the heavy and the less heavy.

"Then nature unfolds further into three phases of the yang category of ☰ (☱ , ☲ and ☳ , strong, middle and lesser in yang); and three phases of the yin category of ☰ ☰ (☰☰ , ☰☰ and ☰☰). These are the six fundamentals of nature which express themselves. These natural energies can positively be symbolized by metal, wood, fire, water and earth. These natural energies correspondingly express themselves in human nature as kindness, righteousness, humility, wisdom and faithfulness, which in turn produce longevity, richness, health, virtue, a peaceful life and a natural death. In contrast to the positive expressions of nature in human life are the negative expressions of sickness, worry, poverty, viciousness, weakness and an early death.

"Not even an excellent leader can unify the good nature within a person or between people; but an individual can work on his or her own spiritual development to move in a positive direction and form positive family and human relationships. Any individual can more fully develop their innately positive endowment by improving their personal intelligence and wisdom, thus reducing the self-trap of negativity in their life.

"There are some beings who cannot be reformed because of their rigid or negative relationship to the natural physical sphere. The way of nature is that beings who are less entrapped have more chance for self-change. Solidification, even in such non-physical areas as thought or conceptual matters, is hard to correct. To be spiritual is to be flexible and attain the potency of self-government. Freedom cannot be attained through a rigid arrangement of the world.

"In attending to one's affairs, one should not become trapped by physical appearances. That which is below the surface, the subtle essence, is the root of the universe. It precedes all forms. Essence precedes; form follows and contains. In human behavior, a good leader moves to attend to the essential. A good student works to attain the essential. An achieved sage embraces the essential."

Wise leaders, rather than rule by rigid laws and punishment, stay in harmony with the nature of the subtle law; thus they can manage the changes of the world and guide people to cultivate and develop themselves spiritually.

From ancient times to today, there have been three kinds of leaders in the world. The highest level of leader attains their own spiritual development before they attend to leadership of the world. Secondary leaders constantly develop themselves spiritually while attending to the work of leadership, because they understand the importance of focusing themselves spiritually. The lowest kind of leader knows nothing about spiritual development. He may be as strong as a lion or a wolf but attains his position by fighting for it, and his solution to the world's problems is war. He is a student of fighting and knows nothing besides fighting. World crises are the inevitable result of this kind of leadership.

From ancient times to today, there have been three kinds of people in the world. The highest kind of people choose the highest level of leader and give him their complete support. Secondary people accept secondary leaders and give them as much support as they can. The third level of people follow the lowest leaders, and the amount of support they give depends on how much pressure the leader puts on them and the world.

The highest level of people choose to follow the highest level leaders; further, they can cooperate with the second level ones and offer to educate the third level.

The second level of people cooperate with the highest level leader, support the second level ones and escape the third level ones.

The third level people cannot even recognize a first-rate leader or cooperate with a secondary one. They can only surrender to the third level, making it their game and becoming a victim of it.

All people should learn the natural truth and live their lives in accordance with it. Leadership and government should function only as the agents of nature. Spiritual direction should be the voice of nature. Then the positive side of people could be released instead of the negative, which creates tension and pressure through bondage to cultural, ideological and religious traps.

"Trivia, the veneer of custom, is a secondary expression of what is essential; it follows the movement of pure spirit in various events. The building of armed forces and various weapons are the trivia of worldly peace. Reward and punishment, benefit and loss, and different penalties are the trivia of government. Rituals and laws, weights and measures, and careful comparison of forms and names are the trivia of public instruction. Bells and drums, ornamental feathers and tassels used to increase the effect of a ceremony are the trivia of making music. The wise ones of ancient times studied trivia, but did not allow trivia to precede essentials.

"The essence of harmony cannot be expressed by the form of a rigid social order such as the leader precedes, the minister follows; the father precedes, the son follows; the older brother precedes, the younger brother follows; the senior precedes, the junior follows; the man precedes, the woman follows; the husband precedes, the wife follows. The true leadership is in subtle change all the time without the need of form or recognition. Yes, one preceding and one following are part of the movement of nature, and from them the sage obtains his understanding. Yet, one superior and one inferior is the artifice of man. In the physical sphere, Heaven is Heaven and Earth is Earth. Which is first and which is second cannot be rigidly decided by human conceptual creation. In the universal nature, the unformed is the first, the formed is the second, yet the formed would again be shaped by the unformed. So which is the first and which is the second? In nature, autumn and winter follow spring and summer. Do spring and summer not also follow autumn and winter? Is there any need for competition? All things change and grow. Their roots, stems and buds, each with its own special form, grow and decay in a constant flow of transformation.

In the ancestral temple, parents take precedence; in government, the most important position takes precedence; in the community, the elders; in matters to be accomplished, the most capable and responsible. Such the order originates from nature. If a person considers themselves part of nature yet disregards the subtle essence of order, thereby disregards Tao. In disregarding Tao, where can he hope to find it?"

CHAPTER SIX

APPLY NO INTERFERENCE

I

A Natural Government

King Wen was sightseeing at Tsang when he noticed an old man fishing.[12] The King watched the man for a while, and he noticed that the old man's fishing wasn't exactly fishing. He did not fish as though he were fishing for something, but as though he continually fished for his own practice of spiritual composure. King Wen immediately knew that this was the person he needed to help rule his kingdom, because he could do it according to natural wisdom. Thus the King wanted to summon him and give the highest administrative position of the government to the old man to hold the reins. He feared, however, that the high officials and his relatives would object. He almost abandoned the idea, but the king did not want to deprive his subjects of such a Heaven-sent leader.

Early the next day, therefore, he mentioned to his ministers, "Last night I dreamt I saw a fine bearded man with a dark complexion mounted on a white horse that had red hoofs on one side. He instructed me, 'Present your throne to the old fisherman of Tsang, then the people may perhaps be cured!'"

The ministers, in awe, said, "That was obviously a description of the King, your late father!"

"Then let us divine to see what is the best thing to do," said King Wen.

"Your Majesty must have no second thoughts," the ministers insisted. "It was clearly the instruction of

---

[12]King Wen, who lived ca. 1191-1222 B.C., is honored as the founder of the Chou Dynasty, 1122-256 B.C. He was one of the ancient sages most often and extravagantly praised by Confucius and his followers.

your late father. We find no need for divination."

So the King had the old man of Tsang escorted to the capital and handed the government over to him. The rules and regulations remained unchanged, and no special commands were issued.

After three years had passed, King Wen went to inspect the state. He found that the local officials had not accomplished anything extraordinary, all dangerous organizations had dissolved themselves and grain was measured using local measure only. The heads of government offices had not accomplished anything extraordinary because they looked on all tasks as equal. There were no dangerous organizations because unity had arisen. Persons entering from other states no longer brought their own measuring cups with them because the feudal lords now trusted local measures.

King Wen thereupon knew that the man was a great teacher and, facing north out of respect, asked him, "Could the methods of government that you use be expanded to include the whole world?" The fisherman from Tsang made no reply and excused himself. To avoid the command he expected to be issued the following morning, he fled during the night and was never heard from again.

Yen Yuan asked Confucius about this story, saying, "King Wen didn't amount to very much if he had to resort to using a dream."

"That is not important," said Confucius. "King Wen had perfected himself; we must not complain about such a small thing! That dream was just a way of getting out of the moment's difficulty."

People listen to dreams more than a rational decision. Both wise and unwise leaders do it. The wise ones fulfill their good dreams. The unwise ones create nightmares and allure their naive followers with dreams which seem too good to refuse.

II
A Developed One

During a visit with Chi Ch'e, Chiang Lu-Mien (a scholar) remarked, "When the Prince of Lu requested my advice, I declined by telling him I had none to offer. But he wouldn't let me go without speaking, and so I had no choice. I don't know whether I was right or not; what I told him was, 'You must be courteous and moderate with others! Promote the people who have the spirit of public service, and do not allow flattery or partiality. Then who among your people will not venture to support you?'

With a laugh, Chi Ch'e said, "As far as emperors and kings are concerned, your advice is right. But as for the virtue and spirit of a great leader of natural wisdom, what you said is like a praying mantis waving its arms in front of an approaching carriage, trying to stop it. It isn't fit advice for a great natural leader. Not only that, but if he conducted himself that way, he would put himself in a precarious position. His palace would be crushed by pressure from all directions."

"If this was indeed foolish advice," Chiang Lu-Mien pursued, "it would please me to receive your instruction about a great leader."

Chi Ch'e replied, "When a great leader of natural wisdom is in the world, he inspires people to educate and develop themselves. With self-education, all improper customs and modes are corrected. Benevolent thoughts multiply and destructive thoughts die out. This is natural, and once things have improved, people do not remember the old way any more. They do not need to look up to a Yao or a Shun, or any external standard, for in doing so they would be diverted from their own integral nature. If you wish to become one with Teh, which is the virtue of your own spiritual nature, you must loosen the grip of your overly active mind which constantly looks for new creations and merits."

III
The Building Of Natural Leadership

Pei-kung Sh'e, a minister of Hwe, was assigned to collect money and labor in order to make a set of bells. He built a platform outside the gate of the territory wall, and in three months the bells were completed,

eight in each of the upper and lower tiers.   Prince
Ch'ing-chi, observing this accomplishment, asked,
"What is your secret in building such a magnificent set
of bells in so short a period of time?"

Pei-kung Sh'e replied, "The assignment was accomplished not by pushing any one or creating any special
tensions.   The power of spiritual unity can accomplish
anything truly valuable and lasting in the world.   In
the midst of unity, what way is more feasible than to
follow nature?   Carving and polishing damages the
original nature of things, then the true value and the
true need of this work is not appreciated.   Thus, when
I took the assignment, I used my spirit to guide my
mind.   Dull, I had no need of special understanding;
calm, I remained myself without attracting attention.   I
bid farewell to whatever went by and ignored the
importance of the work.   I greeted whoever or whatever came and gave help: what comes cannot be denied and what goes cannot be kept.   I drifted with
whatever came in concordance with it, letting each
come to its own end.   Thus I gathered the strength of
the people without imposing upon them.   This is the
way of building the bell towers!"   Prince Ching-chi was
suddenly enlightened by this.   He said, "It is the way
of building true and serviceable leadership.   Is there
any better way than following nature?   What more can
be achieved than the fellowship of the great truth that
you have demonstrated?

"In following Tao, the great truth of universal life, I
wish I could set my spirit and mind in the domain of
Oneness where there is no need for managing the
events of life."

Pei-Kung Sh'e replied, "This is how I was taught to
govern my personal life."

This is to say, all leadership and government
should be natural, not coercive.   To build a good and
true leadership is similar to making this bell tower.

This story gives the model for spiritual practice for
students of later generations.   It is given to instruct the
young ones to sit like a bell, to stand straight like a
pine, to sleep like a bow on its side and to move like a

dragon. In later times in the Taoist or the Shaolin traditions, meditation and chi gong practices were designed as a result of this teaching. The style of Building the Bronze Bell is still a popular and enhancing practice and one used for effective healing in Chi Gong. The bell posture is still performed in the south of my home province Chekiang because of its unifying power.

IV
Nature is One Life

The sea lion, a flipper-legged creature, envies the centipede who has so many legs and a lively walk. The centipede envies the snake which moves smoothly without feet. The snake envies the wind which has no body but moves quickly and with great freedom. The wind envies the eye which travels without even going anywhere. The eye envies the mind who can understand the entirety of the universe.

The sea lion said to the centipede, "I waddle around on my two flippers, but rather clumsily. How are you able to concentrate on coordinating all the legs you have?"

"It is not really a matter of coordinating them," answered the centipede. "Have you ever seen a man spit? The spit falls in globules, some drops as big as hail, some fine as mist, showering down in numerous droplets. So it is with my legs; they work without my having to think about them."

The centipede asked the snake, "With all my legs I could never move as quickly as you, who has none. How do you do it?"

"One's natural condition is not changeable," replied the snake. "I have no need for legs."

The snake commented to the wind, "I can slide along, but you who are formless come gusting down from the North Sea. Then just as quickly you rush away to the South Sea. By what means do you accomplish that?"

"I can do those things," said the wind, "but anybody who can wave at me or kick at me is greater than I; I cannot accomplish that.   However, I am the only one with enough force to snap tall trees in two or blow down large houses.   An accumulation of small failures can grow to become a great achievement.   Only a sage can similarly achieve a great victory."

Is there anyone who can understand the subtler force that moves through all life and the entire nature of the universe?

V
Relying on Big Government and Strong Troops

Men Wu Kuei and Ch'ih Chang Man Chi were observing King Wu's troops.

"King Wu is not equal to the great emperors of the past," remarked Ch'ih Chang Man Chi.   "This is why we are plagued by so many problems."

"When the world was being governed properly, was there any need for troops to keep peace by the force of their presence?" questioned Men Wu Kuei.   "Or did disorder begin first and then after that we proceeded to build such a big army and strong government?"

"If the world was being governed properly," said the other, "what would there have been for a great leader to do?   Now, the actions of the leaders are like putting ointment on a sore.   Generally, only bald men use wigs and only sick people go to see doctors.   A sage would be embarrassed to see a filial son anxiously obtaining medicine to cure his loving parent, because before filial love can be expressed, there must have been some trouble caused.

"In an age of normalcy and wholeness, the skilled and able are not honored and the talented are not employed, because there is no special problem requiring them to show their talent in solving problems. Rulers are like the highest limbs of a tree, and the people are like the deer in the meadows.   Trees do not interfere with the deer who enjoy the peaceful grasses below.   At such a time, people do what is correct without calling it righteousness.   They care for one another without calling it benevolence.   They are sincere and faithful without calling it loyalty.   They are reliable without calling it trust. They do things for one another, but never call it kindness. Thus, they move without leaving any trace and act without leaving any memory of their deeds, because nothing abnormal is happening to them.

"In an age of abnormalcy and confusion, everything is disordered. The mental life of later generations has separated and become split from the wholeness of healthy, normal life. In times of normalcy, does the world need soldiers, generals, troops or weapons? These all express the reality of a world losing its normal sense of unity and organic health. Religions cause people to get sick; this is easily overlooked. Religions are also the doctors and medicine for people who suffer from unnatural physical, mental and spiritual aberrations of our society, while the Great Path teaches one to maintain normal and natural development in their life. A person only needs special support during times of external difficulty; then whatever will work for a short while is taken inside oneself, but that short--term remedy is not the truth of a natural life. Undeveloped people value and respect extraordinary situations, while spiritually developed ones watch and value what is ordinary and natural to life."

Q: So what about normalcy. We live in a world of basic necessities which seems unlikely to change; even the Union of Tao and Man has big financial considerations. Are the teachings of Tao different at this time? Is the Taoist model out of date? What is a practical application for modern times? This model creates dissatisfaction with working and living in modern conditions. If it is at first a normal situation and then becomes abnormal, won't it become normal again by reversing the way it became abnormal? And if the desire for conceptual knowledge is part of what creates an abnormal state, then how can teaching create wholeness and health?

Master Ni: An abnormal life reflects the confused and fragmented vision of the world that leads to a disorganized and disoriented response to life. The state of normalcy is an internal achievement that keeps one centered and whole without being squeezed, twisted or fragmented by momentary situations or changes of the external world.   For example, suppose you have been cheated by someone.   Did it cause you to decide to alter your honest attitudes and sincere nature and learn from the one who has cheated you?   In the end, it would bring about an abnormal change in you.

CHAPTER SEVEN

THE NATURE
OF HUMAN RELATIONSHIPS

I
Natural Harmony

A good son or daughter does not disrespect his or her parents. The parents teach their sons and daughters to be upright and to act accordingly when they are young and they continue to give them advice when they are grown up. A good advisor always describes what he or she sees, while a bad one makes decisions. A loyal administrator does not flatter his lord or the King. This is the essence of loyalty and good work, and by following these precepts, they become the finest of sons, daughters, parents and administrators.

To agree with what is unrightful that a parent or someone in a high position says and to praise what is unjust that a parent or leader does is defined as disloyal action. Most people are apparently unaware that such action would cause the parent or the leader to lose clarity. One who agrees with the extremes of worldly fashion and praises whatever radical action this fashion takes is called a cajoler or spiritual degenerate.

If you call a man a cajoler, he will not like it. If you call him a flatterer, he will be provoked. Yet he is forever both. All such falsity is what the world prefers and, consequently, people do not discourage each other from doing what is not helpful to others, because they do it themselves. For a man to arrange his clothes or change his expression to get into the good graces of the world and yet not consider himself a flatterer, to identify himself in every way with what his friends say and yet not consider himself to be one of them is the height of foolishness.

A person who is aware that he is a fool is not the biggest fool. A person who is aware he is confused is

not the most confused.   The man in the worst confusion will not even be aware of his state of being
when he dies; the woman who is the biggest fool will
not have seen the light of wisdom when she dies.

If three men are traveling and one of them is bewildered, they may still arrive at their destination
because the bewilderment is in the minority.   But if
two of them are bewildered, they will probably become
lost because the bewilderment is in the majority.
Today it seems as though everyone is bewildered;
where can I find direction?   I must keep looking until I
find it and then follow that direction to the best of my
ability.

Most people cannot hear the wise song of the sage;
but when they listen to the popular songs born from
emotional restlessness and disturbance, they are happy,
thinking that they are hearing something good.   In the
same way, the greatest truths are not remembered or
put into practice.   The popular speech that you hear on
television is what attracts most people; as a result they
never listen to speech in its highest and most inspiring
form.   For example, the chaotic sound of two loud,
out-of-tune electric guitars will drown the sound of the
sweetest flute; and the result will be neither melodious
nor harmonious.

Now, since the whole world is bewildered, even
though I know the true path, how can I lead?   If I
know that I cannot accomplish this goal yet try to force
it to happen, this would be but another source of error
and confusion in the world.   Perhaps it would be best
to leave things alone.   However, if I do not work to
help the world, who will?

II
Limitless Natural Virtue

Tang, a high governmental official from the state of
Sung, asked Chuang Tzu to talk about benevolence,
which is also known as kindness.   Chuang Tzu said,
"Tigers and wolves are benevolent."

"How can that be?" questioned Tang.

"The natural love that exists between parents and

their young, like that between the sire and cubs," replied Chuang Tzu, "is that not benevolence?"

"I would like to know about perfect benevolence in people," Tang requested.

"Perfect benevolence," said Chuang Tzu, "does not contain or limit itself to love for the individual; it embraces all people equally."

"Without love for individual people," replied Tang, "it seems to me there would be no fondness or attachment; without attachment there would be no filial piety[13]. Do you mean that perfect benevolence is unfilial?"

"No," replied Chuang Tzu. "Perfect benevolence is much more expansive. Limited words like filial piety cannot describe it. What you are talking about is not only something greater than filial piety; there is no comparison, because the two are scarcely related. If a person is traveling to the south and turns back to look north when he reaches the city of Ying, he will no longer see the mountains in the north. Why? Because they are too far away.

It has been said that it is easy to be filial from one's respect; to be filial out of true love and true affection is harder. To be filial out of true love is easy; to extend this true filial love without one's parents being conscious of it is harder. To extend filial love without one's parents being conscious of it is easy; to forget all concerns about your parents is harder. To forget all concerns about the world is easy; to cause the world to be unconscious of your influence upon it is harder; this is perfect benevolence, because it operates without letting its operations become known.

"True virtue does not do anything; Yao and Shun, both great leaders and teachers, could not come close to its ideal. The influence of great virtue extends for generations, but no one is even aware of its existence. So why do you want to limit yourself to talking only about benevolence and filial piety?

---

[13]Filial piety is the love of sons and daughters for their parents.

"Filial piety, love between brothers, charity, social obligation, loyalty, truth, trust, chastity and honesty are all learned and studied; they are designed to help a person develop their virtue. However, they are inadequate when one wishes to embody the deep truth. It is said, 'Perfect honor includes both the acceptance and abandonment of all the honor a country can give. Perfect wealth includes both the acceptance and abandonment of all the wealth a country can give. Perfect happiness includes both the acceptance and abandonment of all the reputation one can desire.' The one who lives these principles embraces the constancy of truth without giving himself to external changes."

III
The Way of Man and the Way of Heaven

Those individuals who see what can be seen are perfect according to the way of man. Those individuals who see what cannot be seen are perfect according to the way of Heaven.

What is commonplace and yet must be utilized are created objects. What is unassuming and yet must be relied upon are people. What is irksome and unpredictable and yet must be attended to are our affairs and business. What are vague, unthoughtful and inconvenient but yet must be proclaimed are the laws and regulations of a place. What would seem necessary only for relationships with strangers and yet must be observed with those close to us is proper behavior. What seems to apply only to close relationships and yet must be broadened to include all people is kindness and benevolence. What seems confining and yet can be helpful when we understand its purpose is ritual. What is central and important to our lives and yet must be relearned by us is natural living or virtue. What is ever present and yet must be readapted is Tao. What is unformed and yet requires actualization is heaven.

Therefore, the true one of integral wisdom looks up to nature, but does not offer assistance. He perfects himself and his virtue, but does not become involved.

He guides himself in accordance with Tao, holding to no plans. He identifies himself with benevolence, but neither relies upon it nor makes it overly important. He attends to social obligations, but does not overdo it. He responds to the demands of ritual and does not neglect it. He takes care of important affairs and does not neglect them nor make excuses. He brings order to all with regulations and allows no confusion about what is right in the minds of people. He relies upon people and does not belittle them. He uses things and does not neglect or abuse them. Most things are hardly worth using, yet use them we must.

One without a clear understanding of the nature of Heaven will not be able to maintain himself as pure and virtuous. He who has not mastered the Integral Way will find himself without any means of access. He who does not clearly understand the Integral Way has more learning to do! Alas for the one who does not reach it.

What is the Integral Way? It is Tao. Heaven is the way of inaction and compliance; action and entanglement are the way of man. The way of Heaven is essential and central; the way of man is through calculation. The distance which separates the two is great indeed. Reflect on this wisdom and try to understand what it means.

Q: Does compliance mean accepting things as they are? Does inaction mean non-egotistical action?

Master Ni: There are different ways to express the reality. Inaction means to remain in non-impulsiveness, to quiet down one's emotion in order to unite with the universal spiritual unity. Emotionally, it is self-dissolving. Spiritually, it is to root one's deep self with the universal self. It is the way of Heaven. There should be no action extended to create entanglement due to one's own spiritual limitations.

CHAPTER EIGHT

SUBJECTIVITY MEETS OBJECTIVITY

I
Small and Great Understanding

A man named Sun Hsiu went to visit Master Pien Ch'ing-Tzu and complained to him, "In my village no one has ever called me negligent, and even when times were hard no one ever said I lacked courage. But when I worked tilling the fields, it was never a very good year for crops, and when I served in a governmental position, it was never a good year for promotions. I have committed no crime against Heaven or anyone, but I have been exiled from the village. Why did such a fate happen to me?"

Master Pien replied, "Have you heard about how the Perfect Man, one of Integral Truth, lives his life? He forgets his internal organs and disregards what is audible and visible. As though in a trance, he lives beyond the dust and dirt of this world. Without a sense of direction, he wanders about; his job is tending to nothing. This is what is called, 'Action with inaction; growing something, but not supervising or controlling it.' Today most people value knowledge that demonstrates their superiority over others and criticizes what is defective in others. People work at right conduct in order to distinguish themselves from those who are 'wrong.' They act as though they were brilliant, as though they were carrying the sun, moon and stars on their shoulders.

"Sun Hsiu, since you still have a complete body, and have not come upon the inauspicious destiny of deafness, blindness, crippledness, obesity, addiction or laziness, you are more fortunate than most of your contemporaries. Why do you think that Heaven has been unkind? Please, will you leave now. Go away!"

When Sun Hsiu had gone, Pien Ch'ing-Tzu went inside and sat down for a while. Then, looking up at the sky, he sighed. A disciple asked him what was the matter.

"When Hsiu was here just now, I described to him the virtue or nature of the Perfect Man (one of integral nature). I'm afraid he was dumbfounded by what I said and may end up confused or frightened."

"How could that be?" said the disciple, "If he was right and you were wrong, wrong will not cause him to doubt what is right. If, on the other hand, he was wrong and you were right, he brought his doubt with him, and you are not responsible."

"Not so," answered Master Pien. "You don't understand. In time past, a bird perched on the outskirts of Lu. This delighted the lord of Lu, who killed an ox to feed it and had fancy music played to make it happy. The bird, however, was so distressed from the very beginning that it dared not eat or drink. This is called giving a bird the food meant for humans. If, however, one were to feed a bird what a bird eats, it would be allowed to nest deep in the woods and fly above the rivers and lakes, thus feeding on what it likes. In that way everything would be perfectly suited to it.

"Here today, however, was Sun Hsiu, who is a man of small understanding. When I told him about the natural behavior of the highest kind of man, it was like taking a mouse for a ride in a car or amusing a quail with the melody of horns and drums. Of course they would be frightened."

II
Imitation or Natural

When an ambitious and politically active teacher was away in the west visiting the state of Wei, hoping the prince would accept his advice and principles of government, one of his students asked a friend of his, who was a student of a different teaching, "What do you think about the master's trip?"

The latter replied, "Your master will certainly wind up in trouble over there."

"Why do you think so?" asked the first.

"Before the straw dogs are brought forward at the ceremony of the sacrifice," said the latter, "they are kept in bamboo boxes, covered with beautiful embroidered silk. Meanwhile, the impersonator of the dead and the priest fast and practice austerities in preparation for the ritual. Once the straw dogs have been presented, however, they end up being trampled on by passers-by, swept up by the fuel gatherers to be burned. If someone returned them to their bamboo boxes and covered them again with silk and then lingered nearby or lied down to sleep close by them, he would probably have nightmares, again and again."[14]

"Your master has already collected the straw dogs presented by earlier teachers - the worn out, cliche, conventional teaching - and when he goes on excursions with his students, it is the same as sleeping close to the dogs of misfortune. Consequently, the tree beneath which he used to teach is being cut down; he almost lost his life in Wei; he had no appointment in Shang or Chou. These were like bad dreams caused by these straw dogs. Being surrounded in a rural spot by people who suspected him, going without fire and food for a whole week and being on the verge of starvation are like nightmares caused by those straw dogs.

"A boat is best for crossing water; a cart is best for traveling on land. If you try to push a boat across land, you may push for a very long time and hardly move it at all. The past and present are like water and land; the states of Chou and Lu, where those nightmares happened to him, are like a boat and a cart. To practice the customs of Chou in the state of Lu is like trying to push a boat over land: there is tremendous

---

[14]At the ritual of sacrifice, it was a long observed custom to use straw dogs as scapegoats to draw away evil influences and thus to invite blessings and good fortune. They were treated with high regard before the sacrifice but thrown away afterward. To return them back in their fine boxes would only welcome misfortune.

labor with no success and great possibility of harm to the person who tries it. The man who tries to do so has failed to understand the principle of adapting himself to externals; being in harmony with one's surroundings, one moves in freedom.

"Have you ever seen a mechanism called a well-sweep? It is a simple thing, a wood device like a seesaw used to bring up water from the depth of a well. If one pulls it, down it comes. If one lets go, up it swings. It wisely allows people to pull it; it never tries to pull people. So when it goes up and down, it is never accused or blamed by them.

"The rituals and regulations of the Three Great Ones and the Five Virtuous Emperors, sages all, are greatly valued, but not because they were all the same; they are esteemed because they functioned to create order. Those rituals and regulations may be compared to the cherry-apple, the pear, the orange and the citron. Their flavors are all very different, yet all taste pleasant to the tongue. Similarly, rituals and regulations need to change according to the time and situation. If you dress a monkey like a duke, he will bite and tear at each article of clothing until he has removed every stitch. Past and present are no more the same than a monkey and a duke!

"When the beautiful woman Hsi-shih was bothered with heartburn, she happened to frown at her neighbors. An ugly woman was walking by, and seeing that Hsi-shih was beautiful, went home and also frowned at her neighbors. However, when they saw the ugly woman frowning, the rich people of the neighborhood shut their gates and would not go out, and the astounded men took their wives and children and ran off. The woman understood that someone frowning could be beautiful, but she did not understand where the beauty came from.

"I tell you, your master will wind up in trouble!"

III
Accordance with Great Nature
Chuang Tzu said to his friend Hui Tzu, "During

each of the sixty years that Confucius lived, he changed his mind sixty times about doing things. What he had previously accepted as right, he came to consider as wrong; at his sixtieth year, we can be sure that what he approved was not any of the previous fifty-nine disapprovals."

"He worked hard," replied Hui Tzu, "and daily he increased his wisdom. I would say that Confucius was wholeheartedly devoted to learning."

"By being so," replied Chuang Tzu, "Confucius set up a good example for all of us. Unfortunately, his students did not learn from his example. Instead, they held tightly and stiffly to his sayings, without applying them flexibly. Confucius' mind and heart kept improving as he approached Tao, but he himself did not declare his own achievement. He said, 'Talent and wisdom are what we receive from nature. One should do whatever one needs to restore one's own true spiritual nature within the span of one's life.' This is truthful attainment for developing inside rather than just living with externals.

"His own positive living set a good model for living in accordance with the harmonious rhythm of natural proceedings. He was never stuck in his growth or development. Thus, his teaching and behavior, being in a continual state of self-correction and improvement, can be the norm of many generations to come. If one's heart and mind is stuffed with concepts of right or wrong, favor or disfavor, likes and dislikes, linked only with the short-lived goals of life, or if one allows these short-lived and trivial circumstances to direct and cramp one's mind and life, although they may be cunning enough to stop arguments for a period of time, they will not win the mind and the heart of the people for generations to come. Only teaching that is in accordance with the natural universal truth will have no opposition from anyone who is talented and wise. Thus, this teaching can provide great principles and sound rules for all good people under the sky in all generations. This teaching can only win my respect."

CHAPTER NINE

HSU WU-KUEI,
ONE WHO RECOGNIZES
ONLY SUBTLE TRUTH

I
Establishing No Special Identity

Through the introduction of Nu Shang, a state official, the hermit Hsu Wu-Kuei went to see Duke Wu of Wei. Duke Wu greeted him sympathetically, saying "Sir, you must not be well. I suppose the hardships of mountain life have become too much, and so you have decided to visit me."

"I should be sympathizing with you, rather than you trying to comfort me," said Hsu Wu-Kuei. "By trying to fulfill your passions and desires, reveling in your likes and dislikes, you cause affliction or illness to the internal conditions of your nature and existence. However, if you try to deny your desires, or forcibly alter your likes and dislikes, your senses will suffer for the external false change. I have come to comfort you. What reason have you to feel sympathy for me?"

The Duke, looking distressed, did not answer.

After a short while, Hsu Wu-Kuei said, "Let me tell you how I judge dogs. A dog of the lowest category thinks only of catching enough for itself to eat. Its nature is that of a wildcat. One of the middle category always seems to be looking upwards at the sun with self-pride. However, one of the highest category, in accordance with its own nature, acts as though it has lost its identity, forgetting who it is, yet being an unspoiled dog.

"I am, however, much better at judging horses than I am at judging dogs. If a horse can gallop in a line straight as can be, make a curve neatly as an arc, turn a corner as sharp as a T-square, and circle round as smoothly as a compass, then I'd say he was a fine horse, one of the best in the state. But he would still not be the finest in the world.   The finest horse has talents that are perfect with its own nature, but seems perplexed or lost, as if having no identity of his own. In this way he outruns all the others, so quickly you cannot see where he has gone!"

Duke Wu was exceptionally pleased and laughed heartily.

When Hsu Wu-kuei was leaving, Nu Shang asked him, "What you were talking about with the duke? When I talk to him, I discuss the classic books of poetry and history, significant rituals and music, or works on military affairs such as the Golden Tablets and the Six Bow-Sheaths.   I have accomplished matters leading to some success many times over, yet he has never been happy even once.   What did you say that delighted him so?"

Hsu Wu-kuei said, "I only described to him how I judge dogs and horses, that's all.

"Let me explain.   Have you ever heard about the men who are exiled to an relatively uninhabited state? A few days after they have arrived in that place, they are pleased if they see somebody they have been friends with from their home state.   After a few weeks, they are gladdened if they see someone they had only known by sight from their home.   And by the time a year has gone by, they are delighted if they see someone who bears any resemblance at all to people from their home state.   When one is absent from one's people, a certain fondness for them arises.

"A man who has gone into the wilderness and has lived in emptiness and isolation for a long time will be glad if he hears even the sound of a human footfall. How much happier would he be if he hears his own brother or relatives at his side.   I think that it has been a long time since anyone has spoken to him about the pure nature that can be found even in dogs and horses, but which has been lost in men.   What you have valued is far from the true nature of life.   We settle for less and less as we become more and more removed from ourselves.

II

The Comforts of a Pure Life

On another occasion, Hsu Wu-Kuei went to see Duke Wu. "Sir," said the Duke, "for a long time you have been living in the forest, eating only acorns, chestnuts, berries and leeks, avoiding me completely. Is it old age or hunger for rich food that has brought you here? Might my state benefit from your arrival?

Hsu Wu-Kuei said, "I was born to a low position and have never developed a taste for rich food, your highness. I have come to console you."

"Console me?" exclaimed the Duke.

"I have come to comfort your internal gods," replied Hsu Wu-Kuei.

"What do you mean?" asked the Duke.

Hsu Wu-Kuei said, "Heaven and Earth give nourishment to all things and make no distinction between them. To have a high position in human society, therefore, is not necessarily good fortune. And to live in a low position is not necessarily bad fortune. You, as ruler of this state, tax the people to appease the appetite of your senses. Your internal gods will not long tolerate such behavior. The internal gods thrive on harmony and decline from turmoil. Turmoil causes illness. That is why I have come to comfort them. Why are you causing them illness?"

After a moment's hesitation, the Duke said, "I have wanted to see you for a long time now. I wish to love my people and, through good deeds, put an end to war. How can this be accomplished?"

"It cannot be done through the artifice of doing good deeds or providing welfare," replied Hsu Wu Kuei. "Artificial love for people is the root of all evil. Developing one's personal reputation for putting an end to military defense is the source of all fighting. If Your Highness begins in this way, the result can only be disaster.

"While you may think you are being benevolent and benefitting society, in effect you are only causing artificiality. Where there is something to be won, people will try to pursue it; where there is success, there is pride; where there is competition, a battle arises. This is the result of artificiality.

"Anything manipulated to be good by force and willful creation turns out bad. Whatever is artificial is impermanent. Anything done by teaching that merely sounds good does little good, because one's true intention - good or bad - invariably appears in one's actions. Internally adopting forced external standards leads to complications. Conversely, any revolution within your being leads to external fighting.

"Keep no soldiers prepared for battle in your tower of spirits nor infantry near the altar of your natural life. Do not hold any hostility in your heart. Do not try to outdo other people by your skills, plotting or battle. Conquering other peoples and lands to feed your personal desires and your spirit is not a victory. If you must do something, cultivate the sincerity in your heart to engender a correct response to the spiritual and physical needs in your environment. In this way, the people will have no anxiety over death but will be interested in maintaining their good life. Certainly, there is no need to intentionally talk peace or to forcefully put an end to war."

III
Balanced Life

The intellectual man is not happy without new ideas and thought. The rhetorician is not happy without any argument and rebuttal taking place. The examiner is not happy without questioning or investigation. These three are hemmed in by external, concrete situations.

Politicians who attract popular admiration are successful in public office. Men of great strength await trials. Men of boldness and courage enjoy danger. Men with weapons want to fight. Men lacking self-worth seek fame. Lawmakers delight in legislation. Those who lead rituals value appearances. People who are righteous and kind prize human relationships.

The farmer is not content if he does not work in the fields and weed patches. The merchant is not content if he does not have his affairs and sales at the marketplace. Ordinary people work most diligently in their jobs from dawn to dusk. Artisans are most active when using the tools of their trade. If his wealth is not multiplying, a greedy person worries. An ambitious person is anxious if his power and influence are not increasing. But they are only slaves to circumstance, sacrificing themselves to their own possessions. Their pleasure is change, and if an opportunity arises for them to use their talents, they cannot help but act. In such manner they go along with the seasons, being changed by things. Continuing without rest, they are swallowed by the multitudinous things of the world, continuing on in such manner without cease. Isn't this pathetic?

Thus men are always doing something. Inaction, in order to return to their own life nature, is impossible to them. They observe in this the same regularity as the seasons, ever without change. They hurry to destruction, dissipating their vital forces in all directions, never to return. In the end they may discover that the one thing they have not attended to is their personal spiritual growth and development. They will remain in the same life condition without improvement or higher evolution, because they destroyed their opportunity to grow by being too busy for nothing.

Q: Master Ni, in the second section, there was a reference to internal gods. Would you please explain this?

Master Ni: In the past, on several occasions, I have discussed this and put it in my written work. I will still reply to your question because there is importance to it.

In other works, we have talked about the background and development of different religions in the world and the educational systems they offer as the response to external demand resulting from internal impoverishment. Yet the spiritual tradition of Tao began with the attainment of truthful, natural, spiritual knowledge. Initiated in ancient times, people who were born with special spiritual energy usually outlived their relatives, friends and people in the community. They lived in solitude in their old age; thus their internal gods outgrew their physical condition. Most important, their spiritual unity outgrew their internal gods. They had become shiens. A shien is a term for a spiritually developed person, or simply a person of 'supernature' who has attained natural spiritual power. It does not necessarily mean someone with psychic or other powers.

The educational system of Taoism responded to the problem of the external life of the world from the standpoint of internal development. The teaching of Tao examines the spiritual evolution of people. Basically, each individual has been created the same; each has a spiritual nature. How an individual can harmonize his three personal spheres and live in harmony with the external world, was the attainment of the developed ones. This guidance is offered in the writing of the spiritually achieved ones and has also been directly passed down to us. Both are assimilated in the teaching of the Path of Integral Truth. The fact that each individual has a pure spiritual essence which can only be known by the person himself and developed into a spiritual being only from within, by sublimation and refinement. The practice of developing the internal gods has become the secret science of natural life.

The gourd or bottle is a metaphor for the physical being of life, which holds the spiritual entities, and which should not be opened too early in one's life by the specific spiritual practices which can reveal and make them apparent to oneself. General spiritual practices and disciplines are safe enough for young people, but it is better to wait to open the gourd or bottle until one's 'immortal medicine' has ripened. This immortal medicine transforms the internal spiritual entities to a form that can be refined and made ready, around the age of sixty or seventy, at a time when the obligations of worldly life have been completely fulfilled. Then one can live in seclusion or in a quiet place where there are no noisy airplanes in the sky or big cars on the road, and few people with whom you are in contact. Living in such a way, one can nurture the internal gods which have been methodically brought about by the clear knowledge activated in a divine life. This stage of life is the time to follow only the spiritual guidance in Lao Tzu's *Tao Teh Ching*. This is considered the one important cultivation when it is time to be alone.

Otherwise, the one who 'opens the gourd' too soon opens himself to a chaotic, unpeaceful life in the ordinary world, coping with negative disturbances and suffering a double pressure and tension.[15] The danger of opening the gourd too early means that the foundation of your life-being may be shaken, your spiritual entities might be scattered, or evil spirits might invade. Or you just may not know how to handle a new situation in life with such a big group of partners. In my written teaching I have given a safe and gradual way with a blueprint of personal spiritual cultivation and group practice. With the given teaching, complete spiritual development can be reached with the development of the 'red baby.' The secret has also been given in my written work, *The Workbook for Spiritual Development*. This is the way my loving ancestors presented this learning, and so do I, out of universal spiritual nature.

If one concentrates on one's spiritual cultivation on a general level, without opening the 'bottle' (the body), at all, one can still attain the most important achievement. But, you might say, we are modern people; we know that experiencing is believing and would like to experience it. My answer to that is: it is true that until your internal gods attain enough growth, only external gods can be clearly known and directly communicated with. It is important to confirm all the spiritual truth you have gathered in your lifetime. I have proven it for myself, step by step, with tangible proof in my life.

---

[15]For further information on this topic, please refer to the related teaching in *The Uncharted Voyage Toward the Subtle Light*.

I have experienced the truth of knowing the internal gods after first doing general spiritual cultivation for forty years. The books produced in the later part of my life were taken from my experience of this spiritual truth. I have challenged the forbidden code of revealing such a secret when the traditionally achieved teachers would have kept silent about it. I have done so because I am spiritually motivated to save this lost, precious, provable science.

However, I have now accomplished this stage of my work, and it is time to shift to another level of spiritual cultivation. Such a practice can be taught to those who have fulfilled their natural obligation in their personal life and achieved virtuous fulfillment by helping the human world as well as developing themselves. The secret science is a reward to those who have made a contribution in the direction of promoting individual spiritual development to all of society, by helping people learn to live a complete life, fulfilling and integrating all three spheres. Only the spiritual merit of a person can find the door and reach the true teaching of this level.

Q: Master Ni, is 'to open the gourd' a necessary step in spiritual cultivation? What is most important in our spiritual cultivation?

Master Ni: Good question. Scientists, intellectuals and society in general cannot afford to lose this truthful and factual knowledge of the spiritual sphere of human life. In this work, a person is given an opportunity to recognize and re-evaluate their life and reshape their lifestyle. Lao Tzu and other classic works of the early sages gave the answer to your question. As a result of losing important spiritual knowledge, the world has developed differently. Yet, to a serious spiritual student, to open the gourd is one step of self-discovery which is of secondary value to the development of the internal spirits.

The attainment of spiritual unity is most important. You might like to know why, so let me explain it clearly to you. Nature has created people in a wide range of equality. At the middle level (excluding the highly developed and inferior lives), the foundation of each individual life is about the same. The possession of internal spirits is a natural reality of each individual life. For any person, a simple, normal life represents spiritual unity. When death comes, one's spiritual elements scatter. In most cases, it is the scattering of an individual's spiritual elements that causes death. Before death, people still have the chance to experience the disharmony and scatteredness of spirits. You may find an example of this in Shakespeare's *Midsummer Night's Dream*, in which an illustration of this spiritual scatteredness is presented in a dreamlike form. Looking at the paintings of the aged Picasso, I see the reflection of his loss of spiritual unity and centeredness rather than the expression of a new creation. Spiritual unity is contained within the natural form of life. People do not need to do anything. Thus, generally speaking, success in ordinary life resides within the natural unity and integrity of a person.

As for negative people, people who are born sick, and criminals, unfortunately they have some elements within them that they cannot manage. General people sometimes wake up in the middle of the night. If either of these is not for a physically based reason, it must be because of a spiritual reason that they do not know about.

The leaders and followers of most religions do not know whether their spiritual experiences originate from internal or external sources. Thus, they are mixed up and end over-valuing the abnormal experience, interpreting it as spiritual. They are amazed by it and so begin to worship it as spiritual health. When a person has spiritual unity and health, there is nothing to be seen spiritually. Just as the proverb says: "No news is good news." But most people mistakenly value the spiritual problems of an individual or a society and take them for normal. Thus, many religions, natural psychics and crazy people share the same problem of mistaking what is abnormal as good health. Spiritual clarity is expressed in the ordinariness of normal, everyday life.   It is only immature people who are attracted to strangeness.   It is the distortion of healthy spiritual vision that results in the foundation of creating religions.   This confusion will continue until wholeness is achieved and people come back to their own nature.   Each person must return to the spiritual normalcy of his or her own self.   This is the call from the ancient developed ones who lived prior to the beginning of confusion in the world.

For people of spiritual cultivation, the most important thing is their own spiritual unity.   Individual happiness, health and smooth relationships represent an achieved state of spiritual unity.   It is this achievement that is the basic goal of spiritual attainment for most people.

Yet the higher achievement is harder still.   Before becoming a sage, the condition of one's internal spirits is similar to that of an ordinary person.   But now he may experience increased pressure from his internals: it is like an inexperienced but upright man who suddenly becomes the captain of a ship with a full crew of pirates.   The future holds several possibilities: either he can achieve the skills for effective leadership or be fragmented by the internal conflict and rebellion before the ship, his life, is ruined.   This also describes a necessary achievement for each individual.

Now, I bring this to the attention of all serious students: the existence of internal spirits is a reality, both tangible and provable.   I have experienced and practiced a method of knowing and managing these internal spiritual entities; the trouble from doing so was costly.[16]   It is my understanding that to simply open the bottle for its own sake is meaningless.   The most meaningful accomplishment is the transformation and refinement of the gross energies, the 'pirates,' who are

---

[16]For further understanding, please refer to the message of internal spiritual development as revealed in *The Uncharted Voyage Toward the Subtle Light*.

the crew of your ship. Also you cannot expect higher development of your internal spirits without first attaining your own spiritual growth. In terms of unity and balance, you and your internal spiritual entities are not two separated things. Even if you have achieved yourself totally, you still have the external world to face. Therefore, the achievement must be both internal and external; the use and the necessary practicality of following the Great Path of Integral Truth finds its standing point in worldly life. It includes the cultivation of the three spheres: body, mind and spirits. This cultivation includes basic spiritual self-discovery, the development of the internal spiritual entities and the fortification of spiritual unity or center which will support a long healthy life, a life which embraces the possibility of spiritual immortality, of living as the unified universal life evolved by taking essence from physics, using one's own organic foundation of life to reach one's real spiritual heaven.

In the martial arts, a teacher never offers the important skills to students with undeveloped minds. This is crucially applicable to spiritual matters as well. Evil and confused spirits have already pervaded the world, and any responsible spiritual teacher would not support more of that in the world. Otherwise, there is no hope of improving the hell-bent direction of the modern world, where true spiritual knowledge is destroyed and governments follow the prejudice of the immature due to the ignorance and undevelopment of both the individual and society as a whole. Then, what is most important in today's world or, for that matter, any age?

Q: Master Ni, what is the traditional principle for the government of the internal gods?

Master Ni: Lao Tzu's teaching represented maturity of spiritual development. He advocated the non-active mind and embracing oneness in order to live a peaceful and natural life. His influence remained among people of wisdom.

Later, in the Han Dynasty[17], the period of the three Kingdoms and the Tseng Dynasty[18], religious Taoism started with a number of schools whose unified goal was active government of the mind with special training of the internal spirits in order to attain spiritual power. This new religious trend was strong. Many masters achieved magic power and ranked themselves among those with supernatural influence. These magic powers excited the beliefs of the majority of people and they became followers of the religious Taoism; yet no other benefit was given to the followers that could be proven. Later, at the time of the Tang Dynasty[19], these magicians became more respected. It was near the end of the prosperous dynasty that Master Lu, Tung Pien and his friend, Master Cheng Tuan carved the description of the process of complete spiritual achievement on a stone wall in a cave in Flower Mountain where Master Cheng Tuan lived. The carving read:

First, take the nutrition from food and natural energy,
    then let the natural process change the nutrition
    to be sexual energy when you are young.
Second, through training, one transforms and transfers
    sexual impulse to be general vital energy.
Third, refine the vital chi to be shen, spiritual energy,
    and spirits.
Four, prompt all spirits to unite to achieve the highest
    unity within and without.

With regard to the simplicity of following these instructions, what Lao Tzu recommended will be sufficient. With regard to spirit, study to satisfy intellectual knowledge and to prove the spiritual reality. The Shan Ching School of Taoism should be thoroughly researched, along with the teachings of other schools.

---

[17]206 B.C.-219 A.D.

[18]265-419 A.D.

[19]618-906 A.D.

Both Master Lu and Master Cheng's system were acceptable to the people following an organized refining process.

My personal experience has been that, after experiencing the learning and practice that could be reached after many years of effort, I have returned to Lao Tzu's simple way of practice. However, I would not prevent anyone from looking into it, and would offer help to those with qualifications who are ready to prove spiritual reality for the world, if they do so with the purpose of helping others break through the great intellectual blockage of today's people to understanding their spiritual nature. Otherwise, for your own benefit, the great path of the Integral Way as I interpret it is what I sincerely recommend.

CHAPTER TEN

MANAGE THE WORLD WITHOUT PERSONAL INTENTION

I
To Govern Oneself is to Eliminate the Harmful

The Yellow Emperor set out in a horse-drawn carriage to visit Ta-Wai, a god who lived on Mount Chu-tz'u, with Fang Ming driving, Ch'ang Yu assisting the driver, and his friends Chang Jo, Hsi P'eng, K'un Hun and Ku Chi. By the time they reached the Hsiang-ch'eng wilds, the seven sages had become lost and there was no one around to ask for directions. Eventually they saw a young boy herding horses, so they went to him to ask directions. "Do you know the way to Mount Chu-Tz'u?" they inquired.

"Yes."

"And do you know where Ta-Wai lives?"

"Yes."

"This is an amazing boy!" said the Yellow Emperor. "He not only knows the way to Mount Chu-Tz'u, but he also knows where Ta-Wei lives. I would like to ask you about how to govern the world."

"To govern the world," replied the boy, "is the same as what I do here. There is nothing at all special about it. When I was younger, I used to go wandering within the Six Directions, north, south, east, west, up and down, but I incurred a disease that blurred my eyesight. An elder advised me to ride the chariot of the sun and wander in the Hsiang-ch'eng wilds, which I did, so now, my eyesight is improving. I continue to dwell beyond the limitations of the Six Directions.

"Governing the world means just doing what I'm doing. It is nothing special."

"I know that governing the world is not something in your concern," said the Yellow Emperor. "But I would like to know how you think it should be done."

The boy did not wish to answer, but when the Yellow Emperor asked him again, the boy said, "Governing the world is really not different from herding horses. You just dissolve anything in yourself that is harmful to the horses."

Respectfully, the Yellow Emperor bowed before the boy and, calling him Divine Teacher, continued on his journey.

II
True Spiritual Resonance
Is like Harmonious Musical Notes

Chuang Tzu said to Hui Tzu, his friend of intellectual achievement: "If an archer, without even aiming at the bull's eye, just happens to hit it and we call him a skilled archer, then everyone in the world would be called a highly skilled archer like Yi, right?"

"Yes," said Hui Tzu.

Chuang Tzu then continued, "There is no publicly accepted definition of 'right' in the world, but if each person takes right to be what he himself thinks is right, then everyone in the world could be considered as wise as the sage Yao, right?"

"Yes," said Hui Tzu.

Chuang Tzu went on, "Well, four of the schools of thought are as follows: The Confucians believe in society being ordered by a sense of ethics. The Mohists believe in universal love. The followers of Yang believe in the establishment of logic. Lastly, the followers of Ping believe in sheer individualism. With your own philosophy of cognition or the nature of the mind, this makes five. All of you engage in the establishment of a conceptual framework. Now which of you is right?

"Perhaps searching for Tao is like the case of Lu Chu, a teacher active at the beginning of the Chou Dynasty. One of his disciples said to him, 'Master, I have attained your Tao, your spiritual achievement. I do not need fire in winter and can make ice in the heat of summer.'

"'That is merely using the latent power of heat and

cold,' said his teacher. 'That is not at all what I would call Tao. I will give you a demonstration of Tao.'

"Thereupon he tuned two identical long, base-stringed instruments called Seh, and placed one in the hall and the other in an adjoining room. When he struck the Doh note on one, the Doh note on the other sounded. When he struck the Reh note on one, the Reh note on the other sounded. This was because both instruments were tuned to an identical pitch.

"Then he tuned one string so that it no longer corresponded to any of the other notes. When he sounded this string, it started all twenty-five strings of the instrument in the other room clanging. Mastery over the notes does not exist until the differences in the sounds have been produced by tuning. Can we find a similarity in the case of the five schools?"

Hui Tzu said, "The students of Confucius, Mo, Yang and Ping often debate with me. Each of us tries to outwit the others with sentences and quiet down the others with shouts. So far I am the one who has never been proven wrong. How do you find that similar to your Seh?"

Chuang Tzu replied, "A man of Ch'i allowed his son to become disabled and to take a low job as a doorkeeper. Later, he acquired a used wine bottle and protected it with much more care than he gave his own son. He believes he is right in doing what he thinks.

"Another man lost his child and was unwilling to go outside his property to look for him, because he thought he had fulfilled his duty by searching only inside his property.

"A man of Ch'u did not have a house to live in. Someone gave him a place to stay, but he complained about the poverty of the house owner.

"Another man was the only passenger on a boat going somewhere around midnight. The boat had just arrived at its destination, but had not yet reached the shore when the man started to get off. Consequently he got wet, but he picked a fight with the boatman, saying that it was due to the boatman's haste and recklessness that he got wet. He thought he was right.

"The argument among Confucianists, Mohists, Yangists, Pingists, and your own as well, all resemble the positions of these people of self-righteousness. If only objectivity could be adopted by all of you, we might be able to develop something closer to perfection; most people are unaware of this. The standards of right and wrong that have been established by individuals at different places and times all stem from partial knowledge. The integral truth that is universal to all times and places and to all beings are not known or respected by most people now nor will they be in future generations!"

III
The Virtue of Wholeness

When Kuan Chung, a very capable minister, fell ill, Duke Huan, who respected him greatly, went to inquire how he was doing. "Father Chung" he said, "you are very ill. If your illness should worsen, whom should I appoint to manage the affairs of the State?"

Kuan Chung said, "Who do you think could manage them?"

"I believe that Pao Shu-ya could do it," replied the Duke.

"We must choose another," said Kuan Chung. "Pao Shu-ya is a fine man, a person of honor and good character. However, he will not associate with anyone who is not like himself, and he never forgives the mistakes of others. If he managed the state, you would find that he would contend with the people in high positions and distress the ordinary people. It would not be too long before you would have a great entanglement on your hands."

"Well then, who would do well?" asked the Duke.

"I recommend Hsi P'eng, a talented and virtuous one. He forgets about his superiors and remembers those in lower positions than he. He has the ability to forget those in the high positions above him, and to make those below him forget about his own position. He constantly strives to meet the virtue of the Yellow

Emperor and has sympathy for those who are less than himself. By sharing his virtue with others, he is like the sage; by sharing his talents, he proves he is a worthy man. Hsi P'eng will do all right."

Here, Kuan Chung set a standard for a truly capable minister.

IV
The Pursuit of Inner Worth

The King of Wu, boating on the Yangtze River, stopped to climb a mountain famous for monkeys. When the monkeys saw him, they fled in terror and went to hide in the deep brush. There was one monkey who behaved carelessly, as though exhibiting its skill before the King. The King took a shot at it, but the monkey grabbed the flying arrow with its hand. The King then ordered his attendants to shoot at it, and the monkey was soon killed.

The King's friend Yen Pu-i, observing this, reflected: "This monkey, by flaunting its skill and thinking highly of its own talents, displayed contempt for the king and met with its end. I must heed this example and never express arrogance toward others!"

When Yen Pu-i returned, he put himself under the guidance of Tung Wu, a developed one, and learned to keep himself free of superiority, give up pleasure-seeking and avoid fame. At the end of three years, everyone in the State respected and admired him.

CHAPTER ELEVEN

ARTIFICIALITY BRINGS TROUBLE

I
A Good Student

Nieh Ch'ueh saw Hsu Yu, a famous recluse, the teacher of Yao, and asked him, "Where are you going?"

"I'm trying to get away from Yao," replied Hsu Yu.

"Why?"

"Yao is so earnest and so kind to all people that I believe that he will end up being the laughingstock of the state. Eventually, the outcome of his behavior may be that men end up killing each other over their differing opinions. He wants to put me on the throne; that is why I am not staying.

"It is not at all difficult for a leader to attract people. If you love them, they will feel attachment for you. If you benefit them, they will swarm to be near you. If you tell them they are good, they will do their best in their work. But if you do something they do not like, they will immediately depart.

"Affection and personal benefit come as the result of being earnest and kind. There are only a few truly wise leaders who will renounce all philosophies, including the doctrines of love and service. Those of deep vision see the pitfalls of such things. Most people practice benevolence and righteousness with great show; this is artificiality. At its worst, it is equivalent to handing weapons to the evil and undeveloped, because the practice of love and righteousness can be used as an excuse for war and making trouble. Truthfully, to create all kinds of social and religious precepts and regulations for the 'benefit' of the world is like lending invisible knives to people of evil intention in later generations. It also stiffens the growth of the ones who are not evil, but are looking for a creative life.

"Yao knows that leaders of creative philosophies benefit the world, but he does not know that they also harm it. Only those who are superior to good leaders understand this."

Yao finally chose Shun to succeed his leadership.

II
The Pursuit of Plain Virtue

As a student of Tao, I classify the worldly leaders in my own way. There are four types: the witless, who are shallow; the parasites, who are stubborn; and the extremists, who do not take the essence, but only the form; and the True One, who is a student of truth.

"Those whom I call the witless study the ideology of only one school, and feeling wise, are quite pleased with themselves. They believe themselves to be self-sufficient, but do not realize that they have not yet begun to learn truth. That is why I call them witless.

"The parasites are like lice on a pig. They choose a place where the bristles are few and consider it a luxurious mansion or beautiful garden, making themselves at home. Or, they choose a place near the hoofs or joints or down around the thighs and consider it a place for rest and relaxation. They do not know that one morning the butcher will roll up his sleeves, spread the straw and fuel, light up the fire, and they will be cooked along with the pig. Their advancement in the world is affected by similar limits, as is their retirement from it. They are who I call the parasites.

"What I call the extremists are those like Shun. A mutton does not want ants; it is ants who want mutton. Mutton has a strong and dank odor to it. Shun must have accomplished dank things with for all the people to have been so pleased with him. Even though he moved often, each place he lived became a city. By the time he reached the barren wilds near Teng, there were thousands of families following him. Yao heard of Shun's enthusiasm and brought him from the wilderness to succeed him, although Shun was advanced in years, weak in hearing and eyesight. He would not, however, stop working and rest. He is an example of what I call the extremists.

"Therefore the True One, who is the fourth type, was achieved from being a good student of truth. He is not flattered when people approach or group around him; and if they do, he tries not to be friendly with them. He is not too friendly or beneficial to them; yet he is not isolated or withdrawn; thus, he remains dispassionate and impartial. Because he embraces virtue and maintains harmony, he follows along with the world and does not lead. This is what is called the True One. He understands what to do about the ants.

"It is agreeable to strive for what fishes desire, to be left alone in the water. Leave foolishness to mutton. It is better to use your eye to look at itself, your ear to listen to itself, and your heart and mind to turn in upon themselves. The one who can do these things will straighten himself out and be able to make changes in due time.

"The True One trusts the natural development of events. He does not bring what is artificial into the realm of the natural."

III
Silence Teaches More Than Talking

Tzu-ch'i Nan-po, a man of Tao, sat as usual in his chair, leaning on the armrest and staring up at the sky, doing his breathing practice. Ch'eng-tzu, his student, entered and said, "Master, how can one as important as you keep your body still as dry wood, and your mind like dead ashes, rather than working for the benefit of mankind?"

Tzu-ch'i replied, "For a long time, I lived in a cave in the mountains. During that time, after T'ien Ho, King of Ch'i, visited me, the people of Ch'i congratulated him on three different occasions, which is like recognizing him for paying honor to me. I had undoubtedly become known by the people as being a sage, and this reached his ears. What kind of indication could I have given out in order for him to find

out who I was; I did not become a recluse to deliberately pursue fame. Yet, I must have been selling something in order for him to come and buy. Otherwise,
how could he find out who I was?

"I grieve over people losing their own true nature.
I also grieve for those who grieve. I even grieve for
he who grieves for the one who grieves. Because I
have this understanding, day after day I have learned
to keep farther away from the entanglement of showing
myself off and losing my nature."

IV
Silence Teaches More Than Lots of Talking

When Nan-po visited Ch'u, the King commanded
that a toast be made. Sun shu Ao came forward and
stood, holding the wine glass, and I-liao from the south
took the bottle and poured the wine, saying, "Nan-po,
you are wise as the men of ancient times. Would you
kindly speak to us on this occasion?"

Nan-po said, "I am familiar with the great teaching
that does not rely on words, though I have never tried
to talk about it. Shall I now talk about it?

"I-liao from the south once juggled some balls. By
doing that, a disastrous war between the states of Ch'u
and Sung was avoided."[20]

"Sun shu Ao, the prime minister of Ch'u, relaxed
comfortably in his chair, cooling himself with his feather fan. By doing this, the invasion of Ch'u was stopped, and the confronting soldiers put down their arms."
Sun-shu Ao governed so effectively that he was able to
rest in ease."[21]

---

[20]A sovereign in one part of the royal family led a rebellion,
trying get I-liao's support. He began by verbally trying to convince
him, but ended up drawing his sword. I-liao refused to meet his
demands, maintaining his composure by juggling the balls. Thus,
the juggling of the balls symbolizes detachment under threat of
harm.

"I wish to shut up my mouth like a bird with a beak three feet long, that cannot sing well. The truth cannot be spoken.

"Because of the example of these two men, we understand the way of silence. The highest form is attained when all excellence gathers in the unity of nature, and speech stops at what cannot be known. Skillfulness itself, however, cannot share the perfection of nature, and language cannot discuss the integral truth, because it cannot be intellectually defined. Whenever we delineate the conceptual creation of unnatural cultural and religious establishment, attaching names to things, we create something evil.

"An ocean does not obstruct the rivers that flow into it from east of the west land or west of the east; that is its greatness. A sage embraces all nature; his good influence benefits all people. He accumulates nothing, establishing no reputation or fame.

"A dog is not ranked a thoroughbred because of its great barking, and man is not ranked a superior merely because of his great speech. Neither can a good speaker be considered One of Great Nature. That which has become great does not aim at becoming great; only by minding his own nature does he becomes virtuous. He who understands greatness does not exchange himself for things. He who understands greatness returns to himself and finds the inexhaustible; he follows the spiritual development of antiquity to discover the imperishable. This is the essence and the sincerity of the one of great nature."

V
Freedom Must not be Exchanged
For Vain Worldly Glories

Tzu-ch'i had eight sons. He invited his friend,

---

[21]The people of the capital, with great confidence and no fear of foreign invasion, put away their weapons. These two men described by Nan-po dissolved the great trouble of war by saying nothing and are thus great examples of the power of silence.

Chiu-fang Yin, over to see them. He was a person with a special spiritual capability called physiognomy, which enables one to give correct information about people or animals by looking at their appearance. Tzu-ch'i asked him, "Please read my sons' physiognomies for me and tell me which of them shall expect good fortune in his life."

Chiu-fang Yin replied, "K'un will have good fortune in his life."

Tzu-ch'i, pleased, said, "Please tell me how."

"K'un will eat the same food as the duke, with lots of meat, for as long as he lives."

Tears poured from Tzu-ch'i's eyes, who asked dejectedly, "Why should my son suffer such extremity?"

Chiu-fang Yin, astounded at his reply, remarked, "When one dines like a duke, the benefits of his connection may reach his family. This should make his father happy! By your weeping today you are refusing the good fortune."

Tzu-ch'i said, "How do you define good fortune? By having meat or wine? How can you think that eating meat is good fortune?

"The friendship and enjoyment between my son and me is the freedom of wandering between the sky and the earth. Together we take our delight in concordance with great nature. We live on earth, where together we go about, and where we eat our supportive meals. I do not participate in any projects, plots or happenings with other people. We follow the truth pervading the universe, harmonizing ourselves with the external environment wherever we are, not allowing anything to put us in disharmony with it. We travel in unity, without becoming slaves to circumstance. This I consider good fortune. I never thought such treatment from the world of vanity would come to my family. Usually, where there is such a strange fate, there must invariably have been some strange deed that brought it about. This cannot be due to any fault of my son or me. It must be God's will, that is why I sorrow!"

Shortly after, Tzu-ch'i sent his son K'un to the state

of Yen to conduct some family business. As he was traveling, he was captured by bandits. They realized that they would have a difficult time selling him as a slave in his perfect condition, because he might run away. So they damaged his feet and then sold him in the state of Ch'i, to a rich butcher. It turned out that he assisted the butcher in the palace of the duke, and so was able to eat meat until the end of his days.

Fortune and destiny are external. True enjoyment is embracing Tao throughout all circumstances of life.

CHAPTER TWELVE

TSE YANG

I
Spiritual Cultivation

Tzu-lao, a young student who had studied under different masters, came to visit Chuang-wu, a border guard. This is what the guard told the student, with the purpose of enlightening the younger man: "In heading a government one must not to be sloppy; in ordering the people one must not be careless! I used to be a farmer and grow grain. When I plowed the fields carelessly, I got a poor crop in return. When I weeded haphazardly, I also got a poor crop in return. The following year I changed my methods, plowing deeply and thoroughly and weeding very carefully. The harvest was bounteous, providing more than enough to eat for the whole year!"

In the learning of Tao, we take agriculture as the example for cultivating ourselves. Thus, we call spiritual development "self-cultivation." We also use metaphors from alchemy, which is called self-refinement.

Upon hearing about the border guard's comments, Chuang Tzu said, "When it comes to caring for their bodies and managing their minds, people usually do it haphazardly and carelessly. They stray from living a natural life, depart from their inborn nature, destroy their form and spirit, and follow the crowd. He who is careless with his inborn nature will find the passions of desire and hate choking his true nature like overgrown weeds. When they first appear, they seem useful, but later manifest in ulcers, eczema and bloating, causing ill health."

II
Tse Yang

When Tse Yang, a young person, visited the state of

Ch'u he asked I Chieh, a minister of state, to speak to the prince about him with the hope of obtaining an official post. This did not succeed.

Tse Yang then went to see Wang Kuo, a local sage, and asked him to obtain an appointment for him with the prince.

"I have even less chance of obtaining an appointment for you than I Chieh. I Chieh is a man who does not follow a positive way of spiritual development. He is clever, and he is a man who knows how to keep people trusting him. He is attracted to finery and wealth and therefore, he cannot help the king become virtuous. He is capable only out of his own selfish motivation. He is sensitive enough to know what others want. It is like seeing a shivering man; he knows the man is looking for warm clothing; conversely, seeing the person suffering from heat, he knows the man is thinking of a cooling wind. Thus he can keep himself at the side of the King of Ch'u.

"The King is severe and stern. He is as unforgiving as a wolf if one should make a mistake. It takes either a blatant flatterer or a man of utmost virtue to get the King to listen to him.

"Since I Chieh cannot be helpful to you, Kung Yueh-hsiu would probably do better than I to get an appointment for you."

"What kind of person is he?"

"In winter," replied Wang Kuo, "he traps turtles from the river; in summer, he retreats to the mountains. If anybody stops to talk to him there, he tells them, 'This is where I live.'

"A true sage like Kung Yueh-Hsiu can forget about his poverty if there is nothing in his household. When he is in office, he makes kings and dukes forget their noble positions and do what is humble and right. He works quietly, contentedly and carefully on whatever he has to do. He is cordial with all people around him yet remains detached. Even his silence is effective in bringing harmony to a situation. While living with people, people discipline themselves by following his example. All people know their own duty and do not transgress the natural rights of others, thus they are naturally harmonized. He is surely different from the selfish. He will speak for you. This is why I suggest you look for him. Even if you do not get a political post, he can help you by providing a role model. From his example, we see that one can still serve the public in the subtle virtuous way."

III
The Unnaturally Developed World

Po Chu, while studying under Lao Tzu, said, "I would like to travel throughout the world."

After returning from his voyage, he reported:

"The developed people of ancient, natural society credited what success they had to the people; any failure they blamed upon themselves. That is not how most people lead their lives. Presently, leaders make themselves the authority over the lives and deaths of others. They make decisions and do things secretly and then call others ignorant for not understanding. They complicate things and then enforce penalties when people are unable to do them. They set high artificial standards and then punish people for not meeting them. They lengthen other's tasks and then chastise people for not being able to complete them.

"When people's knowledge and vitality are exhausted, they resort to artificiality and unvirtuous behavior. When artificiality starts, there is no ending it. Lack of natural vitality paves the way for artificiality. Lack of true knowledge paves the way for deception. Lack of resources leads to theft. Who, then, can be blamed for artificiality, deception and theft?"

"What you have said seems to make people believe that they do not need to take responsibility for their own unnatural expansion," said the teacher. "This is not the case. Constant self-development is the only way to rise above the troubles of the world."

IV
T'ai Kung Tiao

Shao Chih, a student of knowledge, asked T'ai

Kung Tiao, his master, "What is a society?"

"Society is the relationship between families and individuals who live in concordance by abiding by certain customs," replied the master. "Different elements cooperate to form a harmonious whole. It is also through the unity of the elements that individuality is made known.

"Any one part of a horse is not the horse. It is the combination of all the parts which make up the horse.

"Similarly, a mountain reaches its heights from the joining of many small elements of lowness. A river becomes wide due to the additions of many small streams and creeks. A great man brings together all elements under his authority to form a great work of oneness.

"In regard to his own views, while conscious of their truth, the great man considers the opinions of others. From the union of diverse opinions and viewing the situation impartially, the action that speaks of correctness is recognized.

"The four seasons are each different, but the universal spiritual realm shows no preference for any particular one; thus a year is complete.

"In government, each department has a different function, and by not showing partiality for any certain one, the leader assures that society is well cared for. It would be difficult to make a choice between civil, administrative or military measure of control, but a truly great leader shows no interest in any of them, so their great peace and orderliness is complete and without imbalance. The ten thousand things are all different, but the subtle realm which gives them life shows them no partiality, therefore each performs his function. Thus, there is nothing the subtle realm does not do. Authorities of human society would do well to learn from the profound example of universal nature.

"Seasons begin and end. Generations follow one another. Good and bad fortune alternate, bringing first sorrow, then happiness. How much can a human leader truly govern?

"He who stubbornly does things from his own point

of view will be right in some things and wrong in others. In a forest many kinds of shrubs are found together and on a mountain you see trees and rocks side by side. This is what we call society. Artificial equality damages the nature of a healthy society."

"Is the kingdom then not Tao?" asked Shao Chih, "Can we not call it the principle of integrity?"

"It is not," replied T'ai Kung Tiao, the master. "You see, we talk of creation as being made up of ten thousand things, because that expression denotes an infinite number. Heaven and earth are immense shapes, and yin and yang are immense breaths, but Tao is what embraces all of them. We can call society a part of the universal nature, but there is as big a difference between an artificial society and the natural Tao as there is between a straw dog and a living horse. There is truly no comparison."

"From where exactly do all the creations of heaven and earth arise, what manifests yin and yang?" inquired Shao Chih, the student.

"Yin and yang, through interaction, formation, influence and regulation of one another," answered his master, "bring about all things. Thus the four seasons alternate, giving birth to and destroying one another; love and hate, rejection and acceptance follow one another; and intercourse between the sexes takes place. Danger and safety alternate; good and bad fortune fluctuate; first there is speed, then slowness. There is gathering and later dispersion. The truth of this may be noted; there is the name and the embodiment. When the relations between the opposites and the effects caused thereby lead to exhaustion, they return to their source, only to be born afresh. Intellectual knowledge and language cannot go beyond the material description of existence.

"The student of Tao is not sentimentally saddened by a mature life that is going to pass away or sorrow for how a natural problem has arisen. His mind does not follow the trouble that is not any more existent, and does not re-run the scene of how the trouble happened repeatedly in his mind. He does not argue about what cannot be reached through discussion or intellectual knowledge. All such activities are limited to the surface of the integral truth. Human thought misses the mark."

"There are two schools of thought about existence," said the student. "Chi Chen taught that it is chance that all things are brought about through nature and there is no creator who controls the creation of all things. Chieh Tzu taught predestination, that there is a mystical power above all things that create them. Which is right?"

"Roosters crow and dogs bark," replied T'ai Kung Tiao. "Everybody know that, but no one knows what makes one crow and the other bark, nor why they crow or bark at all.

"So you ask, why? Can it be because of chance? Can it be because of predestination? A person can talk and think about these things for a whole lifetime and not get any closer to Tao. In fact, the talking and thinking are what takes him farther away from the reality of nature.

"One cannot stop the cycles of birth and death. They continue without cease. To describe the 'without cease' in words cannot be done. Chance and predestination are merely artificial conceptual structures projected upon the nature of life.

"Tao cannot be related to concepts or partial existence. If it were related to concepts, it would be limited; if it were related to partial existence, it would have non-existence. We use the word 'Tao' only for human understanding, which is limited.

"Words cannot describe Tao, even if one were to talk all day. It is beyond conceptual understanding and existence. This is why silence is how one may understand its nature."

Another student of Tao heard about this and commented: "This discussion is still intellectual." His elder said, "The subtle truth can be intellectually conveyed through description, can it not?"

CHAPTER THIRTEEN

EXTERNAL STANDARDS

I
Choice Of Following The Subtle Law

External objects cannot be relied upon.   External standards cannot be trusted.

Because of external standards, Lung Feng was decapitated and Pi Kan was executed. They were ethical and moral in their deportment, helped the common people and were loyal to their sovereigns, fulfilling their duty as ministers in the government in such a way that gently opposed the corruption of their superiors. The rulers, therefore, utilized their ethical conduct to trap and condemn them. The external standard of loyalty and faithfulness, and the fame that came with it, turned out to be a snare for two capable persons.

Prince Chi was a strict student of external standards. After seeing the example of Lung Feng and Pi Kan, in order to save his own life, he had to feign insanity. He was a relative of the tyrant, Chou. He realized that rigid external standards cannot be followed; otherwise he would have died wastefully like the others.

Ngh Lai was killed when Chieh and Chou were overthrown. He assisted the corruption of the tyrant ruler and ended up being put to death when his ruler was deposed. The external standard of pleasing one's superiors caused him to meet his end.

All rulers want their administrators to be faithful and loyal, but loyal administrators do not always earn the trust of their monarch.

That is why Wu Yun's body was thrown into the Yangtze River. He continually warned the king about the possibility of the neighboring state attacking the kingdom. By so doing, he aroused the king's distrust and was forced to commit suicide. The external standard of loyalty, taken to an extreme, caused his demise.

The faithful Ch'ang Hung perished in Shu, where the people saved his blood, and after three years it congealed and solidified into green jade. Ch'ang Hung is another whose good advice to his sovereign resulted in his own death. Adherence to the external standard of faithfulness proved fatal.

All parents want their children to be filial, but a filial son is not always loved by his parent, because a truly filial son is an honest son.

That is why Hsiao-chi anguished. Hsiao-chi was the son of a king whose filial behavior earned him only the persecution of his stepmother. The external standard of filial piety brought him grief.

That is also why Tseng Shen wept. Tseng Shen was one of Confucius' good students who, although he was filial, was despised by his parents and mistreated by them. The external standard of filial piety cannot be applied in all circumstances.

II
No External Standard
Can Surpass Natural Harmony

When two pieces of wood are rubbed together, fire is created. If you put metal next to fire, it will melt. When yin and yang are disordered, Heaven and Earth are disturbed. Then thunder will crash, and lightening in the midst of the storm will set tall trees aflame. The opposites of joy and sorrow keep a person disordered. Exhilaration or depression can trap one into inability to accomplish. They trap one's mind between heaven and earth, leaving a person lost in delusion.

It is in the struggle for profit and loss, peace and unrest, good and evil that create the fire in human minds, consuming one's inner harmony. The mind of man is no match for such a fire. The mind is consumed, and for that one, the Way comes to an end.

No external standard should be used in building people or in demanding that people follow short-lived fashion. It always brings more harm than good. The natural harmony of life is higher than any external standard.

III
Standing For Responsibility

During a certain period of time, Chuang Tzu was very poor. He was the director of the state lacquer plantation, which provided natural varnish for the protection of houses and furniture. Three neighboring states conquered his state and divided the land, and Chuang Tzu and his subordinates were not paid their salary. He felt it was still his responsibility to take care of his subordinates, so in urgency, he went to government superiors to ask for help. He went to borrow some grain from the Duke of Chien-ho. The Duke said, "Certainly. The county taxes will be collected soon, and when they are delivered, I will lend you three hundred pieces of gold."

Chuang Tzu was displeased with his offer, saying, "Yesterday while I was traveling here on the road, I heard a voice call my name. I turned around and saw a fish in a rut made by the carriage wheels. I said to him, "Hey fish, what are you doing there?" He replied, "I am a Wave Director from the Eastern Sea. Will you give me a cupful of water so I can stay alive?"

I replied, "Certainly. I am on a trip to Chien-ho now, and when I reach the West River, I will get a barrelful of water and bring it back for you. How about that?" The perch flushed with anger and said, "I've lost the element which supports my life. I have no way to survive. If you can get me just one cupful of water now, I'll be able to stay alive. But even if you promise me the whole ocean for later, the next time you'll see me will be in the dried fish store!"

IV
Narrow Standards Cannot Be Applied to Everyone

Prince Jen fabricated a huge fishhook and attached it to a strong line. His bait was fifty oxen. Traveling to the top of Mount K'uai-chi, he cast his hook into the Eastern Sea. Every morning for a whole year he fished there, but caught nothing. Finally, one morning a huge fish took the bait, dragged the hook down to the bottom of the sea, then rose swiftly up, waving its fins and churning the water until the whitecaps were huge as majestic mountains. The sound could be heard for over a thousand miles. When Prince Jen brought in the fish, he cut it up and dried it, and from Chih-ho to the east and from Ts'ang-wu to the north everyone had enough to eat. Since that time, storytellers are fond of repeating the great tale of the wisdom and strength of the prince.

Most worldly people go fishing for minnows and perch by pursuing wealth, fame and power; these can be easily caught or obtained. Seeking something greater may not come as quickly as those worldly things, but the reward is long lasting. Even Prince Jen had to wait a year before the fish came to the bait; but the result of his patience benefitted many people.

V
The Wise Old Man

A student of Lao-lai Tzu, while out gathering firewood, happened to see Confucius. When he returned, he reported, "There is a man over there who has a long torso and short legs, rounded back and low set ears. He looks like one of those people who try to reform the world, but I do not know who he is."

"It sounds like Confucius," said Lao-lai Tzu. "Go tell him to come over."

When the young Confucius came in, he said to him, "Confucius, get rid of your rigid and narrow views, your dogmatic rules of behavior and your pride and false appearance of wisdom. Then you will be a great man."

Confucius bowed to show respect and stepped back, looking uneasy. Then his face changed expression and he asked Lao-lai Tzu, "Do you think that would help my work and bring me closer to Tao?"

"You cannot bear to see the suffering of one generation," replied Lao-Lai Tzu, "but you are producing even more distress for the ten thousand generations to come!

False benevolence and rigid customs are the ways of undeveloped people who push each other around with position and fame and pull each other into secret plots. They gather together to praise the great Yao and condemn the tyrant Chieh, when the best and safest thing would be to not accept either of them and put a stop to all dispute, praise and condemnation!

"Praise and condemnation are both injurious to the self; the distraction of movement results in diversion from one's true nature. Once one goes against the natural principle of a matter, its natural way is harmed. Once one stirs the peace and serenity of the mind, the mind starts to be uncontrollable.

"The one of true wisdom is natural. He egolessly follows the flow of nature in everything he does. If there is success in any endeavor, he knows that the energy to accomplish it was provided through no means of his own.

"By following the movement of the natural energy, no harm occurs; by thus moving in perfect freedom, there is no evil influence. The one of natural wisdom does not seek great wealth by his actions, so he always achieves success. You, on the other hand, promote external standards to bring about fame and the admiration of others. This is not natural movement."

Confucius was commonly quoted in Chuang Tzu's work. Justly, there are two aspects of Confucius' work. One aspect is the teaching that is written down in books, which primarily promoted humanism and was written when he became older and mature. He made his contribution by preserving the ancient cultural heritage. The other aspect supported the practice of rigid and artificial customs. For example, he supported the custom that a son should mourn for three years for a parent who passed away; and that men and women could not give things to each other by hand unless they were married, etc. Fortunately, all this has been corrected by time. This part of his teaching is denounced by people of Tao whose profound vision saw that any external dogma or practice has a persecuting

influence that would kill spontaneity in later generations. However, Confucius did gain maturity from the
study of the *I Ching* and was inspired by Lao Tzu,
Lao-Lai Tzu and other typical Taoists. The influence of
Confucius' early teachings became very popular by the
time Chuang Tzu started teaching; the work of
Chuang Tzu was meant to correct the students from
the school of Confucianism who were intent on continuing the old social customs. The separation between
these two schools are easily seen: Confucius' school
serves the government, while the students of Tao directly live and work among people, refusing to join the
ancient ruling system.

VI
Godly Foreknowledge
Cannot Replace Human Spiritual Effort

One night, Prince Yuan of Sung dreamed that a
man with disheveled hair entered through a palace
door and said, "I am an envoy from the Great River.
Traveling from the deep waters of Tsai-lu, I was on my
way north when the fisherman named Yu Ch'ieh
caught me."

When the prince awoke, he asked the soothsayers
the meaning of the dream. "It was a sacred turtle who
spoke in your dream," they replied.

"Is there any fisherman named Yu Ch'ieh living in
the Sung state?" he asked, and his aide replied, "Yes,
there is."

"Summon him," said the Prince.

The next day, Yu Ch'ieh went to the prince's court.
Prince Yuan asked him, "What have you caught while
fishing recently?"

"I caught a large white turtle, five feet around."

"Bring your turtle," said the Prince.

When the turtle was brought, the ruler did not
know whether to kill it or keep it alive. Because he
was in doubt, he asked his soothsayers, who replied,
"Kill the turtle for divination; this will result in good
fortune."

Thus the turtle's shell was removed, which when bored for seventy-two divinations, always gave a true answer.[22]

Chuang Tzu said, "The sacred turtle had the capability to appear to Prince Yuan in a dream, but it could not avoid being captured in Yu Ch'ieh's net. Its wisdom brought seventy-two correct answers but it could not escape the disaster of having itself killed.

"From this example, we see that knowledge or wisdom has its limitations. Even spirituality has that which it can do nothing about. A person with the highest wisdom or spirituality is not all powerful.

"Though a person may possess the highest wisdom, there are always dangers. Thousands may oppose him and scheme against him. Fish do not have the knowledge to be afraid of a fisherman's net, but only know to avoid pelicans.

"What ordinary people define as spirit, spiritual, holy, divine, god or goddess are actually external phenomena. They are the misconceptions of spiritual reality. The true spiritual reality of an individual or nature cannot be conceptualized. Once conceptualized, it becomes a conceptual production. Spiritual reality is far more subtle than whatever is able to be conceptualized. At the same time, it is the very thing that is being conceptualized. You may think it is the mind, but it is not. Mind is what is able to be conceptualized, while true spirit cannot be conceptualized.

"When one puts aside small wisdom, great wisdom will manifest. When one stops making false attempts at goodness, he will naturally become good. A child learns to talk naturally without a language professor, because it lives among people who can talk."

Like talking, the good virtues of humanity are natural capabilities. External, rigid dogmas only stiffen and harm what is natural in us.

---

[22] To divine the answers to important questions, small niches were drilled in the shell and heat was applied; the answer was determined from the shape of the resulting cracks.

VII
Spiritual Independence

Chuang Tzu said: "In the neighborhood of the Yen gateway, upon the death of his parent, a son practiced many austerities in mourning which demonstrated his filial piety and ability to follow procedures. The officials therefore gave him a high post in the government. His relatives thereupon all practiced similar austerities, hoping to receive the same honor, and almost half of them died.

"Excellence leads to fame, and fame turns into artificial behavior or notoriety. Crisis or urgency brings about scheming. Obstinacy or stubbornness results in stupidity. Government is effective when there is general consent to its actions, while forceful interference brings forth calamity.

"Spring rains arrive as always, and new plants and bushes push up from under the earth. The life force of most of the plants have been turned under, and now come out again; for that and the most part of nature, nobody knows how it all happens.

"Relaxation brings health to the sick. Massaging the corners of the eyes eases tiredness. Quiet and peacefulness will disperse anxieties. These cures, however, are only necessary for those who are in need. The man who is in good condition does not need them and never bothers to ask about them. When the world is normal, no one bothers anyone else unnecessarily.

"The man of divinity does not pay attention to that which the Sage finds amazing in the world. The Sage does not pay attention to that which the truly virtuous man delights in with regard to his surroundings. The truly virtuous man does not pay attention to how the petty men adapt themselves to the conditions of their society.

"If the eye is not blocked, there is sight. If the ear is not blocked, there is hearing. If the nose is not blocked, there is smell. If the mouth is not blocked, there is taste. If the mind is not blocked, there is

wisdom.   If wisdom is not blocked, one finds Teh, also
known as virtue.

"Tao may not be blocked.   To block is to choke.
Choking causes disorder; disorder harms all life.

"The wisest of creatures is especially careful with its
breathing.   If his breathing is not perfect, nature cannot
be blamed.   It is only man who bothers to close his
openings.   If air does not reach him in sufficient
quantity, it is not the trouble of his body, but of the
individual's absent mind.   Air is supplied day and
night without cease; only man neglects its importance.

"The body is a cavity of hollows arranged in layers.
The heart is the seat of Heaven.   If a house has no empty space, the wife and her mother-in-law begin to
quarrel.   If the mind cannot roam to Heaven, the senses become overextended.

"Those who would be benefitted by living in deep
forests or lofty mountains are simply unequal to those
who expose their lives to the strain of working in the
world.   Being a hermit is not enough, because the
mind does not work well without healthy stimulation
from normal life in the world.

"If one is able to enjoy one's own nature, then
wherever he goes he can still enjoy himself.   If a person is unable to enjoy his own nature, then wherever
he goes he will not enjoy himself.   Some people wish
to enjoy themselves, and so they set their mind to
escape practical life by renouncing the world.   That is
not the achievement of a person of Tao and great virtue.   These people are self-indulgent in their thoughts
and emotions.   They think this is the way.   Such a person does what he likes emotionally, stumbles about and
falls, but does not turn back.   He races as though he
were on fire and does not look in front of him.

"For instance, glorifying past ages and achievements
and condemning one's present life, or vice versa, has
always been the psychological way of people.   Yet if
they were like Hsi Wei Shih, the sage before Fu Shi,
and other spiritually developed ones of that time, they
would learn to accommodate themselves to the age
they live in and the present stage of their development.

"Only one of perfect nature can transcend the limits of human life and yet not withdraw from the world. Such one lives in harmony with mankind, yet suffers no injury himself from it. He disregards the world's teachings. He has something within himself that makes him independent of others.

VIII
A Uniform is Not a Symbol of Development

Chuang Tzu went to the state of Lu for an appointment with Duke Ai. Duke Ai said, "We have many developed people here in the state of Lu, but there seem to be very few men who study your philosophy and methods."

"There are not many developed people in the state of Lu," responded Chuang Tzu.

"But people all over the state are dressed in the clothing of highly developed ones," said Duke Ai. "How can you say there are not many?"

"Their clothing," said Chuang Tzu, "consists of round caps to confirm their understanding of the cycles of Heaven, square shoes to show they comprehend the shape of Earth and jade ornaments of a broken disc that prove they can make correct decisions and take appropriate actions. But a truly developed person may embrace the truth without necessarily wearing that style of clothing, and a person may wear the clothing without necessarily comprehending the truth. If you do not believe me, then I suggest that you issue a proclamation that anyone wearing the clothing of a developed one without practicing the discipline or understanding the doctrine will be sentenced to death."

Duke Ai did issue the proclamation, and before five days had passed, there was no one in the state of Lu who dared wear clothing that announced his spiritual achievement. Only one old man was dressed that way, and he came to the palace. An interview with the Duke was immediately arranged. The Duke questioned him on affairs of state and, although he tried to entangle him with intricate questions and trip him up with difficult problems, the man responded to all situations appropriately.

Chuang Tzu said, "So you see, there is only one man in the entire state of Lu who is a student of truth and wisdom. Do not be fooled by appearances."

CHAPTER FOURTEEN

ON DECLINING POWER

I
Spoiling No Ego

Yao, who reigned from 2357-2258 B.C., wanted to cede his rulership to Hsu Yu, but Hsu Yu refused it. Then he attempted to give it to Tzu-chou Chih-fu, a wise person. Tzu-chou Chih-fu, an achieved man, excused himself from the offer with a correct reason, saying, "I have no objection to being emperor, but just now I am suffering from an illness causing weakness of my body and am engaged in trying to overcome it. So I first need time to heal myself before doing the same for the world. I agree that this position is of supreme importance, yet I will not allow it to harm my life."

The willpower to resist the temptation of worldly power is much higher than the artificial, worldly power itself. Once you become a king, your focus stays at the superficial level of the world and your relationship to it. Such a position does not allow you to go into the depth of yourself. By being a king, the spiritual crisis is the loss of yourself.

Yao finally ceded the throne to Shun.

II
Truly Responsible People

Shun, who reigned from 2257 to 2208 B.C., wanted to cede his rulership to Tzu-chou Chih-po, a wise man, but Tzu-chou Chih-po said, "I have a chronic illness which I have been taking care of, so I have no time to put worldly affairs in order."

Then Shun offered to turn his rulership over to Shan Chuan, a wise recluse. Shan Chuan said, "I live in the center of the universe. In winter, I wear fur clothing; it keeps me warm. In summer, I wear linen;

it keeps me cool.   In spring I plough the fields and
sow the crops; this gives my body work and exercise.
In fall I harvest and store the crops; this gives my body sustenance and relaxation.   When the sun is up, I
work, and when it goes down, I rest.   I move with
great freedom in Heaven and Earth, and my mind is
content with this simple life.   This is my world.   I
have no use for the power of the empire; it would only
spoil the true joy of life!   What a pity that you do not
understand this!"   He therefore refused the throne and
went off to live in the mountains, away from people.

Then Shun offered the rulership of the empire to a
wise friend, a farmer of Shih-hu, who was trusted and
supported by the people. "Sire," said the latter, "I like
laboring work.   The most important thing I know in
my life is to nurture my honest means of life.   I do not
want anything to encourage the swelling of my ego."

Shun was a virtuous leader.   When he discovered a
person who was more competent than himself he
would offer the throne to him.   He was ready to give
the throne to a better, more worthy person at any time.
This was an example of his virtue.

Government is not for everybody, but in the world
there are many unfit people who compete for high positions.   The competition for power has turned into a
socially glorified game.   However, to know and develop oneself should be the first priority in one's life.

III
Sacrifice No Other Lives for Personal Glory

Tan-fu was active around 1200 B.C.   He was the
grandfather of King Wen, developer of the   *Book of
Changes* and a community leader in agriculture.

When Tan-fu was living in Pin, the barbarians from
Ti attacked his territory.   He tried to appease them
with skins and silks, but they rejected them.   He tried
to appease them with dogs and horses, but they rejected them.   He tried to appease them with pearls and
jades, but they also rejected them.   What the men of
the Ti tribes desired was his land.

Tan-fu spoke to the people, "To dwell among the older brothers and send the younger brothers to die in battle, to dwell among the fathers and send their sons to meet death, this I could not do. Remain where you are, my friends. What difference does it make whether you serve them as your sovereigns or serve me? It has been said, 'One must not let that which is intended to nourish one's life become harmful to one's life.'" Then he departed. His people, however, later followed him and in time founded a new settlement at the base of Mount Ch'i.

Tan-fu respected life. One who respects life, even if he has a high position or great wealth does not allow his means of making a living to end up harming his life. One who respects life, although he may be in a humble position or in poverty, will not allow seeking profit to become harmful to his life. Today's men who have a high position or an important title only think about how terrible it would be to lose what they have. They can only see profit, and in doing so, they neglect and risk their followers' lives. Is this not foolish?

The above example shows that only one who loves his life and the lives of all people can be entrusted with authority over other lives. It is wrong to put a wolf in a powerful position. In history, when foolish people have fought hard to put a wolfish leader in power, they have eventually been 'eaten' or destroyed by that leader. In recent history, Mao Tse Tung, a power-thirsty leader, killed a great number of his old supporters in a nation-wide power struggle. The worst thing in his behavior was using the young, naive people to kill many other good people.

The lives of his people are far more precious to the true leader than the possession of territory. Had the people fought the invaders, the community would have been decimated. By the action of withdrawing himself and his family rather than fight, the community moved to the west and grew rapidly. From this the great Chou Dynasty started by Tan Fu was founded, and his descendants enjoyed the support of all the people, becoming emperors of the entire empire, which began a reign of eight hundred years of peace.

IV
The Gentle is Supported

For three generations in a row, the men of Yueh assassinated their strong rulers. The unambitious Prince Sou, fearing eminent death, fled to hide in a red earth cave, and the state was left without a king. The men of Yueh searched for him and trailed him to the cave, but he refused to come out. So they smoked him out by burning mugwort and happily placed him in the royal carriage to be carried back and enthroned. As Prince Sou grasped the strap to pull himself into the carriage, he turned his face to the sky and cried, "Oh my heaven, to be a king! Could I not have been spared such destiny?" It was that he did not wish to be king; he lamented the dangers and rigid life of being a king.

He was the kind of person who would not injure other people's lives or his own safety by establishing himself as an authority. This was why the people of Yueh wanted him as king. They knew that only the one who values his own life can be entrusted over other lives. He was greatly beloved and supported by the people. The ambitious ones were assassinated. The gentle one was supported.

V
Personal Essence is Valued More than Vain Glory

The ruler of Lu, hearing that Yen Ho had attained Tao, considered that his virtue and wisdom might be helpful, so he sent someone with gifts to open up communications with him. Yen Ho lived in a hovel, wore rough clothing made of hemp and was feeding his oxen when the messenger arrived. Yen Ho went out to meet him.

"Is this where Yen Ho lives?" asked the messenger.

"This is Ho's house," said Yen Ho.

The messenger then began to present the gifts, but Yen Ho said, "I think that there is some kind of a mix-up here. You had better go back and check who you are supposed to give them to. It would not be right for an error to occur."

The messenger left and went to check the instructions. When he returned to look for Yen Ho again, he was nowhere to be found.

Men like Yen Ho do not seek wealth nor honor. They do not accept that which they do not deserve.

It is said that the highest essence of truth is used for examining one's own mind and body. One of its good consequences can be to help one's nation or the world, but the actions of emperors and kings are not what is of utmost importance to a sage. Such actions are not considered by the sage as the means by which to nurture the essence of life. Yet many men of today's world endanger themselves and their lives pursuing external attractions such as glory and vanity. It is a pity. The sage always looks carefully to see where he is going before he moves and what the consequences are before he acts. When the world's government is correctly administered, its responsibility is expressed from the inside out, rather than accomplished for external vanity. Only later generations have made government into a field of competition and vanity and thus, all who are ruled by it suffer from it.

Suppose a person took Duke Sui's priceless pearl, which was so beautiful it shone like the full moon in the night sky, and used it to shoot at a sparrow flying by. The world would consider him foolish indeed, laughing at his behavior. Sacrificing something of great value to acquire that which is of small importance is unwise. And one's life is of far greater importance than the Duke's pearl!

VI
Accept No Help Without Deep Knowledge

Lieh Tzu was poor and hungry. One day, a visitor mentioned this to Tzu Yang, the prime minister of Cheng. He told him, "Lieh Tzu is a man of achievement who has attained Tao; however, he is very poor.

Doesn't Your Excellency favor the achieved ones who live in your state?"

Thereupon Tzu Yang gave orders that provisions be sent immediately to Lieh Tzu. When Lieh Tzu saw the messengers come to his door, he bowed to them respectfully but declined the gifts.

When the messengers had gone and Lieh Tzu went in the house, his wife looked at him in astonishment and said, "I have heard that the family of a man of Tao, the achieved one, live without worry. But see how we suffer! The Prime Minister sent us food, yet you did not accept it. Are we not refusing good fortune or denying the blessings of providence?"

"The Prime Minister has never met me," answered Lieh Tzu. "He sent the food because of what other people said about me. If the people were to speak wrongly of me, he might act upon that misinformation. This is why I refused the food."

This is the principle for accepting a favor or gift from anyone. There was eventually trouble among the people of Cheng. A rebellion arose, and Tzu Yang and all of his related friends were subsequently slain. The insistence on a good principle was part of the foreknowledge of Master Lieh Tzu.

VII
Looking For No Favor Beyond One's Capability

When Prince Chao of Ch'u state was forced out of his throne, he went into exile. Among those who left the state was his butcher named Yueh.

When Prince Chao recovered his rule over the kingdom, he wished to reward those who had remained by his side. On the list of those supporters was the name of Yueh.

However, when the reward was presented to Yueh, he declined to accept it, saying, "When the prince lost control of the kingdom, I also lost my butchery. When he was restored, I also regained my post as butcher. Now that I am returned to my job and salary, what necessity is there for any other reward?"

When he heard about Yueh's reply, the Prince insisted that Yueh accept the reward.

"It was not my fault," said Yueh, "that the Prince was expelled from the state, and it was not because of my merit that he was able to return. There is nothing to be rewarded, and I cannot accept it."

When Prince Chao heard about his reply, he ordered Yueh be brought to the palace. Yueh insisted, "The laws of the state proclaim that for a man to be brought before the sovereign, he must have accomplished a great deed or be worthy of great honors. I did not stay to fight the invaders, nor did I accomplish the return of the prince to his throne. When the soldiers arrived, I followed the Prince in exile, leaving the state to save my life. Now, by setting aside the laws of the land in order to bring me before him, neither the Prince nor I will benefit from good reputation."

The Prince said to Tzu Chi, his chief minister, "Although Yueh has a low position, he has the highest principles. Let us promote him to one of the positions of minister of state."

To which Yueh replied, "To be a butcher is to be less important than a minister, and the social position much lower. But I cannot allow the Prince to patronize me. This I cannot accept; it is for me to remain as a butcher." Yueh refused the position.

Yueh, the butcher, has much more virtue than the favor-thirsty politicians of later days.

VIII
Ambitious Expansion Brings About Disaster

The rulers of the states of Han and Wei were engaged in battle over a small piece of territory. Master Hua Tzu went to see the ruler of Han, Lord Chao-hsi, and found him with a worried look on his face.

Master Hua Tzu told him, "Let us suppose that the world's leaders were to meet and write a document saying: 'He who seizes this scroll with his left hand will have his right hand cut off; he who seizes this scroll with his right hand will have his left hand cut off; but he who seizes this scroll will be ruler of the entire world.' Lord Chao-hsi, would you seize it?"

"Certainly not," replied Lord Chao-hsi.

"That is well indeed," said Master Hua Tzu. "It is clear that your two hands are more important than being ruler of the entire world. However, more important than your two hands is your life.

"The state of Han," he continued, "is much less important than the entire world. The small territory that you are fighting over is much less important than the state of Han.

"Yet here you are, fussing and anxious because you cannot gain possession of the small territory, making yourself distressed and endangering your life!"

After a moment's hesitation, Lord Chao said, "Thank you, Hua Tzu. I have received advice from many men about this, but none as sound as yours!"

Master Hua Tzu had the understanding of relative importance, which is the difference between important and unimportant things. Many men risk their lives for power and many lives are lost in struggles over power. What is more important?

IX
Taking No Advantage of Anyone

Shun wanted to cede the throne to Wu-tse, a friend of his from the north who was virtuously achieved. Wu-tse, upon hearing that Shun was looking for him, said, "Shun is a curious fellow. First he supported himself by working in the furrows of the fields, but then he exchanged that good life to work with Yao, trying to benefit the kingdom. Now he wants me to bend to participate in troublesome political life. Rather than take that on, I would sooner drown myself in the Ch'ing-lin River. How can he expect a friend to take on something like that?"

Many people long to have such a special friend from whom they would receive honor and special favors, but not Wu-Tzu. He preferred to keep his own simple virtue.

X
Only Use Force for the Right Purpose

Chieh, who reigned from 1818 to 1766 B. C., was a very corrupt ruler. T'ang, a strong man with the intention of righteousness, decided to remove Chieh from the throne. His motivation was not to replace the evil Chieh for his own personal glory, but to help all the people of the country.

When T'ang was getting ready to attack Chieh, he went to Pien Sui, a recluse, for guidance.

"It is not my concern," said Pien Sui.

"To whom should I go for advice?" asked T'ang.

"I don't know!" replied Pien Sui.

T'ang then went to Wu Kuang, another recluse who had attained Tao, and asked for advice. "I do not know anything about those matters!" said Wu Kuang.

"To whom should I go for advice?" asked T'ang.

"I don't know."

"What do you think about Yi Ying?" asked T'ang.

"Yi Ying is a strong man of perseverance and tolerance. He might put up with some disgrace."

In the end, T'ang went to Yi Ying and together they decided to attack. After overthrowing Chieh, T'ang offered the throne to Pien Sui. Pien Sui refused. He told T'ang, "When you were planning to attack Chieh, you came to me for advice - so you must have thought I had the makings of a thief. Now you want to cede the throne to me, so you must think I am greedy. It is a disordered world I was born into; now a man with no understanding of the Integral Truth twice comes and tries to bring disgrace to me! This is more than I can bear. How can I live under a leadership built by violence? I would rather throw myself in the Ch'ou River and drown than take the bloody throne."

Then T'ang offered the throne to Wu Kuang, saying, "The wise man plans the strategy, the soldier accomplishes the seizing and the benevolent man takes the post of ruler, as done in ancient times. I would like you to rule."

Wu Kuang refused the throne. He commented, "Deposing one's king by force is not righteousness. Bringing turmoil to the people is not kind. Enjoying profit from another man's troubles is not earnest. It is said, 'Do not accept benefit unless it is earned rightly; do not walk upon the earth where Tao, the subtle law, does not dwell.' I cannot accept the position, nor can I bear to stay in your sight."

Power seized by force is not respected by those who attain spiritual development.

T'ang attacked and deposed his king, Chieh, the last ruler of the Hsia Dynasty, and he kept the teaching of Pien Sui and Wu Kuang in his mind. After vainly looking for many years for the right person to be king, the people named him king and the Shang or Yin Dynasty was founded. Tang reigned from 1766 to 1753 B.C. Yi Ying, who aided him, achieved great excellence in public administration.

CHAPTER FIFTEEN

NO DISCOURAGEMENT
FROM HUMANITY'S PAST
AND NO BENDING OF ONE'S NATURE

I
Virtue is the Power

A wise teacher wore clothes of coarse cloth that had been patched a lot over the worn out places. His shoes were so broken that he had to tie them on his feet with cord. When the King of Wei saw him, he commented, "Oh my, it seems that you are really in distress!"

The teacher said, "I may be poor, but I am certainly not in distress! When a man knows about the great truth of life and understands what virtue is but cannot put them into practice, even if he is rich, he is in distress. Worn out clothing indicates poverty, not distress. My lack of material resources is caused merely by living during a time of unnatural development in society.

"Have you ever seen monkeys playing in the trees? They swing from tree to tree, limb to limb, climbing and twirling with great delight. Even a famous archer like Yi would not be able to keep his eye on one of them. But, if they are moved to a prickly bramble bush, they move tensely, glancing from side to side and trembling with fear. The difference is not due to their muscles having become suddenly rigid and losing flexibility, it is just that the difficulty of their position requires the utmost caution and so they cannot fully use their skill or potential.

"Today the situation is the same for man. To live and work under the prickly influence of current social conditions and the control of the state, with all its corruption and wickedness, will bring one to a state of distress! Pi Kan, the virtuous one who was put to death, is an example of this."

II
On Knowing What One Wants

Tzu-chang, a student of wisdom, said to Man Kou-te, a man of greed, "Why don't you think about the things you do?   Conducting yourself in a shameless way will not earn you people's trust.   If you are not trusted, the public will not support you.   If you have no public support, you can obtain no gain or profit in your life.   So for someone like you, if it is profit or fame you are looking for, then righteous conduct is how to get it.   If you decide to give up pursuing profit or fame to return to your heart's true nature, your conduct still bears examination and modification."

Man Kou-te replied, "The one with no sense of shame gets the biggest profit.   The one who inspires confidence becomes famous."

Tzu-chang said, "In ancient days, Chieh and Chou were both tyrant emperors, enjoying the fame, honor and wealth that comes with the position.   However, to-day, if you tell another that his behavior is like that of Chieh or Chou, he will be deeply embarrassed and will not want to believe that about himself, so much are those two rulers despised.

"Confucius and Mo Ti, popular teachers of righteousness, were both impoverished, ordinary people.   If you tell another that their behavior is like that of Confucius or Mo Ti, they will be pleased but protest that they are not worthy of such high praise, so much are those two teachers loved.

"So you see, to be a wealthy king does not mean you will be loved, and to be a poor, ordinary person does not mean you will be despised.   The difference between being despised or loved lies in one's behavior, whether it is righteous or shameful."

Man Kou-te said, "Small thieves are put in jail, but big thieves become lords and emperors.   Teachers and men of righteousness are found right at the doors of the lords and emperors.   Long ago, even though Duke Huan of Ch'i murdered his elder brother to marry his sister-in-law, the virtuous Kuan Chung assisted him with affairs of state as Premier.   Lord T'ien Ch'eng murdered his sovereign and stole his state, yet Confucius accepted money from him. Verbally these men of shameful behavior were condemned by the righteous teachers, but in actuality they were given respect. Isn't the contradiction between their words and actions deplorable? Truthfully, which of the two types of person is bad? Which is good? In either case, the successful man leads, the unsuccessful man follows."

Tzu-chang replied, "If one does not do right, then society will become disordered. There would be no affection for relatives, propriety between the social classes or leadership by the appointed. How will the distinctions of the five human relationships and the six social orders be maintained?"[23]

Man Kou-te said, "Yao killed his oldest son and Shun banished his uncle. Does this show affection between relations?

"King Chieh was deposed by T'ang; King Chou was assassinated by King Wu. Does this show an orderly relationship between kings and ministers?

"We all know that the eldest in a family is the one who is supposed to receive the highest position in transferring the government from one generation to the next. Wang Chi, who was the youngest son and was thus not entitled to inherit the throne, became king. The Duke of Chou killed his elder brother who was plotting a revolt against him. Does this show leadership by the assigned?

"Those righteous teachers, by speaking about equal love for all, make no attempt to maintain the distinctions set out by the five human relationships and the six social orders.

---

[23]The five human relationships are the orderly relationship between kings and ministers, parents and children, brothers and sisters, husbands and wives and between friends. The six disciplinary social orders are: to be a good father and good mother, to be a helpful uncle or aunt, to be a friendly cousin, to be a loving brother or sister, to be a respectful teacher and a faithful friend.

"I may be seeking wealth, but you are obviously seeking reputation."

Unable to come to an agreement, Tzu-chang and Man Kou-te went to Wu Yoeh, one without bounds, for arbitration in the matter. This was his answer: "One of you thinks too much about his reputation, the other about his profits. However, neither seeking reputation nor pursuing gain reflect any true understanding of Tao. The one who will die for wealth is a petty man. The one who will die for reputation is a proud man. Each of them alters their inborn nature by pursuing one thing. They each differ in the way they alter their true nature, but in disregarding the most important thing they have and being willing to die for something external, they are the same.

"Because neither of them embrace Tao, this is why it is said, 'Do not be petty, always seeking more than what you have; instead apply yourself to using what you have been given by nature. Do not be proud and try to adhere to external standards of good; follow what is reasonable in the flow of natural behavior.

"'Do not fix your eyes on one artificial line of behavior or cling to your own interests. Either can cause failure.

"'Do not rush to become rich and do not only apply yourself to your own self-centered accomplishments, otherwise you may be throwing away what has been given to you from nature itself.

"'Whether you are acting rightly or wrongly, maintain your place at the center of things, keeping your mind only on what you are doing, only with the flow of natural vitality. In this way you can turn to face all four directions and flow with all the seasons. You can ramble in the company of Tao.

"'Do not try to be rigid in your behavior. Do not try to make your righteousness perfect. Rigid conduct and artificial perfect righteousness can cause one to lose their true nature. Do not risk your life for external success, or what is true within you will be lost.'

"Let me give you some examples of what I am saying. Pi Kan, who was a loyal minister to the evil King

Chou, had his heart cut out by order of the king because of his faithful but offensive advice of stopping all unscrupulous behavior. Wu Tzu-Hsu, a faithful general to King Wu, had his eyes plucked from their sockets by order of the king for his loyal but offensive advice not to accept a wrongful gift from Yueh. The gift was sent by the defeated neighboring country, Yueh, to distract the King's attention from revengeful action being taken. Both met with misfortune, although they were loyal and wise.

"Chih Kung informed the authorities when his father stole a sheep, but instead of receiving a reward for his honesty was sentenced to death for unfilial conduct. Wei Sheng promised to meet a friend at a certain time on a bridge and stayed to hold true to his promise, although the river flooded. He held tightly onto the stonework of the bridge and drowned. Both met with disaster, although they were honest and trustworthy.

"Pao Chiao, a recluse during the Chou Dynasty, refused to compromise with his corrupt ruler. To avoid living with corruption, he starved to death. Shen Tzu, the prince of Chin, was falsely charged with poisoning his father. Not wishing to expose his father to ridicule, he refused to defend himself and was sentenced to death. Both met with calamity, although they maintained the highest integrity.

"Confucius never took care of his mother, because of the travels he undertook for the teaching of righteousness, until she was about to die. K'uang Tzu never saw his father. Urging his father to act righteously caused his father to exile him, and they never saw each other again. Both met with error because of righteousness.

"These are true stories of the people of past generations which demonstrate to us that the one who rigidly fixes himself on a high standard of behavior and trustworthiness will meet with hardship."

Wu Yoeh paused a moment and then continued, "Sight longs for beauty. Hearing longs for sweet music. Taste longs for flavor. Ambition or desire longs for its gratification.

"A long life lasts around a hundred years; a medium life lasts eighty; a shorter life around sixty. If one considers all the time one spends in sickness, disease, death, mourning, sorrow and problems, there may only be about four or five days a month that a person can laugh and smile and be with the joy of natural life.

"Sooner or later, every person dies. That which lasts forever is heaven and earth. Compared to what lasts forever, our small limited lives are as quick as the passing of a swift steed seen through a crack. This is no cause for discouragement, however. Life is to experience further natural spiritual evolution. The one who can gratify his ambition and enjoy the years given him by nature is one who has attained Tao."

III
Power Resisting Corruption

Yuan Hsien was a disciple of Confucius and was well known for his indifference to living in poverty. He lived in Lu in a house fifty feet around with a roof of fresh grass and a tattered door made of matting. A branch served as door hinge, and broken pitchers hung with coarse cloth were used as windows. Even though the floor was damp from leaks in the roof, Yuan Hsien sat there serenely strumming his lute and singing.

Tzu Kung, a disciple of Confucius well known for his wealth, had a large carriage drawn by huge horses. He wore a white silk robe lined with purple silk. His carriage was too large for the street where Yuan Hsien lived. When Tzu Kung went to visit him, Yuan Hsien was wearing a cap made of bark and slippers with no toes. Carrying a goosefoot staff, Yuan Hsien came to the gate to meet him.

"My goodness," exclaimed Tzu Kung. "You are certainly in distress!"

Yuan Hsien replied, "I have heard that having no wealth is called poverty. It is when one studies and cannot practice what has been learned that a person is in distress. I am poor, but certainly not distressed!"

Tzu Kung stepped back, embarrassed. Yuan Hsien laughed and said, "To act for the purpose of ambition, to form cliques and study for reputation, to teach out of self-interest, to use benevolence and righteousness for one's own profit, and accumulating goods such as carriages and horses - those things I could not bear to do!"

IV
Tao is Normalcy

Tseng Tzu, an achieved disciple of Confucius, lived in the state of Wei. He wore a worn out robe of quilted hemp, his face was swollen and rough, and his hands and feet were callused. He would go three days without lighting a fire for heat. It would be ten years before he wore new clothes. If he straightened his cap, the rim would break. If he pulled his lapels together, his elbows stuck through the sleeves. If he wore his shoes, his heels showed through the back. Yet, wherever he walked, he would sing the hymns of Shang in a voice that filled Heaven and Earth, clear as a bell or chiming stone. He would not be minister to the Emperor nor friend to feudal lords.

He who cultivates his will or purpose forgets his body and seeking profit. He who has attained Tao forgets about thinking.

V
Be Content with One's Honest Support

Confucius remarked to Yen Hui, "Hui, your position in society is very low and your family is very poor. Why don't you get a job with the government?"

Yen Hui replied, "I have no desire to do so. I have fifty acres of farmland outside the outer wall of the city, which is enough to provide food, and I have ten acres of farmland inside the city wall, which is enough to provide clothing. Playing my lute gives me enough joy and studying the Way of the Master gives me enough happiness. I have no need to work for the unnatural ruling order."

Confucius looked abashed. He paused a moment and said, "Hui, I find your perspective enlightening. I have heard that when one understands what is enough,

no thoughts of gain entangle him. When one understands satisfaction, there will be no fear of loss. When
one cultivates what is within him, he holds no position
in society and therefore feels no shame. I have been
studying and promoting these ideas for a long time,
but for the first time, I see someone who lives them. I
am greatly benefitted by what you have shown me."

VI
Inner Health Cannot be Attained by Force

Prince Mou of Wei, who later became a student of
Chuang Tzu, was living in Chung-shan, a rural place.
He said to Chan Tzu, an adept in learning Tao, "Although my body is here beside these rivers and trees,
my mind remains at the palace in Wei. What should I
do about this dilemma?" Prince Mou was apparently
trying, without much success, to live the life of a hermit. He was heir to the throne of a large state. For
him to become a recluse was more difficult than for an
ordinary scholar with little wealth or position.

"Put your emphasis on your life itself," answered
Chan Tzu. "He who considers his inner life and
health to be of utmost importance will find that material possessions no longer matter greatly."

"I know," said Prince Mou, "but I cannot seem to
do anything about my interests."

"If you cannot overcome your tendencies, then it
would be best to follow them!" smiled Chan Tzu. "If
being a hermit is not for you, then it would be well for
you to pursue your natural inclination. To force oneself not to follow one's disposition is like adding one
injury on top of another. People who do such double
injury to themselves do not last long!"

Although Prince Mou did not attain Tao, he may
be said to have been on the way there, because he
learned something about his own nature.

VII
I Direct My Life in Agreement with Tao

When Confucius was in difficulty in Ch'en and
Ts'ai, he went without properly cooked food for a

week. Although his face became thin from tiredness, he sat in his small shelter, playing his lute and singing. Yen Hui was outside gathering firewood, listening to what Tzu-lu and Tzu-kung were saying. "Our Master has been twice expelled from Lu," they said. He almost lost his life in Wei. The people of Sung cut down the tree he had rested under because they so disagreed with his doings. People made trouble for him in Shang and Chou, and now they have surrounded him here at Ch'en and Ts'ai. Anyone who kills him will be pardoned; anyone who takes him prisoner will not be interfered with. Yet he keeps on playing and singing. Is this the way a superior man acts?"

Yen Hui did not know what to say, but went inside and told Confucius, who set aside his lute and said, sighing, "Tzu-lu and Tzu-kung are unknowing fellows. Ask them to come, and I will speak to them."

When they entered, Tzu-Lu said, "I guess you could say that we are all blocked now because the local people have barricaded us in here."

Confucius said, "What are you saying! When a person breaks through to Tao, it is called 'breaking through.' When he is blocked from Tao, it is called 'being blocked.'

"I choose the ways of benevolence and righteousness; unfortunately, we are in the midst of trouble because of the disorder and confusion in the world. But we do not need to find ourselves 'blocked' because of that.

"By cultivation of the inner being, Tao is attained; with Tao, when danger comes there is no loss of virtue. It is the coldness of the frost and the snow of winter which reveal the luxuriance of the pine and fir trees. I regard it a blessing to be in this situation." Then, he turned around and went back to his playing and singing.

Tzu-Lu quickly picked up a shield and began dancing to the music, while Tzu-kung said, "We have not understood that Heaven is so high up above, Earth so far down below and the greatness of attaining Tao like our master!"

The ancients who attained Tao were equally happy in times of success and failure, because their happiness had nothing to do with good or bad fortune. Once one attains Tao, failure and success become like links in a chain. Once one attains Tao, good and bad fortune become like the passing seasons.

To attain Tao does not mean that one has to become impoverished like the wise ones who chose to live in such a poor way, as shown in the last few stories of this chapter. Rather, it is most helpful to examine what is real and what is important i your own life. Those virtuous individuals found that riches were not important to them. Rather than blindly pursuing wealth, it is also right to examine the importance of having money compared to the spiritual condition of your life! What is the function of both money and life? What is the purpose of each of them, and how have you been using them?

CHAPTER SIXTEEN

ROBBER CHIH

Confucius was friends with Liu-hsia Chih, whose younger brother was widely known as Robber Chih, head of bandits. Robber Chih lead a group of nine thousand followers. They terrorized the people of the countryside, tunneled into storehouses, broke into shelters, drove off men's cattle and horses and seized their wives and children. Robber Chih was an extreme example of one who is greedy for personal gain. He disregarded his family and failed to perform sacrifices to his ancestors. These were important rituals in conventional Chinese society; anyone failing to follow these customs was no longer accepted, and Robber Chih rebelled against all of them. Thus, whenever he approached a city, the inhabitants guarded the city walls or fled into their strongholds; all people lived in distress and dread.

Confucius said to his friend Liu-hsia Chih, "A father must lay down the rule of good conduct to his son. An elder brother must teach his younger brother. If a father does not lay down the rule to his son and an elder brother does not teach his younger brother, then the relationship between father and son and that between elder and younger brother loses its worth. You are one of the most competent men of the age, yet your younger brother is Robber Chih, a peril to the world! It is a shame that you, his elder brother, are unable to teach him any better ways. I would therefore like to go to persuade him to change himself."

Liu-hsia Chi replied, "Confucius, you remarked that a father must be able to lay down the rule of good conduct to his son and an elder brother should teach his younger brother. However, even when guidance is given with the strength of conviction or eloquence, if the son refuses to listen or the younger brother does not follow the elder brother's words, nothing can be done. Chih is a man of strength and cunning, power and will. His thinking shifts like the wind. Those who go along with him delight him, but those who go against him infuriate him and incur his abuse. Stay away from him."

Confucius ignored his warning, and taking Yen Hui as his carriage driver and Tzu-gong and a few other students as his companions, he went to visit Robber Chih. At that time, Robber Chih was resting with his followers near Mount T'ai in the late afternoon sun, enjoying a bowl of minced human livers. Confucius arrived, stepped down from the carriage and advanced to one of Chih's servants. "I am K'ung Ch'iu,[24] a native of Lu State. I have heard about the high traits of your leader," he said, respectfully bowing to the servant.

The servant went into Robber Chih's tent to announce his arrival.

When Robber Chih heard who it was, he flew into a rage, eyes blazing and hair bristling. "It must be that scoundrel Kung Ch'iu, who people call Confucius, from Lu! Tell him I said, 'You make up deceitful stories, create fancy phrases and drone on with inane praises about the character of kings Wen and Wu. Your cap looks like a tree branch and your belt is made from the ribs of a dead cow.[25] You drown people with your false theories and misleading 'wisdom.' You eat food that you do not grow yourself and wear clothing that you have not woven yourself. Lips and tongue flapping, you preach about 'right' or 'wrong' until you mislead the rulers of the world and prevent the

---

[24]K'ung Ch'iu was his birth name. Confucius means Master K'ung. 'Con' is his surname, 'fucius' means teacher, a title of respect, like the word Tzu. It should be unified in the translations as Kung Tzu, like Lao Tzu, Chuang Tzu and Mo Tzu. Tzu as a title means master. Tzu as a general word means son or seed.

[25]It was a Chinese custom that mourners who lost their parents should wear such a hat.

scholars from returning to the Source. Your ideals of
'filial piety' and 'brotherliness,' are only your attempt
to attain the favor of the rich and powerful. As such,
in truth your crimes are many. Go home quickly now,
because if you don't leave soon, I will include your
liver in today's dinner."

Confucius sent another message in to Robber Chih,
using words of great politeness for that time, saying, "I
am a friend of your brother Liu-hsia. Therefore I beg
to be permitted to gaze at your feet beneath the curtain
from afar."

After the servant conveyed the message to Robber
Chih, he replied, "Allow him to come in."

Confucius hurriedly went in, declined the mat that
was offered him, and bowed twice before Robber Chih.
Robber Chih, still enraged, sat comfortably in his chair.
His hand was on his sword and his eyes showed the
fury of his temper. With a voice with the fierceness of
a tigress with cubs, he said, "Confucius, step forward!
If I like what you have to say, you will live. But if I
don't, you will die!"

Confucius began to speak. "It is said that in the
world there are three kinds of character traits. The
highest kind of character has a firmly shaped body and
great charisma that inspires all people, young or old,
famous or humble, to bring peace among them. The
second kind of character holds the wisdom of Heaven
and Earth and is able to explain all things and the best
way to do a thing. The lowest kind of character is
brave and fierce, willful and forceful, who attracts a
group of followers or warriors. Any man who possesses even one of these character traits can be above
the majority and call himself a King.

"But you, however, possess the potential for all
three kinds of character. You are eight feet tall, with a
radiant face, shining eyes and deep red lips, pearly
white teeth and a well tuned voice. Nevertheless, the
only title you have is that of 'Robber Chih.' Such a
pity! Listen to me. I have a proposition for you.
Make me your envoy and I will travel south to Wu
and Yueh, north to Ch'i and Lu, east to Sung and Wei

and West to Chin and Ch'u. In those places, I will convince them to create a new, orderly kingdom several hundred miles in size and surrounded by a great wall, where a town of thousands of households will be established and you will be honored as a feudal lord. There, you can lay down your weapons and disband your followers, beginning anew with your brothers and kinsmen, and start again to make sacrifices to your ancestors. Taking such action would be comparable to that of a sage and a gentleman and it is the greatest wish of the world."

Robber Chih, angered, replied, "Kung Ch'iu, step forward! Only men who are foolish, dull or ordinary can be influenced by offers of gain or changed by empty words. The fact that I am big, tall and handsome is a feature inherited from my parents. Do you think I am unaware of that and need your praises? By the way, it is said that those who praise men in front of them also damn them behind their backs.

"You cannot lead me around like a simpleton with promises of gain, a walled state and hundreds of people. Trying to arouse my self-interest in this way cannot succeed. Even if I were given such a state, it would obviously not last long. The Great Empire is the largest walled state, and even though Yao and Shun possessed it, their heirs were left with only the tiniest bit of land. T'ang and Wu were both set up as emperors, but afterwards, their descendants were destroyed. This loss, was it not because their gains and their self-interest had been so great? The worst kind of king or government is no better than my way. They are only practicing a more organized robbery.

"Let me tell you now about Perfect Virtue. In ancient times, there were many birds and beasts and few people. The people nested in the trees to sleep and to escape from danger. They gathered acorns and chestnuts during the day. They wore no clothing; in summer they collected firewood in great piles which they burned in the winter to keep warm. During the time of Shen Nung, people slept peacefully, waking up with wide eyes and clear minds. They lived side by side with elk and deer, planted their food and wove their clothing. They knew their mothers but not their fathers. No thought of harming another could be found in their hearts. This was the height of perfect virtue.

"Even the Yellow Emperor himself could not achieve this height of virtue. In the field of Cho-lu, he fought with Ch'ih Yu of the less developed tribes until the blood formed a stream a hundred li[26] in length. T'ang banished his ruler, Chieh, and King Wu murdered his ruler, Chou. From then on, the weak have been oppressed by those stronger and the few have been abused by the many. From the time of T'ang and Wu to the present day, all sovereigns have been no more than a gang of ruffians and lawbreakers. So what are you doing, cultivating the ways of Wen and Wu, teaching the future generations your hypocrisy with eloquent words and leading the rulers of the world astray? Is it that you hope to attain wealth and power? Ha! With that motive, you are the biggest thief I know. The world may call me Robber Chih, but it should also call you 'Robber K'ung Ch'iu.' You are the friend of all robbers, past and present, who also happen to be called Kings. Can you not see that they are the same as I?

"Your sweetened words persuaded Tzu-lu, the courageous and brash warrior, to follow you. He removed his helmet and unbuckled his long sword to accept your instruction, and didn't the world say, 'Confucius can put an end to violence and evil.' But it resulted that Tzu-lu tried to slay the ruler of Wei, but failed. They hung his corpse up on the eastern gate of Wei. All because of your senseless teaching! You instructed him and all it did was lead him to trouble. Twice they drove you out of your home state; you almost lost your life in Wei; they made trouble for you in Ch'i and besieged you at Ch'en and Ts'ai No one can stand you. Causing all these calamities for yourself and others, what good is this 'Way' of yours? Do you

---

[26]A measurement of one-third mile.

consider yourself a man of talent?   A sage?   What happened that made you come here today?

"Besides leaders like myself, there is no one more admired in the world than the Yellow Emperor.   Yet even he could not maintain his virtue intact, but battled at Cho-lu until the blood flowed like a river.[27] Yao was an unforgiving father, killing his eldest son whom he discovered to be evil.   Shun was unfilial as a son; he married without the consent of his parents.   Yu became half paralyzed from trying so hard to control the great flood.   T'ang exiled Chieh, his sovereign. King Wen was put in jail at Yu-li.   King Wu killed his sovereign Chou.   These six are highly esteemed and respected by the people of the world, yet when we look a little closer, we see that all of them confused the truth within them for gain, turning against their true nature and inborn form, disturbing their original purity. This is shameful![28]

"The world loves to talk about virtuous people. When they do, we always hear the names Po Yi and Shu Ch'i.   Po Yi was the elder brother and was therefore, by custom, heir to the throne, but he thought his younger brother, Shu Ch'i was better suited for the position, so he fled.   Shu Ch'i, however, thought it would be wrong to take his brother's position, so he fled too.   Each fled because their love for each other was too strong.   They both went to Shou-yang Mountain and starved themselves to death, and both remained unburied.   They preferred to die rather than damage their brotherly love.

---

[27]This is a description of the war of early struggle between Han and Ri.   The Yellow Emperor was elected as military leader when he was seventeen.   He won the defensive war and established an orderly society.   Robber Chih viewed this historical event differently, however.

[28]Later writers on the whole recognize these events as historical fact, but offer justifications for them.   Among the early practitioners of Tao, the natural virtuous models were those who lived before the Yellow Emperor.   Confucius, however, somewhat over-promoted the conceptual establishments of Yao, Shun and Yu.

"Pao Chiao made a great display of himself and his 'virtuous' behavior. Rather than acknowledge any unnatural sovereign, he became a recluse, living in the forest and eating acorns. Yet when someone told the King where he was, he decided to commit suicide, wrapping his arms around a tree and standing there until he died.

"Shen-t'u Ti gave advice to his sovereign that was not followed, so he loaded a stone on his back and threw himself into a river and drowned. He said, 'If the sage is not listened to, the country must fall. I cannot help anymore because I am not listened to.' He became good food for the fish and turtles.

"Chieh Tzu-t'ui was a faithful retainer to the Prince of Chin, Duke Wen during his nineteen years in exile. He went so far as to cut a piece of flesh from his thigh to serve the Prince, saving him from starvation. Later, however, when the Prince forgot to reward him, he became angry and withdrew to a forest. The ruler tried to smoke him out so he could recover his friend, but he decided to die in the fire.

"Wei Sheng made an appointment to meet a girl under a bridge. The girl did not appear at the specified time, and although the water began to rise, Wei Sheng would not leave. He clung to the bridge-post and drowned for the sole purpose of keeping his word.

"These six men are no different than beggars, a sliced up dog, or pigs carried away by a flood. They were all trapped by desire for reputation; considering life less important, they failed to remember the Source. They gave up the time that fate would have given them. And they are the ones you promote as examples and praise in front of the people of the world!

"The world loves to talk about loyal ministers. When they do, we hear the names Prince Pi Kan and Wu Tzu-hsu. Yet Prince Pi Kan, who used good conduct and assisted the common people to oppose his ruler, was trapped by his good conduct and sentenced to death by his ruler. Wu Tzu-hsu loyally and repeatedly warned his sovereign about possible attack from a different state, but the king became suspicious of him and forced his suicide. You may call these men loyal ministers, but they became laughingstocks of the world.

"When you really look at all these men, you see that none is truly worthy of respect. So, K'ung Ch'iu, do you think that I should learn from them?

"In your lecture of today, if you tell me some ghost stories or something I have not learned, you can fool me because I know nothing about them. But if you speak about human affairs, there is nothing more you can say, because I already know them so well.

"Now I will describe man's real form to you. His eyes long to see color, his ears delight in hearing sound, his mouth wishes to taste flavors, and his will and spirit crave their fulfillment. A long life for a man is one hundred years. Nature itself never perishes, but there is always a time when a man dies, some sooner than others. A man who cannot gratify his desires or enjoy a long life has not attained Tao. I reject every bit of what you have been telling me! Be gone! No more of your talk. This 'Way' you tell me about is hypocritical, senseless and foolish, not the sort of thing that is capable of preserving the original purity of man. It is all external false creation of no truth. There is no reason to bother discussing it!"

Confucius paused a moment, then replied, "Most people have two possible aspects in their development, the positive (constructive) and the negative (destructive). I dedicate my life to teaching and exalting the healthy sphere. What you viewed is the negative side, or human sickness.

"You and I are both students of history. Before I met the respectful Lao Tzu, who took charge of the historical documents for the Chou dynasty, the learning I received about historical events may have been inaccurate. Lao Tzu truly knows the historical events, and gave us teaching and guidance based on his understanding of the truth.

"I deeply understand that your life is an expression of protest against unnatural social development and the establishment of power structures. There are two ways to gain power: either to use unscrupulous means such as killing and stealing, or through supporting other people by one's good deeds and actions. Most people try to apply themselves to solving the world's problems inappropriately through excessive behavior. However, if we look into the historical examples, we see that the practice of excess leads to unhealthy results.

"For example, it is not constructive that people commit suicide to protest something; this is a negative sacrifice. We respect virtuous behavior that supports an effective life. We would rather follow spiritual health and the right direction in conducting our life than do something excessive to try to change the world or give up completely. It is better to move in the right direction and make a few small mistakes than to move in a totally wrong direction and do a few small right things.

"Therefore, I cannot respect your explanation. At the beginning, I pointed out that you have the qualities of a king who could organize a government and serve people justly. But all you have expressed is disappointment in the past or present human leaders. I do share your understanding. However, history makes inferior people. Superior people make history. It is you and I who have the opportunity to renew history. Yet, my kind of work changes history slowly. Your kind of strength could change history rapidly if you redirect the expression of your life.

"Also, because of the bad quality of human leaders, it follows that the world will be bad. If leadership is built on deluding people, political schemes, depending upon armies, policemen, secret investigative agencies, bribery, threat, concentration camps and assassination to control the population, the situation is created that makes all people depend on the government for a living. It is not healthy if a government is organized in a negative manner with a created, false majority. The resulting world would be like a persecuting holocaust; a realization of hell under a demonic bloody throne. Help can only be had by once again seeing the internal light and doing away with all trouble in order to restore an organic life and organic society. Must people be taught by hard lessons before they can awaken?

"If you could not do away with unnatural development of the world, at least you should not be the one to add to the misery of all people."

Confucius bowed twice, turned and left quickly, his followers behind him. Tzu-Gong, the driver, was a little shaken by the whole scene and fumbled a little when he took the reins, but Confucius remained calm and upright, his spirits undefeated. After their departure, Robber Chih remained silent, astonished by Confucius' words, conviction and bravery.

When Confucius returned to Lu, he just arrived outside the eastern gate when he saw Liu-hsia Chih. "Where have you been?" asked Liu-hsia Chih, "I have not seen you for a few days, and your carriage and horses look as though they have been out. Did you go to see my brother Chih after all?"

Confucius sighed and replied, "Yes, I did."

"Was he not infuriated by your views, as I told you?" said Liu-hsia Chi.

"He was," admitted Confucius. "You might consider that I gave myself some strong medicine without even being sick. I went rushing off to pat the tiger's head and comb its whiskers, and almost didn't escape its teeth!"

Not long after, however, Robber Chih found himself contemplating Confucius' words. Finally, he disbanded his group and with some followers moved to the western wilderness where he started a new, peaceful life as a farmer and hunter. After some years, the community grew with him as its leader. He remained there promoting justice, openness and kindness, enjoying the rest of his life in dignity and free from all curses.

CHAPTER SEVENTEEN

THE TRANSFORMATION OF NATURE

I
The Time For Changes

All lives are in a process of constant development. They are the transformed energy of nature. It is the underlying interplay of light and water that brings about the changes of all lives. It is noticeably the interchange of warmth and cold that keeps all lives changing. Differences in shape, size and length of life become the expressions of the varied natural lives that have been formed. Vegetation and fish are the transformed energy of water. Birds, bears, leopards, monkeys and all animals including humans are the energy transformations of vegetation and the forest. All creatures emerge from the mysterious workings of nature and then return to it again. The physical nature of man, too, in time, returns to the mysterious transforming process of nature, though our spirits always connect with nature. Nature gives, nature takes away.

All human life was brought into the world; long after spiritual development, people became aware that the lower physical sphere of nature is the laboratory that produces all visible phenomena. Gradually, the human mind grew to respond to its external environment through a process of trial and error. The difficulties and challenges of life brought about human development; they represent the darkness that precedes conscious intelligence. Human consciousness and intelligence, however, are preparatory to the development of spiritual discernment. From the development of intelligence emerges the increased potential for a fully developed mind, a mind which can internalize and replicate the natural creative processes and produce body spirits. An individual can learn nature's skill of transforming life energy to produce body spirits, moving that person into the spiritual dimension of the gods. This highest natural convergence of human energy forms a newly integrated spiritual life, referred to as a "shien."

There are many beliefs and practices used to develop oneself. Some are the result of human imagination. The most realistic approach is to learn the unchanging truth of life - Tao. Developed people keep away from the trouble and pain created by religions. From a mature spiritual perspective, most conventional religious ideas and practices are merely emotional toys and playthings of undeveloped minds. Practicing them is an irresponsible waste of time that can cause a person to become spiritually sick.

In modern times, mechanical robots are a refined achievement of our society. Robots, however, cannot gather life experience or benefit spiritually from the wonders of life. Human consciousness can actually be conditioned like a robot by superficial religious customs. It is important to realize that you are the only one who can rescue yourself spiritually from the conditioned mentality of religious thinking. These religious conceptions are traps which reflect the level and responsibility of the teacher and the students who get caught in them. So please choose carefully. The truth of Tao has been clearly elucidated in the work of Lao Tzu and Chuang Tzu as well as in my related material. These teachings do not pull your spirits down in the service of your emotional nature or your desires as do ordinary religions; instead they lift your desires and emotions to the plane of true spiritual integration and development.

II
You Have Never Lived and You Have Never Died

Master Lieh Tzu was traveling along a road and stopped to eat his lunch. As he looked about him, he discovered an old skull. He pulled the weeds away from around it, and pointing his finger at it, he said, "You and I are the only ones who know that you have never either died nor lived. I do not believe that you are unhappy. Is not death the beginning of life, and life truly a type of death?"

III
No Birth Was Received
When Chuang Tzu's wife died, Hui Tzu went to offer his condolences. At the house, he found Chuang Tzu sitting with his legs sprawled out, pounding on an old basin, singing.

"You lived with your wife for many years. She brought up your children and helped you," said Hui Tzu. "It is enough that you are not weeping about her death. But isn't banging on that tub and singing a song going a bit too far?"

Chuang Tzu replied, "When she first died, I could not help being affected with grief. But then I began to think about the beginnings of her life. I looked back upon how her life began and the time before she was born. Continuing on to the time previous to her having a body, then I looked back to the time before she had a spirit. In the midst of the vastness, transformation occurred and she had a spirit. More transformation and she had a body. Still more transformation and birth occurred. Another transformation, and now she is dead. This is no different than the change of one season to the next. She is now resting peacefully in the vastness of nature, but if I were to go around moping and sobbing, it would show lack of understanding about the nature of life. So I stopped."

IV
What Have You to Resent?
Two men, one who had transcended the body and one who had transcended the mind, were hiking together to the top of Mount Min-Po. When they reached the region of the K'un-lun Mountains where the Yellow Emperor rests, one of them suddenly discovered that the other had a tumorous growth upon his left elbow.

"Do you resent this?" he asked.

"No. I don't find anything to resent," said the other. "To be alive is to be a borrower; we do not even own our bodies. If we must borrow merely to live, we know that life is temporary, nothing but a bit of dust and dirt. Life and death are like the procession of day and night. You and I are here watch the process of change occur, and now one change has come to me. What is there to resent?"

V
The Healthy Growth of Soul

When Chuang Tzu was traveling to Ch'u, he saw an old skull by the side of the road, dry and parched but still intact. He poked it with his riding whip and said, "Sir, were you greedy in life but forgetful of good reason, and so came to your end? Were you a noble whose state was overthrown? Did you do some evil deed and end your life to avoid disgrace? Was it poverty, cold and hunger that brought you to this, or was it a natural end of old age?"

After he had finished speaking, he moved the skull over to a sheltered place. Using it for a pillow, he lay down to sleep.

During the night, the skull came to him in a dream, saying, "Your philosophical talk describes the entangled conditions of a mortal and not the reality of the dead. Would you like to hear about it?"

"Yes," said Chuang Tzu.

The skull said, "Among the dead there are no governments nor subjects who are governed. There is nothing that relates to the changes of the four seasons. Eternity describes our existence and knows no boundary. Even an earthly king could not have as much happiness as we do."

Chuang Tzu found this hard to believe. He said, "If Great Nature offered to give you a body, return you to your old home, family and friends, you would choose that instead, right?"

The skull replied, "For what reason would I want to leave happiness that is greater than any person could know? Why come back and take on the troubles of being a human again?"

The words of the skull, Chuang Tzu thought, were reflections on the meaning of physical life. It said that no one should fear the natural event of death. Such unfounded fears distort the healthy growth of the soul.

VI
One Kills When One Fears

With the hopes of persuading the ruler to listen to his humanistic ideals, Yen Yuan went east to the state of Ch'i. His teacher was worried.

"You seem troubled about Yen Yuan's trip," commented Tzu-Kung, one of his senior students.

"Well," relied the teacher, "To this situation I believe the saying of Kuan Chung applies: 'Small bags cannot contain large objects, and short ropes cannot reach the water in deep wells.' You see, fate or destiny assumes pre-arranged forms. The use or appropriateness of a certain form cannot be changed; it has its limitations.

"When he arrives in Ch'i, Yen Yuan will tell the Duke about the wise and kind rulers like Yao, Shun and the Yellow Emperor. Then he will speak about earlier times, about Sui Jen, who discovered fire, and Shen Nung, who discovered agriculture. After listening to him, the Duke will look to see if he has the same capabilities within himself. When he tries to be so but sees that he cannot do it, he will begin to suspect those around him. Because he is in a position of power, his distress and suspicion may lead to killing. Then, what is the good of the trip?

"For you, an ambitious young gentleman hunting for an influential position in the government but who neglects his own nature, I have a story to tell you. It was related by Master Pien to his disciples. A sea gull once perched near the capital of Lu. The Duke saw it and brought it to the temple, where he entertained it by performing the Nine Shao music for it. Then the meat of the sacrifice was prepared for it to feast on. But the bird, looking confused and dejected, refused to eat even one piece of meat or sip the wine, and after

three days it was dead.   This is an example of trying
to nourish a bird with human food instead of with the
food that would nourish a bird.   If you want to nourish a bird, then you let it fly loose in the forest, play
along the banks and islands of the rivers and lakes, eat
mudfish and minnows and live any way it chooses.   A
bird dislikes even the sound of human voices, much
less all the clamor and commotion of composed music.

"Perform the Nine Shao music in the wilds around
Lake Tung-t'ing and birds will fly away, animals will
run off and fish will dive to the bottom of the pond.
It is only people who stay to listen.

"Fish live in water and do well, but if men tried to
live in water, they would surely die.   Because their
constitution is different, their likes and dislikes are different.   That is why the developed ones did not require
the same abilities from each person nor give each the
same duties.   Things were given names according to
their reality and duties were distributed according to
fitness.   This was called a proper relationship with all
things and all others which brings about mutual benefit.   This is what is meant by 'Good fortune stays when
the spokes converge.'   What the world calls good fortune is the result of the support of harmony in a relationship with all."

VII
Strengthen Oneself, But do Not Start Wars

King Ying of Wei and Lord T'ien Mou of Ch'i
made a treaty over the acquisition of a piece of land.
When Lord T'ien Mou broke the agreement, however,
King Ying became enraged.   He was just about to arrange for his murder when Kung-sun Yen, the minister
of war, heard of this and flushed with shame, went
over to him.

"You rule a state possessing more than ten thousand chariots," he said to the King, "but you seek revenge like a ordinary man!   I request command of two
hundred thousand armored troops so that we may attack, take his people prisoner and lead his horses and
cattle away.   I will cause in him a rage so intense that

it will break out on his back like men who develop cancer as a result of intense anger and frustration. Then I will raid the capital city and smash the backbone of his army's resistance."

Hearing this, Chi Tzu, the faithful minister of Wei, was filled with shame. He said, "When a city wall seven feet high is built, destroying it would bring great hardship on all the people who worked to construct it. Similarly, for the past seven years it has never been necessary to call out the military; this peace is the very foundation of your sovereignty. Kung-sun Yen's advice must not be considered!"

Hua Tzu, another dutiful minister of Wei, disagreed with both. He commented, "To attack Ch'i would bring disorder to all that has been achieved, and not to attack would have the same result. And what I say, too, will cause people to be upset."

"Then what should I do?" said the King.

"The only thing is to try to find the Way."

Hearing this, Hui Tzu, the Prime Minister of Wei and a friend of Chuang Tzu, introduced Tai Chin-jen, a developed civilian, to the King. Tai Chin-jen told him, "Does your Majesty know about the creature called the snail?"

"Yes."

"On the tip of its left horn is a realm called Argument and on the tip of its right horn is a realm called Ignorance. They fight over each other's territory and engage in war, slaying thousands, and pursuing one another's survivors for the longest time."

"Humbug," said the King. "This is only a tale."

"Allow me, your majesty, to explain it to you. Do you believe that the universe is finite or infinite?"

"Infinite," he replied.

"Are you familiar with how to let your heart and mind dwell in the infinite, and then, return to the limits of this world, remaining indifferent to its existence? This is how to enjoy true unlimited spiritual expansion and to not be bound by the smallness of insignificant gain or loss."

"Yes," said the ruler.

"In this world is Wei, and within Wei exists the city of Liang, and within the city of Liang there is a king. Within this orderly world, a king is a symbol of highly developed civilization. However, in the days of war, is there any difference between a noble king and the warlike chief of the undeveloped tribe of Maul? When they go to battle, is there any difference between a civilized king and a barbarian? Is there any difference between Ignorance and your Majesty?"

"I am afraid that there is no difference when a war is being fought," said the King.

After the visitor left, the King sat dumbfounded, in silence. The interview over, Hui Tzu came before him. "That visitor is a man of God," said the King. "The wise kings of the past are not even his equal. I understand now. His advice is to strengthen ourselves, not engage in attacking others; then we can enjoy the infinity of independence and freedom, as you have always reminded me. Otherwise, there will be only suffering on both sides. To fight a war is to go against the high law of the precious nature of life. I would like my whole kingdom to enjoy the freedom of no wars rather than to show off our strength to save our pride. This freedom is more important than expansion, which would impose great hardship. So now I have learned to enjoy being lord of a territory as small as the tip of an antenna in a big snail-like world."

CHAPTER EIGHTEEN

ON TEACHING THE SUBTLE TRUTH

I
From Useless Discovery Comes the Useful

Hui Tzu said to Chuang Tzu, "What you talk about is useless!"

Chuang Tzu replied, "One must understand the useless before knowing about usefulness. For example, the earth is vast and broad, but a man only uses as much of it as his feet can cover; this piece of ground you would call useful.

"If, however, all the earth were removed from around his feet until the Yellow Springs (the hollowness) were reached, then would the man still be able to make use of that piece of ground?"

"No, it would be useless," said Hui Tzu.

"Then it is obvious," said Chuang Tzu, "that the useless supports the useful."

The search for truth is like someone standing on Earth looking for the beingness of Earth. Even if he digs every inch of the Earth, he still will not find the beingness of Earth. He is not even aware of where he sets his feet!

II
The Seeing Heart is Commonly Obstructed by Words

Most people take nine out of ten words that are quoted from others as the mark of authority. They believe seven out of ten words of the ancient wise sayings. It is obvious that many people use the values of unexamined convention as the authority to convince others to believe what they say.

Only words spoken with no personal self-interest have any truth to them. Speech that springs from a state of natural harmony flows like grain through a funnel. With no special organization or purpose, it appropriately changes in response to a situation; it is not guided by self-interest, nor from a wish to obtain anything in response. Such natural responses to the environment help people adapt to the fluctuating needs of daily life, and in this way one achieves a state of harmony. If a person is balanced, his words naturally harmonize with his fellow man.

A father would not act as go-between or matchmaker for his own child, because the words of the father would not be as effective as the praises of an unrelated person. People habitually accept the assertion of a third party as truth even when the third party knows nothing about the person or matter involved.

The great teachings of true wisdom are usually unknown to most people, while the false conventional teachings are popularly accepted. This is a great loss, because they lose the opportunity to learn the plain truth of everyday life. The sages do not intend to withhold the plain spiritual truth from ordinary people; it is the fantasies of the masses that compel the truth to be hidden. People are so used to counterfeit money that they doubt the real currency of the truth. It is also very true that people generally only believe what corresponds to their own opinions, and they oppose anything that is different. What is in agreement with their existing views is determined to be "right," and what does not is "wrong." This obscures the recognition and respect for a truly objective standard of "right" and "wrong."

The words of an authority can put an end to any argument whether those words are false or true. They can do this because they are the words of an established elder or authority who has been accepted in the community. An elder can lack requisite knowledge or experience in a situation and be superior only in terms of age, social or financial position. Such a person's judgement will not necessarily be righteous or wise. If such men are not superior in character or personality, they are often people of rigidity and staleness. Nonetheless, they are often trusted by others.

If a person is balanced, his words naturally harmonize with his fellow man.

Once the subtle truth is reached, the language which is used to discuss the truth should be forgotten. The truth is one. Through discussion, words can actively express one's skills and depth. However, the simple wholeness of truth can be buried by too many words. When certain words are insisted upon, the truth is forgotten. It is best to forget the words but reach for the truth.

Similarly, when there is no divergence of minds, there is no dispute, because subjectivity is not involved. Once subjectivity appears, dispute and divergence grow. When a person insists that his own words are right, someone will come along to say they are not right, and someone else will say that they are right. When people cease talking, agreement can prevail. In the presence of talk, agreement cannot be maintained. Even in the presence of common agreement, talk invites disagreement. That is why I say, "Let there be no more talk from any narrow mind."

In dispute, when people take a position, it is because they see that there is something right in it. When other people disagree, it is because they think there is something wrong in that position. We perceive events from different perspectives. Each person's growth and level of development is different, that is all. Nobody should force another to accept what he perceives as right. Proper speech, a balanced mind, fewer words, gentle manners, being open to listen and to what is different brings people in one family together. People become closer by talking to each other, not by having serious, formal disputes. Disputes can separate friends. Natural, open dialogue from the heart as a form of communication is harmonious and brings true peace.

There are many kinds of individuals living in the world. All lives continue by virtue of their difference, like the differences of each leaf on a tree or like a ring without beginning or end. If you choose dispute, you isolate yourself and then must fight for your friends to join you. A new dispute may then evolve from your contentious nature and the new friends who are closest to you will have to leave. Accept the enduring natural harmony which can bring you peace and do not be carried away by your fondness for dispute.

When separation exists between two people, there is prejudice. In this way, the affirmation and denial of right and wrong arise. But how can there be right? How can there be wrong? Each is established by the other. One is only established at the same time in relation to its opposite. Harmony is the integration of opposites. It is like a ring made up of different sections. When opposites unite, they join and form an endless ring. If the two opposites try to separate, the ring cannot stay whole. This is the problem of the subjectivity of the personal ego. The world is stuck in the petty conflicts of ego. The fragments of the ring need to be joined for renewal.

All things originate from the same source and, in their different forms, enjoy co-existence. Beginning and end are part of a single ring and no one can comprehend its end. It reveals the law of natural equalization. A person who is fond of dispute can develop spiritually by learning to tolerate the opinion or reasoning of the other side. Life does not depend on stiff, formal meetings to make things happen. It is in the small-talk of daily life that we respond with an unassertive attitude to all change and learn to cooperate with the organic condition of the world. Someone may work hard to establish himself, but the basic nature of man is equal. It does not matter whether a person is quiet or loud, big or small. Nature, the limitless source of all transformation, does not discriminate.

The fishing net exists because of the fish. Once you've gotten the fish, you can forget the net. The rabbit-trap exists because of the rabbit. Once you've gotten the rabbit, you can forget the trap. Words exist because of meaning. Once you've gotten the meaning, you can forget all about the words. "Where can I find a man who has forgotten about words, so I might have a word or two with him?" The teaching of subtle truth cannot be attached to words.

III
Let Your Internal Harmony be Undisturbed

Tseng Tzu twice held a position in government, each time with a different response. "When I first held office, I was taking care of my parents. The salary was only three fu (approximately 192 bushels) of grain and I was happy," he said. "The second time my salary was three thousand chung of grain (approximately 192,000 bushels), but I no longer had them to take care of and I was sad."

One of the disciples asked Chuang Tzu, "We can conclude, then, that Tseng Tzu was not concerned because the greater salary was not important to him?"

Chuang Tzu replied, "He regarded three fu or three thousand chung to be the same as a sparrow or mosquito passing in front of him, but he was still concerned. If he had not been concerned, he would not have had cause for sorrow. A person without attachment does not grieve."

IV
All Life is Not so Solid or Substantial

Penumbra, the Being of Shadows of a Shadow said to Umbra, the Being of The Shadow, "Just a minute ago, you were looking down; now you're looking up. An hour ago, you had your hair tied up; but now it is hanging loose. Before, you were sitting; now you're standing. Previously, you were walking and now you're still. Why is this?"

The Being of The Shadow replied, "I do them automatically; I don't know why. I do not know how I have come to be. I'm like the cicada's shell and the snake's skin; I look like the real thing, but I am not really so. The shell of the cicada and the skin of the snake are fixed; I, however, do not have any fixed shape. It seems like I have form; yet, I am not formed. I seem to exist but don't. In the firelight or sunlight I come into being; at night or in darkness I disappear and rest. Have you noticed that I depend upon things of form to act? It is true. When things of form come, I come into being; when they go, I go with them. When they live, I live. Have you noticed that the things of form also depend on something else in nature to act and rest?

"Who is it that gives life to form?"

V
Too Full Outside, Too Short Inside

Yang Chu went south to P'ei at the same time Lao Tzu was traveling west to Ch'in, and he went to meet Lao Tzu outside the city. Arriving at the bridge in P'ei, he met Lao Tzu, who was standing in the road. Lao Tzu looked up at the sky and said with a sigh, "At first, I thought you were a person that could be taught. Now I see that it is not possible."

Yang Chu said nothing, but when they arrived at the inn, he presented Lao Tzu with a basin of water, a towel and a comb. He had removed his shoes outside the door and entered, crawling on his knees, to speak with the Master. He said, "Earlier I wanted to ask what you meant by what you said and seek your instruction, but there was not enough time. Now that there is a free moment, may I ask what is my failing?"

Lao Tzu said, "An arrogant bearing and scowling face are your mistake. He who is truly pure behaves as though he were ashamed. He who has abundant virtue, high talent and achievement expresses himself as though he is not enough."

Yang Chu flushed and replied, "I accept your assessment," and bowed, leaving the room.

When Yang Chu had arrived at the inn on a previous occasion, the owners of the inn came out to meet him as he arrived. The innkeeper had a mat ready for him to sit on, his wife had arranged a towel and comb and the guests at the inn moved politely off their mats to let him sit. The other guests who had been warming themselves at the stove stepped aside to make room for him. After Yang returned from his interview with Lao Tzu, however, without noticing him, the other visitors rushed to get the best seats for themselves. This was because he no longer looked and acted like a man of superiority. He had become a truthful person of the Way.

Q: Master Ni, what is the difference, essentially, between this teaching and Christ's teaching of humility? Also, isn't this a teaching that applies only to temporary situations? What is the spiritual advantage of spending more time than is absolutely necessary with crude people?

Master Ni: I do not see how this question relates to the material. If I am allowed, I would prefer not to talk about Jesus. Jesus did not endanger himself by teaching humility; he endangered himself in just the opposite way. He strongly attacked the Pharisees. In teaching Tao, we do not focus upon the teaching of either humility or pride. These are the small ends, not the root. There is no need for a special focus on one or the other.

Yang Chu exemplifies a superficial person with no interior. After receiving Lao Tzu's teaching, however, he was able to immediately gather his essence inwardly. By holding his precious spiritual energy within, it is communicated telepathically to others through a form of magnetism. Yang Chu was therefore suddenly able to change his surroundings.

Yang Chu had prepared himself to receive Lao Tzu's teaching, thus he was ready for the moment of enlightenment in his life. I used to know someone from the time he was a boy. He was a person of some intelligence, but had a lot of pride in himself. He considered himself unsurpassable in many areas of life. Many years later when he had learned more about the Truth, his shining smartness and sharpness disappeared, and he was no longer unsurpassable. He had transformed himself and gathered more depth. Like him, almost all young people are unaware of their rough spots.

The important theme of this chapter is that both the serious spiritual teachings and the informal inspiration of our daily life need to be valued equally. The principle of balance should always be applied in human life. Being overly identified with the spiritual indicates an underlying imbalance in a person.

CHAPTER NINETEEN

THE WISE OLD FISHERMAN

After travelling through the Black Curtain Forest, Confucius and his disciples came to an open flat plain with a waterway. He got down from his carriage and sat down to rest on the apricot mound, a flat-topped hill rising out of the lowland. Now, all were relaxed and at leisure. His disciples took out their books to study, while Confucius at their side played his lute and sang. He was halfway through a song when an old fisherman arrived at the shore. His beard and eyebrows were white, and his hair came down over his shoulders. He stepped out of his boat, walked up the embankment to the higher ground, and listened until the song had ended. Then he beckoned to two students, Tzu kung and Tzu lu, and pointing to Confucius asked them, "Who is he?"

"He is a gentleman from Lu State," replied Tzu lu.

"What is his family name?" asked the old man.

"He is of the K'ung family," replied Tzu Lu.

"What is his occupation?" asked the old man.

Tzu kung answered him, "He is a symbol of loyalty and truth, benevolence and righteousness. He administers ceremonies and music. He understands and clarifies the relationships of man. He respects the sovereign and works to reform the masses. That is his occupation and great service to the world."[29]

"Is he the governor of a state or city?" asked the old man.

---

[29]The social codes, customs, ceremonial activities and music performed by all the people were not unified or regulated. Confucius' ambition was to reinstitute the old conventions and have them followed by all people.

"No," said Tzu Kung.

"Is he a priest?" said the old man.

"No," said Tzu Kung.

The old man laughed heartily and walked away, saying, "That is fortunate. He may be benevolent and full of righteousness, but if he were to establish an external teaching, then the true nature of life would not be seen and great harm would be the result. By so wearying his mind and tiring his body with these things, he not only endangers the truth, but he also jeopardizes his true self and all his descendants. Without a doubt, he is a man severely separated from the Way of Natural Truth!"

Tzu Kung went back to where the group was resting and told Confucius about the man and what he had said. Confucius put down his lute, stood and said, "That man was probably a sage of high wisdom." He walked swiftly in his direction, reaching the shore of the lake just as the fisherman was taking up his pole to push off into the water. Glancing back and noticing Confucius, he turned and faced him. Confucius stopped, bowed twice, and then advanced a few steps.

"What do you want?" asked the fisherman.

"Sir, a moment ago you spoke but left your point unfinished," replied Confucius. "In my ignorance, your meaning is unclear to me. It is my hope that you might clarify it and give some help."

The old man said, "You seem eager to learn."

Confucius again bowed twice and said, "I have been a student since I was young. I am now sixty-nine, yet I have never heard the truth spoken. I am ready to listen to what you might say."

"When creatures follow their own kind, they produce only the same sounds which echo back and forth from one to the other," said the fisherman. "This law of spiritual nature has existed since time began. To explain this to you, I will set aside for the moment my own realm and apply my knowledge to the things that concern you.

"Your concern is the affairs of men. But what is it that you wish to do? Do you want to help rulers gain power in benevolence or do you wish to help those who are ruled restrain the rulers? When the emperor, princes, ministers and people all fulfill their proper functions, the result is good government and order. If they leave their proper places, the result is confusion. When the officials take care of their duties and the people their own concerns, neither causes trouble for the other.

"Unproductive land, houses in need of repair, lack of food or clothing, insufficient funds, arguments of wives and helpers, and disorder between the generations are the concerns of the people.

"Inability to perform a task, administration in a state of disorder, lazy or careless workers, lack of success, and insufficient salaries are the concerns of administrators.

"No loyalty from top administrators, misfortune falling upon the most influential families and the state, artisans lacking skill, low rank in the competitions and inability to maintain a favorable position with the Emperor are the concerns of princes.

"Suffering among the people caused by bad weather, open warfare among the princes causing the people to die, poorly regulated music and ceremonies, loss of wealth, and increasing immorality among the masses are the concerns of the emperors.

"You do not have the authority of an administrator, prince or emperor, yet you take it upon yourself to regulate the social code, customs of general rituals, ceremony and music. You have made yourself knowledgeable about human relationships so that you can have a positive influence upon the mass of the population. Is this not meddling? You have not seen the outcome, but yet you set a goal without knowing whether you offer help to the rulers, the ruled, or the spiritual development of all people.

"One should not help rulers set up unnatural systems of interference so they can apply absolute rulership over others. Nor should one persuade others to accept and obey unnatural control or arouse people's political ambition, distracting them from wholeheartedly attending to their own lives. Reinstituting rigid ideas from the past for a new government, society or religion is not helpful.

"Depending on the place and circumstances, sometimes something may appear to be good and right on the surface. But it cannot also be good and right all the time, in all places, under all circumstances. What can be established on this plane is changeable whenever the time calls for it to change. The establishment of rigid government may be helpful to some people, but to most, it would be harmful and cause obstructions. If it is good for the ruler, it may be bad for the people under his rule; conversely, if it is good for the people, it may be bad for an effective government. Thus, if one succeeds in organizing a strong government, people may still be harmed by it. If one is successful in leading people to develop a system of self-government, capable or effective government may never evolve. There is seldom success when something is approached radically by either a government or the people. Extreme action from either side causes bloodshed. Hasty minds or movement can cause great waste.

"People would all like to find a balanced form of government that would allow for a good and free life and, at the same time, effectively carry out all the important necessities of public affairs for the nation and the world. This is a noble ambition, but it cannot be achieved.

"It is beyond the scope of the human mind and will to manage the personal development of individuals and the collective mental and spiritual condition of human society. A wise and virtuous person will not interfere with the natural growth of people. He will keep his balance. If he is going to become involved in human affairs, he will not assist one side or the other. It is much more valuable for him to indiscriminately awaken all people, rulers and ruled alike, in order to improve the practical sphere of their everyday lives. Personal enlightenment brings Heaven to Earth, not by establishing rigid dogma, but by being serviceable to all people.

"The unwise who considers himself wise and the unkind who thinks he is godly will make trouble for many generations to come. This happens when one blindly imitates what is learned from someone else or when an undeveloped and immature person projects their ill-formed and unnatural ideas onto the naive masses. The worst example of this is the man of speculation who is smart and has the potential to be the first horse in the race, but who is too quick in action and chooses the wrong direction. As a human being he has not yet developed far-sightedness or foresight, and because of his mistake causes damage to all those involved with him.

"A person who cannot take care of himself cannot take care of others. One's focus needs to be first with oneself, then he or she can extend this development to those who naturally respond. If you wish to stand at the pinnacle of your spiritual nature, work inwardly as well as outwardly.

"There are eight defects and four obstructions to individual human growth. It is helpful to examine them carefully in order to keep one's life balanced, at any age. They are:

1. To do or undertake something that is not your concern is meddling in other's affairs.

2. To make unsolicited proposals or assertions is presumptuous and considered too forward.

3. To adapt your mind to someone else's thoughts and arrange your words to echo his or her opinions without deep understanding is a false expression of praise and flattery.

4. To praise or agree with a person, right or wrong, and speak without regard for right or wrong is outright blandishment.

5. To speak about another person's faults and failings is denigrating and unkind and to attack another's reputation with false charges is slanderous.

6. To mischievously separate friends or cause estrangement within a family is malicious.

7. To praise another falsely with intent of harm is to engage in a malicious intrigue.

8. To try to face in two directions for one's own benefit without considering which is right or wrong is called hypocrisy.

These eight defects produce disorder within a society and among people, and cause harm to the person who acts them out in his life. The Virtuous One does not relate with people of this nature and an enlightened authority does not employ them. As for the four worries inherent in our undertakings:

1. To continually try to undertake great things, introducing change into the accepted order, and so enhance avidly your merit and fame is swollen ambition.

2. Insisting that you know it all, that everything be done your way, or grasping what should be available for the use of others is greed.

3. To see your faults but refuse to change yourself despite advice or warning is stubbornness.

4. To praise those who agree with you and to condemn those who are different, refusing to credit them with the virtues they possess, is bigotry.

"These are the four problems that block one's growth. It is not until one has eliminated the eight defects from their personality and abstains from the four evils that a person can begin to be taught."

After quietly listening to the teaching, Confucius sighed heavily. He bowed twice to the fisherman, straightened up, and said, "Twice I was exiled from my home state of Lu; in Wei I was tabooed. The tree I used to rest under in Sung was cut down. A group of people besieged me between Ch'en and Ts'ai. I am aware of no error of my own, so why did these things happen?"

"Well," replied the fisherman, "it is difficult to make you understand.

"Once there was a man who was so fearful of his own shadow and so displeased with his own footsteps that he was determined to run away from them. However, the more he ran, the more footsteps he made, and although he ran very fast, his shadow was still close to him. He then concluded that he was going too slow, so he ran as hard as he could without stopping to rest. The consequence of that action was that his strength failed and he died. He did not know that by going into the shade he would have been free of his shadow, and by keeping still he would have put an end to his footsteps.

"You occupy yourself with rigid ideas of morality like benevolence and righteousness. You sharpen the boundary between what you like and dislike, the changes of movement and stillness, the doctrines of giving and receiving, the emotions of love and hate, joy and anger, yet you cannot avoid damaging your integral nature by triggering those disastrous events that have happened to you. By doing so, you are participating in the same fault as the foolish man who ran so hard.

"When you establish a concept about God, then God dies, because conceptual activity brings deviation. Deviation separates people from the natural integral truth. I suggest that you carefully and gently set your own person and life in order, and protect what truly belongs to it. Care for your body respectfully. Preserve your natural purity. Leave unrelated business to other people; then you will escape entanglement. Now, instead of improving yourself you are trying to improve other people. That will not succeed, but even if it should meet with success, remember that external success means nothing to the deep sphere of life."

"May I ask," said Confucius, respectfully, "what is natural purity?"

"Natural purity is the perfection of truth. It is sincerity in its highest degree. One who lacks purity and sincerity cannot influence others. Thus, one who forces mourning, though he may sound sad, will not arouse grief. One who forces himself to be angry, though he may sound stern, will arouse no awe. And one who forces himself to be loving, although smiling, will create no feeling of harmony. Real sadness can arouse grief even in silence; true anger can impress others without great action; true love can create harmony even without a smile. When a man has Truth in him, his spiritual power can move the external world. That is why Truth is so greatly valued.

"When Truth is applied to human affairs, then in serving our parents, our behavior is naturally loving and filial; in serving our sovereign, our behavior is naturally honest and loyal; at the time of celebration, we are naturally merry and joyous; and in the hour of mourning, we are naturally sad.

"The object of our actions is as follows: of loyalty, to serve another successfully; of celebration, to provide joviality; of mourning, to express grief; of serving parents, to fulfill their needs. If the service is accomplished, no trace needs to remain of the action. If the needs of one's parents are fulfilled, the means do not matter. If a celebration causes laughter, the exact dishes and cups to be used are not fussed over. If real grief comes in mourning, the detail of the ceremony is not significant.

"Ceremony is the invention of the mind of man. Our natural purity, however, is given to us from the spiritual nature of the universe. It cannot be changed. The true one of natural wisdom models himself upon universal nature and values his natural purity; he is independent of human urgencies. Foolish men do the opposite. They are unable to follow universal nature and instead fret over human affairs and matters by holding artificial standards. Consequently, they suffer the fluctuations of morality and never reach the goal. You, like many people, were taught deceit at an early age and are late in hearing the Integral Truth."

Confucius again bowed twice. He said, "It has been a blessing to meet you. Please allow me to follow you as a servant, so I might continue to learn from you."

"It is said," replied the fisherman, "that if a person is an appropriate companion, one may travel with him into the depths of Tao. But if he is not, it is best to remain alone so that no harm occurs. Perhaps some other time. Continue to work on your learning. Excuse me, I must go now." The old fisherman pushed away from the shore in his boat, and disappeared among the reeds.

Yen Yuan brought around the carriage and Tzu lu held out the reins, but Confucius kept solemnly quiet and waited until he could no longer hear the sound of the boat pole; the ripples on the water were stilled before he mounted the carriage.

Tzu Lu asked him, "Master, I have had the privilege of serving you for a long time, yet never have I seen you treat any person like this. When you're with the great rulers and sovereigns of state, you are always treated with the greatest respect, seated on their level, yet even so you yourself show an air of disdain. Yet before this old man, you do not speak before politely bowing twice. Haven't you gone too far? None of the students understand it. Why did you act that way?"

"You are slow to understand," replied Confucius from the carriage. "You have studied ceremony and social obligation in the books for a long time, but have kept your rigidity. Let me explain.

"To meet an elder without showing respect is impolite. To meet a sage and not honor him is to lack benevolence. Only one who has perfected himself sees others humble themselves before him. Only humility coming from purity of intention will bring achievement of the Truth.

"Tao is the source from which all creation springs. When it is disregarded or neglected, it means death;

when it is followed, it means life. To go against it in one's endeavors brings failure; to follow it brings success. A sage thus honors Tao wherever he might be. The old fisherman possesses Tao and has enlightened me. He is certainly worthy of all respect."

CHAPTER TWENTY

THE UNITY OF ONE'S LIFE BEING

I
The Truth of Life Cannot be Artificial Creation

A very old tree was cut to make bowls for serving sacrificial wine. They are covered in blue and yellow patterns, and the left-over wood chips are thrown into the ditch. If you compare the sacrificial bowls with the chips in the ditch, you will find them greatly differing with regards to beauty and ugliness, yet they are alike in suffering the loss of their original nature. Robber Chih, the model of evil, and Tseng and Shih, model citizens of elite society, are far apart in deeds and virtue, yet they are the same in having damaged their original nature.

There are five conditions under which one's natural function of good sense and original nature might be damaged. One: when the different colors confuse the eye and cause unclarity of vision. Two: when the many notes confuse the ear, dulling the hearing. Three: when many odors confuse one's sense of smell. Four: when the different flavors dull the palate, impairing the sense of taste. Five: when preferences and dislikes disturb the mind and cause the original unity to become disturbed. Then one's mind becomes fickle and flighty, and the array of choice unsettles the heart and causes agitation in one's life. The five senses, if not correctly applied, would all disorder the normal flow of life. The results are the same when the followers of different conceptual and religious schools go striding around, thinking they have really achieved something. They preach acceptance or rejection of sensual appeal to attract different followers, and each thinks his way is the truth that others should follow. What they teach tempts people to abandon their own intrinsic truth that is revealed in simply living a normal and natural life.

If the externally established standards they offer cause people hardship, and in the process of adjustment to those standards they damage their own nature. Can it really be said that they have achieved the truth of life? If so, then the pigeons and doves and quails and owls that are put in cages have also found the truth of life.

With likes and dislikes and all kind of sensory enjoyment, you impair what is inside. Meanwhile, you pile up what is on the outside by dressing up in fur caps or high heeled shoes, fancy accessories, long skirts or fine neckties. The inside is stuffed up like firewood crammed in a wicker basket; the outside is covered over with wraps and ornaments; yet you stand in this tangle of concealments and proclaim that you have attained the truth of life? If so, then the imprisoned men with their chains and barred cells, and tigers and leopards in their pens and cages have also gotten hold of the truth of life!

II
The Example of the Old Man of Han Yin

A student of one of the popularly established teachings went south to the state of Ch'u. On his return to the state of Chin, he passed through the town of Hanyin. There he saw an old man who had prepared his fields for planting. The man had dug an irrigation ditch, and he was using a pitcher to pour water into it for the irrigation. It was a lot of work with very little result.

"Good day, sir. If you install a machine here," said the student, "in one day you could irrigate a hundred times more than you have accomplished with that pitcher. It does not take much effort to operate, and the results are excellent. Would you like one?"

"What is it like?" asked the gardener.

"It is made of wood," replied the student, "it is heavy in the back and light in the front. It draws water up like you do with your pitcher, but in a continuously flowing stream. It is called a well-sweep and is used everywhere in China."

Thereupon the gardener calmly said, "This way is one way. I use it to train myself to manage my mind. You know, the use of machinery can madden and overextend one's mind. I enjoy doing this because my body and mind can work together in unison. The same harmony of body and mind exists in any simple task of the same nature. No secondary instrument should overstress one's mind and disrupt one's life. Let us differentiate between the importance of simply taking care of one's own life and serving society in an emergency or in a pressing task; in the latter, one might consider the use of mechanical force. However, the most important thing in life is learning to manage and discipline oneself before putting one's hands out to manage any machine. Unless that is done, it would be spiritually dangerous. The overuse of machines in personal life can seduce one to taking short cuts in one's life, pursuing one's purpose through the use of contrivances.

"I was taught by my master that wherever you find contrivances, you would also find contrived situations and wherever there were contrived dealings, there was a contriving heart behind the matter. If there is such a heart in a man, he is not completely pure and uncorrupted. When this is the case, his spirit is restless and his inner gods are not steady; then, Tao, the subtle integral nature, does not provide support. It is not that I do not know of such machinery, but I would be ashamed to let my body become idle and my mind become widely active."

At this the student was taken aback and said nothing. Then the gardener asked him who he was, to which the student replied that he was a disciple of a famous master.

"You must be one of those who enlarges his external learning, trying to be a sage, who attempts to put himself above the masses and plays and sings songs to gain fame in the world. Your kind ignores your own inner gods, breath and body! If you cannot even take care of yourself, how will you be able to help the world? Don't waste the time I have for honest living, but go away!"

The youth turned pale and silently went off, not at all pleased with the rebuff the man had given him. He travelled many miles before he recovered his usual appearance and composure.

"What sort of person did you talk with back there?" asked one of his fellow students who was traveling with him. "What startled you so much that it took you so long to recover?"

"I used to think that our master was the only teacher in the world," replied the youth. "I did not know about this man.

"Our master says that one of natural wisdom seeks practicality in accomplishment, which means minimum energy used in such a way that obtains maximal results. But the man I met today aims at Tao, the Integral Truth, in order to perfect his personal virtue. His personal virtue being perfect, he goes on to perfect his physical form and then his spirit. Perfection in high spirit is the way of the Sage. Like an ordinary person, he does not know the end of his life journey. He is a person of simplicity and purity; such a person is not concerned with external accomplishment, profit or contrivance. People like him do only what their will directs them to do, and go only where their heart and mind dictate. Even if the entire world were to praise his life, he would pay no attention. Even though the entire world were to criticize his life, he would not be bothered by it. Neither criticism nor praise can add or detract anything from him. He is a man of perfect virtue in integralness. As for us, we are moved only by our impulses."

He went back to Lu to tell his master about it and said, "I wonder if I am correct. That man seems to have achieved the practice of integral spirit, the ancient spiritual art that is called the Integral Way."

The master replied, "He is one of those who cultivate the way of spiritual unity. You had a right to be startled, but how would you and I know anything about the practice of Tao while we are still students of the contemporary world?

"One who attains the integral truth would also keep pace with external changes in order to maintain spiritual unity. One must adapt to the changes of the times. Practically, it is to say that the highest one can maintain the unity of his spirit and also accommodate the changes of different circumstances. He allows his spirit to remain in original simplicity while experiencing worldly life. By doing nothing extra, he attains the wholeness of nature.

"To further describe this practice, one who follows the Integral Way knows the first thing and is also able to extend to the second. He looks after what is on the inside and also what is on the outside. One of true purity can enter into simplicity and return to his original nature through no extra action or doing, renew his nature and embrace his spirit, and in this way proceed happily in his life in the everyday world. He is complete when embracing oneness as he moves through the world. He leaves no trace behind. Though the depth of the Integral Way is not easily understood by intellectual study, you and I certainly need to learn about it."

CHAPTER TWENTY-ONE

THE HIGHEST SWORDSMANSHIP

The King of Tzao was fond of swordsmanship. He called for the best swordsmen in the country to come to his door, which they did in great numbers. Contests of swordsmanship were continually conducted in the royal palace day and night. Although the list of those killed and wounded was over a hundred each year, the king never tired of watching and enjoying the sword-fights. For years his interest and pursuit in this activity continued.

His son, the future successor to the kingdom, began to worry about his father's pastime, as there were matters of great administrative importance that needed attention. So he put out a proclamation offering a thousand gold pieces to the person who could stop his father's habit. The single response to this announcement was a recommendation that a master by the name of Chuang Tzu was the only one who could help.

The next day, the prince sent a messenger with a thousand pieces of gold to Chuang Tzu, along with a summons to the palace. However, when the messenger extended the money to him, Chuang Tzu refused to accept it.

The messenger said, "You are a very wise man. If you do not take the money, the prince cannot ask you to do this favor."

Chuang Tzu replied, "The prince wishes to use me to stop his father's favorite game. As an ordinary person, after accepting the money, if I go there and say something that displeases the king, my life would be in danger. Then what good would the money be? If I say something that pleases him, and supports his interest, then what use of me? I think it would be better for you to find someone who likes money more than I. It is better for the prince to send somebody that the king will listen to, rather than myself, a scholar."

The messenger told him, "The prince said that his father likes to challenge excellent swordsmen."

"I am good enough with swords," responded Chuang Tzu, "but not very good in pleasing Kings."

"The King's type of swordsman, "said the messenger, "is the kind who has short hair in disarray, sideburns that stick out, a tilted cap. He wears a short jacket, walks with his eyes wide open and talks in a rough manner. He does not think that any conquering force could come from a gentleman. What he enjoys is physical."

Chuang Tzu said, "If you would really like me to do the job, then you must make me look like those people: the same manners, same words, same way of dressing, same appearance. Then perhaps I can help you." You see, Chuang Tzu did not decide to go to the palace for the money, but to help. He wanted to see if he could face a person and conquer his desire.

Chuang Tzu went to meet the prince and the two of them went together to see the king. The king, with a sharp sword in his hand, was waiting for new swordsmen to arrive. When Chuang Tzu entered the royal house, he walked like rough people do, and as he approached the king, he did not follow the proper manner of kneeling down in front of him.

A little taken aback, the king said, "For what do you come to see me?"

Chuang Tzu replied, "I have heard that your majesty is fond of swords. What I can do is considered fine swordsmanship."

The king asked, "How strong is your skill?"

"With my sword," declared Chuang Tzu, "every three steps, I can kill one person, continuing on for ten thousand miles, and no person can stop me."

At hearing this, the king became extremely excited. "In that case," he stated, "there is no opponent that can equal your authority."

Chuang Tzu continued, "My way of swordsmanship is this: when the sword is in my hand, I keep my mind still. Any movement is a spontaneous reaction to an external circumstance."

The King directed him, "Please use my guesthouse and rest. Await my order and I will let you have a formal contest with my best swordsmen."

First the king conducted a contest among the swordsmen in the palace to select the most excellent among them for competition with Chuang Tzu. After seven days, more than sixty persons were wounded or dead. Five or six people were selected as the contenders. They were waiting, sword in hand, for the summoning of Chuang Tzu, who was called and entered the hall.

The king told them, "This is the day of the contest. I would like to see you try your skill, your art of swords."

Chuang Tzu said, "I have been waiting for this contest a long time."

The King instructed, "Tell me about the sword you will use. What is its length?"

"The sword I use can be long or short," replied Chuang Tzu. "However, I have three kinds of swords. I will let you choose the one that is best to use."

The king responded, "So you have three kinds of sword. I would like to know what kind they are."

"My swords are graded. The first one is used to handle ordinary swordsman and general people. The second sword is used by dukes and princes to produce governing power. The highest sword is used by the emperor to give ruling power."

The king hesitated a moment and said, "How do you use them?"

"To utilize the sword of ordinary people," said Chuang Tzu, "first I need to put my hair in disarray and make my sideburns stick out, pull my hat down a little bit, widen my eyes and wear a short jacket. In this way, when I stand in front of people they will notice my physical strength. I have the power to pierce the throat of the opponent, cut people's heads off and take out their livers and lungs. Using this kind of sword is the power of brutality and is therefore no different than two roosters or crickets fighting each other. If in this way people are going to die, it helps neither the world nor oneself."

The king listened, then said, "How do you use your second sword?"

Chuang Tzu said, "Let me tell you about the second level in my art of swordsmanship. A higher level in swordsmanship uses intelligence and bravery as the two sides of the sword's blade. It uses righteous and capable ministers as the body of the sword and the orderliness of society as the back of the sword. It uses the sincerity, earnestness and clarity of the leader himself its ring and uses the special courageous people in his army as the handle. When I utilize this sword, nobody can compete with me. When I raise this sword, nobody can see its extent. If I lower the sword, nobody can see its depth. When I move it, nothing can stand in its way. With this kind of sword, all people in my territory obey definitely and faithfully."

The king was now a little bewildered and a little enlightened. The kind of swordsmanship he had admired of the first kind of sword caused lots of killing, yet many people in his country rebelled and made trouble. By using the second sword, people would still obey their ruler, but not out of fear of being physically conquered. The king understood more or less what Chuang Tzu said about this higher swordsmanship, which would mean he would be able to live happily in his territory without killing or threatening people.

Chuang Tzu continued without interruption. He said, "But the second sword is still for people who have the small interest of occupying a small territory and becoming a small king; it is only organizing a small government, organizing a small population and making oneself the top of a small world like the tip of a snail's horn. Now I would like to explain about the sword used by a great emperor.

"This third type of sword uses the high mountain and deep river as each side of its blade. It utilizes the harmony of the highland people as its back, and the harmony of the lowland people as its ring. It makes the peace of the surrounding countries and kingdoms as its handle. The one who uses it follows orderliness and harmonizes with the natural cycles. His government follows the order of the alternation of yin and yang. He who utilizes it supports the growth of all people. Nothing can stop this kind of sword. When you use this kind of sword, you can touch the clouds above. You can reach the depths of the ocean below. With the depth and sagacity of the person who uses it, this is the sword of the leader of the world."

The king, after hearing his description, understood fully that conquering through the physical competition of killing is not the best way.

"You mentioned the sword and art of ordinary people," the king said, "but apparently you are not in the place of ordinary people. You mentioned the sword and art of dukes and princes, but apparently you are not of dukes and princes, and do not wish to be. You mentioned the sword and art of emperors, the top of the entire world. It seems that you also do not wish to be like them either. Tell me, please, what sword do you use?"

Chuang Tzu said to the king, "Your majesty is interested in knowing the invisible but most useful sword of a person of spiritual cultivation. Its existence is known only to an achieved student of universal, eternal life. It is the capability of the developed spiritual discernment that sees through the shallowness of the human world. Sympathy and compassion that spring from love for people are the two sides of its blade. The wholeness of virtue is the body of the sword. The creative cycle is the ring of the sword. Individual personal spiritual cultivation and one's continual development is the handle of the sword. With spiritual knowledge, he enlightens his life. With reaching the depth of nature, he enlightens his mind.

"The small use of this sword is as follows: to take nutrition from experiencing an awakened life and transform it to wisdom, which can cut away all the vexation and self-aggrandizement of one's mind. It defends one from the harmful influences that would damage one's natural organic vitality and enables a person to extend his spiritual energy into the realm of unlimitedness. A limitless life is not something that is confined by human conception. The idea of a man with strong contempt who has the ambition to be a king or even the emperor of the entire world is leading a limited life. Forgive me, my great majesty, for speaking so. However, unlimited life is a life lived in all time and all space.

"Then, the big use of the sword is to raise it to the heights, where it breaks the darkness of all ages and of all people, then to lower it to the depths, where it breaks through the obstacles of the next generation in the world. As a devoted practitioner of this precious art of the spiritual sword, held certainly in my hand, it must not be a bloodthirsty sword of undevelopment, but the sword of true spiritual development. This is the swordsmanship I respect and enjoy most."

CHAPTER TWENTY-TWO

TRUE SPIRITUAL ACHIEVEMENT

I
Spiritual Achievement is not for Show

Lieh Tzu, an achieved man of Tao, was traveling to Ch'i, but halfway on his journey he turned around and returned home. By chance he met his friend Po-hun Wu-jen, a developed man. "Why did you come home so soon?" asked Po-Hun Wu-jen.

"I became afraid," answered Lieh Tzu.

"What were you afraid of?" asked Po-hun Wu-jen.

"Well, I ate at ten different inns," said Lieh Tzu, "but five would take no payment for my meal."

"Why does that cause you to be afraid?" inquired Po-hun Wu-jen.

"A man who is only half-achieved internally has not really solved all aspects of himself," replied Lieh Tzu, "but his outward appearance may assume a polished air that masks his heart and mind. It is a brightness that is externally visible which naturally attracts attention and respect from others; this radiance overpowers men's minds and makes them careless of their treatment of him. People might easily honor him or pay him more respect than they would an older, wiser person who is more developed but who shows it less. The pleasure taken in this attention starts the downfall of one's moral nature. One should first conquer his own heart and mind so that he can disregard his desire for authority and seniority which are always precursors of trouble.

"An innkeeper earns his living by selling soup. The profit he makes from that business cannot be very much, yet look at his response towards me. Think what would have happened if I had been seen by a prince or the ruler of a state. Such a man works hard for the benefit of the nation, and he would have immediately assigned me tasks and burdened me with the responsibilities of his administration. That is what frightened me."

"Sounds like you understand the situation well," said Po-hun Wu-jen, "but even if you stay at home, people will gather around you."

Not long afterwards, Po-hun Wu-jen went to Lieh Tzu's house and found the shoes of many people outside his door.[30] Po-hun Wu-jen stood there for some time facing north, resting his chin on his upright staff. Then he went away without saying a word. The servant who was in charge of receiving guests went in and told Lieh Tzu. Lieh Tzu ran after him, barefoot, catching up with him at the gate. "Now that you've come all this way, can you help me?"

"There is nothing that can be done. As I mentioned, here they are, gathering around you. You could not force people to come; neither can you prevent them from coming. But how did you influence them? There is certainly some influence at work here. And what good is it to you? By so moving others, you invariably upset your own basic nature. He who influences others is in turn influenced by them. None of those staying with you can be at all helpful; their chatter is only a kind of human poison. The unawakened and unenlightened cannot help each other because they are not alive to the situation around them.

"People of talent are overworked and intellectuals worry too much about how to help the world. Those with no talent have no ambition. Like an unmoored boat, they uncommittedly wander about, with no concern for where they are bound."

In order to cause no imbalance to one's basic nature and his society, the achieved one offers service for just a certain period of his life or in a very informal way.

---

[30]The Chinese at this time politely removed their shoes before entering a house so they could sit on mats on the floor.

No personal establishment is sought in his way of giving service.

II
Intellectual Mindedness Parts Brothers

There was a man named Cheng Huan who became a scholar after three years of study and then took a stand for the philosophy of his school. The benefits of his education extended to three families (his own, his mother's and his wife's, all of whom learned to read). His younger brother then became a member of a different school of philosophy, but whenever the two doctrines were discussed at home, the father always sided with the younger brother, Ti.

After ten years of argument over the different conceptual beliefs and his father always taking the side of the younger brother, Cheng Huan committed suicide. His father then dreamed that Cheng Huan came to him and said, "I helped your other son become a scholar, who then became a member of a different philosophy. Look at my grave, where the catalpas and cypresses have already borne flowers. I have influenced Ti to have an education, and the philosophy I stand for is better." The argument was not stopped, even by death; at least the father was so impressed.

When Heaven rewards a person, it does not reward him with a conceptual structure but empowers the spiritual nature of the man. Heaven does not reward a man for what he believes conceptually but for what he is. The life nature of all people is the same at the beginning - original nature - but expresses itself differently under different influences. Insisting on those differences, however, is artificial and establishes separation, confrontation and conflict; it is those artificial cultural creations that cause deviation from one's true nature.

A person who regards his abilities as being from himself, forgetting the influence of his parents, thinks of himself as different or better than others. It is like the story of the person who dug a well in Ch'i and pushed away the other drinkers, forgetting that nature provides water for the thirst of all people. That is what is meant when it is said, "The present generation is made up entirely of Huans, the intellectually minded people."

If one becomes self-satisfied with one's worldly achievements due to one's own ignorance, in the case of those who claim to have attained Tao it is even more the same situation. A man who truly identifies with virtue is not even aware of it, much less the man who is identified with Tao. The ancient ones called this "escaping the punishment of nature."

The trouble with Huan's family was that each member of the family learned something conceptual and became so stuck in his own way that they could not see each other any more. This is how worldly separation comes about. People are not balanced enough to let things pass, keeping an open mind to what is new and real in life. Tao is what teaches people the openness that allows conceptual and spiritual experiences to pass. The story shows the insistence on man's artificiality and the ignoring of one's inborn nature.

A true sage reposes in that which provides rest for him, not in that which does not provide rest. The world reposes in that which does not provide rest, such as all kinds of evil competition, not in that which does provide rest.

III
How to Slay a Dragon

Chu P'ing Man spent a thousand pieces of gold to learn the skill of how to tame dragons from Chih Li. At the end of three years he was perfect at this art, but there was no opportunity for him to show his skill.

This story shows that one who learns the subtle achievement in Tao will find no opportunity to show it off. It is too big to be seen by people in general.

IV
One Portion of Artificiality, One Portion of Separation

A student, referring to Chuang Tzu's teaching, said, "To know Tao is easy; to keep from talking about

it is hard." To know and not to speak is spiritual integrity.   One attains the integral nature by understanding yet not putting it into words.

To know and to speak provides service to humans,
but putting into words what cannot be spoken creates
some artificiality.

The ancient developed ones followed the subtle law
and thus were natural, not artificial; they dissolved conceptions, not established them.

The learning of Tao is like studying the art of
taming dragons. Beginners do not know how to apply
their profound learning in the practical daily affairs of
life.   Truthfully, the principle of Tao is a great path,
the way that allows everything to pass.   One should
not allow anything on the way to become an obstacle,
especially conceptual dogma and variable phenomena
of everyday's nature and experiences.   You can learn
principles and they can be useful in your life, but there
is no way to make a show of a principle.

The story about taming dragons shows how to take
one's life as its natural wholeness, which cannot be
fragmented or conceptualized merely by intellectual
habit. Partiality is unable to represent the wholeness of
life. If a powerful, alive dragon is killed and cut apart,
no longer does the wholeness of the dragon exist, but
only bones, flesh and other parts; the life is gone too.
An intellectual approach cuts the subtle integral truth
of life. The subtle truth confirms the way of Heaven -
the unharmed wholeness of the nature of life - rather
than the fragmented intellectual rules of man and the
world. The world's way is to follow conceptual acts,
not the nature of Heaven.

A dragon is your own life force.   To tame the
dragon takes great skill. This skill we call Tao. People
who attain Tao are those who have tamed their own
life force and can enjoy riding it. This skill demands a
great deal of patience, otherwise the dragon does not
listen to you, but you will be carried away
purposelessly to any treacherous condition. Chu Ping
Man is a student of dragon taming, but to him, to slay

the dragon would be much simpler than to tame it because he was a typical impatient person. However, he set his first purpose into learning the skill of taming the dragon. If he had not done that, he would have finally become a slaughterer of dragons. Truthfully enough, the world's campus is full of that type of student. With a heavenly spirit and wholeness of mind, one can enjoy all human spiritual and conceptual creations. With an artificial mind and spirit, one is locked into an artificial shape.

V
Hold Nothing

A true sage accepts that certainties are uncertainties. He does not insist on anything unchangeable because he does not like to be involved in shallow dispute. Therefore, he is not up in arms to start with, which means he avoids the state of mental disturbance which arises from stressing something other than the real.

People generally regard uncertainties as certainties. They try to make what is changeable by nature into something fixed and unchangeable. Therefore, they are constantly up in arms, being stimulated or disturbed about something. One who is accustomed to behaving in this way rushes to arms for even the slightest cause. To thrive thus on conflict is to perish.

That is why the sages went unarmed. They knew that what seems to be indispensable is dispensable. However, the masses treat the dispensable as indispensable, thus they are always armed. Their actions are self-seeking.

VI
Great Truth is Beyond Wrappings

The understanding of the man of little knowledge never rises above cards and gifts, letters and bribes. His mind is cluttered with trivial things, yet he thinks he wants to know the depth of Tao, to blend form and emptiness together in the Great Unity. Such a person becomes trapped by time and space; living in the world of objective existence, he does not know the essence of the Great Truth.

One of perfect nature, however, lets his spirit return to the time prior to the Great Beginning and reposes in perfect freedom.   He flows like water to the clear depths of the infinite.   All man's intellectual understanding can be encompassed in the tip of a hair; but nothing of the Great Peace can be so limited.

VII
The Truly Great Sages Make no Noise

When Confucius was travelling on his way to the capital of Ch'u, he spent the night at an inn at Mt. Ant. Next door, several men and women were rushing around, making preparations for a move. His student, Tzu Lu, asked him, "Who are those people and why are they in such a great rush?"

"They are the followers of a sage," said Confucius. "He has concealed his light of wisdom so that he could live among the people, hiding himself in his work in the fields and marketplace. His behavior may resemble that of other people, yet in his heart he does not go along with the times.   His reputation as a sage has faded, but not his goal of spiritual development. Though his mouth speaks, his mind remains silent.   It is I-liao from the South."

"Shall I go next door and invite him over?" asked Tzu Lu.

"Don't.   He knows that I am on my way to Ch'u, where he is sure I will recommend that the King summon him to service. He thinks that I will expose him. He would be bothered if people knew who he actually is.   This is why he is moving away.   He would not like to hear my words, much less see me in person! What makes you so sure he is still there in the house, anyway?"

Tzu Lu went next door to look and found the house empty.

This is a great example of a spiritually developed one who lives an ordinary life without distinguishing

himself in any way. Such an achieved one never needs
to show his achievement. He can work in the fields as
a farmer or in the marketplace as a businessman. He
does not need to label himself as an achieved one. He
does not need special attention from others nor look for
recognition from anyone.

VIII
Spiritual Power has no Sign
Confucius decided to write the history of the time
between 722 B.C. and 403 B.C. He included the big
events of the princes and dukes of the period and entitled it, "The Period of Spring and Autumn." He went
to see three historiographers, Ta T'ao, Po Ch'ang-ch'ien,
and Hsi-wei about Duke Ling of Wei. He then asked:
"Duke Ling of Wei was so habituated to drinking and
seeking his own pleasure that he ignored governing his
state and its leading families. He was so habituated to
going hunting that he did not keep appointments with
other lords. Why was the posthumous title of Ling
given to him?"[31]

Ta T'ao replied, "It was an accurate description."

Po Ch'ang-ch'ien said, "Duke Ling had three wives
and would bathe with them and have fun in the same
tub, but when Shih Ch'iu, a developed spiritual person,
appeared in his court to offer his teaching, the Duke
received him in person and respectfully attended Shih
Ch'iu without anger for being interrupted from his
pleasure with his wives. He promptly walked away
from merry-making to present himself respectfully before a worthy man. He could have been proud and
presumptuous, but he was not like most spoiled kings

---

[31]Ling means spiritual power or foreknowledge. It was an
ancient custom that once a ruler or an important official passed
away, a new title was given to his soul according to what he had
achieved in his lifetime. This is why the proverb says, "A person's
worth is not decided until the lid of his coffin is put on." It is only
a judgement from the public, yet public opinion can sometimes be
incorrect.

and dukes. This is why he was titled Duke Ling, because he was not confused or caught between personal fun and respect toward a spiritually achieved one."

Hsi Wei said, "When Duke Ling passed away, we divined to see whether he should rest in his family graveyard, but received an unfavorable sign. Then we divined to see if Sand Hill was the right location, which is someone else's property, and received a favorable answer. Digging down quite deep, we found a very old stone plate carved with a message which someone apparently had previously buried there. When we had it washed and examined, we discovered the inscription which said, 'This land will be chosen for the burial of Duke Ling. He did not choose his own family graveyard because he had no confidence that his sons would have the capability to protect it.' From this it would appear that someone with real spiritual foreknowledge was alive a long time before Duke Ling had been called Ling."

This person leaves no name behind him even though he had excellent achievement in spiritual foreknowledge. A life that contains its own truth does not require recognition from anyone and can never be accurately described by anyone.

CHAPTER TWENTY-THREE

DIGNITY AND FAVOR SEEKING

I
A Good Government

Duke Ai of Lu asked Yen Ho, an achieved one, "If I were to make a school of thought or a religious practice the pillar-like support for my kingdom, would the State benefit by it?"

"It would be a most hazardous action to take," replied Yen Ho. "In the end, this teaching would become nothing more than a matter of outward display and specious expression, having the appearance of a genuine thing but being in reality, artifice. The government as well as the common people would come to prefer believing in the flowery words rather than seeing reality. This is like mistaking the branch for the root: taking the accessories as if they were of main importance. In this way, you would be treating what is absurd as the truth. People would lose the connection with their true hearts. People would be filled with a kind of idealism or spiritual fantasy. People would also learn to disguise their true selves. Do not do anything that can cause people to leave the truth and study the false. There is no benefit in it, either now or in the generations to come.

"The key to governing others lies in one's ability to constantly practice self-effacement; one must learn to govern with no regard for one's own self. Merchants and traders have not been able to do their work with the highest of ideals, which is self-effacement. Government must do it. A good government guards society from extreme trends and unhealthy influences, taking care not to start any itself.

"A bad school colors people's thoughts; a good one keeps them pure. Thus a good school is not forceful or imposing on anyone. Similarly, a bad government enslaves people, while a good one develops them. Thus a true government is not forceful and imposing.

"A truly good school is like having no school. A truly good government is like having no government.

"It would be better to stay natural rather than adopt a religion or a school of thought. Otherwise, it will be hard to maintain good order. Once superficial standards are established, people see only the external punishments inflicted by humiliation and the deprivation of freedom; but they cannot see the internal punishments that are inflicted by anxiety and remorse and the deprivation of the freedom of mind and spirit. Fools who incur external punishment are treated with metal bars. Those who incur internal punishment are devoured by the conflict of emotions, mind and spirit. No one likes to be behind wooden or metal bars, yet however smart or clever a person may be, he foolishly creates conceptual bars inside himself and thus cages his own soul. It is only the pure man, who is perfectly normal and maintains his normalcy through self-cultivation, that can succeed in avoiding both. Thus he is the one who can enjoy freedom of mind and spirit."

II
Virtue Distinguishes a Person, not Rank

One of spiritual development said, "Generally, an undeveloped heart and mind are a larger obstacle and present more difficulties than do mountains and rivers. Nature has its regular periods of the four seasons, day and night. Man has a certain exterior but his nature is hidden within. That is why although some look all right, they are really addicted to slavery. On the other hand, some are fully matured, but look undistinguished. Others may be apprehensive, but have a firm understanding of a situation. Some look like they are in control, but are lax; others look weak, but are ruthless. That is why some approach righteousness and benevolence as though they were thirsty for it, but in fact, they avoid their virtuous natures as though they were fire.

"Because appearance does not reveal one's character, a ruler will send his men to a distant place on a mission of public welfare so that he can observe their loyalty. He will employ their talents close to home to observe their respect. He will allow them to handle troublesome affairs so that he can observe their ability. He will seek their advice on important matters to observe their knowledge and wisdom. He will move up a schedule to observe their devotion to duty. He will entrust them with money to observe their integrity. He will inform them of danger to observe their faithfulness. He will get them drunk to observe their deportment. He will place them in disreputable surroundings to observe their morality. After these nine tests have been applied, it is clear who is the superior man and who is the inferior man.

"Most men look for the honor and glory of official positions. But Cheng K'ao Fu, when he received his first appointment as preliminary minister, bent his head when he approached people. On receiving a promotion to a higher position, he hunched his back to people. On receiving his third promotion, he scurried along the side of the path instead of in the middle.

"Men of ordinary character, on their first appointment, become self-important. On their second, they put on an act from their vehicles. On their third, they treat their own fathers like servants."

III
Spiritual Virtue is the True Form of a Life

One of the greatest sources of benefit is a skill of natural excellence which becomes conscious of itself. Such self-consciousness brings about introspection, which can help a person see what can be done to avoid stumbling and falling.

One of the greatest causes of destruction is the intentional virtue of an outwardly looking mind. By only looking outward, the great power of self-inspection is destroyed. Any person who intentionally tries to be virtuous practices only what he likes and condemns what he does not like. The worst thing someone can do is to believe and actually follow some ready-made conceptual principle that will block his mind, because spontaneity is the essence of real virtue.

By being subjective about what is in the mind, one cannot objectively face the reality in front of him, and his work will fail to make a true contribution.

Trouble and mistakes have five sources: the partial use of any of the five receptive organs, the senses. Worst among mistakes is the partial use of one's mind: the subjective mind that approves only of its own perception, forming its own preconceptions, and rejecting any other facts. Conversely, the other partial use of one's center is the mind which attends only to the superficial, which perceives only external establishments and ignores the internal. It is important to find depth by balancing the two.

It is said in the Yellow Emperor's secret guidance that one who is able to keep watch for the five 'thieves' of the senses will have a good life. Thus, do not be carried away by sensory pleasure and superficial observations. Your inner virtue is the pivotal point which maintains your balance. To practice inner virtue means to remain true to yourself and always balanced.

There are eight causes of failure, three elements of success and six sources of punishment.

The eight causes of failure are these: a heart that pursues external beauty, working only on having a particular handsome appearance, having a tall stature, possessing great strength, exhibiting great style, being full of grace, practicing great bravery and being a dare-devil - any of these can cause trouble in a person's life. When one surpasses other people in any of these areas, one may also become proud. Pride is a sure ticket to failure.

The three elements of success are as follows: modesty, compliance and humility.

The six sources of punishment consist of: wisdom and knowledge, and the recognition that come with them that causes you to pull the focus to yourself; bravery and decisiveness, and the resentments they incur by benefitting only one group of people or one side of people's opinion; and benevolence and righteousness that cannot satisfy some of the people and leaves other people out. These six work together and can bring you punishment.

He who has mastered the true form of life has all things revealed to him. He who understands the value of intellectual knowledge is wise. He who comprehends the Great Destiny of the Universe becomes part of it. He who is limited to the Lesser Destiny of an individual human remains with it.

IV
A Detached View of Life

When a developed one was about to die, his disciples expressed a desire to give him a magnificent burial. The teacher said, "I have Heaven and Earth for my coffin, the sun and moon for my burial furnishings, the stars and constellations for decoration, and all creation to accompany me to the grave. With the preparations for the burial already made, what is there to add?"

The developed one, who enjoys the plain reality of life, does not respect the old custom of overly luxurious funerals for the nobles.

V
Non-Assertiveness Rescues Stubbornness

If a person adopts an absolute standard of evenness to apply to that which is only relatively even, his result will never be absolutely even. If he adopts an absolute criterion of right to apply to that which is only relatively right, his result will never be absolutely right. If he tries to establish peace through acts that are unpeaceful, he will not attain peace. If he attempts to prove something that cannot absolutely be proven, then no proof can be established.

A person who trusts their senses alone is a slave of external objective existence. One who is also guided by their intuition can find the true standard in life. Insight has long been the victor where vision suffers defeat. The senses are so much less reliable than the intuition, yet fools hold to their sensory-based opinions of what is good for the world. They eventually find that the results are only superficial.

He who intellectualizes his mind is a tool of things, but he who is inspired by nature commands them.

VI

A man named Ts'ao Shang from the state of Sung was sent by the King of Sung as delegate to the state of Ch'in. When he left, he was to have been given only four or five carriages, but the King of Ch'in was so impressed by him that he received a hundred vehicles from the sovereign.[32]

When Ts'ao Shang returned to Sung State, he went to see Chuang Tzu to show off. Chuang Tzu was not home, but Po the Straight, a disciple of Chuang Tzu, greeted Ts'ao Shang, who said, "I'm no good at living in small apartments and barely scraping by for a living. Being favored by the great ruler of a state of ten thousand chariots and returning with a hundred of them for myself as a prize is what I am much better at!"

Po the Straight said, "When the king needs medical treatment, he calls his doctors. If it is an abscess to be drained or an infection to be cured, the attending physician may receive one carriage. The lower down the area to be treated, the more carriages are given. Judging from the large number of carriages you've received, it must have been his piles that you were treating. Only by brown-nosing him would you receive such a favor. Please leave our teacher's house now!"

When Chuang Tzu returned home, Po the Straight, described the visit to him. Chuang Tzu asked him, "Do you admire him or are you jealous of him?"

"No sir," he replied, "I do not like worldly politicians of low character who would do anything to hook up with someone in authority to try to gain their personal favor."

---

[32]This story took place during a time when Ch'in kept expanding into its neighboring states with no self-restraint.

VII

A man had an interview with the King of Sung, a cruel and short-visioned king, and was presented with ten vehicles. He then showed these off to Chuang Tzu. Chuang Tzu warned him, "Over by the river there is a poor family that earns its living by weaving. One day the son dove into the deep waters and found a valuable jewel, worth thousands, and brought it home. His father said to him, 'Go fetch a stone so we can smash and destroy it. Such a valuable jewel must have been located in deep water somewhere close to the jaws of black sharks. The sharks must have been sleeping or else you would not have gotten it. You can be sure that if the sharks had been awakened, there would not have been an ounce of you remaining!'

"Well," continued Chuang Tzu, "the state of Sung is now in much deeper trouble than those waters, and the king is much more violent and unpredictable than the black sharks. To get the vehicles, you must have seen him while his cruelty was sleeping. If you ever awaken it, you will be killed and cut up!"[33]

VIII

Someone who was just named to a high position in the royal court of a tyrant sent gifts to Chuang Tzu with an invitation to celebrate his new office. Chuang Tzu responded, "Have you ever seen an ox taken to the sacrifice? Before that event, they decorate him with ribbons and flowers and allow him to feast on grasses and beans. But when they are ready to take him to his calling, he certainly wishes that he were again a young, lonely calf in an ordinary living condition!"

---

[33]Sung was Chuang Tzu's home state. The event occurred before the state of Sung was first split and then ceased to exist after the king had lost the support of his people. Because of his cruelty, the people did not fight hard enough to resist the invaders.

CHAPTER TWENTY-FOUR

HUI TZU
A GREAT TEACHER OF LIBERAL MIND

Chuang Tzu was attending a funeral where he passed by the grave of his old friend, Hui Tzu. Turning to his helpers and disciples he said, "Once there was a plasterer who, if he got even a tiny bit of mud on the tip of his nose, would call for his friend Carpenter Shih to slice it off for him with his adze. Shih would accept the assignment and proceed to remove the tiny spot of mud without causing any damage to the nose, while the plasterer stood there relaxed and undisturbed.

"When Lord Yuan of Sung heard of this, he summoned Shih and asked him, 'Can you do this for me, too?' But Shih replied, 'It is true that I once had the ability to do that, but it took two persons to achieve it. Now the partner I have worked with has gone; I no longer have a man with such great trust who will allow me to apply my adze to his nose.' Clearly carpenter Shih was politely suggesting that Lord Yuan could not keep from flinching if he applied the adze to him.

"Like Shih, since the death of Master Hui Tzu, I have no one like my great friend to work on. There's no one I can discuss deep things with any more." This was Chuang Tzu's deep feeling and his sincere appreciation for his friend who had an equally liberal mind, though he was of a different nature. Chuang Tzu enjoyed his spiritual development by following Lao Tzu's teaching of the Integral Way. Hui Tzu enjoyed using the dialectic method of thought and applying it in disputes as well as practical matters, and he accepted the position of Prime Minister of the kingdom of Wei. Chuang Tzu did not enjoy narrow political involvement; however, they were good friends.   They often made fun of each other.

Once Hui Tzu said to Chuang Tzu, "The Prince of Wei gave me a seed from a large gourd.   I planted it and it produced a huge fruit, the size of a five-bushel basket.   But if I had used the gourd for storing liquids, it would have been too heavy to lift.   If I had cut it in half to use for ladles, the ladles would have been so large I couldn't have dipped them into anything.   The gourd was uselessly large, so I broke it up and threw it away.   This is like your teaching of the Integral Way of Tao."

"Hui Tzu," replied Chuang Tzu, "it is you who do not know how to make good use of large things.   This reminds me of the man of Sung who had a formula for making lotion for chapped hands.   He and his family were silk-washers and they had used it for generations.   Well, a fellow from a different place heard about it and offered him a hundred ounces of silver for the formula.   He called his family together and said, 'We have never made a large quantity of money silk-washing, but now we can make a hundred ounces of silver in one day!   Let us give the formula to the man.'

"So they gave the recipe to the man who soon thereafter notified the Prince of Wu about it.   At that time, the Prince of Wu was at war with the state of Yueh.   The salve was used in a naval battle fought at the beginning of the winter; by applying the salve, the soldiers' limbs were not stiffened by the cold and they were thus able to defeat their enemy.   The man received a reward of territory and a title.

"The capacity of the salve to heal chapped hands was the same in both situations, but its application was different.   In one situation it secured a title and land for a man, while in the other it enabled a family to wash silk for many generations.   Similarly, the teachings of Tao can be beneficial to many people.

"Now, as for your large gourd, you could have made it into a raft to carry you across rivers and lakes. That would be better than complaining that it is of no use. If, however, you keep worrying about ladles, you will remain a man with a head full of underbrush."

On another occasion, Hui Tzu said to Chuang Tzu, "Sir, I have a large tree that is worthless. Its trunk is so irregular and knotty that it cannot even be measured to be used for planks, and its branches are so twisted that there is no way to divide them evenly. It stands right by the roadside, but no carpenter ever even looks at it. Your words are like that tree: big, unwanted and useless."

"Hui Tzu," rejoined Chuang Tzu, "have you ever seen a wildcat crouched in wait for its prey? When it jumps about in all directions, it gets caught in a trap or dies in a snare. It is so intent on one thing, it loses sight of all else.

"Teaching with a particular intention of benefitting personal purpose would cause one to run into traps of desire and unreasonable ambition. Doing things and giving help without any particular intention creates no pressure for people or oneself; thus, one may remain free. The great path of teaching serves all people in one great direction. For what purpose could it be narrowed down to a specific race or to see only certain results?

"You are attacking my teaching for being undefined and not easily understood. I accept that, because I do see the value of detachment in teaching and service, in giving and in personal life. Why should I be like a wildcat with a big intention?

"There is also the yak, which with its huge body, can be very helpful in accomplishing big tasks. However, it is useless for catching mice.

"You have a big tree and are concerned about its uselessness. Why not plant it in a barren land? Then relax and do nothing by its side, lie down and take a free and easy sleep under its shade. There, axes will never shorten its life. Its uselessness keeps it from harm."

At a different time, Chuang Tzu and his dear friend Hui Tzu strolled together along the wide stream of Hau. The water was clean and lucid, and at the bridge, they enjoyed watching the fish swimming freely in the water. After watching for a quiet moment, Chuang Tzu exclaimed, "How happy the fish are!"

"You are not a fish, how do you know the fish are happy?" retorted Hui Tzu.

"You are not me, how do you know I do not know the fish are happy?" answered Chuang Tzu, and the two of them had a good, hearty laugh together.

Hui Tzu was a man of many talents whose knowledge, if all written down, could fill five carriages. However, almost all of his writings were lost. His life was a model of the spirit of liberty. His thought could challenge common people and also help them push through to see the truth. Here is his view of the universe:

"The integrity of the universe is greatness in its ultimate form. There is nothing beyond it; it is infinite. At the same time, the integrity of the universe is smallness in its highest form. There is nothing more within it; it is infinitesimal. Yet, the greatness of universal integral nature can be found and completely contained in the smallest particle of the universe. Conversely, the smallness of universal integral nature can hold the entirety of the multi-universe with its endless time and boundless space, always expressing the undistinguishable oneness."

The next is his dialectical view: "That which has no thickness cannot heaped up into a pile, yet its breadth is measurable in millions of miles. From the view of greatness, Heaven and earth have the same lowness; mountains and flatlands are equally level. The sun seen at noontime is the setting sun. The moment something is born, it is dying. The likeness of things partly unlike is called lesser likeness of unlike. The likeness of things altogether unlike is called the greater likeness of unlikes.

"The direction South is infinite, yet it has a limit to its infinity. (This means that any direction is infinite, but when the sense of infinity is applied, it becomes definite and no longer infinite.)

"I can go to Yueh today and have arrived there yesterday. (Yueh is a place in the south. One starts a journey today but one has arrived yesterday. It is the cyclic sense of time he applied.)

"Joined rings can be separated. (This means a cycle is a continual curved line formed by the accumulation of small dots.)

"The middle of the world is north of Yen and south of Yueh. (It means the center of the surface of a ball can be at any set point.)

"Let unity embrace all creation, for Heaven and earth are not separated."

Hui Tzu devoted his intelligence to deep intellectual pursuits. People had a high opinion of his wisdom, and there were few people in the world who were his peer. His only true peer was Chuang Tzu, who responded profoundly to his stimulation.

Hui Tzu was much more advanced than the philosophers of many other schools of his time. He could apply his integral vision to destroy all shallow, established conceptual relativity; he was powerful in talking and in debating. He saw that the general mind is not thorough. He did not hesitate to start a discussion with anyone because he knew it could be a way to reach a common understanding among people.

The famous logicians Huan T'uan and Kung Sun Lung were not Hui Tzu's peer. They could out-talk others, but they could not subdue their own hearts and minds. This was due to the limitation of their minds. Yet by grasping only one statement of Hui Tzu, one might be enlightened if one could only breathe away the words presented.

In the south lived Huang Liao, who questioned why Heaven and Earth did not collapse or fall apart, and what activated wind and rain, thunder and lightning. Hui Tzu, without stopping to think, began to reply, touching upon each of the ten thousand things with his deep vision, expounding on without stopping, in great quantities of words. In searching for the truth of nature he never gave up; his deep vision arrived at the truth that contradicted but completed other men's partial views. Such deep discussion does not sit well with ordinary minds. One who is weak in inner vision, though strong in intellectual information concerning external things, walks a crooked road that reaches nowhere. If we examine all accomplishments from the point of view of great nature, we see that the exertions of most rhetoricians do not begin to touch the truth and seem instead like the empty buzzing of mosquitoes and gnats. What service can they therefore offer the world? Their scope is limited by not reaching the truth as did Hui Tzu.

Hui Tzu deserves to be regarded as the fore-runner of the school of liberated thinking: he opposed rigid thought and he was a great example of the liberal spirit exploring for truth. Anyone who can show great respect for the Integral Way will have come nearer the truth by not getting stuck in the playground of language, which has only relative scope. However, one cannot find dependable inner peace with such relative means as words and concepts, even if motivated by the desire to help others break through their own conceptual cages.

Hui Tzu's method of discussion seems contradictory to the Way of Great Unity, yet it can help break through conceptual blockages. He went on tirelessly separating and analyzing the ten thousand things, and in the end he made the subtle integral truth known by his skill in exposition. He was not someone who abused and dissipated his talent without ever really achieving anything. Chasing after the ten thousand things fragmentedly, never turning back to the truth of one's life but establishing one's philosophy or religious faith, is like trying to shout an echo into silence or separate form from shadow.

Hui Tzu investigated all creation, but made us discover him and conclude his great work of the dialectic method for reaching Tao, a method derived from the content of the *I Ching*. First you have what is afirmed (———), then comes the denial (— —); finally comes the combination or union of what is affirmed and denied to establish a new unity (○). The *I Ching* is the common source of philosophical faith developed in ancient China. The forerunners of Tao employed the *I Ching* in its original diagram form, without written words. Confucius employed the *I Ching* with worded explanations, while other schools of thought utilized the dialectic method of the *I Ching*, as, for example, the schools of Hui Tzu and Moh Tzu. All of these can supplement each other in the explaining of Tao, the subtle ultimate truth, to general learners, making it approachable and of service.

PART TWO

WHERE THE WORLD SHOULD GO

CHAPTER TWENTY-FIVE

SPIRITUAL SELF-CULTIVATION
AND BALANCED WORLDLY SERVICE

I
Breaking Off All Limited Conceptual Frames

In the great ocean in the North, the water takes the form of a large fish. It is known as Kun and is many thousand li in length.[34] This fish then transforms itself into a large bird known as Peng whose back measures thousands of li in width. After accumulating sufficient energy, the bird rises and its wings obscure the sky like clouds.

When the sea begins to move like the tide, the bird migrates to the dark abyss of the South where it forms the Heavenly Lake. The Book of Marvels of Chi records all kinds of unusual happenings, stating that when Peng flies southward, after creating a storm that spans three-thousand li of water, it rises upon a whirlwind to a height of ninety-thousand li and begins a flight that lasts six lunar months.

Peng travels far above with bits of dust blowing about in the strong winds, and the sky's color is deep blue. Is blue the sky's real color or does it only indicate its unattainable distance? When the bird looks down, what he sees is the same blueness.

Unless water is sufficiently deep, it cannot support a large boat. The same is true of air; if there is not enough depth, it cannot support a large bird. For Peng, a depth of ninety thousand li is necessary. Then, with clear sky above and nothing blocking it, it begins its flight to the South.

Hearing about Peng, a cicada laughed heartily and said to a little dove, "When I make an effort to fly, I

---

[34]One li measures approximately one-third mile.

can reach the elm tree over there, but sometimes if I do not reach it immediately, I fall to the ground. What is the purpose of going up ninety-thousand li and why bother to go to the South?"

When someone goes to a nearby field, he only needs to take enough rice and food for lunch and he will return with his stomach as full as when he left. One who travels a hundred li, however, must take enough food to last overnight, and one who travels a thousand li must carry enough provisions for three months. What do two little creatures like a dove and a cicada know? Small knowledge does not encompass greater knowing any more than a day spans the length of a year.

How do we know this is true? A mushroom that lives a single morning does not know the change between day and night. The summer cicada does not know the change between spring and autumn. Their years are short. In the state of Chu, however, there lives a caterpillar whose spring and autumn each last five hundred years. And long ago there was a tree known as a Large Sharon which had a spring and autumn that each lasted eight thousand years.

Today, Peng-Tzu is famous for living eight hundred years and he is thus used as a standard of comparison for those seeking longevity. Isn't it pitiful that some people are sad they cannot live as long as he?

In 1766 B.C., Emperor Tang spoke to Ch'i of these things, saying: "In the North there is a great sea. In it is a great fish called Kun, thousands of li in breadths and I know not how many li in length. There is also a bird called Peng, with a back like Mount T'ai.[35] Its wings spread across the sky like clouds. Upon a whirlwind, this bird soars up to a great height of ninety thousand li. With only clear blue sky above and below, flies toward the southern waters."

---

[35]One of China's most famous sacred mountains, situated in Shantung Province.

When a quail heard of this, he laughed and said, "What can that foolish creature be trying to do? I rise a few feet into the air and come back down again after flying around the reeds; this is the longest and best flight possible. Where on earth is he going?" The quail's words describe the difference between small and great. A man who creditably fills a small governmental position, is a model of virtue in his neighborhood or exerts a righteous influence over the ruler of the state might have the same pride as the quail. Sung Jung-Tzu, the achieved one, would not feel so proud, even if the whole world praised him, nor would he be affected if the whole world blamed him. Sung knows the difference between intrinsic and extrinsic, true and false, internal and external, honor and disgrace. It is rare to see such a man in this world.

Lieh Tzu, another achieved one, could travel by riding the wind. He knew how to become very light, and could stay aloft for as long as fifteen days. But although Lieh Tzu was able to put an end to walking, he still depended on the wind for his transportation. If he had been one who could ride upon the subtle truth and follow the natural fitness of eternal life, there would have been nothing on which he needed to depend. Thus it has been said, "Man in his highest form is selfless. Gods, who were once men, have no interest in achievement. One of natural wisdom takes no interest in fame." Worldly joys and sorrows cease for the one who advances into the everlasting life of transcendental peace.

The practices of "Transformation of Kun and Peng" and of "Lieh Tzu Riding the Wind" were esoteric teachings passed down strictly to the spiritual descendants of Chuang Tzu and Lao Tzu.

II
Spiritual Reality of Life is More Important Than Reputation and Position

In 2356 B.C., Emperor Yao wanted to cede the empire to Hsu Yu, a highly developed sage. The Emperor said, "If torches are left burning when the sun and moon are shining, is this not a waste of light? If irrigation is continued in the rainy season, is this not a waste of water? Now that I have found you, sir, the empire will be at peace and the world will enjoy order if you would but assume the throne. Recognizing my own deficiency, I turn the world over to you."

Hsu Yu replied, "Since you took up the reigns of government, sir, the empire has enjoyed tranquility and peace. If I were to take your place, I would establish a reputation from it. But reputation is only a shadow cast by the reality of life. Should I live in the light of reality or in a shadow? The weaverbird, building its nest in the great forest, occupies no more than a single branch. The mole quenches its thirst from the river, but drinks only enough to fill its belly. I have no use for the throne or to rule over the world. Even though a cook may not manage his kitchen well, the priest who comes to bless the food should not leap over the wine casks to replace the cook or interfere with something that is not his responsibility."

III
The Inner Divinity of Each Individual

Chien Wu said to Lien Shu, a person of natural wisdom, "I heard Chieh Yu, a developed one, say something that didn't make any sense at all. I was greatly startled by what he said, which seemed to speak of a magnificence unknown to the mortal realm, of a vastness like the star-filled sky, which quite startled me."

"What did he say?" asked Lien Shu.

"He said that on the Mountain of Neglected Vision there lives a divine one whose flesh is white and cool like ice or snow and whose behavior is fresh and youthful like a virgin. He eats no food from the earth but lives instead on air and dew. He rides on clouds with a team of flying dragons and travels beyond mortality. His inner gods are so congealed that he is concentrated in divine oneness. His personal power is strong enough to drive off corruption, sickness and plague from all things; his presence can even cause

189 ATTAINING UNLIMITED LIFE

crops to flourish. To me this is insane talk; I cannot believe or make sense of it."

"Your reaction to words like his is a typical response," said Lien Shu. "A blind person cannot admire beautiful pictures and a deaf person cannot enjoy music. Blindness and deafness do not apply to the physical world alone; there is also a subtle blindness and a deafness of the mind. Your words reveal that kind of blindness. A divine one of integral nature cannot be comprehended by people who are spiritually blind and deaf. Would you have a divine one of natural wholeness trapped in the triviality of the world? One who is filled with all virtues expresses the integrity of the universe.

"Things that exist in a particular form cannot harm the integral nature of a divine one. If a flood were to rise as high as the sky, it would not drown the unity of a divine one. If a drought were so severe that metals ran liquid and mountains were scorched, it would not burn the integralness of a divine one. Out of only the dust and ashes of such a one, you might make two great sages like Yao and Shun. But a divine one would prefer to remain far from the world, its continual affairs and struggling, and its desire for worldly reform."

This describes the passing of Tao. The virgin is the inner wholesome pure energy of each individual being. By nurturing the inner being, one attains spiritual development. In later generations, the statue of the Goddess of Mercy, Quan Yin, came to symbolize this personal, inner spiritual energy.

IV
A Life Itself is Whole
A man from the state of Sung, in the north of ancient China, designed some stately looking ceremonial hats intending to sell them to the people of the State of Yueh in the southern part of China. However, the custom of the men of Yueh was to wear their hair in a certain short style and to tattoo their bodies, and thus they had no use for hats. Emperor Yao, the wise

ruler of all under Heaven and the peacemaker of all earth, visited the four sages of the Mountain of Neglected Vision. After seeing these sages of integral nature, he returned to his capital, which was north of the Teng River, and found that the worry and burden of governing his empire in the conventional way had disappeared. This shows that something of use in one place or time is not necessarily fit for another.

V
The Truth is Too Great to Grasp

The high truth may be too great to grasp, yet an integral person is someone who, in the course of his life, maintains the natural spontaneity, kindness and flexibility of his original nature. Such a person has a deep connectedness to all of being alive. There is a sense of wholeness or completeness in his or her presence; there is also a depth of wisdom. One who has lost these qualities through worldly contact or undigested life experiences seems twisted or distorted by comparison; something about them seems lost, unfocused or not correctly put together.

A person living in the modern world can restore his original nature by carefully and diligently improving and integrating himself and his life. This can be accomplished through a process called self-cultivation which is described in detail in my other books.

The source of this teaching is the tradition of the ancient spiritually developed people, passed down through numerous generations, notably through two great masters, Lao Tzu and Chuang Tzu.

The life of nature is like water; it is free-flowing and can transform into oceans, lakes, clouds - even fish and birds - and then back into water. The concordance of nature is manifested in a cycle of , transformations, like an immense creature containing all things.

Nature can transform itself and yet maintain its integrity. This cannot be understood by any short-lived creature limited by the form of its own life, like the cicada, dove and quail or someone limited by an ordinary, habitual mind like Chieh Wu or with a rigid intellectual mind, no matter how bright or clever.

CHAPTER TWENTY-SIX

THE UNITY OF OPPOSITES

I
The Breath of Nature

Tzu Ch'i of South City sat in repose, leaning on his armrest. Looking up at the sky he breathed deeply, engaged in the breathing practice, as if he lived alone in the world without any company. Later, after he had been restored by his quiet sitting, Yen Ch'eng Tzu Yu, his student, stood in attendance by his side and said to him, "How can you make your body like a dried tree and then have it refreshed, and your mind like a heap of dried ashes and then have it rekindled? The man who was leaning on the armrest before is not the same one who is here now and emanating such a beautiful radiance."

"Tzu Yu," replied Tzu Ch'i, "your question is valid. You notice that I dissolve myself, but how can you understand it? Ah! The spiritual energy of people is like music. Perhaps you have only heard the music of man, and not that of Earth. Even if you have listened to the music of Earth, you may not have heard that of Heaven."

"Please explain," requested Tzu Yu.

"The breath of nature," said Tzu Ch'i, "is the wind. Sometimes it is inactive, but when it is active, every opening in the earth sings with it. Have you ever listened to its song?

"The caves and hollows in hills and forests, the nooks and crannies of large trees, the gullies and ditches in open ground are like nostrils, mouths and ears, like jugs and cups, like pipes and tubes through which the wind rushes, blowing, howling, groaning, singing, whispering, whistling and murmuring; first treble, then bass, now hushed, now thunderous, until there is a pause and silence reigns. Have you ever witnessed a turbulence such as this among the trees?"

"Well," began Tzu Yu, "since the music of Earth consists of nothing more than the wind moving through holes, and the music of man consists of breath moving through pipes and lutes, what then is the music of Heaven?"

"Although there is only one wind, its effect upon the different apertures is not the same," replied Tzu Ch'i. "As it blows on the ten thousand things, each can be itself and take what it wants for itself. But who makes the sounds? Heaven is not something apart from Earth and man. Heaven is a name of the subtle force given to the natural and spontaneous functioning of earth and man."

II
The Naturalness of Man

Tzu Ch'i continued: "Great knowledge encompasses the wholeness of life or the whole situation. Small knowledge encompasses only a part or a section. Great teaching is universal, clear and simple. Small teaching is particular, screeching and quarrelsome.

"In sleep, a person's spirits communicate with the body. In waking life, the body is activated by the spirits.[36] During the day, people are subject to mental disturbances such as indecision, lack of depth, concealment, worry, fear and apprehension. The mind flies forth like an arrow, the self-named arbiter of right and wrong. With fixed intention, as though one had signed a contract, one remains firm, sure of attaining victory. Later, one's spirits fade like autumn leaves, passing away like flowing water, never to return. Finally, when the failing mind draws near to death, nothing can change the fact that he shall no longer see light.

"Delight and anger, happiness and sadness, prudence and folly come to us by turns in ever-changing

---

[36]Personal spirits are termed 'hun' and 'po,' two subtle forces that assist each other.

qualities. They come like the music from the hollows and caverns. Day and night, they alternate within us, but we cannot tell from where they come. They are the means by which we live; without them we would not exist. Without us they would have nowhere to express themselves, but we know not from where they arise. It seems as though they have a master, yet we find no trace of one. Is their master outside our being or within? That such a power exists is clear enough; we can perceive its function, but its form is invisible.

"Consider the human body with all its parts. Which part does a person appreciate most, or does he use all parts equally? Is not each part of equal value to him? How do they operate - do they govern themselves or are they subject to a hierarchy of leadership? Surely there is some true Master among them, but whether you succeed in discovering his identity or not does not add or detract from the truth of his existence. Whether we know the functions of this Master or not does not matter to the Master himself.

"By coming into existence in this mortal form, and with the exhaustion of this form, the function or purpose of this form will also be exhausted. To be troubled by the events of daily life, to rush through life at a gallop without knowing where to look for rest, seems most pitiful. To work without stop and then, without living long enough to enjoy the harvest, to be all worn out and then suddenly to be gone, heading for the unknown, is this not good reason for grief? In old age people cling to being alive, but to what advantage? The body decomposes and the mind goes at the same time; this is our real cause for sorrow. Can the world be so dull as not to see this or am I the only one who is dull?

"If one accepts conventional feelings and thoughts as the criteria for one's own attitudes and behavior, then no one would have a personal criterion to insist upon. There would then be no need for people to learn from each other. However, if one takes one's own feelings and thoughts as the guidelines for one's life, then even a fool will have his own standard for living. To be in the clutches of 'right and wrong' before one has attained true knowledge of life is like someone saying, 'I went to Yueh today and was there yesterday,' to make yesterday's experience as today's reality, or like describing where nowhere is. These are things that even the wise Great Yu[37] would fail to understand. So how can I understand them?"[38]

Tzu Ch'i continued, "Speech is more than breath; it has meaning. Take away meaning and you could not say it is speech. Without meaning, would you be able to distinguish the sounds from the chirping of young birds?

"How can the integral truth of nature be so hidden that we can speak of it as being true or false? How can speech so obscure the truth and contain the sense of opposites? How can the integral truth of nature go away and yet remain present? How can speech exist and yet be so absurd?

"The integral truth of nature is obscured by our lack of understanding. Speech obscures truth by the luster of this world, hiding its essence beneath the one-sided meanings of words and phrases. Thus arise the affirmatives and negatives of the different schools, mainly the disputes of the Confucian and Mohist about the new direction for the old society. Each one denies what the other affirms and affirming what the other has denied. The person who wishes to balance affirmative and negative, one with the other, must do so by the light of integral nature.

"As the subjective is also objective, and the objective is also subjective, each indistinguishably blended with

---

[37]Yu was a famous engineer of antiquity who lived ca. 2205 B.C. He rechanneled the Yellow River so it would not flood and he also divided the ancient Chinese territory into nine areas, each with its own natural aspect.

[38]The mind should be neutral, free from all judgments and opinions, ready only to accept things as they are, not as they appear to be.

the other, it becomes impossible to say whether either really exists at all. Without their correlating positives and negatives, subjective and objective are united as the very axis of the integral truth of Tao. When that axis passes through the center at which all infinities converge, the positive and the negative, the objective and the subjective, both blend into an infinite One way. This is why it has been said that there is nothing equal to the light of universal integral nature.

"Everything has an opposite. When something extends itself, it cannot help extending its opposite side as well. While this fact cannot be seen by the person on one side, it can be seen clearly by someone on the opposite side. Therefore, good or bad, right or wrong, the truth is born of oneself but cannot be seen by oneself. It can be seen, however, by standing opposite oneself. Integral vision, therefore, does not forsake one side by insisting on the other. It does not forsake 'this' or 'that,' nor does it insist on either 'this' or 'that,' because the truth of the matter is they are interrelated.

"In any situation involving the relationship of a pair of opposites, there is a point of balanced clarity between the two poles. When this point is insisted upon, however, it then becomes one pole of a new set of opposites.

"If we can observe, with balanced clarity, the interdependent relationship of two opposites, when the positive contribution is discovered, a converged new point appears. Yet the new converged point cannot be insisted upon, because then a new opposite point will sprout. So you see, new opposites continue to be brought about by firmly establishing any one point. Open-mindedness, therefore, is what naturally dissolves the negative confrontation of opposites by absorbing each of them.

"If one insists on the old, on the past, then a new vision cannot be received. What is born, therefore, should be allowed to die; what is affirmed should be denied, and what is denied should be followed by a newly affirmed position. People will isolate one thing out of a whole group or one time period out of a whole event and think that their chosen position reflects the entire situation. Someone else will think this is wrong. This is not the way of those who have attained truly useful wisdom and who know not to cause or allow waste or sacrifice on the part of the believer or user of the situation. Someone who has attained non-conceptual wisdom keeps himself at the pivotal point, letting right and wrong pass while he remains rooted at the deep core of all superficial, constant, changeable phenomena.

"There are those who insist on arguments such as 'a finger is not a finger,' meaning it is just an abstract idea, or 'a white horse is not a horse,' meaning that white is a color and the horse is an animal, so a white horse cannot present the common idea of a horse. This type of argument that makes distinctions between a solid object and a conceptual image or between a particular existence and a common idea are not direct and clear.

"The unspoken language of truth is always direct and distinct. The statement that a finger is not a finger needs no argument. Saying that a red or a white (i.e., particular) rose is not a rose (i.e. the common idea of all roses) sufficiently does the job of distinguishing between one particular rose and 'rose.' It is clear that a lily is not a rose and that a camel is not a horse. Sometimes, too many names for the same object can cause confusion, so sages look for the real things through the clouds of colorful names that surround it.

"Always reach for the direct truth, the fact. 'A rose by any other name is still a rose,' and 'a fast horse is still a fast horse.' People who play with ideologies bring conflict, duality and trouble upon themselves and others. Ideological discrimination and separation can harm one's integral spirit through confrontation, endless conceptual struggle, and personal as well as political antagonism.

"One of integral nature can see that the universe is but a finger and the totality of all things is but a horse."

The order of the long established ancient Chinese society crumbled at the end of the Chou Dynasty.[39] The changes began in 722 B.C. and continued to the peak of the warring period around 400 B.C. Different schools of thought then emerged to express different opinions on how to establish a new order. The strongest argument was between the ideologies of the Confucian school and the Mohist school.

The Confucian school advocates a social order established on the peace between kingdoms with respect to the traditional center, the Chou Dynasty. Their idea was to have an orderly society which developed from clans into a community, then developed further into a larger society. The basis of the orderly society is dependent upon wise leadership and moral education by elders of their youngsters, with the emperor as the central figure. Confucius and his followers wished to revive the cultural achievement and moral leadership achieved by Yao and Shun, who were wise leaders in ancient times of peace and orderliness, using their spiritual influence to rekindle the dying Chou Dynasty. This school of thought was employed to try to prop up the fallen central authority of the declining Chou Dynasty.

The Mohist school advocates conventional spiritual faith in God and a universal love that makes no distinction between tribes of people, considering the world as one family. Its basis is unified social order supported by strong organization and moral discipline. Mo Tzu, the leader of this school, was a philosopher in the fourth century B.C. He wished to restructure society based on the cultural achievements and selfless leadership of the great Yu, who was a prominent fighter and leader during the great flood in his time.

The attitude of the Taoist school, as distinctly expressed here, suggested the unimportance of the dispute between the two other schools. It advocates the natural harmony of healthy social development without

---

[39]1122 B.C. to 256 B.C.

returning to any former establishment. There is the subtle path pointing the right direction for the development of human society. Any artificial institution would express an impulse of the human mind which competes with the traceless natural path of growth. In many places in his work, you will find that Chuang Tzu expresses his belief that Confucius sells ancient hats to modern people, hats that no longer fit the time. Chuang Tzu advocates stopping all wars and allowing naturally virtuous developed people to become leaders and take care of society. Coming from this historical background, Chuang Tzu was not someone who groaned without pain; trouble existed then as it still does today. Taoists continued the work of Lao Tzu, suggesting that each individual seek universal harmony and a natural way of healthy life.

IV
Freeing Ourselves From Argument

"What is adequate, we call adequate. What is inadequate, we call inadequate. A road is made by the action of people walking on it. Things are what they are and they are called so. What makes them what they are? Making them the way they are makes them so. All things have that which makes them the way they are.

"We can never know anything but phenomena. Things are what they are, and their consequences will be what they will be. Viewed from the standpoint of Tao as the integral truth, whether you point to a small stalk or a great pillar, a leper or a beautiful woman, they are all one. Their dividedness is their completeness. Their completeness is their impairment. Nothing is either complete or impaired, but all are made into one again. Only a person of far-reaching wisdom can recognize their unity. Such a person has no use for categories, but relegates all things to what is constant. The constant is useful; the useful is the passable, the passable is the successful, and with success all is accomplished. A person of far-reaching wisdom relies upon this alone. He relies upon it and does not know he is doing so. This is called the integral truth.

"From a sea shell we can hear the sound of the ocean. From a drop of sea water we can taste the entire ocean. On the tip of an eyelash one carries the weight of the Himalayas.

"To wear out one's intellect by stubbornly holding onto the idea of the individuality of things, and to not understand that all things are One, is illustrated by the story 'Three in the Morning.'"

"Would you tell the story, 'Three in the Morning?'" asked Tzu Yu.

Tzu Ch'i replied, "A keeper of monkeys said that each monkey was to have a ration of three chestnuts in the morning and four at night, but the monkeys were very unhappy with this. So the keeper said they could have four in the morning and three at night, at which all the monkeys were satisfied. The number of chestnuts was the same, but there was a reconciliation to the likes and dislikes of the monkeys. This illustrates the principle of being in a subjective relationship with external things.[40]

"The true sage of integral truth thus adapts himself to the subtle law of the universe and regards opposites as identical. This is called following the course of the unity of opposites.

"Those who have achieved transcendence see that matter exists, but only as phenomena. It is merely a relation, or rather the result of a relation between our living souls and the Subtle Origin.[41] Is it not true that living souls and the Subtle Origin are One? When a

---

[40]Three means community ownership advocated by Mo Tzu. Four means family ownership advocated by Confucius. Neither are of true benefit. True benefit is the wisdom which advocates that all individuals should attain spiritual development instead of relying on the controlling rational promises of food or sociological support.

[41]It has been called 'The Great First Cause' by early Western philosophers.

person is made a prophet, must he be unmade as a man?"

After many years Yen Ch'eng Tzu Yu, the student, said to the venerable teacher of South City, Master Tzu Ch'i, "After one year of receiving your guidance, I became simple and natural.   After two years I could adapt myself as needed to fit whatever situation I was in.   After three years I understood.   After four my intelligence developed, and after five years it was complete.   After six years the pure natural spiritual energy gathered to assist me.   After seven I reached the divine source.   After eight life and death no longer existed.   After nine, I reached perfection."

V
The Natural Spiritual Reality is Beyond Argument

"Nature is perfect.   Tao does not declare itself; a perfect argument does not express itself with speech. Perfect benevolence does not show itself through actions.   Perfect honesty is not constant.   Perfect courage is not always unwavering.   The utterances of greatness are not articulated; its argument uses no words, its benevolence is amoral.   No matter how clear, man's utterances are not expressive.   When used in argument, his speech does not hit the mark.   He does not achieve benevolence through constancy, and his uprightness does not inspire confidence through disinterestedness.

"The Tao that is the integral essence of the universe and that is visible is not Tao.   If it is made clear, it is not the Way.   Charity with a certain end loses its object.   Absolute honesty lacks truth.   Absolute courage misses its mark.   These are, you might say, round with a strong tendency to be square.   Therefore, knowledge that knows that it does not know is the highest form of knowledge.

"Who knows the argument that can be argued without words, the utterance that cannot be articulated? He who understands this may be said to be of God. He is poured into without ever becoming full and he pours forth without ever becoming dry.   He does not know the source of his capacity. This man is one who nurtures the inner light.

"The integral essence of the universe has never manifested itself except through the self of all things and all lives. A true self is beyond the shallowness of individuality."

Most individuals look outwardly for what is right and wrong. Thus, arguments are established among intellectuals and differences in ideology are incessantly produced. Although they perceive a distinction between right and wrong in their thoughts, there is truly no end to the expedition or the relative sphere. Unless one works to understand the function of the conceptual mind, he fails to know that all differences and opposites share the same origin, and all voices come from the same silent source. This is how ancient Taoists set the direction of self-cultivation in attaining spiritual development.

CHAPTER TWENTY-SEVEN

NOURISHING THE ESSENCE OF LIFE WITH INTEGRAL SPIRITEDNESS

I
I Do Not Know

Yeh Ch'ueh[42] asked Wang Ni, a highly achieved one, "Do you know for sure that all things are fundamentally the same?"

"How could I know that?" answered Wang Ni. "Can you know what you do not know?" Wang Ni refuses to discuss it, because discussion disturbs one's unity with the wholeness of nature. For a person who is in a harmonious relationship with nature, all of life shares the same root.

"But how can I know?" replied Yeh Ch'ueh. "Can anything be known?"

"How could I know?" said Wang Ni. "However, reluctantly, I will speak to you of this. Who is to say whether what is known as knowledge is not really ignorance - and that what is known as ignorance is not really knowledge? A person who sleeps in a damp place will get lumbago and die, but an eel will not. For a man, living in a tree is difficult and hard on the nerves, but not for a monkey. Of the man, the eel and the monkey, which one lives in the right place or the best location, in an absolute sense? Human beings eat vegetables and meat, deer eat grass, centipedes eat crawling things, and owls and crows eat mice. Of

---

[42]Yeh Ch'ueh was the teacher of Shu Yu, to whom Emperor Yao offered his throne. Yeh Ch'ueh was also the student of Wang Ni. The following conversation was recorded when Yeh Ch'ueh was still a student.

these four, whose taste is right, in an absolute sense? Monkeys pair with monkeys, bucks with does. Men admire beautiful women at the sight of whom a fish will rush down to the bottom of the stream, a bird will soar high in the air and a deer will scurry away. Who determines the standard of beauty? In my opinion, the standards of human virtue and morals, right and wrong, positive and negative, harmful and beneficial are so obscured and confused that it is impossible to actually know anything."

"If even you do not know what is harmful or wrong," exclaimed Yeh Ch'ueh, "then is one of integral truth also without this knowledge?"

"One of integral spirit," answered Wang Ni, "is a being of spiritual completeness, a divine person. Were the ocean itself to become scorched and dry, he would not feel hot. Were the Milky Way to freeze solid, he would not feel cold. Were the mountains to be split by thunder and the earth to be shaken by storm, he would have no fear. Such a one can mount the clouds of Heaven and with the sun and moon before him, roam beyond the limits of the external world to where life and death, much less what is harmful, have no effect on him."

Conventionally, it is told that Bodhidharma introduced the Zahn (Zen) sect to China in the sixth century. It is said that Bodhidharma interviewed King Liang Wu[43] in Kwang Zhou. The King asked, "Who is this?" Bodhidharma answered, "I do not know." However, here, from the first section of this chapter, you can find the true source of Chinese Zahn Buddhism. It is the old bottle of wine, newly labeled. When Buddhism came to China, it was a dualistic spiritual institution, a worshipping religion, the so-called big vehicle. In meeting the arrival of this religion, the initiators of Zahn Buddhism responded by teaching the Integral Way, as advocated in Chuang

---

[43]502-550 A.D.

Tzu's work, keeping the true but forgotten teaching alive but dressing it in different clothing.

II
The Wholeness of Nature is My Life

Chu Ch'iao was talking with Chang Wu Tzu, an ancient developed one who lived under the shade of an umbrella tree.

"I have heard that one of natural wisdom pays no attention to mundane concerns, neither seeking profit nor avoiding loss. He never asks anything of man. Without questioning, he follows Tao, the wholeness of spirit, the entirety of being. Without speaking, he speaks, but, when he does speak, he says nothing. He travels beyond the limitations of the dust and mire of this world. These words sound incredible, but I do believe them to be the description of one who embodies Tao. What do you think?"

Chang Wu Tzu replied, "Even the wise Yellow Emperor would not have understood these words. People, however, often hear words and then jump to conclusions or try to hurry things. They see an egg and expect to hear a rooster crowing. They look at a bow and arrow, and already expect to eat roast duck. You are too hasty in forming an opinion. I will give you a brief explanation, so listen well.

"The wise one uses the sun and the moon for his support and holds the universe in his embrace. He blends all things into one great harmonious whole. High positions and favors, which are greatly valued by common folk, are ignored by him. Despite the disturbances of ten thousand years, he remains himself, unified in oneness. Even if the universe would come to an end, he would continue to flourish.

"Can it be that love of life is just illusion? Can it be that the one who fears dying does not realize that he has been lost and is now on the way back home?

"Lady Chi was the daughter of a border guard. When she was first taken to the state of Chin she wept until her dress was soaked with tears. But after living at the royal palace with the Duke and eating rich food, she wondered why she had cried so much. Similarly, the dead may wonder why they had been clinging so tightly to life. In the attainment of Tao, one surpasses one's conceptual mind. The power and the joy cannot be known or recognized by one's conscious mind, because such a person lives with pure and complete spirit.

"A person dreaming he is about to eat a sumptuous feast wakes up only to become disappointed and weep. Those who dream of disappointment and weep may wake up to enjoy a day of hunting. While people dream, they do not know that they are dreaming. Some, during a dream, try to interpret the very same dream. Only upon awakening, do they realize it was only a dream.

"Only he who is fully awake knows that this life is just a dream. Fools think they are awake now, and spend their time trying to differentiate things, calling one man a king, and another herdsman or peasant. How dense! The man who does the naming is a dream; and the people he gives names to are all dreams, too. I am a dream myself. This type of talk is considered strange, yet, after perhaps ten thousand generations, a man of integral truth may appear who will know its meaning.

"Suppose that you and I make a bet about something. If you win, are you sure that you are right? If I win, am I necessarily right and you wrong? Or are we both partly right and partly wrong? Or are we both completely right and completely wrong? Neither you nor I can know this; other people are bound to be even more ignorant.

"So then, who could arbitrate between the two of us to decide this matter? If we hire someone who agrees with your viewpoint, he will side with you. How can such a person arbitrate fairly? If we hire someone who takes my view, he will side with me. How can such a person arbitrate fairly? If we hire someone who differs with both of us, he will express a third point of view and will still not be able to decide between us. If we were to hire someone who agrees with both of us, he would be unable to decide between the two sides. Since, then, neither you nor I nor even another person can fairly decide, do we continue to look for a fourth?

"The wise ones said, 'Whether the constantly changing voices arrive at agreement or not, harmonize them with Heaven and Earth; set them in accordance with vastness, that they may end.' By that they meant, when a person embraces the unity of universal spiritual nature and depends upon it, he will then adapt perfectly to whatever happens in his life, and so peacefully lives out his years. Such dependence does not seem like dependence.

"What do we mean when we say to embrace the unity of universal nature? It is this: if right were really right, it would be so clearly different from what is not right that there would be no need for argument or discussion about it. If so were really so, it would be so clearly different from what is not-so that there would be no need for argument or discussion about it. The condition of harmony is found only in the all-embracing unity of universal spiritual nature, the Subtle Origin, where all differences of positive and negative, right and wrong, this and that cease to exist, and only oneness remains.

"Thus, leave arguments for fools. Do not worry about time or etiquette, right or wrong. Be moved by universal spiritual nature in your life."

III
The Interrelationship of All Lives

The Light said to the Shadow, "First you move around. Later, you rest. Next you sit down, but at another moment you get up. Why do you have such fluctuation of purpose?"

"I do not know," replied the Shadow. "I depend upon something else to generate my actions. That 'something else' depends, in turn, upon something further which causes it to do what it does. My dependence is like scales to a snake or wings to a cicada; the snake and the cicada do not move of their own.

Thus, I cannot say why I do one thing and not another, because it is not from me."

IV
The Spiritual Nature I Live With, Is It Me?

Once the young Chuang Tzu dreamt that he was a butterfly, fluttering and flying about. His knowledge was that he was truly a butterfly; he was conscious only of following his inclinations as a butterfly and was unconscious of his individuality as a man. Suddenly he awakened, and there he was, unmistakably Chuang Tzu. But after that, he did not know whether he was a man dreaming he was a butterfly or a butterfly dreaming he was a man.

V

In the first section of this chapter, Chuang Tzu taught the spiritual achievement of the ancient developed ones in response to Mo Tzu's teaching of worshipping God and obeying Heavenly will. Belief in God was the grassroots of Chinese spiritual faith in ancient China.

Confucius compiled the "Books of History" which are a collection of the official declarations of Yao, Shun, Yu and the early documents of the Chou Dynasty. According to the material he collected, we know that the ancient people and leaders deeply believed that God is the highest authority of all lives. The Emperors, being called the Sons of Heaven in all the different generations, were considered the elder brother of all people. They were seen as being assigned by God to take care of all lives for Heaven, since all people are children of Heaven. It was a strong belief that anything that went wrong on earth such as a drought, earthquake, big fire, disharmony of the society, etc, expressed that something was wrong in the personal moral state of the emperor in his private life and public administration. All the bad things that happened in the world were seen as his personal fault. Thus, an earthly disaster was considered a sign of the shortcomings of the emperor, and the emperors had to publicly admit the inadequacy of their spiritual achievement and moral fulfillment which had caused the trouble. Oppositely, if the emperor was truly highly achieved and of moral strength, nothing disastrous would happen and the world would be peaceful and happy, in which case he was considered to be blessed by Heaven above him. The emperors of later generations, however, always thought they were of heaven, but forgot they were also of the people.

Emperor Chieh[44] and Emperor Jow[45] were removed from the throne by people because of their corrupt personal lives. Their downfall was brought about by their losing the power of rational thinking because of the influence of one of their wives.[46] They disregarded the good advice of their ministers and friends, and followed the advice of one woman who was not familiar with the affairs of state. To be an effective head of state, a person must be able to accept and evaluate advice and information from many sources. By refusing to do this and by focusing on the counsel of only one woman, they slowly became corrupt. According to the ancient standard, an emperor represents heaven and must have the heavenly quality of impartial and equal love, qualities which they lost by their narrow focus on one woman. It may be interesting for modern people to see that it was not because they had too many wives that they lost their power, but because they excessively loved only one woman.

Wine making was invented to celebrate the success of overcoming the tremendous flood under the leadership of the Great Yu. The Great Yu himself stopped drinking, setting a standard that it was unwise to drink more than three tiny cups at a social rite. However, these two young emperors, Chieh and Jow, later would

---

[44]1818 - 1766 B.C.

[45]1154-1121 B.C

[46]At that time in Chinese history, it was customary for a man to have several wives.

enjoy bathing in wine, eventually going so far as to make a pool containing wine. They ignored the good advice of their ministers and also neglected the ancient administrative rule of beginning the day at dawn. It was custom for all the ministers and administrators to gather at dawn in the big convention hall to wait for the emperor; who, in the case of Chieh and Jow, did not arrive until noon. Because the emperor is considered an example to the people, both Chieh and Jow went down in Chinese history as examples of evil emperors. Generally, the imperial seat was more stable than this; there was usually no competition for a job that most people did not enjoy. This was why in Chuang Tzu's written record, Yao looked many times for someone to replace him. Filling this position was not a playful competition like the elections of modern times; the selection came from public recognition of one's virtue and the prudent recommendation of the previous emperor.

Political ambition did not exist until the Period of Spring and Autumn[47] and the Period of Warring[48] at the end of the Chou Dynasty. During this time, the emperor was no longer a model of perfect morality, but in a powerful position of "I can do what I desire." Then all the kings began to compete for the position through warring with each other.

Mo Tzu believed that the poor example set by the feudal kings and lords was the heart of the spiritual and moral downfall of the people. He inexhaustibly dedicated himself to spiritual work to revive the faith of Heaven. With his extremely devoted example, he organized followers and promoted his political counsel of peace and non-aggression among the kingdoms. During both the Period of Spring and Autumn and the Warring Period, the minds of developed teachers were unified and responded in trying to correct the situation.

---

[47]This period began in 722 B.C.

[48]Beginning 403 B.C.

The most important teachings from China were developed during that critical time.

Among all those teachings, the most popularly accepted ones were the teachings of Confucius and Mo Tzu; both shared the same goal with regard to the Integral Way. They wanted to guide the people out of their troubles and promote a balanced way of life. That is to say that all three had the same goal, only it was accomplished with a different approach. Confucius' focus was the development of the moral nature in people; he favored an educational approach to reach that goal. Mo Tzu's focus was the extension of man's consciousness and conscience to meet heavenly consciousness and conscience; he favored the religious approach of enhancing a faith in Heaven. The Integral Way unites both and corrects their tendency to become one-sided and superficial, turning into empty shells and rigid formalities.

The Integral Way is to interpret Tao. The subtle path for all generations emerged through the efforts of Chuang Tzu, a great mind and universal talent who adopted the teaching of Lao Tzu for his main direction. He raised the banner of everlasting peace. He suggested that following Tao is a way to do away with both the competition between people and God, and the competition between people themselves. One can continually be supported by the natural world through the high consciousness of respect for nature, because human beings are a part of universal nature.

In the work of Chuang Tzu, in Chapter 25, the first chapter of Part II in this book, he communicates that freedom is the essence of natural life. He warned against establishing any shallow and narrow institution that would damage the organic nature of human life. In the second chapter, he did not aim to function as peacemaker between the different teachings of Confucius and Mo Tzu, but with his own deep vision unite their differences with his exceptional understanding and unshakably valuable advice.

In Chapter 27, he exclusively addressed Mo Tzu. He used the teachings of the Integral Way, the spiritual development from the long trusted faith of God, to admonish Mo Tzu's effort to revive the dualistic religious practice of worshipping God. He explained that the separation of God and Man was a conceptual mistake, just a tool for the convenience of the intellectual function. Because of the idea of separation from God, the people of later generations lived one-sidedly, in an incomplete life of spiritual undevelopment. The teachings of the Integral Spiritual Way, also called the Union of God and Man, are seen in the example above given by Wang Ni in the first section of this chapter. Mo Tzu himself, we can trust, presents a good example of the union.

Faith in God is a very old Chinese religious custom that has been continued in religious Taoism. Following the main teaching of Mo Tzu, many new leaders have refreshed this old belief in succeeding generations. However, in later times, they became confused by worldly religions. This is clearly shown in the existing temples of "worshipping" Taoism in Taiwan and other Chinese overseas communities. The Integral Way, also known as Tao, is the spiritual achievement of the ancient Chinese sages; the word Tao was later usurped and misused by new leaders in later times who had reshaped the old religions. After studying my books and hearing my lectures, some of my readers or friends became overly enthusiastic and made trips to China or Taiwan to visit the religious Taoist temples with the hope of learning more about Tao, the Way. But they knocked on the wrong door; they are totally different spiritual practices that use the same name.

An ordinary Chinese temple belonging to the Taoist religious sect is a place that projects internal states onto its many statues and altars. It is a place for people to worship, to look for oracles and obtain the services of channeling. Before 1967, the existent Tao Kuan in mainland China lowered its purpose, combining its function with that of a general temple in order to receive support from the local community.

For your knowledge, there are two kinds of Taoist temples. In an original Tao Kuan people do spiritual cultivation with a Master who teaches individual development. In a pure Tao Kuan (House of Observance of the Integral Way), a student or a number of students of Tao live and work on their development.

CHAPTER TWENTY-EIGHT

HARMONY WITH ALL LIVES
AND
AGREEMENT IN ALL ASPECTS OF LIFE

I

Your lifetime is limited, and petty intellectual knowledge is endless. To exhaust your limited life energy in the endless and overwhelming pursuit of petty intellectual information is pointless. If you understand this and still strive for petty intellectual knowledge, you will certainly be exhausted!

If you do well by society's standards, do not do so for the sake of fame. If you do something that does not meet external standards, avoid feeling disgrace. Locate a middle course and live according to what is constant. This is how to stay in one piece and live a long and happy life. In this way, your body and mind will be sound, you will fulfill your duties and live out your years.

II

The cook of the feudal lord Liang was cutting up an ox. Every shift of his hand, every move of his shoulders, every step of his foot, every thrust of his knife, every tear and cut in his work and every sound made by the blade was in perfect harmony: rhythmical, like the famous dance the Mulberry Grove; synchronous, like the chords of a beautiful melody of a great music.

"Excellent," cried Liang. "The skill you apply to your trade is extraordinary."

"Your majesty," replied the cook, "I have devoted myself to learning the Integral Truth of life. It is the root of all skills. Many years ago, when I first began to cut oxen, I saw them as whole animals before me. But after only a number of years of practice, I no

longer saw an animal as one piece; I saw it already
divided into sections.

"Now I work with my intuition rather than my
eyes; perception and understanding have come to an
end, and my spirit moves freely. I rely upon eternal
principles. I follow the natural constitution of an
animal, guiding my knife through the openings and
hollows, following along with the way things are. I
never cut into even the smallest tendon, much less a
joint.

"A good cook must change his knife once a year,
because he cuts with it. An ordinary cook must buy a
new one about once a month, because he chops with it.
It's been nineteen years that I have had this knife;
although I have cut up many thousand oxen with it, its
edge is as good as the day it left the grindstone. You
see, at the joints of the animal there are always small
spaces and since the edge of the knife is without thickness, I have only to insert that which is without thickness into a space. If you insert what has no thickness
into a space, then there's plenty of room for the blade
to move in. In this way I have kept my knife fresh for
nineteen years.

"But when I come upon a complicated place, I am
extremely cautious. I fix my gaze upon it, steady my
hand and gently apply the blade, moving it with great
subtlety until the part yields and falls to the ground.
Then I remove my knife, stand up and pause. Carefully I clean it and put it away."

"Magnificent," cried the prince. "From the words of
this cook I have learned the secret of how to care for
life by living with the Integral Way."

III

When an old master died, his friend Ching Ye, a
developed person, went to mourn his death.   He
voiced three wails at the funeral and then left.

A disciple of the old master asked him, "Were you
not a friend of our Master?"

"Yes, I was," replied Ching Ye.

"Do you consider what you did a suitable expression of grief at our losing him?" asked the disciple.

"I do," said Ching Ye. "I had believed that he was the greatest man among men, but now I know it is not true. When I went in to mourn, I found old persons weeping as though it were their child and young people crying as though it were their mother. To have cultivated the emotional attachment of a group like that, he must have done something in violation of the spirit of universal nature, indicating that he forgot the source of all life.

"Your master came because it was his time to be born and he left because it was his time to die. If one is content and can accept birth and death, then grief and joy have no stronghold. In the spiritual tradition of the old days, death was thought of as liberation from the bonds of physical law."

IV

An ambitious young student who wished to save his fellow people from political hardship and turmoil, went to his teacher so that he might render his service to humanity by attempting to influence those in political power. He asked his teacher's permission and guidance in his mission.

"What do you plan to do?" asked the teacher.

"I understand," answered the student, "that kings are selfish and interested only in power, and are thus engaged in power struggles most of the time. They are also cruel to their opponents; this shows that the welfare of the people is not their ultimate goal. They refuse to see their own faults, and as a result people are dying. Their corpses lie about like a meadow devastated by fire. The crisis is now at an extreme stage.

"I have heard you say, 'A person of high morality leaves an area that is well ordered and goes where there is chaos in order to be of service to others. Outside the doctor's gate are many sick men.' I want to use your guidance as my principle in the hope that I

can restore a normal, healthy, good life to the people
of this area."

"You will only create a dangerous situation for
yourself!" cried the teacher. "You wish to talk about
the 'yielding' principle to the power-hungry leaders?
Do not go there just to increase the trouble! No developed one would risk disturbing the spiritual unity of
Tao within himself. That is something that cannot be
handed out; if it were, it would lose its unity. In
losing one's inner unity, one becomes unbalanced. This
causes a disturbance, from which there is no escape
when it reaches its extreme.

"The developed people of ancient times first attained spiritual integrity for themselves and then
helped others attain it. When you're not sure that
you're confirmed and strengthened in Tao, how can
you attend to the lives of those who are not? Also, do
you know why perfect, natural action becomes twisted
and how knowledge is demonstrated? Perfect, natural
action is twisted by the lust for adventure and fame,
and knowledge is demonstrated out of an interest in
dispute. Those who chase fame crush one another, and
those concerned with knowledge become instruments of
contention and dispute. Fame and knowledge are
instruments of disaster and neither is conducive to
virtuous behavior. More importantly, the high quality
of a man's sincerity may be well-established, but he
may not yet understand human nature and spirit; he
may not be striving for renown, but he may not yet
understand the way the human mind and temperament
works. So, if he insists on speaking of benevolence,
uprightness and moral standards in the presence of
one of those tyrants, in whatever disguise of beautiful
slogans or political 'isms,' this only amplifies the other
man's inferiority in contrast to his own excellence. He
would be called an agitator or a reactionary; thus, he
will bring disaster upon himself.

"Let us suppose that this leader is actually a man
who appreciates worthy people. What use would he
have for you to change things in his world? Before
you even said a single word, he would certainly take

the opportunity to win a victory for himself. Your eyes will become glossed over, your expression will become drained, your words will stick in your throat, and your attitude will become more and more meek until, in your mind, you end up supporting the one you originally opposed. This is what is called 'adding fire to fire' or 'adding water to water,' which is also known as 'augmenting the excessive.' Once you begin making concessions, they will endlessly continue. You will be diminished in power, and the tyrant will not believe the integrity and sincerity of your words in the least.

"In history, there was a tyrant who killed a man of very faithful words. Another murdered a virtuous man who had approached him straightforwardly, in the same manner he would have used to face himself. The victims were both men who cultivated virtue, but by being solicitous of the welfare of other people, they came into conflict with their superiors. Their solicitous actions drew them into the limelight instead of concealing their good intentions and deeds. Their superiors had to get rid of them in order to save face and guard their reputations.

"In another historical situation, one leader attacked the highland countries while another attacked the lowland countries. Homes were desolated and families destroyed, yet the attackers fought on, never checking their ambition for victory and gain. These men were seekers of fame and fortune. Have you not heard of them? If even the most brilliant of men fail in their efforts to resist the lure of adventure, fame and fortune, do you think you are likely to succeed? You must have some plan in mind for what you want to do, though, so go ahead and tell me what it is."

"My plan is to remain humble and respectful, and keep my focus of concentration while working hard. By this I would win the trust of one of the kings," replied the student.

"It will not work," said the teacher. "So you think you can gauge this man's feelings and influence his mind! If you are seen as demonstrating your quality of perfection and become thus visible, his response will be uncertain. Even though this leader seems impressive on the outside, he has uneven and unpredictable reactions. Ordinarily, his actions are unopposed; he manipulates others to satisfy his own mind. With him, even an approach that is gradual and subtle, advancing a little each day, will not succeed, much less a great display of strength. He would not change by either approach. Although outwardly he might make a show of compliance with your beliefs, inwardly he would stay the same."

"In that case," replied the student, "while maintaining myself inwardly righteous and correct, externally I will adapt to the situation as a companion of man. Thus being fully formed internally, I would do my work by using the examples of the sages of antiquity.

"I learned that he who is inwardly righteous is a companion of Heaven, and he who is a companion of Heaven loves all people, because all people are equally children of Heaven. However, I will adapt myself to the situation and be a 'companion of man.' Such a person shakes hands, smiles, and exchanges pleasantries; such are the rituals followed by people. Everybody does it; I will pretend to be one of them, because ordinary people do not criticize those who conform.

"I would do my work through the examples of the ancient sages. I will speak in lessons and scoldings, but since they are words belonging to the ancient ones, even if I am direct, I will not be blamed. Can I proceed in this way?

"No," replied the teacher. "Your plans lack prudence. You have not seen what is needed. You can probably get by without incurring any blame or harm to yourself, but that is all. You will not influence him to the point at which he will cease to function according to his own self-interest and ambition."

"Then," said the student, "I have no further direction and ask your guidance. What is the proper way?"

The teacher said, "In order to be trouble-free or to live a personally trouble-free life, one must learn to fast with the purpose of controlling one's hasty and

impulsive tendencies. This is an important discipline
for all spiritual students."

"My family is poor," replied the student. "For many
months we have not eaten any meat nor consumed any
wine. Isn't that fasting?"

"This is the customary fasting of external religious
observances," answered the teacher, "but it is not the
fasting of the mind and spirit."

"May I ask," said the student, "what is the fasting
of the mind and spirit?"

"I will tell you what it means," replied the teacher.
"Do you think it is easy to do anything while you have
a mind full of ideas? If so, you deny the Subtle Law.
Spiritual fasting enables a person to become aware of
the universal subtle law and behave correctly.

"Cultivate unity in your everyday life and for your
special purpose. Make your will have only one purpose. Make your mind as though it were an indi-
visible whole. The practical application of this is to let
hearing stop with your ears and the workings of the
mind stop with itself; don't listen with your mind,
listen with the energy of your pure spirit, the vital
fluid which informs the whole self. The ear is limited
to ordinary hearing, the mind to rational hearing, but
spirit is empty and awaits things unconditionally. The
spirit offers an empty existence, passively responsive to
externals. In such emptiness, only Tao, the subtle
truth, can abide. And that emptiness is the fasting of
the mind."

"Then, what blocked the understanding of this
method," said the student, "was a sense of my individuality. If I had achieved the use of this method, a
sense of myself as an individual would have disappeared. Is this what you mean by emptiness?"

"That's it," replied the Master. "If you can go into
this man's surroundings without offending his own
self-love and be accepted, you would automatically say
the right thing. Be cheerful if he hears you, passive if
he does not listen to your words. Living simply, in
this way, in a state of complete indifference, you will

220 ATTAINING UNLIMITED LIFE

be near success. Where there is no opening, there is
no poisoning.

"It is simple not to walk; what is difficult is to walk
without leaving a trace. It is easy to be false when
you work for men, but hard to be false when you
work for Heaven. You have heard of flying with
wings, but have not heard about the kind of flying that
is done without wings. You have heard of men being
wise with knowledge, but not of the knowledge that
does not know.

"When you look upon things unconditionally, your
uncommitted mind will produce understanding, and
good fortune will manifest. If you do not wait patient-
ly and keep still, you would be doing what is called,
'sitting still and rushing around at the same time.' The
body sits but the mind continues to race. Let the
channels of your senses be to your mind what a win-
dow is to an empty room. Where there is penetration
to the interior through the ears and eyes and exter-
nalization through the mind and knowledge, the high
spiritual essence of universal nature will not come to
dwell. Where the supernatural finds shelter, man will
find shelter too. This is the way to regenerate one's
spiritual vitality.

"It was that practice which the virtuous leaders Yao
and Shun used. It was the secret of the success of Fu
Hsi and Chi Chu, two great spiritually attained ones in
the early stages of human life. It would be beneficial
if it were now adopted by mankind in general, who
stand in such great need of regeneration and spiritual
development."[49]

In this section, three attitudes were discussed. The
first was of the student of Confucius and the second
was of the student of Mo Tzu. The third was Chuang
Tzu's suggestion to them. We have already reviewed

---

[49]Yao reigned from 2357 to 2258 B.C., Shun reigned from 2257
to 2208 B.C. and Shen Nung reigned around 3218 B.C.

the social background of the teachings. There were a few important key teachers that we will date for your better understanding.

1. Lao Tzu, whom it is estimated was active around 571 B.C. His life was very long. He still appeared in the court of China with a wish to stop the king's ambition around 250 B.C. His advice to human society is to follow the universal moral law and forsake all conceptual creations that have caused people to fight one another.

2. Confucius, who lived from 551-479 B.C. He promoted the reestablishment of social order according to the conventional humanistic principle.

3. Mo Tzu, who lived from 501-416 B.C. Mo Tzu teaches the obedience of Heavenly will. Here in the second plan discussed by the student, the Mohist approach of "the fellowship of Heaven," "the fellowship of man" and "learning from the example of the sages" was evaluated.

4. Mencius, who lived from 372-289 B.C. He continued Confucius' social goal by traveling among the different kingdoms, teaching the humanistic doctrine of Yao and Shun. He was active at the same time as Chuang Tzu. Though it was a great humanistic approach, Chuang Tzu foresaw the failure in his work. Chuang Tzu did not negatively comment on him but instead expressed the common direction of spiritual development of all people.

5. Chuang Tzu, who died around 275 B.C. In this section Chuang Tzu, among the differences of the influential schools, pointed out the practice of spiritual fasting to those who love people and wish to give their help to the world. His clear vision sees that without the practice of spiritual fasting, whether with a humanistic approach or a religious approach, the world will not improve its lack of good quality. Heavenly Will also cannot really be known; as a matter of fact, it is

too easily replaced by man's will. In the case of the latter, the world will go nowhere, but continue to suffer from the old traps. It is truly valuable for spiritual teachers and students to practice spiritual fasting in order to prevent misguiding oneself and others.

CHAPTER TWENTY-NINE

A MAN AMONG MEN

I

Tzu Kao, Duke of Sheh, a student of wisdom, was about to go on a mission to the Ch'i State. He told his teacher, one of the spiritually developed ones, "My sovereign is sending me to accomplish a most important task. I shall be received with great respect in Ch'i, but the people there will not take the same interest and responsibility as I and will be in no rush to do anything about the matter. One cannot force even an ordinary person to act, much less a king, therefore I am edgy and alarmed.

"You have told me that in all matters, either large or small, there are few men who are able to reach a mutually beneficial outcome, and only those who remain on the path of integral mindedness succeed. There are few situations in which one is not glad to see the matter completed. When it is still unfinished and incomplete, there is sure to be anxiety about something unforeseen arising. If you do not succeed in the matter, you are bound to endure the judgments of others. If you do succeed, there is your own excitement and worry of success to contend with. Only the person of a highly developed nature, a virtuous person, can be free of anxiety and attract no harm under these conditions.

"I am a person who eats simple, plain and healthy foods. I never use cooling drinks because I have an even temperament and also wish to preserve my health. However, this morning I received my orders, and this evening I find myself drinking ice water. I am hot with anxiety, excitement and worry. I am already concerned about the judgments of others. So it seems that harm is already befalling me from internal causes. Have you some advice to give me?"

"There exist two sources of protection in the world," the one of natural wisdom replied. "One is fate; the other is one's duty. A child's connection with its parents is its destiny and its love for them cannot be severed from his heart. A person's obligation to his work is duty. There is no way under Heaven to escape these two. The way one's destiny and duty can become a source of protection and safety is this: to take care of one's old parents, whatever one's situation happens to be, and to serve one's boss without preference to the task, focusing on accomplishing the service. In either case, you do what needs to be done; this is called filial piety and loyalty. And in accomplishing your destiny and fulfilling your duty, serve your own heart so that neither joy nor sorrow, like nor dislike grow within you to trouble you, but cultivate the ability to accept the inevitable - this is virtue. Virtue should be understood in this sense as the exemplification of Tao.

"Now a person often finds himself in a situation over which he has no control, needing to do things he would rather avoid. But if one simply focuses on his work, forgetting about himself, his mind may be kept in control; love for life and hate for death will not trouble him. This is where a person may find safety.

"Also, keep these things in mind. All your communications, if personal, should be made with sincerity. If you must communicate with someone from a distance, you must invite loyalty by your words. Sometimes, messages will have to be transmitted by someone. One of the most difficult things to do is to transmit messages, being the go-between for two people who are either happy or angry. Whether the matter is happy or harsh, the message is usually overdone; in it there will usually be an excess of compliments about the good points or insults about the bad points. Excess brings about disorder, and when disorder occurs, confidence is lost; disaster for the intermediary is the result.

"Thus, let your message be simple statements of fact, without extra expressions of feeling. Do not transmit exaggeration, and your risk will be decreased.

"When people get together to play games of skill or contests of strength, they begin friendly and carefree, but usually end up either angry or frustrated. If they go on too long they start resorting to trickery so that they can beat each other. Similarly, on festive occasions, drinking is orderly in the beginning, but the good order degenerates as the evening passes and things get out of hand. All events have the same tendency: people begin with good intent and sincerity, but end up with antagonism or disillusion. From small, simple beginnings comes big tumult or turmoil.

"Words can bring either success or failure. Speech is like the wind that arouses waves and sets them in motion. Once in motion, divergence from the original goal is possible. Divergence can cause anger. Like the gasping cries of an animal facing death, a person will end up finding himself speaking dishonest words with an air of fury. Thus, we see that the anger springs forth from careless or crafty talk, or words less than honest. Similarly, if we are too particular in what we demand of another, we will see his straightforward anger or his unconscious response of careless behavior or resistance. With such occurrence, the end result may be disaster.

"This is why it is said in one of the ancient books, "Do not diverge from your instructions. Do not force any issue. To depart from an order can endanger the outcome of a situation. An inadequate or improper completion of a matter cannot be changed later. One cannot be careless. Let yourself move without fear by taking refuge in having no alternative. This will preserve you from harm from either side. Nothing is as reliable as following destiny, even if it seems difficult."

In this section, Chuang Tzu expressed his support for the worldly undertakings of students and friends. He cannot be mixed with the example of shunning personal and social responsibility.

II

Yen Ho, a virtuous man from the Lu State, accepted a position as tutor to the eldest son of Duke Ling of the Wei State. Before he began, he said to Chu Poh Yu, one of the spiritually developed people and the Prime Minister of the Wei State:

"This young man lacks virtue. If I cannot find a way to prevent him from acting in an unprincipled way, the state will be in danger. However, if I restrain or antagonize him in any way, my personal safety will be in danger. He can see other people's faults, but has not enough intelligence to see his own. I do not know what to do; have you any suggestion?"

"This is a good question," replied Chu Poh Yu, the developed one. "You must be very careful. The place to begin is with yourself. Outwardly, adapt yourself to the situation, but inwardly, hold to your own principles. However, be certain to guard against letting the outward adaption penetrate within, and the inner standard becoming visible outwardly. In the first case, you will fall, be overthrown and destroyed. In the latter case, you will clash with him; you will be discussed, fault will be determined and you will be condemned. Your reputation will suffer. Therefore, if he acts like a child, you act like one too. If he is reckless, do the same. What he does, you do also. In this way, you will be able to lead him to where his faults will be corrected.

"Have you heard the story of the praying mantis, who angrily stretched out its arms to prevent an approaching carriage from coming? It had such a high opinion of its ability that it became blind to the limitations of its strength. Be very cautious. If you offend others by showing superiority, you will probably come to harm.

"Those who keep tigers do not dare give them live animals as food, because killing arouses their anger. Neither do they feed them whole animals, because tearing them apart stimulates the tiger's fury. This is why the periods of hunger and fullness are also carefully watched. The tiger is of a different species than man; but man must also be carefully and appropriately handled, because when aroused to anger by being opposed, he is equally unmanageable.

"Those who love horses sometimes pamper them too much. Often, mosquitoes or flies trouble the animals. Sometimes, in trying to kill a mosquito, a groom will unexpectedly slap the horse, resulting in the startled horse breaking his bridle, bumping his head and bruising his chest. Moderation can bring success; overdoing can bring disaster."

III

A skillful carpenter was traveling to the state of Ch'i. On reaching Ch'un-yuan, he saw a serrate oak next to the village shrine. It was considered a sacred tree by the local people because of its great age and giant shape. Several thousand oxen could have rested in its shade. It measured hundreds of yards around and was taller than the hills. From each of its dozen lowest branches a boat could have been made. A crowd of people were around it, but the carpenter paid no attention, continuing on his way without stopping.

His apprentice looked at it for a long time and then ran after carpenter Shih, saying, "Since I came to serve you, Master, I have never seen a tree so beautiful. But you did not even look at that tree. Why did you ignore it?"

"It's not even worth talking about," replied his master. "That tree is good for nothing. Make a boat of it, and it would sink. A coffin and it would quickly rot. Furniture and it would soon break down. A door and it would sweat. A pillar and it would be worm eaten. It is a wood of no quality, and it is of no use. That is how it got to be so old."

When the carpenter returned home, the sacred oak appeared to him in a dream, saying, "What trees are you comparing with me? Other useful trees? In the case of pear, orange and apple trees, as soon as the fruit is ripe, the tree suffers loss and destruction. Big branches are split and small ones broken off, bringing great misery to the tree. Such trees do not last the length of their natural life, but are caused to perish prematurely. All this from their usefulness and their entanglement with the world around them.

"The pain and trouble they suffered was because they were useful to people's idea. Therefore, they could not maintain the natural span of life. All unnatural suffering is invited by people of worldly thought. As if that were not enough, they extend their worldly thought over other natural lives to cause them unnatural suffering, in the same way as they have. And so it is with all things."

The tree continued, "For a long time my goal was to become useless by people's standards. Many times I was in danger of perishing by being cut by human hands, but finally I succeeded in achieving my pursuit. My uselessness to people turns out to be my own great usefulness. But if I had been useful earlier by people's hands, I would not have grown so huge.

"You and I are both objects of natural creation, but how can you, one object of the creator, judge another as being useless? Life is nature. In nature, all things have their usefulness in some way, although some things may not be useful to you, in your human form. Nature accepts all. Thus, one should be like nature. No one should deny the nature of others. "Useful or useless is not decided by people. People are so narrow and lack depth, setting the standard and judgement for another natural being, even among themselves. What you have said about me, is it not against the truth of nature?"

IV

When a teacher of great devotion and worldwide spiritual reformation was arriving in the Ch'u State, the rather eccentric Chieh Yu, thought by some to be a madman, passed by his door, singing, "Oh phoenix, O noble bird, how can it be that your virtue has fallen? To the future you cannot hasten, to the past you cannot return.

"When the world is on its natural course, good people succeed. When the world is without the normal natural cause, the good must look for survival. In times like the present we do well to escape trouble. Good fortune is light as a feather, but nobody knows how to maintain it. Misfortune is heavy as the mountain, but nobody knows how to avoid it. Desist teaching men virtue! It is dangerous to mark the ground and then run off. Don't spoil my own walking, I walk a curved road, so watch you don't step on my feet.

"The mountain trees bring harm upon themselves by growing straight and tall; the oil in the lamp causes itself to be consumed because of its flammability. Cinnamon can be eaten, so the tree that produces it gets cut down; the tree which produces lacquer can be used and so gets chopped apart. All people know the use of being somebody, but nobody understands the usefulness of being nobody."

The teacher said to his students after he had left, "I know he is right about the world. I know the result of my effort to change the world into a better place may not be seen. I admit it is foolish to undertake a task that cannot be accomplished by one person only. Yet I still do it, but not for my own cause. I do it for the cause of all people. I have learned from the great Lao Tzu that moral teaching must be done without the establishment of one's self in the teaching. Great things can only be accomplished when one does not dominate.

"Nature has offered me the magnificence of my life. I feel my life will have some significance if I can offer it to the lost children of nature. My teaching comes from nature; I use nature to teach. I do not try to establish my own ideas to impose on the nature of people. They have long been twisted, in a state of deviation from their natural form. My goal does not include any external establishment; my way is not in imposing institutions. The Integral Truth is self-evident, even before discussion.

"As an individual person, I don't assume my life as being either useful or useless, great or small, somebody or nobody. I live my life in the Creative, as Heaven; it has endowed its nature in me. I do not feel I have exhausted the use of life. When I live in the path of universal subtle integration, it does not matter what my life situation is. If I am allowed to live the entire sum of lifetimes of a natural span, I continue to extend the universal virtue in me to all people. I am not discouraged by the fact that the world is how it is. I am going to continue to fulfill the natural moral harmony in me to share with my fellow people of the world."

A student rose and bowed to him and said, "We will all remember this as our guidance for life and the spirit of our work in the world. We will not shrink back from the difficulty of being righteous. We will not interrupt our moral effort in our personal and social behavior. We will not sneer at people's foolishness. We will be on guard against our own foolishness so that we may not be harmed by evil pressure from any source, internal or external. We will not be negative, only thinking or conscious of troubles. We like to be positive; in any moment of difficulty, we are still able to see the light. We will be responsible in our life. We will be faithful in our learning. We will fulfill our naturally-endowed virtue and extend it in all aspects of our life. We identify our life with the Integral Way as in your example. We are nothing but beings of the integral nature of the universe. We continue the universal great life through our small lives. We do not look to make a single establishment, we follow only the path of universal subtle integration and harmonization."

CHAPTER THIRTY

INNER VIRTUE, NOT OUTER FORM, DISTINGUISHES PEOPLE

I

In the state of Lu, there was a man named Wang T'ai who suffered political persecution and was severely punished by having his toes cut off. His students numbered as many as those of the most popular teacher of the time.

Ch'ang Chi, a student of the popular one, said to his teacher, "Wang T'ai has been physically damaged, yet like yourself, he teaches half the state of Lu. I have heard that although he neither gives sermons nor discusses, those who go to him feeling empty always leave feeling full. They say that he teaches the doctrine which words cannot describe, that he has fullness of mind even though his body is not normal. Simply, he is a higher model than a teacher. He has no self-pity or other psychological problem. He is positive in his life. What kind of person is he?"

"He is one of natural virtue," replied the teacher. "I should have sought his instruction a long time ago. I will go now to seek his wisdom. If I approach him as my teacher, many others will follow who are not even my equal. Not only will half the state of Lu come along, but the entire world; so we'll all become students of his teachings."

"The man has been disfigured," replied Ch'ang Chi, "and yet people consider him to be a Master. Is he different from ordinary men? Is it that he uses his mind in a different way than others?"

"Although life and death are powerful, they cause no change in him," answered their teacher. "If Heaven and Earth were to end, it would be no loss to him. He has found how to become free from imperfections, so that he does not change with the rest of creation.

He sees clearly into the place where there is no false-hood so he does not shift with external things; he remains with the source."

"I do not know what you mean," said the inquisi-tive student.

"If you look at the forms of life from the point of view of differences," replied the teacher, "it is like comparing a liver to a gall bladder or measuring the distance between the state of Ch'u in the North and the state of Yueh in the South.

"From the point of view of their sameness, however, all things are one. This is the position of Wang T'ai, which is what he learned from his teacher. Thus he is no longer troubled by what he perceives in his eye or ear; his heart and mind delight in perfect harmony. He directs his mind toward virtue and beholds all things as if they were one, without observing their differences or inconsistencies, looking only at their unity and not noticing what might be lacking. He regards the loss of his toes simply as a bit of mud thrown back to earth."

"Then he devotes himself to virtue, and uses his virtue to perfect his mind," said Ch'ang Chi. "In other words, by applying what he has learned he has gained complete command over his own heart and mind, and by this means he has achieved constancy of heart. Yet his virtue seems to be completely personal. I do not understand why people think so much of him."

The teacher replied, "People cannot see themselves in running water, but they use still water as a mirror and thus observe themselves. Only that which is still in itself can awaken stillness in others. Of all things which receive their life from Earth, only pines and cypresses are examples of constancy, for they are green in all seasons. Of those who receive their life from Heaven, only Shun is the model of propriety. By being able to keep his own life correct and orderly, he helped bring order to all lives.[50]

"Fearlessness is often proof that one has taken refuge in the origin and source of all things. If a warrior battling boldly against armies and disciplining himself for the purpose of attracting fame is considered fearless, then what about the man whose influence extends over heaven and earth and all things? For him, it is as though his lodging is his body with its narrow channels of the senses; he brings himself to know that all things are one. That man should be considered even more fearless. On any day he chooses, he can depart from the earthly realm. Other men naturally flock to him on their own; he makes no effort to attract them. People gathering around him so are but an indication of the quality of his inner virtue."

II

Shen T'u Chia had his foot cut off and was badly disfigured by tortures suffered from a political ruler. He was a fellow student, with Tzu Ch'an of the state of Cheng, of the teacher Po Hun Wu Jen.

Tzu Ch'an said to Shen T'u Chia, "When I leave first, you stay here a while. When you leave first, then I will stay behind." Tzu Ch'an, as a high political leader, did not want to be seen with Shen T'u Chia.

The next day, when they were together again in the lecture hall, Tzu Ch'an said, "When I leave first, you stay a while. When you leave first, then I will stay. I am about to go now; are you going to wait or not? You have not been showing any respect to the Prime Minister. It seems you believe you are my equal."

"Oh my," replied Shen T'u Chia, "I did not know that there was a state official in our class. Perhaps you think that because you are a government official you

---

[50]Shun was a virtuous civilian. By his service and help to his neighbors, he became naturally, if unofficially, recognized as a teacher and leader in his community. People flocked to him even before he was chosen by Emperor Yao to be the successor of his virtuous, responsible leadership.

must be put before others. I have been taught that a mirror is bright when there is no dust and dirt on it; if any dust settles on it, it loses its brightness. I have also been taught that one who associates for a long time with those who are wise will come to be without fault. You have been improving yourself here in the presence of our Master, yet you say such a thing. This is not right, is it?"

"It is interesting that one like you talks this way," retorted Tzu Ch'an. "Next you will be trying to act like the virtuous emperor Yao. One would think that you have enough to do to take care of your own faults," he said, sneering at his disfigurement.

"There are many who mask their shortcomings so that they cannot be seen by others," replied Shen Tu Chia. "But there are few who admit that they have faults. To embrace what cannot be changed or improved, plainly and quietly accepting one's destiny, whether it be great or humble, is the great achievement of a virtuous person. It takes one of true excellence to achieve this. If a person is standing in front of the bull's eye when the talented archer, Yi, is shooting, he will be hit; it is a matter of fate if he lives. There are many men who make fun of me because of my disfigurement. This used to cause me to become furious, but since I have studied with our Master, their words no longer bother me. Possibly our Master has purified my character. Regardless of that, however, in the nineteen years I have studied with him, he has never made me aware that I am missing a foot.

"You and I are here to study what is internal to man. Why then, are we wasting time talking about what is external? Perhaps the reason our Master keeps me in the same class with you is to show me the minor problem in a great man like you."

At this Tzu Ch'an became uneasy. Changing the expression on his face, he requested, "Please, say nothing more about me being great." Tzu Ch'an felt ashamed but accepted the valuable instruction of the other man.[51]

III

There was a man in the state of Lu named Shu-shan who's foot had been cut off.   Limping along, he went to see a proud young teacher.

"Because of your carelessness," said the teacher, "you have caused misfortune to come to yourself. How do you think you will benefit from coming to me now?"

Shu-shan replied, "I did not understand about working hard, so I was careless in my behavior which resulted in my losing a foot.   I have come to you today because I still have something worth much more than a foot that I want to preserve.   There is no man or thing that Heaven does not cover; there is no man or thing unsupported by earth.   I expected that a master would have the qualities of both Heaven and Earth. I did not expect to hear those words from you."

"Please accept my apology," said the teacher. "Won't you come in?   We can discuss the important teachings."

But Shu-shan left.

The young teacher told his students, "Be diligent, my disciples!   Here is Shu-shan, a man who has had his foot cut off but who is still looking for wisdom so that he can make up for his former conduct.   Those who are intact should make even a greater effort to learn."

Shu-shan then went to see an old achieved one and related to him what had happened. "The young teacher has certainly not yet achieved the stage of integral

---

[51]Tzu Ch'an was later became a political leader and model minister in the sixth century B.C.   Under his influence, the state was so safe and the population so virtuous that articles lost on the roadside were not picked up or taken by others, and people could even leave their doors unlocked at night.

nature and virtue, has he? He impresses me as only seeking fame and reputation, being ignorant of the trouble they cause a person."

The old achieved one answered, "He needs to learn that life and death, acceptable and unacceptable are one and the same. It would be well if you could free him from that illusion."

Shu-shan said, "When Heaven so chooses to punish him, how is one to set him free?" He was making fun of the young teacher. Shu-shan had only been mistreated by man, not by heaven.

IV

Duke Ai of the state of Lu said to a wise teacher, "In the state of Wei lives an ugly man named T'ai T'o. The men who live with him like him and make no effort to have him move away. Many of the women who are acquainted with him have told their parents that they would rather be his concubine than any other man's wife, no matter how rich or handsome the other man might be.

"T'ai T'o never preaches or tries to teach anyone, but he empathizes with them. He is neither powerful and able to protect people, nor is he wealthy and able to feed them. He is not well traveled or well educated, but all people like being around him. He does not take the initiative in anything but is simply very agreeable.

"Wondering if he was different from ordinary men, I sent for him to come so I could get to know him. He was certainly very ugly. Only a short while had passed, though, before I understood the kind of person he is. Before the year was over, I came to trust him greatly and offered him the position of Prime Minister when it became vacant. He accepted, but with an air of sadness; he was quite hesitant about it, and it seemed almost a refusal. When he answered me, his speech was vague and evasive, and he acted rather uncomfortable about the matter. Despite my presentiment, I turned over the office to him. However, in a very short time, he left without a word and never returned.   Since he left I feel crushed, like there is no one there with whom to enjoy living and working in the state.   What sort of man was he?"

The wise teacher replied, "When I was sent to the state of Ch'u to accomplish some matters, I saw some piglets trying to nurse from the body of their dead mother.   After a short while, they stopped to look at her and then, all of them ran away, because they found her different than themselves.   She was not the same as she had been before.   In loving their mother, they didn't love her body, but that which made her what she was: the spirit that moved the body.

"When a man has been killed on the battlefield and people come to bury him, he has no longer any use for his weapons and shield.   When a man has had his feet amputated, shoes are no longer of value to him.   In these cases, the function of the things is gone.

"It is the ancient custom when women are selected to enter the royal harem for their nails to remain unpainted and their ears unpierced in order to maintain their originalness.   Also, when a man has just taken a wife, he is kept within the palace borders and no longer sent on dangerous missions.   If it is so important, and so much care is taken to keep one's body completely whole, then much more care should be taken to keep one's virtue whole!

"T'ai T'o is a man who says nothing and gains people's trust.   He has no accomplishments yet is loved by others.   Sovereigns would like to delegate their states to him and are only afraid he will not accept.   It must be the power of his wholeness, although there is no form to his virtue."

"What do you mean by the power of wholeness?" asked the Duke.

"Life and death," replied the teacher, "up and down, triumph and disaster, poverty and wealth, virtue and vice, good and evil, hunger and thirst, heat and cold; all these are the changes taking place in the world, the work of fate.   They follow each other in our presence day and night; no knowledge can determine their origin.   These temporal things should not be allowed to disturb one's equanimity or gain entrance to one's spiritual center, the mind. If one can learn to harmonize with them and enjoy them, master them and never be without joy; if one can do this without cease and make his life spring forth with gladness, blending with all and creating the moment - this is what I call the power of wholeness."

"What did you mean when you said his virtue has no form to it?" asked the Duke.

The teacher replied, "Water that is still can serve as a model of virtue without form. The water remains quiet and does not overflow. Similarly, virtue is the creation of perfect harmony. It does not extend itself. Where it takes no outward form, man likes to remain."

Some days afterwards, Duke Ai told Min Tzu, one of the wise teacher's students, "When I first took the throne, I used to face south and play lord of the world, governing people and being concerned about their lives and deaths. I believed that I understood everything about life perfectly. Now, though, after having heard the words of man in his highest and most perfected form, I fear that I lack these qualities in myself and I shall be negligent and lose my natural integrity unless I continue with his teaching. It results that I am not truly lord over your teacher; it is an excellent friendship that we have."

V

A hunchback named Wu Ch'un was an associate of Duke Ling of Wei. Duke Ling became so pleased with him and accustomed to him that when he looked at normal men, their bodies seemed malformed. Another man, this one with a goiter as large as a cantaloupe was acquainted with Duke Huan of Ch'i. Duke Huan became so fond of him that when he looked at well-formed men he thought their necks were too thin.

Wherever excellence or virtue abides, appearance and form are forgotten. Generally, however, men do not forget what should be forgotten and they forget what should not be forgotten. To forget one's virtue and the virtue of others is a true loss. When people do not forget what they normally forget, they have a godly memory. It means that if one can forget his riches, nobility and importance of position, and can be with anyone or in any environment without distinction, his virtue is certainly complete.

VI

Chuang Tzu thus concludes, "Technical knowledge without the wholeness of virtue creates many problems. Agreements without virtue are merely ink on paper. Favor without virtue is bait. Friendliness without virtue is only a skill for better bargaining. Developed people do not scheme; they have no use for cunning. Living with nature, what need do they have for agreements in ink? Complete in themselves, why would they listen to artificial standards? They do not engage in the pursuit of extra profit; what need have they for bargaining? In other words, an achieved one contains his own true enjoyment. For him, bad knowledge is the source of trouble, promises are bait, favors are patches and social skill a trap.

"An achieved one's survival is supported by Heaven. He sees things as the work of nature and accepts what nature offers to him. He who is thus nourished has little need for human artificiality. He wears the form of man but is without human passions. Wearing the form of man, he associates with people, but being without human passions, questions of right and wrong do not affect him. Small in form, he stays with men. Great in stature, alone he perfects his spirit."

Upon hearing Chuang Tzu say this, Hui Tzu said to him, "Are there really men who have no passions or emotions?"

Chuang Tzu replied, "Surely there are."

"But," argued Hui Tzu, " if a man has no passions or emotions, how can he be considered a man?"

"He is given his expression by the subtle realm," replied Chuang Tzu, "and nature gives him a body. How would he not be called a man?"

"But if he is a man," repeated Hui Tzu, "how can he have no passion?"

"What you mean by passion or emotion," answered Chuang Tzu, "is not the same as what I mean. By a man without passions I mean one who does not allow his own likes and dislikes to disturb his internal balance, but adapts to whatever happens, letting things be the way they are. He accepts the universal spontaneity without needing to add anything extra to his nature."

"But," asked Hui Tzu, "if he doesn't do anything, then how can he keep himself alive?"

"The subtle realm gives him expression," replied Chuang Tzu, "and nature gives him form. He does not permit things to disturb his internal balance. But right now, you are using your intelligence to pursue external things and thus wearing out your mental powers. 'Nature gave you the vision to see the whole, but you only talk about hard and white, the division between the appearance and the quality of a thing.'"[52]

However, in Chuang Tzu's guidance on how to nurture one's spiritual essence, he had already pointed out that one should not waste one's spiritual energy pursuing enormous quantities of irrelevant knowledge nor involve oneself with enormous insignificant activities, neglecting one's self-cultivation and spiritual growth. He then discussed the middle path of life by which one can support and preserve oneself, enjoy a natural length of life and sustain those to whom one is related. This path is not reached by attracting fame through the force of egotistically or negatively driven desire, nor by constantly dodging laws, no matter how senseless or artificial they may be. Spiritually, of course, no one else has any authority over your life, but in matters of everyday necessity, you must respect the natural right of other lives. Above all, when you wish to maintain authority over your own life, in worldly life, you must not go against any artificial

---

[52]He is talking about an important philosophical thought of Hui Tzu. This is friendly teasing between the two of them.

human law that could harm you. Your self-dignity requires that you not be in conflict with artificial laws in order to maintain your spiritual freedom. You must not resort to using the power of artificial human laws, nor, if you should ever be threatened by the worldly circumstances of such laws, should you ever use those laws to your personal advantage.

Those who, through blind circumstance of internal drive or by accident of uncontrollable external situations, have damaged their bodies should not give up on themselves spiritually. Spiritual completeness is more important than physical form. Whatever your physical situation is, one should cultivate to attain one's spiritual completeness. For example, Helen Keller was blind, deaf and dumb, incomplete in form. But she was complete in spirit, while many others with beautiful figures, who have a perfect form, are spiritually blind, deaf, dumb or crippled. The incompleteness of their spiritual energy usually makes such a person a nuisance to all. All of us who suffer from spiritual incompleteness should make Miss Helen Keller our model; she achieved herself as a goddess although she was in a troubled form. She is a truly Holy Lady.

For all my readers and friends, including those with beautiful or complete forms and with a generally sound mind but who pull themselves down to taste the endless bitterness of psychological problems of the fear of life or disappointment in oneself, please look up to the example of Helen Keller. Whenever you are in difficulty, feeling desperate, take her example as inspiration and learn to keep going as she did. In truth, she is greater than any of the figures of worship in a conventional church. Because of her life and spirit, she can be regarded as holy as any held in esteem by conventional churches. Her accomplishment was great because she is an example of a whole life and not just of one single event visited upon someone, like giving birth to a famous son. This is human affection; it is not spiritual achievement that can be made an example for human spiritual life. A single event in the life of a person does not demonstrate high spiritual achievement and therefore does not serve as a good example, although religious statues are made of such people. My concern is that the statues and the religious faith they engender mislead people and does not bring them to understand how to improve themselves and spiritually. People should learn to develop the divine quality in themselves. Many people, in general life, render selfless service to mankind in a broad range of behavior and can be considered good examples. It was their divine qualities that earned them long respect. I trust the helpers in my work all have this divine quality. Their truthful spiritual goal is usually ignored in the life of most people.

In this chapter, Chuang Tzu protests the custom prevalent in his time of punishing people by physically damaging them. He extends great sympathy to those who have suffered such damage and offers them his spiritual encouragement.

Every individual must go through self-cultivation in order to attain spiritual sovereignty over their own lives. Even if you have been physically damaged, by natural or other causes, your spirit is still intact and whole. Those who have not been damaged and whose lives are in good condition have no excuse for failing to attain spiritual development.

CHAPTER THIRTY-ONE

SPIRITUAL DEVELOPMENT

I

He who knows what his innate nature is has attained a high degree of understanding. Knowing his innate nature, he lives there. Knowing what man is, he uses his knowledge of the known to find out the unknown and lives the natural span of years allotted by nature without being cut short in mid-life. This is the result of the perfection of knowledge.

Intellectual knowledge, however, causes anxiety, because it must be confirmed before it is recognized as being correct. It is not certain that this confirmation will occur. Natural wisdom, on the other hand, grows from close attendance to the experience of life. It does not appear before or after the experience but is immediate, being intrinsic to the experience itself. Such natural wisdom is, in fact, spiritual energy. It is the best of all guidance and will appear to your vision at exactly the right instant. This wisdom comes directly from your spiritual source; it cannot be learned beforehand. How, then, can I know if my knowledge of what I know as Heaven is really human and what I call human is really Heaven?

The relationship between God and Man can be put in three ways: First, to leaders of the world, God is man's ambition. Second, man, in spiritual unity, is the existence of God; and third, to people of spiritual cultivation, God is the spiritual achievement of people. People are "gods before they develop spiritually." Gods are "people after they develop spiritually." In natural, spiritual reality, God is "man with spiritual completion," and man is "God with spiritual decrease."

Before there can be spiritual development, there must first be a man of truthful nature. What do I mean then by a man of truthful nature? The man of universal natural truth in ancient times did not resent poverty nor did he grow proud in plenty. He acted without calculation and made no rigid plans in order to insure a particular result. If a man of natural truth commits an error, he has no cause for regret; when he is right or meets with success, he is not self-satisfied. He can climb the highest peaks without fear, enter water without getting wet and walk through fire without being burned. With spiritual development he is able to integrate his being with Heaven.

In ancient times the man of natural truth slept without dreams, and he was free from worry in his waking hours. He ate without great interest in seasonings, and his breathing grew deeper and deeper. Such a pure, natural being breathes with his entire organism, not just superficially. Ordinary men breathe shallowly, in their throats; that is why, if they are arguing with someone and are defeated, the words catch in their throats. As their desires and ambition become strong, their organic wholesomeness becomes weakened.

The ancient men of natural truth neither loved life nor hated death; neither life nor death was a cause for celebration nor sorrow. They simply came and went. They never forgot where they came from, nor did they seek to quicken their return there. Quietly they played their allotted parts and lived each moment fully. If they received something, they took pleasure in it, yet could easily give it back again and forget about it. This is what I call the spiritual development of people: not, by one's desire, sacrificing natural morality, nor by believing in God, creating pressure in a man's life. This is what has earned my greatest respect.

A person of spiritual development has a mind that is open and free. His expression is calm and his forehead not wrinkled with worry. He is cool like autumn, yet warm like spring. His joys and angers occur like the four seasons, at the proper time. He fits so well with the rest of creation that he may not be noticed. He is in harmony with all things.

Therefore, if a naturally developed person is forced to call out troops, he may overthrow any evil government and he will not lose the support of the people. The benefits he provides eternity do not come from love of his race or shallow beliefs; he acts out of what is right, and people are naturally benefitted. A truly achieved person does not delight in success only. A benevolent person does not show favoritism. A truly great person does not calculate for opportunity, but maintains his good qualities all of the time. A gentleman knows how to accept loss. One of good quality does not only think of his reputation. A person who loses touch with his original nature and who's life is not harmonious with that nature is unable to master his own life being.

Hu Pu Hsieh, Wu Kuang, Po Yi, Shu Ch'i, Chi Tzu, Hsu Yu, Chi T'o and Shen T'u Ti, all ancient respected ones, were men who could make room for others and let them feel at ease, but who failed to live long and natural lives themselves.[53]

In ancient times, the man of natural truth maintained a proper attitude with regard to others, but did not fraternize with them. He appeared wanting, but accepted no favors. He seemed very independent, yet he was not stubborn. His stillness inspired calmness in his surroundings. He was open-minded, but did not follow fashion. His relaxation made him appear contented. His actions were natural responses.

His patience and tolerance made him seem a part of his environment, but he maintained his aloneness and self-potential. He enjoyed solitude. His outward

---

[53]These eight men were famous and respected in their time, but they became overly renowned for their wisdom. Six of them drowned themselves rather than accept the thrones of unnatural rulership offered them by the Emperor. Two of them starved themselves to death because they did not approve of a new order established through violent means. They all chose dying to express their objection to a situation. Chuang Tzu, however, has pointed out that death is not a proper solution to life's problems.

appearance came from his great reserve of goodness within him. He seemed to desire silence, but that was because he understood the limitations of language.

Men of natural truth could agree on the basis of laws, social ceremonies and rites and could use them as tools for maintaining and guarding the social order of undeveloped people in a natural society. Such tools have aided people's progress through life. Such a man could accept the use of intellectual knowledge when there were affairs that needed to be taken care of. Intellectual knowledge could be a useful accessory, but morality and virtue have always been the basic guides. When natural morality is followed, even issuing a death sentence could be done out of kindness. The man of natural truth considered wisdom as doing what is timely and virtue as doing what is reasonable. It may appear that the men of natural truth worked in their own interest, but they led truly worthy lives.

He had his likings, but maintained his oneness with nature. He had his dislikes, but even so he still maintained his oneness with nature. He treated people and things as one with nature by maintaining himself as one with nature. He treated people and things that were not one with nature by still maintaining himself as one with nature. To be one with nature is to be the companion of Heaven. Not to be one with nature is to be the companion of the animal, a degradation of Man. When one's animal nature and Heavenly nature do not compete but unite together, one may be said to have achieved the integral nature of a whole being, the description of the men of natural truth. They are people of spiritual development.

II

Life as well as death have their fate. They are as constant as the succession of dawn and dusk. They are functions of nature; they are things that man cannot change; they are the inevitable changes through which all creatures must cycle. If people look upon nature as a parent and feel a personal love for her, they should extend that love beyond universal nature to the Subtle Origin of all creatures. If people can look upon their nation as more important than themselves and are willing to give their lives for her, then why aren't they willing to broaden themselves to become a whole person of integral nature?

When a pond dries up, fish that are left stranded on dry ground spray moisture on one another and wet each other with spit. But wouldn't it be much better if each were by itself in a lake or a river? Similarly, rather than praising Yao, the great and wise Emperor, and blaming Chieh, the worst tyrant, and involving oneself in bitter argument over which is right and which is wrong, wouldn't it be better to forget both of them and attend to the development of one's own integral nature?

Nature has given us bodies, provided us with work, with repose in old age and with rest in death. Thus, our death and our birth come from the same source.

III

You hid your boat in a ravine and your valuables in the water, convincing yourself that they would be safe; but in the middle of the dark hours someone carried them away and in your sleep you did not know that happened. You do not realize that no matter how well you conceal things, there is always a chance of losing them. If you were to keep the world in your control, so that nothing could get away, this would not be like the constant subtle law of all things. One who is overly self-protective, shunning true responsibility, or who has decided to live motivated only by self-interest, cannot achieve his purpose. He has lost all.

IV

To have taken a human form is a cause for joy. But a human life undergoes multiple transformations. Therefore, those who are truly developed delight in that which can never be lost but which always abides. One of integral nature roams where all things have their being. He enjoys his youth; he enjoys his old age. He enjoys the beginning; he enjoys the end. All people would like to learn from a person who is carefree in any circumstance. So why don't we learn from the integral truth, from Tao, to which all lives and things are tied and on which all change and nonchange depend?

V

Tao, the integral nature of the universe, is trustworthy and is free from any particular movement or form. Tao is transmittable and can be embraced by anyone. It is attainable but invisible. It has its own source, its own root in itself. At the beginning of time, when the sky and the earth first appeared, Tao was there. It gave birth to innumerable spirits and gods; it gave birth to Heaven and Earth. To Tao, the highest point is not high, and the lowest is not deep. It existed before Heaven and Earth, yet one cannot say that it has been here for long. It is more ancient than antiquity itself, but it is not aged.

VI
Humans can Attain Spiritual Development

Hsi Wei attained Tao. He was able to be one with universal truth.[54]

Fu Shi attained Tao. He was able to go deeply into the vital nature of the universe.[55]

For people of spiritual development, their virtue is perpetual like the Big Dipper; it has never failed to keep refreshing itself in its course. They are also like the sun and the moon, who are not easily exhausted.

---

[54]Hsi Wei was one of those who exemplified the life of oneness with nature. He was thought to have lived before the time of recorded history. He was one with the subtle light and was thus called Hsi Huh - the gentle light.

[55]Fu Shi, who was inspired by nature, laid down the principles of Yin and Yang, the basic pattern of universal change.

Therefore, K'an P'i attained Tao and then entered the sacred K'un-Lun mountains to become one of divine life.

P'ing Ie attained Tao and then wandered in the Yellow River to become the deity over the water.

Chien Wu attained Tao and deathlessly dwells on Mount T'ai.

The Yellow Emperor attained Tao. Soaring upon the clouds, he transformed into a spiritual life in high Heaven.[56]

Chuan Hsu[57] attained Tao and was thus able to continue his spiritual life in the mystical realm.

Hsi Wang Mu, the Mother of the West, attained Tao by cultivating herself at Shao Kuang. No one knows the exact beginning or end of her achieved life.

Yu-jan attained Tao and connected his long spiritual life with that of the North Star.

Peng Tsu attained Tao and physically lived from the time of Shun until the time of the Five Powers[58].

Fu Yueh attained Tao and went from being a captive to becoming a great and helpful minister to Wu Ting, rendering invaluable public service to the world.[59] He had attained the energy of a star in one of the twenty-eight constellations. He rode on the energy of the star and charioted the sky.

---

[56]The Yellow Emperor is the most creative, helpful person in ancient Chinese society, the father of Chinese culture. He lived ca. 2697 B.C. and among other things is said to have invented and designed clothes, wheeled vehicles, social order and natural integrated medicine. He is said, generally, to have begun the healthy civilization of his people. Lao Tzu's teaching has been attributed to him. Later generations have regarded him as the first promulgator of the integral path continued by the ancient sages such as Hsi Wei, Fu Shi, Shen Nung, etc.

[57]2513 B.C., the grandson of the Yellow Emperor.

[58]From 2255 to the seventh century B.C., or about 1500 years.

[59]During the Yin Dynasty, 1324 -1266 B.C.

All of this is to illustrate the spiritual possibility in each human's innate nature, which can be further developed.

The above list of divinities was made by Chuang Tzu. Most of them rendered good service to the world. None of them are those who sit in dark corners to suck their thumbs. The teachings of Chuang Tzu cannot be mixed with those of people who make excuses from accomplishing even general moral and natural fulfillment.

VII

Tzu Chi of South City was in pursuit of his spiritual development and went to see a specially achieved lady, Nu Yu, wishing to learn from her. He said, "You enjoy a great old age, yet your complexion is like a child's. How can that be?"

Nu Yu replied, "I have attained Tao."

"Can I attain Tao by studying it?" asked Tzu Chi.

"That is not possible," answered Nu Yu. "You are not a man with that temperament.

"I would like to tell you of my experience teaching someone. You perhaps know Pu-liang Yi. He is one who has the talent of an achieved person but not the way of an integral person, whereas I have the way of an integral person but no intellectual depth. I wanted to teach him to be one of wholeness. However, teaching wholeness even to someone who has the potential of being a sage is no easy task. But I began, instructing him for three whole circles of solar rotation. After that, he was able to put the world and all things of being at a distance, outside himself. Following that, I continued for seven more whole circles of the sun. After that, he was able to put things near to him outside himself. When he had accomplished that, I continued explaining to him for nine more whole circles of the sun, at which point he was able to go beyond life. Next, he was able to achieve the morning light, and then went on to know his own solitude. Following that, he was no longer bound by time and was able to enter where there is no life or death, where killing does not end life, nor does prolonging life add to one's existence. In this state, he is always accompanying, greeting, destroying or creating. It is called Active Unity.   It means to attain completion following action."

"Where did you learn all of this," asked Tzu Chi, an eager student and himself a teacher of meditation.

Nu Yu replied, "Since you are a scholarly type, I will use a scholar's rhetoric in answering your question. I will point it out for you this way so that your mind may comprehend it. One may learn it from the son of Facilitating Ink (i.e., books) who learned it from the grandson of Repeated Narration (the storyteller). The latter was taught by Clarity (the creative mind). Clarity was taught by Whispered Secret (the purpose) who learned it from Purity in Use (spiritual inspiration). Purity in Use learned it from Exclaimed Wonderful (great appreciation) who learned it from Subtle Understanding. Subtle Understanding learned it from Going-in-the-Indistinguishable-Mystical-Oneness, who learned it from Where-You-Dissolve-Yourself.

"The other way you can learn it is from Desire to Know. Desire to Know learns it from Prudent Investigation. Prudent Investigation keeps learning from Total Concentration. Total Concentration finally develops the coordination of the whole being from inside and out through Constant Practice. Constant Practice enables you to reach Unknown Profundity, who makes you become the Void of Artificial Knowledge. The Void sends you to join with the Infinite!"

CHAPTER THIRTY-TWO

THE WISE PEOPLE

I

When four developed friends - the wise Su, Yu, Li and Lai - were talking together they made the following resolution: "We will befriend those who know the origin of nothingness as their head, life as their backbone and death as their buttocks, and who know that life and death, existence and destruction are one thing." Then they looked at one another and laughed. Since each of the four shared the same understanding, they all became good friends and assisted one another when it was needed.

Some time later, Yu became ill, and Su went to see him. "Amazing," said the sick man. "See how the great transformer has changed me? My back is so hunched that my bowels are at the top of my body and my cheeks are close to my navel. My neck is below my shoulders and my braided hair points upwards towards the sky. The entire balance of my organism is disordered. Nevertheless, although there is this disharmony of yin and yang within me, my mind is not perturbed." Then he dragged himself over to a well where he could see his reflection and continued, "Just look how the Great Transformer has turned me around."

"Are you fearful?" asked Su.

"No," answered Yu. "What is there to fear? Before long my body shall decay. Maybe after some time has passed, my left shoulder will become a rooster, and I'll noisily greet the approach of morning. It could be that my right shoulder will become an archer's bow, and I'll shoot down an owl for some delicious eating. Perhaps my buttocks will eventually become the wheels of a cart and my inner gods may turn into horses who will then lead the way.

"I was born because it was my time to come here. I am now leaving in accordance with the nature of the universe. Following nature is my contentment; thus, happiness and sadness do not trouble me. Such acceptance of life's requirements or conditions is called 'Release from Bondage.' Many cannot attain this freedom because they are so entrapped by their material existence. However, no matter how hard people try, they cannot evade Nature's directive. Because it is natural, why should this type of change bother me?"

Later, Lai became ill and was gasping, being on the edge of death. His wife and children had gathered close by him and began to cry. Li, who had come to ask how he was, said, "There is nothing about his transformation to be afraid of. Please move back and stand quite a bit away. Let us not disturb the process of change." Then, leaning against the door, he said, "The Lord of the Great Transformation is truly marvelous. I wonder what you will become now? Do you think he will make you into a rat's liver or a bug's arm?"

Lai said, "A child obeys its father and mother, going where it is directed by them, whether north or south, east or west. Yet, more powerful than one's father and mother are the alternation of Yin and Yang. Truly, the parents of man are nature itself. Now that it has brought me to the verge of death, if I were to try to refuse, it would only show spiritual undevelopment on my part. The Law of Great Transformation has given me a bodily form, labor in my life, ease in my old age and now is ready to give me rest in death. The same goodness which brought me into life is now bringing me back to be nothing. I am treated fairly.

"If a talented blacksmith was working his craft, and the metal he was using was to jump up and say, 'I insist upon being made only into a sword to be used by a great general,' they surely would be inauspicious words. If I were to say to the keeper of the law of the great transformation, 'I want only to be a man,' it would surely show undeveloped character on my part. In my view, Heaven and earth are but the biggest

furnace and the natural transformation is but the for-
ging. What could I be made into that would not be
the right shape for me? Soon, I will peacefully drift off
to sleep, and wake up again."

Here I would like to point out the important view
of the universe of a Taoist, which differs from the
Bible. In the Biblical creation, what the creator made is
fixed. Adam is created first and Eve is made from
Adam, etc.; there is no change. The Taoist view is that
nature or life is a great transformation. Nothing can
refuse it. In literature or poems, sometimes we refer to
the Lord of the Great Transformation, which is another
term for nature. The Law of Great Transformation
means the alternation of Yin and Yang: what is latent
will become apparent and what is apparent will become latent. It generalizes the interchange of all things
and describes the general background of all lives.
There is no exception to this law.

*Q: This is a beautiful story, but how is it possible to have
such a severe physical imbalance and not be mentally affected, if one is an integral being? I know that it is possible
to remain detached from pain or disorder, but how could the
equilibrium of the mental sphere be unaffected by something
in the physical or spiritual sphere?*

Master Ni: This is to illustrate what a person can
achieve in spiritual concentration with great self composure. Nothing can bother him. He is beyond the
disturbances of life and death; his spiritual achievement
can over-power anything that is happening to him.

II

The four wise men Sang Hu, Meng-Tzu Fan, and
Ch'in Chang were conversing and said, "Who can join
without joining? Who can do and yet not do? Who
can soar to heaven and roam in the mist, go beyond
the limits of space to wander through the infinite, forgetting about life?" Then they looked at one another
and laughed. All three sharing good understanding,
they became good friends.

Not much later, Sang Hu died. A nearby ceremonial master who lived nearby sent one of his chief disciples, Kung, to attend Sang Hu's funeral. Upon arriving, Kung found Sang Hu's two friends there. One
had composed a song while the other accompanied him
on a lute. They sang together as follows:
"Oh, Sang Hu.
Oh, Sang Hu.
You have already returned to your true form,
while we stay here as men. Oh!"
Kung rushed in and said, "How can you sing over
a corpse? Why haven't the ceremonies begun?"
The two men looked at each other and laughed,
saying, "What does he know about ceremonies?"
Kung returned and reported the incident to his
master. Kung asked, "What sort of men are these who
pay no attention to proper behavior? Not only was
their personal appearance incorrect, but they were
singing in the presence of a corpse without showing
any respect. I do not know what word to call them!"
"Kung," replied his master, "these men wander
beyond the customs of life; my travels remain inside
them. Since the two opposite poles of beyond and
inside do not meet, I should not have sent you there.
"These men are of the kind that are at One with
nature, enjoying themselves as they flow with the
universal natural energy, the breath that fills all forms
of life. Life is to them as something that is left over.
Death is to them like the breaking open of the big
tumor. They do not take life as specially interesting
and death as specially uninteresting; they take the body
as a tree for their free spirit to perch on.
"Their focus steadfastly remains on the unity of all
things because their view of physical life is as a union
of many composite elements. They ignore the reactions
of their internal organs of passion, which are their
stomach, liver, gall bladder, and in women, female
organs. They do not rely alone on the information
gathered by their eyes and ears.
"Traveling back and forth through all eternity, they
do not admit a beginning and an end as two absolutely

separate things. They stroll far beyond the dusty and dirty mind that other people play in, wandering free and easy in the realm of non-interruption. You cannot expect such men to trouble themselves with the social rituals and ceremonies that are designed to entertain other people."

"But if this is the case," gasped Kung, "why should we bother performing ceremonies?"

"It seems that we are limited by our own nature," replied the master. "However, we may be able to develop ourselves and increase our wisdom, thereby changing our destiny."

"How does that work?" inquired Kung.

"Fish are born in water," replied the master. "Man is born in the path of healthy natural and social life. When fish swim in water, they find their food provided. When people seek to live with universal nature, they find their lives strengthened and renewed, and live enjoyably. This is why it is said that fish forget each other in the rivers and lakes, and people forget each other in the path of non-discriminated life."

"What about those who have spiritually achieved themselves and who have spiritual powers?" asked Kung.

"Man is a miniature Heaven. God is a grand-scale man. Such men," replied the master, "are extraordinary on earth, but ordinary to Heaven, hence the saying that the worst being in Heaven would be the best on earth, and the best on earth, the worst in Heaven. Man is a miniature Heaven. God is a grand-scale man."

To be a ceremonial master was conventionally the side job of a Confucian scholar. Chuang Tzu, here and in the next section, purposely wished to correct the common tendency of people to make a show of funerals and weddings. In the Chinese society, it was a custom to do things for 'face,' which developed into a bad habit.

III

On another occasion, another student asked the

master, "When Meng Sun's mother died, he wept, but with no tears. He mourned, but did not grieve or suffer anguish. He wore the garments of mourning, but did not wail. Although in those things he seemed lacking, he became known in the state of Lu for the depth of his mourning. I do not understand this. It seems that he did not mourn at all."

"Meng Sun did all that was required of him," said the master. "He has made progress toward the natural truth of life. He does not make a great outward show of mourning. Ordinary people do everything possible to exaggerate their emotions. General social etiquette is associated with artificial religious customs, but a man such as Meng Sun maintains a natural balance in harmony with all situations.

"Meng Sun does not bother himself with where we come from or where we go to. He does not concern himself with whether to engage in the pursuit of life or approach of death. He has accepted that he has been transformed into a human; now he is simply waiting to see what further transformations will take place. When one is at the point of change, how does he know that he is changing? When one is not changing, how does one know that change has ended?

"Meng Sun adapts himself physically to the changes of the body and avoids any injury to his mind and spirit, thus keeping his soul free from damage by the passion of emotion. He regards changing form as he would regard moving to a new house; thus he does not consider death as real. When he sees others weep, however, he may be naturally moved to tears, too. Meng Sun, alone, is a fully awakened person. You and I, however, may be living in a dream from which we have not yet awakened.

"Because he knows how to treat life and death as equals, he can embrace the oneness of nature and become enduring. He is thus different from other people. People see me in the shape of a human being and make friends with me, but do they know whether the temporary physical form they see is really me? We express ourselves, saying, 'I did this, I did that,' but how do we know that the 'I' we talk about truly has any substance to it?

"Each person is subjectively conscious of his own personality; but is he, in fact, that which he is conscious of being? If you dream you are a bird that flies in the sky, it seems real; then if you dream you are a fish that dives to the depths of the ocean, it seems real, too. How, then, can you tell whether you are now awake or in a dream?

"A smile occurs because a pleasant sensation has been felt. The smile itself does not depend on your arranging it beforehand. After you have already burst into laughter, it is too late for you not to laugh. Therefore, flow with the natural course of change, and do not exaggerate or overdo the sadness produced by the change of death. Then you can enter the vast bosom of nature and become one with the universe which uses change to maintain its everlastingness."

IV

Yi Erh Tzu went to see Master Hsu Yu. Hsu Yu asked him, "What did you learn from Yao?"

Yi Erh replied, "Yao told me that one must live a life of benevolence and righteousness, according to what is right and what is wrong."

"Then what are you looking for here?" asked Hsu Yu. "If Yao has already smoked you with ideas of benevolence and dyed you with ideas of righteousness, then what do you want from this path of freedom and natural life?"

"He may have instructed me as you say," answered Yi Erh, "But I would like to see if there is something for me to learn here."

"It is not possible for a man who has lost his sight to appreciate a thing of beauty," rejoined Hsu Yu. "Nor can a person who is color-blind enjoy the blue and yellow embroidery on a silk robe."

Yi Erh responded, "The famous beauty Wu Chuang's indifference to her fine appearance, the muscular Chu Liang's disregard for his physical strength, and the well-studied Yellow Emperor's abandonment of his intellectual knowledge were all brought about by a process of carving down and reshaping. How can you know whether Heaven has not brought me here to have me cleared of the coloring of the smoke and dye so that I am able to follow the Way?"

"Ah," smiled Hsu Yu, "there is no way to know that, but I would like you to consider something. The Master I serve helps all things and beings and does not consider his actions as benevolence nor duty. He acts in accordance with the moment, passing on his blessings to all generations yet not thinking of his actions as righteous. He is an elder to antiquity, but he is not old. With Heaven he covers all things, with earth he supports all things, and although he is the one who creates all forms, he does not think of himself as skilled. This is the level of my Master, the one you should seek!"

V

A student of the Integral Way said to an instructor, "Teacher, I've learned!"

The teacher said, "What do you mean by that?"

"Now I am beyond social ceremonies, advertising and propaganda!"

"That's good, but you still aren't there yet."

At another time the two met again and the student said, "Teacher, I've learned!"

"What do you mean by that?" said the teacher.

"Now I am beyond benevolence, righteousness, any dogmatic attainment and intellectual achievement!" replied the student.

"That's good, but you still haven't gotten there."

Once again, the two met each other and the student said, "Teacher, I've learned! I can sit down and be beyond everything!"

The teacher, with a look of astonishment, said, "What do you mean when you say you can sit down and be beyond everything?"

"I can be free of my body," answered the student. "I have abandoned my power of intellect and reasoning; by thus dismissing body and mind, I am one with the absolute. This is being able to go beyond everything."

"If you have arrived at Oneness," exclaimed the teacher, "you must have arrived at the point of no preferences. If you have become so developed, then you must be a being with no beginning and no ending. And if it is true that you have accomplished this, then I would like to learn from you!"

VI

Yu and Sang were friends. Once, after it rained without stopping for ten days, Yu said to himself, "Sang is probably in difficulty," and he prepared some food and took it to his friend. When he arrived at Sang's gate, he heard someone playing the lute and singing or crying:

"Father? Mother? Heaven? Man?"

It sounded as though it took a very great effort to produce these words.

Yu went in the house and asked him, "Why are you singing a song like that?"

"I am trying to figure out what brought me to this point," replied Sang. "My father and mother would certainly not wish me to be so poor. Heaven covers all beings impartially and Earth bears all life equally; Heaven and Earth surely wouldn't single me out among all others. I want to know how it happened, but I have not been able to understand. Here I am in my extremity! But I should not accept this fate or destiny. A decent worldly life should be the contribution of everyone. I seem to have isolated myself from the supportive natural order. It must be that I have not been supportive enough; that must be what caused this absence of support. Therefore, I do not deserve help from anyone."

"Dear friend, please do not blame yourself. You have made many good attempts to improve your situation, you just have not found your way yet. In your

case, you are not lazy or crazy.   In all people's lives,
there are times of low cycles and times of higher ones.
Truthfully, not all the sweetly scented flowers bloom in
the spring; some blossom in later seasons.   Please
accept the help that I can give you at this time."

CHAPTER THIRTY-THREE

THE TRUE MASTER

I

Yeh Ch'ueh[60] was questioning his teacher, Wang Ni. Yeh Ch'ueh asked Wang Ni four questions, who did not answer any of them. In silence, the truth would be expressed to him; so Wang Ni remained quiet but answered with the integralness of his spiritual nature.[61]

This response made Yeh Ch'ueh jump with joy. His delight came from the fact that he finally realized that when one's intellectual faculty is over-grown, one's spiritual energy becomes blocked. He went straight out and told Master P'u-I his discovery.

Master P'u-I said, "Is it only now that you have found that out? Emperor Shun did not attain the greatness of Fu Hsi, who discovered the basic principle of all existence: the unchanging truth of the constant change of matter. Shun was zealous in his charity for all mankind, but although he succeeded as a leader, his teaching never rose above the worldly level to the realm of the divine 'not-man.'

"The great Fu Hsi was peaceful when he slept; he had so completely closed all channels leading to the spiritual self, that he remained whole when he was awake. He could accept that sometimes people thought him a horse and other times an ox. His wisdom and

---

[60]Yeh Ch'ueh was the teacher of Hsu Yu to whom Emperor Yao (who reigned from 2357 to 2258 B.C.) looked for guidance.

[61]This is a method used in teaching the integral truth. Later it was demonstrated by many masters, both in the tradition of Tao or in the tradition of Zen Buddhism which was a later transformation of Chuang Tzu's teaching. However, true attainment must be proven by adepts. One cannot pretend to be a achieved by imitating silence and giving no answer.

feeling were trustworthy and above suspicion. His virtue was true. He never sank to the level of the worldly. He was a true sovereign of life in the pattern of
Tao."

II

Chien Wu went to see the somewhat eccentric
Chieh Yu, who some people considered to be mad.
Chieh Yu asked him, "What does your teacher Jih
Chung Shih tell you these days?"

"He says that the leaders of the people should devise their own rituals, standards, laws and principles,"
replied Chien Wu. "Then all people will obey them
and their lives will be transformed for the better."

"This is useless advice!" exclaimed Chieh Yu.
"Attempting to govern the world like that is like trying
to wade across the ocean, thaw an icy river or make a
mosquito carry a mountain!

"When an achieved person sets out to help others,
he is not concerned with externals or with the thought
of how to rule people. When a sage, one of integral
nature, is in the position of leadership, he does not
govern what is on the outside. First he perfects himself, and then with his virtue he can accomplish what
needs to be done. He becomes sure of himself before
he acts and the completion occurs passively, without effort of any kind. All he does is make sure that things
can do the job for which they are intended.

"Birds fly high in the sky to be far from the threat
of man's arrows. A field mouse burrows way down
under the ground where men cannot dig or smoke it
out. One must be even more sensible than those two
creatures!"

III

Tien Ken, The One Rooted In Heaven, was traveling
on the sunny side of Yein Mountain. When he reached
the shore of the Liao River, he happened to meet The
One Who Is Unnameable and begged him for his teaching, requesting, "Please, tell me how to govern the
world."

The One Who Is Unnameable cried, "Get away from me! What kind of question is that? I am just about to place my heart beyond the reach of the world, to flow with Heaven, to ride on the wings of the Bird of Vastness out beyond the six directions, front, rear, left, right, up and down, on an excursion into the Realm of Perfect Freedom where I would live in the Field of No Boundary. Why are you disturbing my mind with your talk of governing the world? Is the world not you or me? Am I not a world; are you not one also?"

Nevertheless, Tien Ken persisted to ask him again. The One Who Is Unnameable replied, "Do not set your mind on the pursuit of fame and fortune alone, but maintain your life completely by your own spirit. Let your heart and mind be occupied by nothing. Be naturally and spontaneously obedient to the subtle law of life and tolerate no subjectivity or personal views. Then the world will no doubt be well governed."

IV

Yang-tzu Chu went to see Lao Tzu and said, "If a man were strong and brave, swift and smart, knowledgeable about the principles of things, never tiring of studying the Way, he would compare with an enlightened king, would he not?"

"Sounds like he is trying to imitate the wise ones," replied Lao Tzu. "A person like you describe has only the talents of a craftsman, who only wears out his body and mind. The tiger and leopard are killed because of the beauty of their skins. The cleverness of the monkey and the ability of the dog to chase cause them both to be put on a leash. This is not the equal of an enlightened one."

"How, then, does the wise one govern?" inquired Yang-Tzu Chu.

"An enlightened one," answered Lao Tzu, "has good merit and achievements that spread over the world, but he does not look upon them as his own accomplishment. His great capability to transform touches all people and things, but he does not make anything dependent on him, nor does he take credit for his

266 ATTAINING UNLIMITED LIFE

achievements in order to gain praise or reputation. He lets everyone discover their own enjoyment in life. His strength comes from a place that cannot be measured by any instrument. He finds his own joy in the nothingness of the subtle essence. The true government of such a person is invisible to the physical eyes of the people."

V

In the state of Cheng there was a shaman named Chi Han who could tell whether people would have a long life or die early, have good fortune or misfortune, and if ill people would live or die. He could also predict events to the day with great accuracy. The people of Cheng used to run away when they saw him coming, but the young Lieh Tzu went to see him and was so amazed that, on his return, he said to Master Hu, his teacher, "I used to look upon your teaching as the best one, but now I know something even better!"

"You think you know all about Tao," replied Hu Tzu. "You do not realize that I have only taught you the outward form and not the essence. Without roosters in your barnyard, what sort of eggs do you think the hens are going to lay? People do not believe a show-off; they can see right through you. Bring your friend with you tomorrow so he can see me!"

So the next day Lieh Tzu brought Chi Han to see Master Hu. When they came out, Chi Han said, "I am sorry to tell you that your master has not much longer to live. He will only have about ten more days. I am astounded; he is nothing but wet ashes."

Sadly weeping, Lieh Tzu went in and told Master Hu, but Master Hu said, "Just now I appeared to him as the outer shape of a mountain, silent, calm and motionless. Closing off the vital force, I prevented him from seeing the energy of Tao within. Bring him again tomorrow."

The next day, they came by again, but this time Chi Han said to Lieh Tzu, "It is a good thing for your teacher that he met me. He is better now and will recover. I saw that there was some healing power."

Lieh Tzu went in and told Master Hu what Chi Han had said. The master replied, "Just now, I let a little of my vital energy run out of my heel so he could observe the life force. I will show him a little more of the power of the transformations of nature which work deeply. Bring him here again tomorrow."

On the next day another meeting took place. As they were leaving, Chi Han said to Lieh Tzu, "Your teacher is always different! I have not been able to come to any conclusion about him. If he will try to be a little more steady, I will come to see him again."

When this was repeated to Master Hu he said, "I showed myself to him just now in a state of harmony and stability as Balanced Breath. Where swirling waves unite is the abyss; where still waters gather is the abyss; where running waters meet is the abyss. There exist nine names for the abyss; I have shown him three."[62]

On the next day Chi Han and Lieh Tzu came once more to see Master Hu, but the shaman, bewildered and confused, fled.

"Go after him!" cried Master Hu, and Lieh Tzu ran after Chi Han but could not catch up to him. When he returned he told his master that Chi Han had run too fast.

"Just now," said Master Hu, "I showed myself to him as Tao appeared before time was, not yet emerged from the source. He saw me as a great void, existing of itself. He did not know me. He became unsettled, and so he left."

After this happened, Lieh Tzu decided that he had not even begun to learn anything. So he set about applying himself earnestly to his work. He performed all tasks without thinking of preference, took no personal interest in the affairs of the world and eliminated what was artificial from his life. He did not go out of the house unless it was necessary or make a pilgrimage to

---

[62]This describes the depth of chi movement of an achieved person.

a holy land. He was happy doing the small chores and did not think of them as insignificant, helping his wife take care of the household. He did not think it was lowly. He was devoted to earnest life, and in such simplicity and peace he reached full development.

The true master is the person who has achieved mastery over his life, death and so-called fortune. This is beyond the capability of a psychic.

VI

This is what Master Lieh learned from his teacher, Master Hu: Don't create a great reputation for yourself, don't create a lot of schemes or strategies, don't accept any great commitment, and don't try to master the intellectual mind. Develop your understanding of the integral way as unlimitable. Let your heart and mind enjoy freedom where no obstruction is placed in your path. Whatever you have is bestowed on you by nature; do not think that anything you have attained is beyond nature. Anything you think you have attained, if it is against nature's doing, is not truly beneficial. The heart and the mind of the developed one, once applied, reflects things as they are, without welcoming or rejecting them; it does not conceal the things that it reflects. It can therefore maintain its complete function without being damaged by anything external.

VII

The deity of the southern sea was called Shu, The One of Immediacy. The deity of the northern sea was called Hu, The One of Suddenness. The deity of the central zone was called Hun Tun, The One of Undifferentiation.[63]

Frequently, Shu and Hu met at the territory of Hun Tun, and for this generosity, wished to return the favor. They said, "Every man has seven holes in his

---

[63]The term "Hun Tun" is generally used to designate the state of matter in the pre-Heaven stage, before separation and differentiation into visible phenomena. Here Master Chuang Tzu uses it to tell us something else in the story.

body for seeing, hearing, eating and breathing. Hun Tun is the only one without any, so we will drill some for him."

So every day they drilled one hole; but on the seventh day, Hun Tun died.

The seven holes refer to the seven orifices of the face. With over-expansion of sensory pleasure, one destroys the balance of one's center. Hun Tun refers to the spiritual center or subtle origin. This story illustrates Lao Tzu's teaching of shutting the doors, closing the outlet and maintaining oneself spiritually whole, without being pulled away by sensual desires.

This story illustrates that the over-development of the human intellect which is the root of all disharmony and the source of jealousy and competition. All the perils and crises of human history have been caused by it. To an individual, an overly developed intellectual function brings both knowledge and comparison, which can result in aggression, tensions, frustration, depression, disappointment and an inability to move smoothly and carefully in life, etc. The ancient masters of the integral way supported balanced development of body, mind and spirit in which negative, narrow, destructive and excessive intellectual tendencies were weeded out.

CHAPTER THIRTY-FOUR

HUMAN AFFAIRS

I

The young and ambitious heir of Duke Wei went to learn from Chuang Tzu. He stayed in Chuang Tzu's house, and was given all the ordinary chores to do for many long years, without being given any special instruction. On one occasion, he requested, in a very formal manner, "Sir, may I know something more about Tao?"

Chuang Tzu replied, "Tao is the principle of naturalness, harmony and efficiency; one who is one with it does not extend personal intellectual and emotional energy as interference. If you know how to apply it to governing a country, the government will function well. If you know how to apply it to your work, then you will work efficiently. If you know how to apply it to the delegation of duties, everyone will do well in their job. If you know how to apply it to personal relationships, there will be growth and mutual benefit. If you know how to apply it to your life, you will be productive and satisfied.

"Tao is the path of natural growth that constantly proceeds and supports everything that moves in a positive direction. Tao, the integral way, enlivens all things. Wherever it is found in the world, people take good care of each other and their abilities find appropriate expression. When people keep to Tao, all tasks are accomplished easily.

"There are many ways which describe how the positive, enlivening energy of Tao manifests in the world. Godliness is to act without thought of personal gain. Virtue is to help others without selfish intention. Natural kindness is to love other people and care for all things without thought of oneself. Greatness is viewing people and things without discrimination yet with respect for their differences. Broadness is to not limit oneself to any extreme. Wealth is being able to enjoy great variety. Positive discipline is to keep your focus on Tao at all times. Perfection is to harmonize, not run counter, to the natural way of things. However, most truthfully, the person who follows Tao will find that he or she is safe from fault or blame.

"Tao is the subtle potency which supports the positive relationship of all things. Virtue, also known as Teh, is the connecting link between the common interest and the individual. One who embodies Tao is called One of Great Virtue. When he is a leader of others, he lets them find the work to which they are best suited and which displays their talents. When he is a leader of society, he does not interfere with the positive direction of life so that the world will develop in a healthy way. If he is a leader in government, he maintains a balanced heart and mind so that the world will enjoy peace."

"Sir, may I venture to interrupt you. So far all that you have mentioned seems to be abstract, hard to digest and absorb into my personal life. How does it relate to me?" queried the young man.

Chuang Tzu smiled and said, "You must practice Teh, which is virtue. One of Great Virtue remains in harmony with his spiritual nature. He would be ashamed to be a master of facts or intellectual knowledge without embracing the subtle law that is hidden behind all facts. With both, his understanding reaches divine clarity. His spiritual mind is activated; he moves forth only when some external thing has need of him. He can also cause things to respond to him when help is needed. It is said, 'Achieve mindlessness within yourself through spiritual cultivation, and all things will come to your support.' One of Great Virtue thus has no need to strive for fame, position or wealth. He is not bothered by either affluence nor poverty. He does not look for worldly glory; his glory is knowing that all things are one, and life and death are only phases of the same existence.

"One of Great Virtue is peaceful and harmonious, broad and boundless. He sees in darkness. He hears where there is no sound. He sinks to the lowest depths, where things have their beginnings, and to the highest of heights, where the spirit finally soars. Thus, he stands at the junction point between all people and phenomena; he supplies their wants selflessly. He observes the race of life in freedom, both its beginning and its finishing-point. The largest and the smallest, the longest and the shortest, the boundless and the infinite - that is Tao."

The young prince's face turned red and he said, "Sir, I have been here a long time and learned to do all the minor things of daily life. Are they associated with Tao and Teh?"

Chuang Tzu continued, "The capability to do useful work is called skill. Individual skills can fulfill the needs of society. Skill can be demonstrated in effective administration of people and things. Skill is connected to the circumstances of life. The circumstances of life are connected with one's own duty. Duty is related to virtue, virtue to Tao, and Tao to each individual. The heir of a prince might learn the skills of a civilian, but only those who live an earnest, truthful life will not be defeated."

After some time, Duke Wei was defeated in war. The heir of Wei was not defeated because he lived a good civilian life.

II

The wise Yellow Emperor wandered north of Red Lake and visited the K'un-lun mountains. After he had returned south, he discovered that he had lost his mystical pearl. He hired Li Chu, who was exceptionally good with colors and sounds, to find it, but without success. He then employed Che-o, who was especially refined in speech and argument with great convincing power, to find it, but again without success. Finally, he asked Shang Mang, whose mind was exceedingly dull, and he was successful.

"Strange indeed," said the Emperor, "that Shang Mang, the mindless one, should be the one who was able to find it!"

Intelligence, sharp eyesight and speech are roads that lead away from one's spiritual center. Only in a state of mindlessness can one regain one's mystical pearl and embody it completely.

III

Emperor Yao went to visit Hua, a place in Shan-Shi Province. The border guard of Hua said, "I see you are a man of great blessing. My deepest respects to you, sir. I hope that you enjoy a long life."

"No thank you!" replied Yao.

"Then I wish that you enjoy many riches," continued the guard.

"No thank you!" replied the emperor.

"Then I wish that you have many sons!" returned the guard.

"No thanks!" replied Yao.

"A long life, lots of money and many sons are what all men want," cried the guard. "How is it that you do not want them?"

"Many sons mean many worries," answered Yao. "Plenty of money means lots of concern, and long life involves much unpleasantness. These gifts do not advance my natural virtue, so I prefer to do without them."

"At first I took you for someone of great wisdom," said the guard, "but now I find that you are merely a good man. Nature brings forth many lives and gives each its own function. If you were to do the same with many sons and daughters, what cause would they give you for worry? Similarly, if you allowed people to enjoy your wealth with you, what concern would it bring you?

"A true one of natural wisdom can dwell anywhere in nature, just as a free bird does. He also travels like the flight of a bird that leaves no trace behind it. When the subtle law pervades the world, he lives in harmony with all things. If the world is in confusion

274 ATTAINING UNLIMITED LIFE

and turmoil, he cultivates virtue in solitude. Should he
weary of this world after a thousand years, he rises up
and riding upon the clouds, goes into Heaven where
the three troubles of age, wealth and offspring do not
exist and where he can enjoy eternal happiness. What
concern is there in that?"

Thereupon, the border guard allowed Emperor Yao
to continue on his way.

The three troubles refer to the negative side-effects
produced by the ordinary blessings described above
which bring about worry, trouble and suffering. However, one who rides in the carriage of the great virtue
can come and go, cruising through all changes as if the
three troubles did not exist at all. The seven-foot physical body is not forever; it is not worth mentioning the
so-called problems associated with it.

The border guard was certainly in an inferior position to the Emperor, but his spiritual development was
greater than that of the one who was socially higher
than he. Tao can be found as the baseline; it is the
teacher. What is being pointed out here is that problems can be created from personal attitudes. Everything has its own position. A person of Tao would
live the humble life like the border guard of Han. He
would not follow a rigid spiritual practice like one who
was not yet developed. Tao is a broad approach to
life; true upliftment comes not from social success but
from internal development.

IV

Before time began, there was non-being. There was
no name for non-being, yet out of it arose One. It was
the formless subtle energy, by virtue of which things
are what they are. It is called Teh; it is the process by
which function and capacity become distinct from the
subtle, formless source.

Within the formless One there is subtle distinction
between yin and yang, yet they embrace each other
closely. This is called natural fate.

Fate lies in formation. At the time a thing is formed, its fate is also shaped: long or short, black or white, and so forth.

The form of life is produced by that which is in a state of constant change, and form itself is but one short cycle of endless change. Form temporarily holds the moving spiritual elements and has its own law of change that corresponds to the law of the universe at large. If a person attains spiritual self-awareness by refining and developing his own nature, he can return to Teh, the perfect condition of life, and the process of creation and transformation will be a perfectly natural, smooth voyage.

By continual development, one reaches the Subtle Origin and becomes one with universal life. Such a one leaves no trace of himself and seems to know nothing. This is known as non-separation or subtle virtue when one lives harmoniously in the world. Having one's own individual nature (which is already a second nature), and cultivating this nature to become identical with one's original nature is the goal of attaining Tao. The original, unconditioned, pure life is like birds that unconsciously join in the chirping with other birds; to thus be joined with the universe, without being conscious of it, is complete virtue. This is in accordance with integral virtue, the assimilation of the subtle truth of the universe.

V

A student asked Lao Tzu, "There are some people who cultivate Tao according to rigid rules of right and wrong, so and not so. They follow the intellectual function which separates hardness from whiteness, as though those things could be detached from the object. Can such people be called men of natural wisdom?"

"What they do can be applied to a different category," replied Lao Tzu. "It is nothing more than mental skill; it would wear out the body and soul alike. The skill of a trained hunting dog brings it toil, because it is kept captive by man instead of being free.

The intelligence of a monkey causes its removal from the mountain and also to the world of man.

"My friend, you cannot hear what is impossible to explain. Those with a head and two feet, but no organ that is spiritually receptive, are many. Those who are attached to the concept of a solid body find it hard to understand the formless Tao. The mind that is occupied with physical beingness cannot readily accept or be open to that which is formless and unembodied.

"To move is to rest, to live is to die, to rise is to fall, but people cannot understand this. The cultivation of the self belongs to each individual. To be unconscious of the existence of things and of Heaven is to be unconscious of one's own being. He who is unconscious of his own being embodies the universal integral truth."

VI

Chung Mang, a student of the great teaching, started traveling toward the ocean and met Yuan Feng, a student of the small teaching, near the shore of the Eastern Sea.

"Where are you going?" asked Yuan Feng.

"To the ocean," replied Chung Mang.

"What will you do there?" asked Yuan Feng.

"The ocean cannot be filled by pouring something into it nor emptied by taking something out," said Chung Mang. "I am simply going to study and enjoy it. I am going to learn to be infinite."

"But don't you care about the world? Surely you must have some ideas about how to straighten it out," said Yuan Feng. "Please, tell me how one of excellent intelligence should govern the world."

Chung Mang replied, "He assigns people to office according to propriety and promotes them according to their ability. He always considers the facts in any situation. All people understand clearly what their leader is doing; they also do what needs to be done and what they are told to do. If he practices his teaching in his own life, the whole world will manage itself. He calms himself and does not trouble himself over making his wishes known; thus, no one in the world fails to follow him. This is the way a man of intellectual achievement would govern."

"But what about a man who reaches the level of virtue?" asked Yuan Feng.

"An individual who fulfills the integral nature of any situation is a person of virtuous fulfillment," replied Chung Mang. "His rest is free of thought and he moves without anxiety. He has no recognition of right and wrong, good and bad, beautiful and ugly. His delight is to see all people sharing and profiting equally in life. People stay around him like children who have lost their mothers or travelers who have lost their way. He has more than enough wealth, but does not know its source. Such is a man of perfect virtue."

"Now," said Yuan Feng, "I would like to know about the one who reaches the level of the divine."

"A divine, integral being," replied Chung Mang, "rides upon the subtle light of the universe. His personal existence can no longer be discerned. This is called 'absorption into light.' Acting in harmony with his nature, he fulfills his earthly destiny. He lives in oneness with both God and man. This is called 'envelopment in wholeness,' or 'undifferentiation.'"

CHAPTER THIRTY-FIVE

THE KING AND THE MINISTER OF LIFE

I

The Heart is as the King of life. The Mind is as the capable Minister of life. When they come together, there is heavenly joy.

A wise leader is a man who has attained a powerful and great mind. A virtuous social worker is a person who has an open, loving heart. The union of a truly wise mind and virtuous heart is the greatest sovereign who brings about a blessed world. It is the same for an individual; the cooperation of the mind and heart of one person will organize his or her natural healthy life.

It is the law of nature to keep moving without stagnation; this is how all things grow and reach completion. It is likewise the way of wise people in power to keep society moving and allow no stagnation. Such wise leaders are supported and befriended by all. They hold no stiff conceptual attitudes in their leadership that would cause people to become prejudiced, hence they treat all within the seas with equality. Similarly, for an individual, it is the way of a healthy mind and heart to keep moving with life, allowing no stagnation to block their growth.

They who comprehend the way of nature to keep moving, who follow in the footsteps of one of natural wisdom and who realize the virtue of a leader will be harmonious and reposeful in their actions. Through them all things will be harmonized and thus all things will be accomplished.

The heart of a wise leader of the world and the heart of a wise individual life are always composed and calm. This is the result of cultivation. Nothing can disturb their equilibrium, hence their heart remains unperturbed and unruffled, which allows the mind to make correct decisions.

A calm mind is like water in stillness; its clarity is like a mirror, reflecting every single hair in one's beard and eyebrows. Similarly, it is like the water in a carpenter's level, which gives the accuracy of balance to all construction. If water thus derives lucidity from stillness, how much more do the faculties of the mind benefit from quietude? Repose, tranquility, stillness and placidity are the profundity undisturbed by universal phenomena. The calm mind of a wise leader becomes the mirror of the world, allowing no confusion from any emotion or infatuating conceptual creation.

He attains the level of the unconditioned, from which comes the conditioned. With the conditioned comes order. The serene mind is uncommitted and, while uncommitted, has complete clarity. Clarity is what allows one to fulfill duty. Once inner tranquility has been established, outer movement results from necessity and thus without injury to the organism; from such movement comes attainment.

From repose and non-impulsiveness comes doing nothing extra that would cause deviation or diversion from the natural subtle course, which cannot be seen when impulsiveness is followed. From doing nothing extra comes possibility of action. When non-impulsiveness has been achieved, the organism reacts spontaneously and unconsciously. Doing nothing extra is happiness; where there is happiness no cares can linger and life is long. Hence, good decisions and balanced actions come from a healthy mind with lucid energy.

Rest, peacefulness, stillness and the fullness of impetus stored in inaction are the spiritual root of all things. To understand them is to become a wise and virtuous leader such as Yao and Shun. The perception of this is the virtue of great world leaders. Practicing these virtues, a spiritually developed one helps himself and others. Though he has the virtue of a world leader, he remains a civilian in his correct way of life, producing healthy effect in helping the world.

280 ATTAINING UNLIMITED LIFE

Fully comprehending the subtle virtue of the universe, meaning the spiritual serenity by which all things are brought to maturity, and bringing it to realization in your life is called the great principle of being in accord with nature. Such a person harmonizes with nature, and by doing so brings equitable accord to the world and harmonizes with people as well. To be in harmony with people is human happiness; to be in harmony with nature is the happiness of a divine one.

Chuang Tzu has said, "This is the Master Teacher from who I learn, who provides everything in the universe without participating in violence, who benefits all creation without calling it benevolence, who assists all time without considering it duty. An elder to antiquity, he is not old; creator of all forms, he does not consider himself skilled.

"While quiet, he enjoys the virtue of universal yin energy; while active, he shares the same movement as universal yang energy. This is his joy; this is called Heavenly Joy. Whoever knows the joy of Heaven knows how to find his happiness in nature; for him life is nature in operation and death is harmonious transformation. Finding his happiness in nature, he is harmonious with God and man, and holds no grudges nor grievances; nothing in the spiritual plane punishes him and nothing on the material plane entangles him. It has been said, 'He moves like Heaven: ceaseless revolution, without beginning or end. He rests like Earth. To him, both action and inaction are natural. Mental balance gives him harmony with all creation.'"[64]

"The quality of a wise leader takes nature for its model, is guided by Tao and always dwells in centeredness. Being centered, he can govern the world and still has ample energy, whereas one of unnatural

---

[64] This signifies that in repose, one extends oneself to the whole universe and is in relation with all creation. This is the happiness of a developed person. This is what enables the mind of the wise and virtuous leader to cherish the whole world.

action finds that his energy is insufficient for dealing with the tasks of administration. The leaders of long ago were greatly respected for their centeredness.

"If the leader, the heart, practices action (effective centeredness and balance), and if his minister, the mind, practices action (effective movement), the result would be great accomplishment. On the other hand, if a leader practices action and his minister is inactive, the leader will be left unsupported and isolated, and there will be no accomplishment. A leader as the heart must practice effective centeredness and balance in order to administer the world. The minister as the mind must practice effective movement in order to serve the interests of the world. This is an unchanging principle.

"Thus, the great leaders, although their knowledge can extend through the universe, are not troubled in mind. Although their eloquence could reap many benefits, they keep quiet. Although their abilities could win praise from the four corners of the earth, they do not act.

"Heaven does not mean to give birth, yet all lives and things are formed and nurtured. Earth does not mean to grow anything, yet all things grow. The wise leader of the world practices spiritual inaction and makes no interference, and the world follows an order that is natural. There is nothing more profound than Heaven, nothing richer than Earth, nothing greater than a wise and virtuous leader."

Therefore, the virtue of a wise and virtuous leader makes him the peer of Heaven and Earth. Supported by nature, with all people bowing to him, he smoothly passes on his journey to eternity.

CHAPTER THIRTY-SIX

ORGANIC NATURE

I

The Yellow Emperor had been on the throne for nineteen years. His government was so open, just and benevolent that his commands were followed throughout the known world. At that time, he heard that Kuang Cheng Tzu[65] was living on Mount K'ung-t'ung. He immediately went to visit the sage and said, "I have heard, Master, that you possess Perfect Tao. I would like to ask about this. It is my wish to invoke the beneficial influence of Heaven and Earth in order to produce good crops to feed the people. I would also like to learn how to control the two forces of nature, yin and yang, so that all living things may be protected and grow. How is this done?"

Kuang Cheng Tzu said, "What you say you want to learn is the substance of God, but what you really want to do is control the fragments. Since you began governing the world, rain has fallen before clouds form in the sky, plants and trees shed their leaves that haven't yet turned yellow, and the light from the sun and moon has become weak and sallow. You are only a talkative intellectual who has no more depth than a puddle - what good would be accomplished in telling one like you about Perfect Tao?"

The Yellow Emperor bowed and withdrew from the presence of the teacher. He left his throne and went to a solitary hut, used white rushes for a mat and spent three months in retreat and seclusion. Then he went again to see the Master. Kuang Cheng was lying down, facing south, the direction the ruler of the world usually faced. The Yellow Emperor approached him

---

[65]Tzu means Master, and it is sometimes a part of a name.

humbly by advancing on his knees. He bowed his head twice and said, "I have heard that you, Sir, have mastered the Way, which means you have attained Tao, perfectly. I would like to ask about the attunement of the body. What must I do to live a long life?" Kuang Cheng Tzu jumped up quickly. "An excellent question!" he cried. "I will tell you about perfect Tao.

"The essence of perfect practice to reach Tao is mysterious; its magnitude is silent and obscure. Do not be looking and listening; keep your spirit in quietude, and your body will correct itself. Keep still, be pure, do not exhaust your body or disturb your essence; then you can live a long time.

"Value that which is within you and block that which is without; too much knowledge will harm you. Then I will lead you above the Great Light to the origin of Yang energy and guide you through the Gate of Mystery to the origin of Yin energy. These powers control Heaven and Earth. Guard and preserve your life and everything else will flourish. As for myself, by guarding unity with Universal Nature and abiding in harmony with the earth I have stayed alive for twelve hundred years without suffering any decline."

The Yellow Emperor bowed and said, "Master, I believe you are God." The Master replied, "The spiritual self is eternal, though men believe it mortal. The spiritual self is infinite, though men believe it finite. The spiritual self is the condensed universal spiritual nature. It is Tao. Those who attain Tao are the authorities of life in this life and divinities in Heaven. Those who do not attain Tao, though they may see the subtle light in their lifetime, will return to earth.

"All living things arise out of the dusty world and return to dust, but I move through the doors of eternity into the realm of the infinite. My radiance is the brightness of the sun and moon. My breath is the life of Heaven and Earth. Men are born and die, but I abide forever."

II

The Spirit of the Clouds, while traveling eastward
through the branches of the divine tree, Fu-Yao, happened to meet Hung Mong, the One of Vital Principle.
The latter was hopping up and down and slapping
himself on the ribs. Observing this, the Spirit of the
Clouds said, "Who are you, old man, and what are you
doing here?"

"Enjoying myself," replied Hung Mong, without
stopping his activity.

"I would like to ask a question," continued the
Cloud Spirit.

"Oh dear," exclaimed the One of Vital Principle, in
a tone of dismay.

"The relationship between Heaven and Earth is out
of harmony," said the Spirit of the Clouds, "The six
breaths of wind, rain, warmth, coldness, darkness and
light are not properly attuned and the four seasons will
not stay in order. I desire to attain attunement with
the six breaths so I may provide nourishment for life.
How can I do this?"

"I don't know!" cried Hung Mong, all the while
continuing to hope and slap his ribs; "I don't know!"
He shook his head.

So the Spirit of the Clouds received no answer. But
three years later, when again traveling east through the
state of Sung, he met up with Hung Mong a second
time. The Spirit of the Clouds was well pleased; going
quickly to meet him, he said, "Did you forget about
me, Heavenly Master?"

He then bowed twice and requested instruction, but
the latter only said, "My wanderings have no pursuit.
My roamings have no particular purpose. I do not
bother to know where I am going. As an unbound
wanderer, I merely stroll about in this manner, and
simply enjoy watching the harmony of great nature.
What do I know?"

"I am also a wanderer," answered the Spirit of the
Clouds, "but people depend on me and follow me.
Unavoidably I am a leader, and it is for their benefit
that I request instruction."

"If you disorder the normal makeup of nature and disturb the natural order of conditions," said the One of Vital Principle, "then the Dark Womb will not reach its fulfillment. Instead, animals will flee, birds will cry, destruction will befall the vegetation, and even insects will experience disaster. Ah, this is the fault of men who do not respect nature in their government."[66]

"That is true," replied the Spirit of the Clouds, "but what can be done?"

"Return to fundamentals!" exclaimed the One of Vital Principle. "Go back to the root, to the natural state of inaction that accomplishes all things."

"It is not often that I see you, Sir," continued the Spirit of the Clouds. "I request the kindness of further advice."

"Nurture your heart and mind. Live in perfect freedom, and everything will be automatically harmonized. Drop the worry of your body. Eliminate intelligence. Forget about the differences between yourself and other things. Be completely one with the Natural Breath. Release your heart and mind and loosen the sensitive spiritual agents within you. Give no thought to the existence of your soul; then the ten thousand things will return to their root without even realizing it. Being unconscious of it, they will never again become separated from it. To experience consciousness is to be separate. If you try to know it, you have already departed from it. Never ask its name or peer into its affairs, then all things will live naturally and flourish."

The Spirit of the Clouds said, "You have kindly benefitted me by your virtue and taught me by your silence. All my life I have been seeking, and at last I have found." He bowed, stood up and said goodbye, and went away.

---

[66]The Dark Womb refers to the spiritual origin. It is also the vital origin. Here "dark" refers to what is deep and hidden.

III

The common worldly type of people welcome those who are like themselves and dislike anyone different from themselves. The reason for this is that they are determined to distinguish themselves from the majority. But if this is how they go about it, how can they ever be distinguished from the crowd?

To exalt oneself above the majority in order to gratify personal ambition and ego is not as good as letting the majority be uplifted by their collective talents. Collective effort is preferable to being restrained by the limited talents of one individual.[67]

Those who desire to have all the advantages and profits of establishing an ideal government in the world - like the three dynasties of Yao, Shun and Yu - do not see the real troubles these rulers faced. Most men who turn out merely to be political leaders do not have a deep knowledge of world problems, but nevertheless try their hand at matters and put the world at risk. That is no better than trusting luck. Has this ever occurred without bringing a country to grief?[68] There is not one chance in ten thousand that the state will be preserved and protected, while their chances of bringing it to ruin are ten thousand to nothing or perhaps greater. Such, unfortunately, is the ignorance of most leaders.

Leading a society within a vast territory is a great responsibility. The one who is not limited by collective and territorial values will not misguide people or misuse the resources of their land. He understands how to be different from most people so that he can lead them. It is healthy to keep a society organic and to let the land remain organic also. This principle applies not only to governing the world, but also to the life of an achieved individual. He is one whose organic spirit

---

[67]This is the advantage of true democracy over individual heroism.

[68]Consider the many famous and strong leaders of this kind in history who met with disaster.

can freely extend even beyond the six directions, and he can travel over the earth, unrestrained in coming and in going. This truly distinguishes a man from the majority and is the highest attainment of spiritually developed people.

The principle of integral nature taught by the great sage to all people is as a shadow is to form, as an echo to sound. He only responds when questioned, and then he makes himself a mirror and pours out all his thoughts to reflect the world back to you. He dwells in the realm of no preconceived answers, no attachment to any response and no image kept in his reflecting mind. He moves in no personal direction, subtly rescuing you from all your rushing back and forth. He continues to wander among people to break through their darkness of no spiritual light. He is the one who leads people to pass in and out of the boundless and to be as ageless as the sun.

His individuality or form is in concordance with that of ordinary people and thus he does not appear distinguished in any way. His true self blends with the Great Unity, which is selfless. Being selfless and without distinction, what is it that makes him distinguished from the majority?

Those who see what is to be seen are wise men. Those who see what is not able to be seen are companions of the universe.

CHAPTER THIRTY-SEVEN

THE ILLUSTRATION OF TAO

I

Pei Meung Ch'eng said to the Yellow Emperor, "When your Highness played the Han-ch'ih music in the forest near Lake Tung-T'ing, at first I was frightened. I listened some more and I relaxed. By the end, I was awed, speechless and overwhelmed. I even forgot the existence of the music and my life and the universe."

"Your description is close to the truth," replied the Yellow Emperor. "The first part was played through Man, tuned to Heaven, accomplished with ceremony and propriety and established in great purity.

"Music in its highest form, perfect music, first begins by adhering to a healthy human standard; then it moves with the pace of the divine, is harmonized to the flow of the universe, continues in accordance with the five virtues and then evolves into spontaneous expression. After that, the four seasons rise, one after the other, and the grandeur of harmony comes to all creation.

"The four seasons arise in sequence; all creation lives cyclically. For every flourishing there is a decline: spring and birth, summer and thriving growth, autumn and withdrawal, winter and death, these four all form a natural pulsation. First clear, then mixed, yin and yang fluctuate, the sounds flowing like light. Then came a rousing sound, like a thunderclap which startles the insect world. Continuing, there was no point which could be called the beginning or the end; living, sinking, rising, on and on, with no break. Such constancy is infinite, and so you became afraid.

"I continued playing, harmonizing yin and yang illuminated by the grandeur of the sun and moon. Although the sounds may be quick, lengthy, soft or loud, gentle or strong, the changes of tempo and volume are equal in importance, and since there is no climax to the music, it is infinite. It pervades the valley and the gorge. It closes the openings and shelters the inner gods, the spiritual agents of individual life. Adaptable to circumstance, its clear tones can be heard from immense distance. Therefore, the ghosts and gods keep maintaining and the sun, moon and stars continue in their orbits. When the melody exhausted itself, I stopped; if the melody continued, I went on playing. Thus the music was naturally what it was, independent of myself, the player.

"When you concern yourself about it, you are unable to understand it. Wishing to gaze upon it, you cannot see it. If you attempt to pursue it, it is impossible to catch it. Unconsciously, it abides in empty space everywhere. You stood dazed in the emptiness, leaning on a tree. When a body fills with empty space, it becomes joyful; with this joy, one is relaxed and refreshed.

"I played the last part with refreshed notes, attuned to the flow of spontaneity. Therefore, it seemed chaotic; arising in a mass, springing forth like a burst of water from the depths. It was deep, cloudy as though there were no sound. Beginning nowhere, the melody rested in emptiness; some would call it dead, others alive, some fact, others fancy. It meandered and twirled, shifting and moving in all the directions; constant yet changing.

"Confused and awed by it, people turn to the ones of wisdom, for the wise have a deep understanding of things and are themselves in harmony with eternal law. This is how the wise ones find joy in nature. When the physical mechanism is not entangled by extra force and is in its harmonious natural action with all vital organs complete, this is the music of Heaven. en.

"Being without words, it is a source of delight and refreshment for the mind. This is why the Lord of Yeng so exalted it: 'Listen, it has no sound. Look, it has no form. It fills Heaven and Earth and encompasses the six directions.' You wanted to hear it, but unable to comprehend its true existence, you became awed and overwhelmed.

"The music first caused fright which brought its corresponding element, respect.   Then it was played with gentle comfort that let you drop all worries.   And lastly, awe, which brings about an absence of sense and all thought vanishes.   An absence of sense and being without thought will deliberately bring you to Tao, the oneness of the original universal vitality, into which you can be absorbed."

II

At age fifty-one, the bright and respected Confucius had not yet learned Tao when he went south to P'ei to see Lao Tzu.

Lao Tzu said, "So you have come.   I hear that in the north you are considered a sage.   Have you reached Tao?"

"Not yet," responded Confucius.

"In what manner have you sought it?" asked Lao Tzu.

"I have spent five years," replied Confucius, "researching ancient social and governmental systems and cultural influences, but did not succeed."

"Where else did you look for it?" continued Lao Tzu.

"I spent twelve years," answered Confucius, "seeking it in the principle of the yin and yang, also without finding it."

"Of course," rejoined Lao Tzu. "If Tao could be presented, all people would present it to their leader. If Tao were something that could be offered, everybody would offer it to their parents.   If it could be told, everybody would immediately tell his brothers and sisters. If Tao could be given, everybody would give it to their sons and daughters.   This is impossible for the following reason.   Unless there is the suitable endowment within, Tao will not stay.   Unless there is outward correctness, Tao will not operate. If the external situation is unsuitable for the instruction of the internal, the truly achieved one does not seek to teach.   If the internal being is unfit for the reception of the external, the true student does not yet seek to receive.[69]

"Fame is easy to attract, but dangerous to oneself, so do not build it up. Kind help and social obligation are like way stations; you may stop there for one night, but to stay too long would only bring criticism, argument or trouble.[70] In ancient times, one of integral nature and virtue made kindness a path to be walked over and social obligation as a lodge to take shelter in, but neither were his true abode. He wandered in uncommittedness, ate in the plainness and simplicity of life, and strolled in the garden of no unfulfilled obligation or deficit. Free and relaxed, his home was spiritual inaction; plain and simple, it was easy for him to live. Having no unfulfilled obligation to others, he did not put anyone under obligation to him. Such a one lives with the grace of God.

"Whoever thinks that wealth is of ultimate importance can never give up money.[71] Whoever thinks distinction is of ultimate importance can never withdraw from fame. Whosoever takes a personal interest in power can never delegate it or bear to hand over authority to others. They are anxious while holding it, distressed if they might be losing it; they fail to take warning from the past and see the foolishness of their pursuits. Such men are punished by their own natures.

"Anger and kindness, taking and giving, scolding and instructing others, power of life and death - these eight are the means to attain righteousness and uprightness. Only one who can adapt himself to the changes of fortune without becoming stuck has the capacity to use them. It takes one who is correct

---

[69]The subtle essence of Tao is conveyed telepathically, so the master must be sure that the student's mind is prepared and ready to receive it before passing it to him.

[70]This also refers to public office.

[71]e.g. decline a position with a high salary or bear the loss of money.

himself to be able to correct others. To him whose heart is not cultivated in such a way, the door of divine wisdom will not open."

III
Confucius visited Lao Tzu and spoke of his ambition to make all people move in accordance with benevolence and social obligation.

Lao Tzu said, "The dust in a windstorm can so blind a man's eyes that Heaven, Earth and the four directions all seem to change places. Just as mosquitoes keep a man awake all night with their buzzing and biting, it is the same with any effort that externally demands that people become benevolent and righteous. The highest instruction is to guide the world back to its own original simplicity, and like the wind, move in freedom and naturalness, allowing virtue to establish itself. Why waste one's energy; such action is like searching for a fugitive while beating on a big drum!

"The snow goose remains white without taking a bath every day. The raven is black without having to dye itself. The original simplicity of black and white has no need for argument. One's great fame and the gathering of people's attention does not tell the true stature of a person. When a pond dries up and the fish are left on dry ground, wetting them with a little splash of water cannot be compared with having left them in their native rivers and lakes in the beginning."

IV
After he returned from his trip to see Lao Tzu, Confucius did not say a word for three days. A disciple finally asked him, "Teacher, when you visited Lao Tzu, in what direction did you persuade him?"

"It was not a matter of persuasion. When I saw Lao Tzu, I saw a dragon," replied Confucius; "a dragon, which when coiled shows his body in its perfection, and uncoiled displays his patterns in their perfection. Riding upon the clouds of Heaven, it is nourished by yin and yang. I just stood there looking in awe. Do you think I was going to persuade Lao Tzu in any direction?"

Upon this the disciple remarked, "So it is true; there really are those who dwell quietly, still as a corpse, and yet look like a dragon, and whose voices are like thunder and yet have the silence of deep pools? I, too, wish to meet him!"

V

On his next visit Confucius said to Lao Tzu, "I have been working with the six classics of *Poetry, History, Rites, Music, Changes,* and *Spring and Autumn.* I have spent a lot of time on them and know their contents well. I have traveled to see seventy-two different world leaders and presented each of them with discourses on the wisdom of the ancient sages and leaders as presented in those books. I have specially included material from the lives of Chou and Shao, who were the highly responsible and effective prime ministers of the early Chou Dynasty; yet not a single one of those seventy-two has in any way followed my advice. Is it that world leaders are so difficult to instruct, or is it just that wisdom cannot be presented clearly?"

"Luckily," replied Lao Tzu, "you did not come across any really wise leader of mankind. The six classics are only the footprints of ancient sages; they are not the true essence of their personal development. And what are footprints? They are something made by the foot; they are not the foot itself.

"Let us take a few examples. Two fish hawks gaze closely at each other without blinking, communicate, and their young are produced. The male of a certain insect chirps one way while the female chirps another way, and then their eggs are laid. And there is another animal which, being a hermaphrodite, is both male and female and reproduces itself. One's inborn nature cannot be changed, but it can be influenced; destiny cannot be changed or altered; time does not stop. The fundamental study is Tao. Tao, the subtle law, cannot be obstructed. Once you attain to Tao, everything goes

right.   Without it, like being on the wrong road, nothing goes right."

During three months following this visit, Confucius
did not once step out of his house.   Then he visited
Lao Tzu again and said, "I have it!   I have attained!
Birds lay eggs, fish swim, insects bite, and when a
younger brother is born, his big brother becomes jealous.   Every development proceeds according to certain
fixed laws.   It has been a long time since I have respected the natural subtle law that governs life.   If I
myself cannot follow this subtle law, how can I move
people in a direction that the laws of nature would
approve?   It is useless to try to use force to do anything.   Nature is ever a subtle doer."

Lao Tzu said, "Ch'iu, you are enlightened!"

VI

Confucius devoted his life to collecting the ancient
relics from different sources and compiling them into
six classics: *Ballads, History, Rites, Music,*[72] the *I Ching*[73]
and the *Book of Spring and Autumn.*

The latter volume was based on the major events
caused by the competitive feudal lords who no longer
accepted the leadership or control of the central government of the Chou Dynasty and describes the internal
changes within each individual state during the period
of 722-403 B.C.   In this influential history book, Confucius promotes the principle of supporting the central
government, the Chou Dynasty.   However, using his
standard, he established an historical misperception
because he failed to look at the reality of change.   He
judged the state governments and lords, praising some
and condemning others.   In other words, in this book,
Confucius tried to support the declining central government of the Chou dynasty by condemning the current
separating state governments.   He expected to see a

---

[72]This volume was lost.

[73]This is generally translated as the *Book of Changes.*

return to the glory and unity of the dynasty through convincing the states to conform to the present, but weakening, center.

Now, many years after he had written these books, being a renowned person with many followers, he wished to preserve all his work in the royal house of the central government of Chou. Tzu-lu, one of Confucius' disciples, told him, "I have heard that the chief of the Royal Historical Archives, the respectful Lao Tzu, is now retired and living at home. If you wish to place your work in the Archives, you might go to see him again. With his influence, after he sees your work, you may be able to achieve your purpose." It is not hard to understand that at that time, an ordinary person's work was very unlikely to get governmental recognition and protection.

"Excellent idea!" said Confucius, pleased at an opportunity to see Lao Tzu again. The next day, the two of them took the carriage and went to visit Lao Tzu. Lao Tzu seemed unimpressed with his work, so with the purpose of convincing him, Confucius unwrapped his twelve books, which included the Six Classics as well as his material for teaching the six arts of writing, driving, shooting, calculating, conducting ceremonies and performing music, and began expounding on them.[74]

After listening to Confucius, Lao Tzu nodded his head and said, "These books should be kept; but as for yourself, do away with your ambition. You cannot expect all generations to follow the same rite or one custom, especially if they are regulated by the official, imposing force of a government. I recommend that you study the cyclic law of nature as described in the *I Ching*. If you apply the objective knowledge from the *Book of Changes* to worldly matters, you will understand

---

[74]At that time, books were written on wooden or bamboo strips and bound by leather straps. A single book, therefore, would fill a large part of a carriage.

that it is necessary to be objective with regard to the changes. You see, the influence of the central power of society has declined. Your dream of returning to a powerful center shows that you have not objectively used the practical knowledge of the law of changes. Thus, the energy you have put into your writing will not bear correct fruit.

"In your *Book of Spring and Autumn,* you promote an artificial and unnatural morality.   Nothing in the world is forever strong enough to hold this big world together.   Everything must follow the law of natural rhythm, including any artificial establishment which was once strong and in control.   Artificial morality is fulfilled by external influence only when the influential factor is strong enough.   Natural morality is universal and is fulfilled without a command from anyone. This truth remains the same throughout the ages.

"A truthful historian is a student of history.   His sacred duty is to keep the record of facts and explain them without extending personal preference.   Learning the historical lessons for which people have paid dearly is valued as objective historical experience, and it is the compass for future generations to find their way."

Confucius bowed deeply and remained in quiet reflection, while his student Tzu-Lu went forward to see Lao Tzu.   After Tzu-Lu bowed to the master, Lao Tzu inquired, "Young man, what is your question?"

Tzu-Lu said, "The Three Great Ones[75] and the Five Virtuous Emperors[76] took care of the world and led people in different ways, though they were similar in receiving praise and acclaim from the people.   I am told, sir, that you do not agree about their greatness. May I ask why?"

"Young man, come closer.   What do you mean that they ruled in ways that differed?"

---

[75]Fu Shi, Shen Nung and the Yellow Emperor.

[76]Tchun Suh (2514-2358 B.C.), Ti Kau (2436-2366 B.C.), Yao (2354-2256 B.C.), Shun (2257-2208 B.C.) and Yu (2205-2297 B.C.)

"Yao turned over the throne to Shun," he answered, "and Shun gave it to Yu. Yu wore himself out in his duties. The leadership of the government of these three was recommended and selected by the previous emperors with the recognition of all people.

"T'ang, however, ended up going to war because the last emperor of the Shaw Dynasty[77] was corrupt. King Wen obeyed Emperor Jow, not daring to overthrow him, but his son King Wu turned against corrupted Jow[78] and refused to remain loyal because of the corruption. His revolution succeeded, and a new central government was established. Therefore I say that they were not the same. But they received the same support from all people as truly great leaders."

Lao Tzu said, "Young man, I will tell you how they influenced the world with their leadership.

"In ancient times, under the government of the Yellow Emperor, nothing was promoted that might disturb the hearts of the people. People remained with their nature. Thus, if people did not weep at their parents' death, no one saw anything wrong with it. In other words, people honored what was internal to a person and did not look for external displays.

"The government of Yao, led the hearts of the people to become affectionate. Therefore, according to the classes of relationship, if there were those among the people who decided to mourn for longer or shorter periods according to the degree of kinship to the deceased, the people saw nothing wrong in this. The sense of family became very strong. The meaning of life became narrowed by a preference for personal kinship.

"The government of Shun promoted the knowledge of right and wrong, causing rivalry among the hearts of the people. Therefore, the wives of the people

---

[77]2207-1707 B.C.

[78]The last emperor of the Sarng Dynasty which lasted from 1766 to 1121 B.C.

became pregnant and gave birth in the tenth month as always, but their children learned to talk much earlier than usual, and before becoming toddlers, they began to distinguish people. At that time, early death appeared. Unnatural rivalry caused people to develop exceedingly fast to cope with their living environment and thus, premature death appeared.

"The government of Yu promoted intelligence, causing the hearts of the people to change. People believed that each man had his own heart and that resorting to use of weapons was acceptable. Killing a thief was not murder because every man in the world must look after his own. This resulted in great disorder; many schools of thought and religious emphasis came forward, creating for the first time rules of unnatural ethical behavior.

"I have given you some examples of how the Three Great Ones and the Five Virtuous Emperors ruled the world. Only the earlier leaders can be considered truly great leaders who did not interfere in the lives of people. People at that time enjoyed the freedom of human life.

"The later rulers were worse. They made too many institutions which bound people, causing them to lose their freedom and accept the limits of their rulership. You may call it leadership, but their ruling, in fact, plunged the world into the worst confusion. The intelligence of those later rulers after the Three Great Ones blotted out the brightness of the sun and moon, sapped the vigor of hills and streams, and overturned the round of the four seasons. Their evil intelligence was more fearsome than the tail of the scorpion; down to the smallest creature, not a living thing was allowed to rest in the true form of its nature and fate. And yet, they considered themselves superior. Was it not incredible, their lack of shame?"

Upon hearing his, Tzu-Lu became totally aware that the rulers of the time of the Three Great Ones were truly sagacious leaders and the Five Virtuous Rulers were superior as leaders. The Five Virtuous Emperors in early ancient times, however, were responsible for making the people expect a good emperor and a good king, instead of respecting their own independence and freedom.

From the above story, let us review the timeless guidance that Lao Tzu pointed out 2,500 years ago. Confucius believed that the key to restoring the peaceful order of a society was to have all people and all feudal lords politically obey the leadership of the central government, the emperor. He cited the examples of the governments of the Three Great Ones and the Five Virtuous Emperors to support his theory. Lao Tzu did not agree with his theory that the peaceful order of society must rely on a strong and capable government. He agreed with Confucius that the ruling of the three great ones was truly great, because their rulership was non-disturbing to the people, and more like having a wise neighbor than a government. The Five Virtuous Emperors were capable in their time, gradually instituting and shaping the leadership of a complete monarch. They established a dualistic society: the rulers and the people. However, because they were responsible and earned the trust of people, slowly, people came to depend on the government and waited for the government to tell them what to do.

By writing *The Book of Spring and Autumn*, Confucius revealed his shallow understanding of human history; this was before he met Lao Tzu, who deepened Confucius' vision. Unfortunately, by this time, the influence of what Confucius had previously taught had already taken form in the thoughts of many people.

Lao Tzu's principle of the peaceful order of the world does not rely on a powerful or capable government. It depends on each person's spiritual maturity to enjoy their own peaceful nature. It is better to have people stay with their own peaceful nature than to have a powerful government impose a peaceful order on society. This springs from Lao Tzu's truthful knowledge which came from long years of experience gathered before written history appeared. Thus Lao Tzu's teaching and writing have his historical perspective, so he did not think the key that Confucius held was correct.

This describes the main difference, therefore, of the influence in Chinese history between Lao Tzu's teaching and Confucius' teaching. Confucianism worked for the government to obey the emperor whether he was virtuous or evil, right or wrong. Confucius' theory supported the monarchial system until the early part of the twentieth century. Although its form had changed, the monarchial influence still existed in the 1970s. However, through the personal will of the rulers, millions of people lost their lives because their thought was considered different from the positions of the strong rulers.

The followers of Lao Tzu's philosophy, the so-called Taoists, remained in civilian life, working among people to improve Chinese practical life, as, for example, by the practice of holistic Chinese medicine. From thousands of years of evidence, Lao Tzu's deep vision and foresight deserves our great respect and the willingness to continue this effort. Improving our own spiritual situation and that of other people is the only possible solution for a peaceful and healthy human society. Lao Tzu does not set up hope that any external authority can achieve that purpose, nor does he trust that external religion can further this goal. He advised the direct spiritual cultivation of each individual self. He taught that spiritual unity can be reached first by individual spiritual development; that is, first attain unity within, then universal spiritual unity can be achieved externally.

After internal spiritual self-sufficiency is reached through each individual's spiritual cultivation, then, self-contentment - with a foundation of a good practical life - will bring about true joy in living. Material abundance alone cannot achieve the completeness of life. Without achieving spiritual sufficiency, the aggressive hand of human desire will continue to destroy whatever good order has been set externally.

It was too late for Confucius to take back his teaching. His image was used to support the strong monarchial systems generation after generation in China. Unfortunately, there were only a few individuals who truly understood the Taoist teachings and its theme of the spiritual development of each individual. Politically, it has never agreed with monarchial rule. According to Lao Tzu, it is natural virtue that government serve the people, instead of making people serve the government. People are the center, the main body of human society, not the government and rulers. This natural position has been usurped. It is an artificial morality which makes all people obey the king or the persecuting party; it is natural true morality when the leaders obey their own natural virtue rather than ride on the shoulders of their people. A government is composed of people; unless all people become spiritually achieved, neither worldly peace nor harmonious progress can be made!

Q: In the second section of this chapter, it says that Tao cannot be given. Yet, it is explained that the teacher presents it to the mind of the student. How can this be?

Master Ni: This means that Tao is not something tangible that can be passed around. It is the mind after developing its comprehension; then enlightenment can reach it, even in the daily ordinary matters.

CHAPTER THIRTY-EIGHT

THE LEARNING OF TAO

I
Innate Human Love

Chuang Tzu says: He who holds to true rightness does not lose his original inborn nature, which is Tao. He who would attain the perfection of non-deviation from nature should never lose sight of the natural conditions of his existence. For him what is joined is not united, and what is separated is not apart; what is long is not in excess, and what is short does not lack anything. Just as a duck's legs, though short, cannot be lengthened without causing agony to the duck, nor a crane's legs, though long, shortened without bringing distress to the crane, that which is long in the nature of humankind cannot be cut short nor that which is short be made long. There is no reason to be distressed over this.

Forced benevolence of heart and forced social obligation are surely not part of our true nature. Just think of the distress they must cause the one who practices such unnatural behavior.

Heaven and Earth continue in their constancy, the sun and moon illuminate with their brightness, the stars and planets rest in their orbits, the birds and beasts keep to their flocks, and trees and shrubs hold firmly to their patch of ground. One has only to go along with virtue in one's actions, to follow the truth of nature in one's journey and one is already there. To be glad and joyful; to embrace universal love and be impartial - this is the true form of human love and righteousness. Why raise the banners of human love and righteousness as though you were beating a drum and searching for a lost treasure? You will only confuse yourself.

II
True Sages Are Hard To Recognize

Shih Ch'eng Ch'i visited Lao Tzu and addressed him thus: "Having heard, sir, that you are a man of natural wisdom, I gave no importance to time and distance to come and visit you. During the hundred days of my journey, the soles of my feet grew thick with calluses, but I did not delay in coming. I have found upon arriving, however, that you are not a man of natural wisdom. While rats feasted on your leftover rice, you turned your sister out of the house, and though you have no lack of food, both raw and cooked, you continue to pile up and amass more material goods."

Lao Tzu remained silent and did not respond. The next day Shih Ch'eng Ch'i came again and said, "Yesterday I was rude to you. Today I do not understand why."

Lao Tzu replied, "I make no claims of possessing either the skill of cunning nor heavenly wisdom. Had you called me an ox yesterday, I would have considered myself an ox. Had you called me a horse, I would have considered myself a horse.

"If men classify you truthfully and you reject their classification, you only double the reproach. My humility is natural humility, not humility for humility's sake. I always dress the same. I am opposed to changing outfits."

Shih Ch'eng Ch'i stepped back in respect. Then he stepped forward, also with respect, and said, "I would like to request your instruction for self-cultivation."

Lao Tzu said, "Your face is mean, your eyes angry, your mouth gaping, and your bearing is haughty and self-satisfied. You look like a man riding a tethered horse; his body is there, but his mind is elsewhere. Painstakingly checking everything over, you think plotting and planning is wisdom, and you make a show of superiority. This type of behavior causes others to mistrust and fear you. In certain areas of the country, any person who acted in such a way would be immediately regarded as a thief!"

III

Lao Tzu said, "Tao exists in all things both large and small; from this comes the wholeness of natural creation. How vast is Tao! There is nothing that it does not embrace. How deep! It is unfathomable.

"Form, virtue, benevolence and social duty are correct, but are only trifles compared to the spirit. Who, except a person of integral nature and virtue can know and strengthen these things? The world of an integral being is vast, yet it never enmeshes or entangles him in difficulty, because he does not participate in the competition for power. He sees clearly into what has no falsehood and is unswayed by all thought of gain. Having brought to a peak all that is true in himself, he confines himself to essentials, to fundamentals, to the source. He thus places his own considerations outside of worldly concerns and keeps himself beyond the competition of all creation; here his soul is carefree, in consonance with Tao and in harmony with natural virtue. He is above all artifice. He is one who is real, thus he can put himself outside conceptual divergence and not interact with things that are wearisome. Being thus free from unnatural competition, he maintains his integral nature and does not suffer from the fragmented cultures and religions of the world. His inner gods are never disharmonious, because he is one with the truth of natural universal life.

IV
Books May Give an Example,
But You Need to Grow Yourself

"Some books are what the world values as truth, but books are only words. The valuable part of words is the thought they convey. Thought contains something which cannot be conveyed in words, yet the world values words as the essence of books. Though the world values them and assigns them a price, yet the way in which the world values them is not the sense in which their true value exists.

"That which the eye can see is form and color. That which the ear can hear is sound and noise. Unrealistically, people of this generation think that form and color and sound and noise are the way to know the essence of Tao. Yet that is not the Way. Those who are wise do not speak, and those who speak are not wise. The world can only obtain true knowledge from that which cannot be seen or heard or spoken.

V

One day, Duke Huan was reading in his palace when a wheelwright who was working nearby put down his hammer and chisel and, mounting the steps, said, "Whose words is Your Highness studying?"

"I am studying the teachings of the sages," replied the Duke.

"Are these sages still living?" asked the wheelwright.

"No," answered the Duke, "they have died."

"Then the words Your Highness is studying are only the chaff and dregs of the ancients," rejoined the wheelwright.

"No common person has permission to comment on what I do or what I read," exclaimed the Duke. "Explain yourself or you shall die!"

"Let me take an example from my own trade," said the wheelwright. "In constructing a wheel, if you work too slowly, it will not be properly shaped. If you go too fast, the spokes do not fit well. You must go the correct speed. If you use the mallet too gently, the chisel will slide instead of catching the wood, but if you use it too forcefully, it digs in tightly and will not move like it should. You must do it neither too gently nor too hard, and there must be harmony between the mind and hand. Words cannot explain this skill; the way to do it is certainly an art. This is not something that I can teach or give to my son; it is not something that can be learned from talking about it. So now for seventy years I have been chiseling and continue still.

"So therefore, the words you are reading there must be the chaff. When old men died, they left behind

what they did not need. The way I see it, books alone
are not all the learning!"

VI

An ancient achieved one attained spiritual centeredness. He recognized no beginning, no end, no number
and no time. Because he changed each day to harmonize with all things, he was utterly unchanging, so
at no time did he ever part from his inner nature.

Anyone who ambitiously tries to learn from nature
will never learn well; he will end up in a blind alley
and become a victim of his own fantasy. How can he
then attain harmony with all things?

A true one achieves the different existences of Heaven and Man. He pays no attention to the beginnings
or externals. He harmonizes with his generation and
so does not bring trouble to himself. He takes things
as they come and is never blocked in his forward
movement. How can we become like him?

A wise student who follows his teachings is not
confined by them; thus he can complete his endeavors.
He receives no title, but he knows that chasing or
intentionally attracting fame is a violation of one's
self-nature and leads one into the realm of alternatives
instead of into constancy and perpetual peace.

An achieved student said, "Be done with schemes,
plotting and planning; then you will be able to help
yourself and nourish your nature."

Another achieved student said, "If there were no
days, then there would be no years. With no inside,
there is no outside." To forget one's ego is to forget
the trouble of the world.

VII

In the stage when matter did not exist, and when
nothing was added to the only existent single unique
energy, this is the stage of pre-Heaven, of Indistinguishable Oneness, of the unmanifest Subtle Origin.

At the stage when the "involution of unified one
energy into form" takes place, matter occurs; matter is
unconditioned and has no artificial description or

boundaries. This is the stage of after-Heaven and involves the subtle law of Yin and Yang. All of creation is ordered and harmonized, admitting the existence of separate entities but maintaining no conditions of right and wrong.

"In the third stage, matter became conditioned, but opposites were still unknown. It was when the partiality and preference of the human mind appeared that the sense of integralness began to decline. With the decline of the sense of integralness, individual bias arose; boundaries were recognized; right and wrong were decided according to individual bias. The individual's integral spirit was severed, and the poison of emotional bias became the root of all motivation. This stage in the growth of human intellect saw the birth of antagonism, confrontation, preference, separation and disharmony.

"Do the states of rising and falling truly exist? Labeling things as right or wrong weakens one's integral nature, but in weakening the integral spirit, do such preferences actually exist or not? If they do, then the result is heard in the perfection of Chao Wen's lute playing.[79] Without these preferences, we would not have such perfection.

"During the time of Chao Wen's lute playing and Master K'uang's rhythmic drum,[80] music was an expression of universal harmony and sublimity. It was not rooted in emotional or physical stimulation. The inspiration and direction of human intelligence has changed now, and the focus and direction of creativity have diverged from the inspiration and experience of nature as an integral whole. The influence of these Masters has lasted and will still be popular in later ages, even though human intelligence will be inspired and led in a different direction from true spiritual

---

[79]Chao Wen was a famous ancient master of music who lived 2800 years ago.

[80]Master K'uang was another master of music at that time.

achievement and the integral truth of universal life. When people develop ideals and ideologies that are confusing, they dedicate their lives to confirming opposition to "hard and white," which makes no positive contribution to human life. With the emergence of such a philosophy, the ancient spiritual knowledge of wholeness began to dissipate. Subsequently, sons devoted their lives to understanding the philosophies of their fathers, but were never truly benefited by them.

"One of integral truth aims at the light which brightens the darkness, not the torch of chaos and doubt. One of integral truth accepts things as they are even if, to the ordinary person attempting to establish values, they appear chaotic and doubtful and in need of clarification. In other words, he does not take a subjective view only, but understands the position of the opposite side as well. This is called using the light. It is not to say he does not use things, but that he relegates all to what is constant. This is what it means to use clarity.

"What remains are words and speech. Do they fit into either category of opposites? Regardless of whether they fit or not, they will polarize to one or the other and will thus seem as though they existed of themselves. It would be gratifying to hear speech without such category.

"If there was a beginning, then there was a time before such a beginning, and thus a time before the time of the beginning.

"If there is existence, there must also be non-existence, and if there was a time before existence, then there must have been a time before the time of existence. So when non-existence came into existence, would it have belonged to the category of existence or that of non-existence? I do not even know whether the words I have just spoken have actually been spoken or not. The existence of all contraries is man-made.[81]

---

[81]Chuang Tzu regrets all philosophizing.

TAO OF WELLNESS STORE

13315 WEST WASHINGTON BLVD., SUITE 200

LOS ANGELES, CA 90066

PLACE
STAMP
HERE

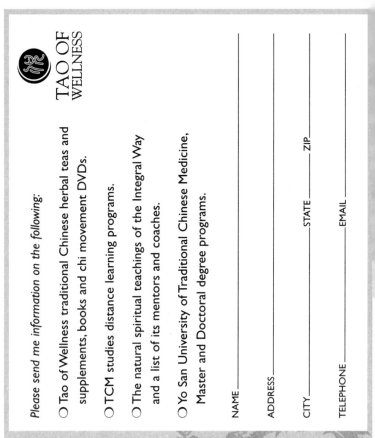

Please send me information on the following:

○ Tao of Wellness traditional Chinese herbal teas and supplements, books and chi movement DVDs.

○ TCM studies distance learning programs.

○ The natural spiritual teachings of the Integral Way and a list of its mentors and coaches.

○ Yo San University of Traditional Chinese Medicine, Master and Doctoral degree programs.

NAME _____

ADDRESS _____

CITY _____ STATE _____ ZIP _____

TELEPHONE _____ EMAIL _____

TAO OF WELLNESS

"Thus, there is nothing under Heaven greater than the very tip of autumn goose down. A vast mountain is the smallest of things. No age is greater than that of a child who dies in infancy. P'eng Tzu lived to be eight-hundred and he died young. The universe and I arose at the same time; thus, I am one with all that it contains.

"If all things are one, why have words? If all is one, how can there be any discussion about existence and non-existence?[82]

If we go on splitting, diverging, multiplying, even the cleverest mathematician won't be able to clearly distinguish where a number ends up, much less an ordinary man whose conceptual mind is active. The thought that all things share one life establishes one thought; the person having such a thought establishes two; and the objective reality becomes three.[83]

To engage in splitting, divergence and endless multiplication is to depart from Tao, the truth of universal integrity and the integrity of universal essence. To avoid such progression, you must put yourself into subjective relation with the external.

---

[82]The conceptual function of the mind muddies one's personal spiritual unity. Its attitude is that the universe lives through 'me,' and all things share one life with me. If this is actually attained, life is a matter of positive realization. There should not be anything to escape, yet human thought cannot conduct conceptual escape by causing weakness. For example, one universal life is the high truth. Everyone does share life with everyone else in the deepest sense. Spiritually, it is a matter of realizing this in a positive way.

[83]This is to say, what is spiritual and what is conceptual are two separate categories. They should not be confused with each other. If the conceptual faculty is applied to spiritual reality, it weakens one's spiritual sensitivity and directness of vision. People then degrade their own spiritual capability by substituting false conceptual creations for spiritual truth. This has been the great mistake of most people, including many spiritual leaders of the past and present.

"Before conditions came into being, Tao was. Before the existence of definitions, there was speech. Tao has never been located, and words have never enjoyed constancy. Words divide things between right and left, relationship and obligation, discrimination and acceptance, emulation and contention. These are called the Eight Categories. They apply only to the material sphere, not to the completeness of integral being.

"For one of integral truth who lives beyond the limits of the external world of phenomena, the Eight Categories exist, but are not recognized. One of integral truth is recognized within the limits of the external world, but is not limited. One of integral truth describes the wisdom of the ancient ones, but does not justify by argument. Thus, classifying, he does not classify. Arguing, he does not argue. One of integral truth keeps his knowledge within, while ordinary men set theirs forth in argument in order to convince each other. Therefore, it is said that in argument the integral one does not manifest himself. Others try to establish their own subjective view. The integral one embraces things; ordinary men discriminate among them and then parade their discriminations before others. Those who discriminate fail to see.

Because the one who has achieved spiritual integralness knows that all things exist both objectively and subjectively, but it is impossible to start from the objective. Only from subjective knowledge is it possible to proceed to objective knowledge. The objective, therefore, emanates from the subjective, and the subjective is dependent on the objective. When there is birth, there must be death. Where there is death, there must be birth. Where there is acceptability, there must be unacceptability. Where there is recognition of right, there must be recognition of wrong. When one is possible, the other is impossible. When one is affirmative, the other is negative.

"In as much as we think the opposite side is wrong, the opposite side thinks we are wrong. The opposite side can think what is right or wrong, and it is the same with us. But is the opposite side truly right or truly wrong? On this point there is actually no difference between our side and the opposite side. If you can see that there is no true confrontation at the heart of a situation, you have reached the spiritual point of learning the integral truth. One of natural wisdom does not insist on the constant alternation of yin and yang. He illuminates all people with the light of the integral truth. A state in which subjective and objective no longer find their opposites is called "the hinge of the Way," or the pivotal point. When the hinge fits into its socket, it can respond endlessly. Its "right" can then be endlessly expanded and its "wrong" can endlessly extend in the opposite direction.

"As what is subjective is also objective, and the objective is also subjective and each is indistinguishably blended with the other, does it not then become impossible to say whether either of them really exists at all? Without correlating positives and negatives, subjective and objective are united as the very axis of the integral truth of Tao. When that axis has passed through the center at which all infinities converge, positive and negative alike blend into the infinity of Oneness. Hence it has been said that there is nothing like the light of universal integral nature. As Lao Tzu said: the one who argues does not know the Integral Truth; the one who does not argue knows the Integral Truth.

BALANCE IN LIFE

I
The Fountain of Life

Two friends were having a discussion. Ambitious and Never Content said to One of Natural Harmony, "Never has there existed a human being who has not promoted his own fame and sought his own wealth and advantage. You see, the reason for this is that if a man is rich, others gather around him. If they gather around him, they become subordinate to him. If they are subordinate to him, they honor him. Everyone knows that to have others working for you and honoring you is the way to enjoy the greatest security, comfort and general happiness for your entire life.

"How is it, then, that you, my friend, have no inclination toward these things? Is it that you are not smart enough or is it that you are unable to do it and therefore go for being spiritual and virtuous, though in the back of your mind you are still remembering renown and comfort?"

His friend replied, "I hope that even those like you who are determined to succeed in life still notice that there are those who live life in an extraordinary way. They maintain a set of guiding principles to examine the past and present and hold standards for making clear what is right and wrong. They are noted for the naturalness and correctness of their behavior and speech.

"But it seems that the people you generally respect and praise are people of the world who change as the world changes, discarding what is most valuable, and abandoning what is most worthy of honor. They live very mundane lives, thinking that there is something that has to be done, and declaring that this is the way to insure long life, comfort and happiness.

"In admiring the latter, you have missed what is most important in life by far. The disturbances of sadness and anguish, excitement and gaiety are of no help to the body. The strain of worry and terror, the euphoria of happiness and triumph do not help one to become enlightened. By acting with involvement instead of disinterest, all these difficulties are visited upon you. Therefore, even if you received the total honor paid to an emperor and possessed all the wealth in the empire, you would not escape disaster."

Ambitious and Never Content replied, "Riches are of the greatest use to man. It takes him to the ultimate beauty and the greatest power, things which a virtuous one or sage could never acquire. With wealth, a person can avail himself of the courage and strength of other people and to make himself fully potent. He can apply the wisdom and advice of other people to add precision and timing to his own decisions. He can appear virtuous because he is supported by other people's virtue. Without sitting on a throne, he still has power and authority over the world.

"You know, music, beauty, rich food, power and other pleasures do not require study before they can be enjoyed by a person's mind and body. No one needs a teacher for instruction on what he likes and what he deplores, what to seek or what to avoid. It is instinctive in every person. Why would anyone give up what he liked or wished to follow?"

"A man of true wisdom," replied the One who Values Natural Harmony, "acts for the sake of others and does not overstep certain bounds. If he has enough, he does not try to obtain more, because he has no use for more. If there is not enough, however, then he seeks what is needed, striving but not considering himself greedy. If there is a surplus, he might give it away. He could refuse the whole world and not think himself as great or as a highly virtuous individual. To him, neither greed nor virtue have anything to do with standards imposed on him from outside, but represent a turning within to observe what is internal to himself. He may be given the power of a worldly throne, but

will never use it to degrade or lower others. He may
be given control over the wealth of the whole world,
yet he will not use it to take advantage of his fellow
man.   By calculating risk, trouble and anxiety and
considering what may be contrary and harmful to his
inborn nature, he may decline something that is offered
to him, but not out of a desire to become famous for
his decision.

"When the wise Yao and the kind Shun occupied
the throne, peace lasted. They did not try to be great
nor did they allow the position to harm their existence.
They were natural, that is all.   The ancient hermits
Shan Chuan and Hsu Yu both declined the throne
when it was offered them.   Their refusal was not,
however, an empty gesture; they did so in order not to
bring harm to themselves.

"In all these cases, each individual adopted the
beneficial course instead of the harmful one, and the
world calls them virtuous and great.   They may enjoy
such renown, but none of them were striving for a
reputation."

Ambitious and Never Content said, "But in order to
have a reputation like theirs, does a person need to
punish his body, depriving oneself of its sweetness and
pleasures?   To live like this would be equivalent to
being a sick man who lives in trouble and can never
enjoy himself."

"True happiness or serenity," replied the One who
Values Natural Harmony, "is to be found in balance.
Too much or too little of anything can cause a problem. One can look to be wealthy - it is all right - but
not to be overly possessive.   The ears of a man of
great possession resound with the melodies of sweet
music and his mouth is stuffed with rich food and
wine.   However, in the pursuit of pleasure, he forgets
his business, he forgets what he ought to care about,
and he forgets what is more important in life. This is
called confusion.

"The man of great possession eats rich food and
drinks fine wine until his breathing is as heavy as that
of someone carrying a heavy load uphill. This is what

is called misery.

"In his craving for riches, he overtaxes his body and mind. In his desire for power, he drives himself into a frenzy. In his use of comfort, he becomes weak. This is called illness.

"Even after he has accumulated enormous quantities of goods and money, because of his habit of desire for wealth, he continues on and cannot stop. This is called disgrace.

"Yet, although having no use for all the money he has collected, he would not stand for any loss. This is called unhappiness.

"At home he is in terror of the pilfering thief: abroad, always wary of the bandit or mugger. He is forever on edge at home and never ventures out alone. This is fear.

"The six dangers of fear, unhappiness, disgrace, illness, misery and confusion are the greatest of the world's harms, yet such a man never considers them until after the hour of misfortune has arrived. His reputation vanishes; although his ambitions were gratified, his natural powers are now exhausted and nothing but the possessed shell of wealth remains and disaster comes. Though he seeks his inborn nature with everything he has and exhausts his wealth in hopes of returning even for one day to untroubled times, he cannot.

"Therefore, he who looks for fame will find that it is nowhere to be seen. He who desires gain will find that it is not to be had. To entrap oneself and spend one's life pursuing them, is this not foolish?

"One who abides with the natural truth of life, when in hardship, is able to forget his poverty. When affluent, he is able to forget his high position and wealth and does things humbly. He goes along with healthy situations and is merry. He remains calm and unattached. He finds happiness in the progress of other people, all the while remaining firmly in his true self. Thus, although he is silent, he can promote peace, and by his presence people may come to trust each other as father and son. From his passivity comes an active influence for good. Thus does he differ from an intellectual.

"The one who abides with the natural truth of life understands that the universe is one single body. All things are one to him. It is his inborn nature to penetrate to the center of a complication and round it out. Whether or not he takes action, he remains the same. He makes nature his teacher, and men make him their teacher.

"The intellect is a great worrier. One who abides with the natural truth, however, instead of worrying, knows how to take effective action immediately.

"For a beautiful woman, other people are the mirror in which she sees herself. If no one tells her she is beautiful, she does not know it, but whether she knows it or not, her delightfully good looks remain the same, and other people do not stop taking pleasure in her beauty. This is the nature of things.

"The love of a person of natural truth for his fellows likewise finds expression among mankind. If nobody told him that he were a loving person, he would not know that he loved others. But whether he knows it or not, whether he hears it or not, his love for his fellow man is without end, and mankind finds great security in it. This is also the nature of things.

"The old country and one's old home are wonderful sights to a traveler's eyes. Even if most of it is a scorching desert or a wild tundra, his eye will still be glad. How much more, then, is the gladness that comes from hearing the teaching of Tao after much longing and finding the truth after many lifetimes of searching. How much greater, then, is the joy of the soul upon rediscovering one's true nature after a long time of self-cultivation. Neither one's true nature nor the great path of Tao look to be adored as though they were a high peak towering in the midst of the mountains and oceans of people, inviting admiration and devotion. Instead, wearing plain clothes, working and living among the mountains and oceans of people, those following this path of life never raise themselves up high to invite admiration, because they have reached something that is unseen, unheard and untouched by many others.

II
Examples of Independence

When Po-li Hsi was having a hard time he did not let low wages or inferior position enter his mind to build up walls of self-pity. He fed the cattle, and the cattle grew fat. This made Duke Mu of Ch'in marvel at Po-li's spirit, and he turned the government over to him, despite his lowly position.[84]

Shun never allowed thoughts of life and death to disturb his mind. By maintaining a healthy spirit he had the ability to influence others. Although Shun's parents and brother repeatedly attempted to kill him, he was steady with regards to behaving in a filial manner, and is thus a good example of maintaining balance in a negative situation.

Hunchback Su's chin was close to his navel, and his shoulders were higher than the top of his head. His head was a bit twisted so that his braided hair pointed skyward, his five vital organs were upside down, and his two thighs were thin like ribs. He earned enough to eat by taking in sewing and laundry. By winnowing and sifting grain, his earnings would have been enough to feed a family of ten. When the sovereign summoned warriors to defend the security of the state, the hunchback was ready to go while many men of strength and good health wished to shun this social obligation. But Su could not be of use in the army, nor could he be assigned a job when large public works were undertaken. Yet, when distributions were made to the ill, he refused the ten bushels of grain and ten bundles of wood that were offered him. This

---

[84]Po-li Hsi was a statesman of the seventh century B.C. and was taken captive when his state was overthrown. For a time, he led the life of a cowherd, but his worth was eventually recognized by Duke Mu of Ch'in, who made him Prime Minister.

hunchback could support himself and stand sturdily as
an excellent independent man and enjoy his full span
of years, while many normal people deform themselves
morally and mentally by their own actions. From him,
we find a good example of inner strength truly being
able to balance external weakness.

When the Main Commander Kung-wen Hsuan, who
was the general of the right, saw his new assistant
commander, the general of the left, control his chariot
skillfully, he was startled and said, "What kind of man
might this be? How did you come to be without a
foot? Did it come from birth or was it caused by
man?"[85]
"It was natural; it was not caused by any man,"
replied the general, remaining in the Commander's
confidence and maintaining his own confidence equal
to that of any person with a complete body. "Though
nature has given me only one foot, I make full use of
it. I feel I am still as complete as anyone else born of
nature."
This made Commander Kung-wen Hsun thoughtful,
because there are many people who are physically
complete but who become full of self-pity when their
mood changes; such people never fully enjoy their own
nature. This one-footed person enjoyed himself more
than those who were in one piece and had inflicted
mutilating punishments on themselves, unpunished by
either Heaven or man.

The swamp pheasant sometimes must go ten paces
for a peck and a hundred steps for a single drink, but
even so it would rather do that than be in a cage.
Caged, even though you treat it with great kindness, it
still misses nature. Most people do not know that they
are caged by the institutionalized society and the
artificial world. They lose their natures and are not

---

[85]In ancient China, the punishment for murder was to amputate
one foot.

content with the life of the natural world. Their spirits become low and they become like the caged swamp pheasant without even knowing it.

Thus we see the importance of spiritual cultivation. It is to keep one from being caged in artificial society or one's own delusions about oneself. We should learn from good examples to develop a strong inner being to balance external defects. Such people had no delusions about themselves or life. Be like the swamp pheasant who wished to return to its true nature.

III
The Truthful Knowledge of Life

Duke Huan was out hunting in the fields with Kuan Chung driving his carriage, when he saw a ghost.[86]

The duke grabbed Kuan Chung by the hand and gasped, "Kuan Chung, what do you see?"

"Nothing," replied Kuan Chung.

When the Duke got home, he became ill and did not go out of the house for several days.

A gentleman of Ch'i named Huang-tzu Kao-ao, a man of natural development, came to see him and said, "Your Grace is worrying for nothing. How could any ghost have had the power to harm you? This could not cause you to become ill.

"If a man's vital breath becomes scattered and does not return, then he suffers a deficiency of spiritual essence. If it rises and fails to descend, he becomes to be moody, irritable and easily angered. If it descends and fails to rise, he suffers from forgetfulness. If it neither rises nor descends, but is stagnant in the middle of the body near the heart, then he becomes ill."

The duke said, "Do ghosts exist?"

"They might. But in your case, something else is

---

[86]It was a delusion. A man in a high position who has too much wine, too much sex, too much tension and who does many things against his own nature weakens his spiritual energy. Thus he becomes negative and suspicious, and his vision becomes distorted.

more important. To nourish one's life, the first principle of importance is to maintain your heart and mind in peaceful union. If this union is disturbed, the result is mental and spiritual disease. The second important principle is to nurture the vital energy of the body by rectifying the mind. To nurture the mind by maintaining it in peace is to nurture the vitality of the whole life being. Let this be good advice to you in recovering from this illness and in your daily life. Then you will not see any more illusions."

The Duke said, "In my case, I do not consider my vitality weak. It was what I clearly saw. The ghost must really exist. Do you believe that ghosts exist?"

At this moment, Huang-Tzu totally understood his client's characteristics, so he said, "Indeed, they do exist. In deep water there are some called lih, the delusion of darkness in the deep water. The ones that exist in stoves are called tchi, the delusion of the transforming fire. In the heap of trash just inside the farmers' barn is where the one called Lei-t'ing lives; the harmful vapors are what forms his figure. In the northeast corner the ones called Pei-a and Kuie-lung jump around, and in the northwest corner is where I-yang sleeps. In the well is Kang-hsiang. In the hills live the kind called Hsin. In the mountains lives K'uei, and in the marshes lives P'ang-huang. If you go to the fields, you will see the kind called Wei-t'o.[87] He may have been the one you saw.

The Duke requested, "What does a Wei-t'o look like?"

Huang-tzu answered, "It is as big as a the hub of a wheel, tall as a house and wears a purple robe with a red cap. It is very ugly. When it hears thunder or the sound of an approaching carriage, it jumps up with a start. Anyone who sees it will become a powerful

---

[87]The word 'Wei-ser,' when pronounced correctly in Chinese, means 'disfigured snake.' Huang Tzu is deliberately saying the word differently, as 'Wei-t'o,' so that the meaning of his communication to the Duke is not too direct.

king, the leader of all other kingdoms."

The Duke's face brightened, and he said, gladdened, "That must have been what I saw!" Then he straightened out his clothes and sat up. Before the day was over, his illness had gone away.

It was the ambition and desire of the duke to be the strong king reigning over all the lords which caused him to see a ghost. The image of the ghost was his own projection, an image shaped within himself over a long period of time. Duke Huan of Ch'i became the first one of the many dictators who emerged after the central government, the Chou Dynasty became weakened in influence. Duke Huan imposed his will upon the other feudal lords in 679 B.C., and he truly became a political monster. His real disease was the monstrousness of his political ambition.

Generally, healthy people do not see visions. If a vision is seen, it is the reflected spiritual image of the person himself. You see, spiritually we shape ourselves by each thought we think; our thoughts manifest in the subtle sphere of our life energy. It is dangerous to shape ourselves wrongly. Spiritually, a low character of spiritual undevelopment would see a monster.

Since the publication of the work of Chuang Tzu, we find many idioms in the Chinese language which come from his book. It has become a common expression to call one who uses a superficial and untruthful approach with someone as 'playing Wei-t'o.' Spiritually undeveloped people are often dictators in their nature; by being self-righteous, they will not listen to anybody else. They extend their friendship to people untruthfully and play Wei-t'o with them; this occurs among friends and other harmonious relationships and even between husbands and wives and family members. This is partly why the world situation has not made any big changes spiritually although material life has improved; perhaps it has only improved the capability to create more monsters.

The book written by Chuang Tzu is a great book.

It has very much influenced Chinese literature. His real teaching bears a simplicity and eloquence in the original writing, which was crafted in such a way as to mask the contents so that it could be preserved. It was kept out of the main stream of thought and out of the destructive hands of monarchial governments over the generations. There are a few spiritual heirs who live as recluses and do not like to play Wei-t'o with the dreamy dictators. Those spiritual heirs have passed down the meaning of the book. This is why in the teaching of this tradition of truth, the first discipline is to stop playing Wei-t'o to anyone on important occasions, because almost all the people of the world have become Wei-t'o.

The amiable Chinese majority played Wei-t'o with Mao Tse Tung, but finally they were slaughtered by his dictatorship which surpassed all dictators within China as well as abroad. At least six million people had their life taken by playing the game of Wei-t'o with him at the beginning. This time these games did not work, though it had worked in other generations when it was played with other dictators and the people's lives were spared. In his own poems, he expressed his enjoyment and satisfaction with his dictatorial achievement, which was far greater than that of the famous successful dictators, the first emperor of Chin,[88] Emperor Wu of the Han Dynasty[89] and all others. This gives you an idea of what his soul was like and the extent of his sickness!

---

[88]246-209 B.C.

[89]140-86 B.C.

CHAPTER FORTY

BE DETERMINED IN SELF-CULTIVATION

I

Self-assured and conceited, willfully constrained, arrogant in action, isolated from the rest of the world and its customs, elevated in speech, sullen and critical, preoccupied with indignation - such is the life of the cynic or scholar, worn and haggard, whose heart is closed and who lives in his mountain valley and means to end it all.

Benevolence, social obligation, loyalty, truth, respect, economy and humility all being preached - such is the matter of religious culture that has been created by social programmers, teachers, some scholars and missionaries. Because their faith is only conceptual in nature and lacks true application in everyday life, social problems have increased.

Talk of their wonderful accomplishments, winning fame, moves and countermoves, setting superiors and inferiors straight - such are favorite pastimes of court scholars, party men and patriots who hunger to extend the boundaries of their own influence and stir up the conflict with others.

Living in the wilds and idly passing the days in personal enjoyment is mere reaction - such is the indulgence of those who turn their backs upon the world and flee their generation.

To exhale from different organs, cleansing the old and inhaling the new, to move like a bear and stretch like a bird - these are the activities of those who conduct the breath throughout their bodies, who practice stretching exercises, develop their physiques and seek longevity without working for their spiritual growth and the fulfillment of their moral obligations. These are still incomplete practices in the tradition of Tao.

When the aim is that of establishing a balanced integral being, individual longevity becomes a side-effect of the practice of Tao.

If one is interested in higher things in life, but not in abusing the mind; in improvement, but not in standards of righteousness and etiquette ; in orderliness, but not in notable deeds or fame; in enjoying one's leisure time, but not in lounging by rivers and beaches; in longevity, but not in breathing and stretching exercises - then nothing will be disregarded, and one will have everything one needs.

When a person has reached the freedom of infinity, good things come along. This is the way of nature. This is why it is said, "Calmness, simplicity, silence[90] and spiritual inaction constitute the balance of nature and the virtue which realizes Tao in one's life. In this the sages rest, and in that rest lies balance, stability and effectiveness." Where there is calmness, balance and stability, anxiety cannot enter and malicious forces cannot arise. Thus one's spiritual nature is protected, and one's unity remains undamaged.

It has been said, "The birth of a sage is the movement of Heaven. His death is only a transformation of physical existence. When still, he shares the same perfect nature as yin; in action, he shares the motion of yang. He does not push himself forward in search of happiness, so his actions do not become the source of misfortune. He rouses himself in due response to circumstance. He acts when necessity in the external environment occasions it. He disregards knowledge and purpose and follows only the reasonableness of nature.

"He incurs no disaster or entanglement, thus nothing injures him, he has no enemies, and he is not bothered by evil spirits. In life he floats, in death he rests. He does not ponder or plot things that could never happen. His honor does not draw attention to him. He does not take credit for the good he does.

---

[90]Freedom from ambition and too much desire.

"His sleep is without dreams, his waking hours without worry. His spirit is pure and clean, unconfused by desires. His soul never wearies. In simplicity and with an unoccupied mind he joins the virtue of nature itself."

It has been said, "Happiness and sorrow can be destructive influences that damage one's virtue. Joy and anger lead one astray from Tao. Love and hate, like or dislike, denote a lack of natural balance which is most perfect when there is neither worry nor rejoicing."

Being completely concentrated and without any change is quietude in its highest form. Being free from stubbornness is the highest form of detachment. Having no worldly contacts is calmness in its highest form. By not contending with anything, one arrives at the highest state of unity with all.

It is said, "If one's body is made to toil without rest, it will become exhausted and wear out. If one's spiritual essence is used without stopping, it will grow tired and such weariness will bring depletion."

Pure water is clear, and if nothing causes it to stir, it will be level. If it is dammed and not allowed to flow, however, then it will cease to be clear. Thus it symbolizes nature's action and heavenly virtue.

It is said, "To be pure and clean, unmixed with anything else; to be uniform, simple and tranquil, - this is the best care for one's spirit."

II

The man who possesses a sword forged in Kan or Yueh[91] will keep it in a box and store it in a safe place. He will not use it because it is such a great treasure. Keeping the highly prized sword with its sharp blade in a box means one should not expend one's spiritual energy on unworthy things. With this special care, it produces a power that goes beyond the blade alone. Pure spirit extends to in all directions; there is nowhere it does not reach. Above, it embraces Heaven; below,

---

[91]These places were famous for craftsmanship in swords.

it encompasses Earth. It influences all that is created, yet it has no form. It has become Oneness by merging into the universal divineness.

The way to purity and whiteness is to guard the spirit. Whiteness means there is nothing mixed in; purity means the spirit is never impaired. He who can embody purity and whiteness may be called the true man or one of natural truth.

Treat it as a good swordsman does his finest sword; respect it and never be negligent with it, and you will become one with its pure essence. The one who cultivates his spirit with purity will communicate and mingle with the heavenly order. As the proverb says, "The ordinary man values gain, the man of integrity values name, the worthy man honors ambition, and the true sage prizes spiritual essence."

III

Those who would like to return to their original inborn nature through worldly studies or religion, and those who put their hopes in mere financial gain or trust religious fantasy to reach enlightenment are blind and dull.

The ancient developed ones who cultivated Tao derived their knowledge from stillness. When it arose, this knowledge was not applied to any special purpose, thus it may be said that out of knowledge they derived stillness. When knowledge and stillness mutually produce each other in this way, then harmony and order develop naturally. Perfect, natural behavior is virtuous. Being virtuous is harmonious. To follow Tao is to attain the natural orderliness.

Natural behavior accepts everything, so benevolence springs forth. Tao embraces all things, so social responsibility arises. Where these two are established, loyalty is born. From inner purity and truth arises its expression, harmonious music. Sincerity is expressed by ceremony. However, if too much emphasis is placed on the emotional conduct of ceremony and music (either religious or mundane), the world will be plunged into confusion.

If one tries to correct others when their own virtue is confused, they set up a task for themselves that is impossible to meet. By acting with incomplete virtue in relation to others, the result will be that the completeness or unity of one's own nature will suffer along with the outer object of one's attention.

Living with Oneness and indifferentiation, the ancient developed ones enjoyed tranquility. At that time, yin and yang harmonized with one another and peace was known. Spiritual beings made no mischief for man, and nothing harmed all of creation. There was no premature death. The four seasons alternated smoothly. Humans had great wisdom, but they had no use for it. This was the time of the highest form of unity. At that time, spontaneity was uninterrupted, there being no calculation nor planning.

There was a time, however, when virtue began to decline. It started with Sui Jen, the man who discovered the use of fire. Later, Fu Hsi developed herdsmanship, horse riding, cooking, the eight diagrams which symbolize the universe and the use of the written word. He learned net-making from watching spiders and developed selective marriage for eugenic purposes. When these two men stepped forward to take leadership of the world, there was obedience but unity no longer existed.

Virtue continued to decline with Shen Nung, who further developed agricultural skills. With the Yellow Emperor clothing, medicine, acupuncture and the compass were developed. He also united the government and gathered together spiritual knowledge and practices of ancient achieved ones. When he stepped forward to take charge of the world, there was protection but disobedience arose.

Virtue continued to decline, when Yao, who was always looking for advice from achieved ones and divine beings, stepped forward. At that time there were divinities living on the top of Mount Kun Lun. In that period Shun was using farming to support himself and developed a great cooperative community, thereby attracting the notice and trust of Emperor Yao. Together they began systems of government and moral reform to transform the world, and the sweetness of purity and simplicity came to an end.   The integral way was pulled apart for the sake of people pursuing the mere name of goodness.   Virtue was imperiled for the sake of noble conduct that was engaged in adventure.   What was natural was abandoned; thinking began.   There was knowledge, but mind against mind brought instability to human life.   Culture, the colorful ornament of nature, was slapped on, with the realm of intellectual knowledge heaped on top.   This artificial layer of culture destroys what is natural and essential; the realm of external knowledge suffocates the natural mind.   Under their influence people became confused and their lives disordered; they had no way to return to the true form of their nature.   They lost an awareness of the Subtle Origin of universal life.

From this we can see how the world has lost Tao, and Tao has lost the world.   By what means can a man of Tao advance in the world?   By what means can the world advance in Tao?   Although sages no longer become hermits in the mountains, their virtue is hidden anyway.   Since true virtue is no longer respected by people, the virtuous one does not need to hide, because people do not recognize him.

There is no need for a developed person to hide and worry that people will offer him a throne or entrust him with the responsibility of the world as they did in ancient times.   In this day and age, people like to make friends with someone who, as far as they can tell, is virtuous and trustworthy, but they do not support a truly virtuous, moral person in the top level of government.   Today, that job is reserved for those whose character is a combination of a wolf and a fox.   How can a virtuous person protect himself?   When a person of such mixed character is in the highest position of responsibility, what security can one hope to have?

This is how the world becomes worse; it deteriorates when it does not choose leaders based on virtue.   Most people do not even like their own sons and daughters to become virtuous and pure-minded. Thus poison is served to the youngsters at the "dinner" table. How can you expect the next generation to improve the world? Who is responsible? Can you change the prospect of the future without first changing the subtle programming in your own everyday life?

The spiritually developed ones who hid themselves in ancient times did not conceal themselves and refuse to be seen. They did not refuse to speak. They did not refuse to share their knowledge; it was just that the people of their age had become too twisted to understand it. If it had been the destiny of the world at that time to accept their teaching, they could have accomplished great things. However, it was not so; they only experienced hardship in the world. Thus the ancient developed ones fell back upon their own resources and in repose, merely waited, and kept themselves alive.

Those who practiced this did not use eloquence to decorate their knowledge, nor did they use their knowledge to stir up trouble in the world. They quietly kept to their own spheres and returned to their inborn nature. What else could they do?

The Way has no use for petty conduct. Perfect, natural action does not deal with petty facts. Petty conduct injures one's virtue. Petty practice injures the Way. Therefore, it is said, "Cultivate yourself; that is all." A person who has complete happiness is one who has fulfilled his desire.

When the ancient developed ones spoke of attaining their desires, they did not mean great carriages and high-sounding titles. They meant that their delight with life was full and that it could not be augmented. Now, however, when men speak of the fulfillment of ambition or the attainment of their desires, they are referring to external things, not their inborn nature and fate. External fulfillment may happen to come to you from time to time, and when it comes, you cannot keep it from arriving. Likewise, when it departs, you cannot keep it from going. Carriages and titles, therefore, are not reasons for becoming proud and arrogant, and hardship and poverty are no excuse for becoming a flatterer. If you find the same joy in one situation as you do in another, you can thus be free of care instead of being sorrowful when things that came your way take their leave. If your joy depends on chance, it will always be fated for destruction. Thus it is said, "There are many people who destroy their lives seeking things and lose their creative energy in worldly pleasures. These are the people who are upside down in their behavior."

IV

Does perfect happiness and bliss exist on earth? Are there any people who truly enjoy life? If there are, what are they like? What do they do? What do they enjoy, avoid, seek, promote, like and dislike?

The world honors long life, wealth, high position and a good name. It finds happiness in a life of ease, rich food, fine clothes, beauty and music. It looks down on poverty, early death and lowly work. It complains when people do not enjoy security, when there is no rich food to eat or fine clothes to wear, when there are no beautiful sights to see and no music to hear. When people are without things which please the physical frame, they are miserable indeed, yet this is foolish. Physically we can, and most people do, get along very well without these extras.

People who are rich wear themselves out accumulating more wealth than they can possibly use. From the point of view of what is necessary to support our bodies, is this not going too far?

High ranking officials spend night and day scheming and wondering if they are doing the right thing. From the point of view of what is necessary to support our bodies, isn't this also going too far?

Human life always has troubles, concerns and worries. The very old have worried so long about dying that they have become confused about life. They have spent their time worrying instead of living. They have not achieved anything by their suffering; from the point of view of living a long life, this is missing the mark.

Patriots and martyrs who sacrifice their lives are considered to be highly honorable in the world's opinion. As a third party to the situation, can you be sure whether such a thing is true goodness or not? If it is, it does not enable them to enjoy life. At least perhaps they can think that by their death they enable others to enjoy life.

It has been said, "If your good advice and warnings are not heeded, give way or depart quietly without arguing." Wu Yuan continually warned his king about the potential for revenge from the neighboring state of Yueh, but his warnings provoked the king's suspicion, and he was forced to commit suicide. Had he not insisted, however, he would not have been remembered for his outstanding loyalty to the king. So what is goodness, after all?

When you talk about how most people find happiness, I do not know whether that happiness is truly happiness, or if it is sorrow. Most people find happiness in following the majority, racing around and doing the same things that other people do; but it seems more like they cannot stop themselves from behaving this way. Can all these people who are doing the same thing be happy? I have not understood yet, though, whether it is happiness or sorrow. Is there truly anything called happiness?

To me, perfectly natural action (inaction) is true happiness, but people do not appreciate it at all; it makes them miserable. True happiness must not come from stimulation. It comes from inaction. Happiness gained from stimulation is artificial, relative and not absolute. It usually has its negative side too. It has been said, "Happiness in its highest form is not happy. Praise in its highest form is no praise." When something exists, so does its opposite. Therefore, if you have happiness, you also have misery. However, without happiness, there is no misery; being in a "neutral" state, therefore, is to be in one of "perfect

happiness," but there are not many people mature
enough to appreciate and enjoy such a state.

It is impossible to know for sure what the world
will or will not approve of, yet perfect natural action,
spontaneous spiritual knowledge, can determine right
and wrong. If happiness consists of being alive, only
perfect natural action assures survival. Spiritual awakening enables us to be conscious of real life.

Consider this: Heaven has its purity and earth has
its stillness. From the inaction of these two, all things
are transformed and brought to birth. Inaction, thus, is
vast and infinite, yet it has no form.

All things spring from inaction, thus it has been
said, "Heaven and Earth do nothing extra, yet there is
nothing which they do not accomplish." Among men,
however, who can attune their lives to inaction?

V

A foot steps on only a small area of ground, but it
relies on the ground not stepped on for the entire act
of walking. A man's intelligence is limited, but it is
from his untutored or unformed mind that he extends
his learning to what is meant by Heaven.

Learning from the creativity of Heaven, the receptivity of earth, the unfolding of natural truth, the balance of universal life, the natural instinct of all lives,
the reliability of the rotation of the heavenly bodies
and the universal subtle law - this is what is called the
attainment of perfection.

The heavenly creativity is forward moving; thus it
is from Heaven that we learn to be creative. The
receptivity of Earth dissolves all differentiation; thus it
is from Earth that we learn to be receptive. The unfolding of natural truth expresses itself in each life;
thus it is from natural truth that we grow. The balance of the universe provides natural stability to all;
thus it is from the universal nature that we learn to be
supportive. The natural instinct of the universe stimulates all lives to grow; thus we learn to do nothing to
harm our natural instinct such as living in an unnatural
way. Nature routinely and reliably moves in cycles

without stagnation; thus we can adopt our lives to the cycles of nature and keep moving forward. The subtle law of the universe increases its binding force upon those who are forceful; thus we learn to be gentle and soft and to give ourselves more room in moving.

When one knows all of these, one's learning is complete. When one can apply them all, one's life is perfect.

Further, by following the developed subtle light within, one may trace one's way back to Heavenly nature and see the subtle origin; it is Tao. All things begin from this universal source of vitality. It is inexplicable, with nothing to explain. It is unknowable, with nothing to know. From the unknowable, however, we reach the known. But when the knower and the known are totally immersed in one another, the burden of knowing something without being able to actualize it in one's life no longer exists.

The investigation of these things should be neither limited nor unlimited; undertake it from the unconditioned mind. In such vagueness and undefinedness, one would reach the reality unchanged by time. We might call our great guide the personal development of ourselves.

With our doubting hearts, we learn them. With the certainty that we find, we dispel our doubts. When doubt is dispelled, conviction gives forth true strength.

CHAPTER FORTY-ONE

BROADENING ONE'S SCOPE OF VISION

I

The time of the autumn floods had arrived, and all the streams and rivulets poured into the Yellow River. The banks became so far from each other that it was impossible to tell a cow from a horse if one were standing on the opposite side.

The Spirit of the River smiled and laughed because of the joy he felt with all the beauty of the earth being gathered to him. He traveled eastward with the river until they reached the ocean. There, looking out and seeing no limit to its size, his expression changed. As he gazed over the great expanse he sighed and said to the Spirit of the Ocean, "There is a proverb that says, 'The one who knows half thinks he knows the most.' Now I know that this saying applies to me.

"When I used to hear people ridiculing the stiff practice of the ancient rituals of Confucius or mocking the rigid moral realization of Poh I, I did not believe them.[92] But now that I have come to see you and know your great size, I understand that I would have been in great danger if I had continued the way I was, like the limitations of Confucius and Poh I. If I had

---

[92]Poh I was considered a model of righteousness. He was the elder of two brothers and heir to the throne of an ancient community of spiritually developed people, but he declined rulership as he considered his brother more capable as a ruler. His brother would not accept the throne because he was not the heir, and the two of them became hermits. Later, they chose to die of starvation rather than live with the newly established Chou Dynasty which had dethroned Emperor Jow, the corrupt tyrant, which according to moral standards was an unjust revolution.

not reached your gate, I would have been laughed at by those who truly know what greatness is!"

The Spirit of the Ocean replied, "A frog that lives in a well cannot understand the vastness of the ocean. A well-frog's understanding is limited to the well in which he lives. A summer insect that lives no longer than one season does not know about the ice of winter. You cannot speak of Tao to a cramped scholar who is restrained by the intellectual instruction he has received. But you, my friend, now that you have wandered from your limited experience and seen the size of the ocean, you know your own smallness, and therefore we can speak of greatness.

"The ocean is the greatest body of water beneath the blue sky. It accepts the contents of all streams and rivers, but never overflows. It constantly gives forth water and is being drained, but never becomes dry. None of the seasons cause it change; floods and droughts do not affect it. It is, therefore, much greater than any river, stream or brook, but I dare not boast; for in the universe, I am no more or less different than any small stone or a tree on the side of a great mountain. All of us receive our shape from the universe and our lives from the Yin and Yang. There is nothing for me to boast of.

"The Four Seas are to the universe what a few blades of grass are to a vast meadow. The Middle Empire[93] is to the ocean what a single seed is to a granary. Of all the ten thousand things, man is only one of them; and of all the number of people living on the earth, eating its food and traveling about, each individual is only one of many. Compared to the size of the universe, he is as small as the tip of an eyelash on the body of a horse of a great herd of horses.

"All sizeable things that brought war to the five great emperors and the three kings and all small things that bring grief to the benevolent man and cause work

---

[93]Middle Empire (Middle Land or Middle Territory) is the name the Chinese people gave their nation.

for the responsible man are the same size in regard to their importance. Poh I gained reputation by declining the throne and Confucius appeared wise to others by his talk of peace, but the ample pride of such a man of importance and stature is the same size as the pride of someone of small accomplishment. Do you not see that you are swollen with self-importance because of the size of your flood waters?"

"I see," replied the Spirit of the River. "So the universe itself is great and the other things are small and unimportant."

"That is not the depth of the truth," said the Spirit of the Ocean. "Dimension has no limits; time has no end. Conditions are variable and terms are changeable. This is why the wise man does not consider the small as too little nor the big as too much; he looks into space and understands that dimension has no limits. He does not grieve over the past or rejoice for the future to come, because he understands that there is no end to time.

"He understands the changing nature of fullness and emptiness, and therefore does not rejoice upon receiving something, nor grieve if he loses something, because he knows there is no constancy to the amount of possessions one owns. Neither does he rejoice upon succeeding nor sorrow if he fails, because he knows that success and failure are not fixed conditions.

"He clearly perceives that there is no real separation between life and death, but that both are part of the normal road for everyone; he does not rejoice over life or grieve at death, for he also knows that terms are not final.

"It cannot even be said that the tip of a eyelash is a measure of smallness or that the universe itself is a measure of great size," he continued. "What man knows cannot be compared to what he does not know. He ends up in confusion because he tries to compare the time of his short existence to the time when he did not exist, and tries to measure the smallest of small and the largest of large."

The Spirit of the River said, "I have heard tell by educated men that the infinitely small has no form and the infinitely large cannot be measured. Can this be true?"

The Spirit of the Ocean replied, "When what is tiny looks at what is big, it seems infinitely big. When what is big looks for what is tiny, it cannot see it. The tiniest of the tiny is minute, and the biggest of the big is gigantic. We use those terms, but being relative concepts, they rely on circumstance for their definition.

"Thus, both minute and gigantic things possess form. A thing without form cannot be visualized by the mind. But that of great importance which cannot be discussed with words nor pictured by the mind cannot be categorized by terming it 'minute or gigantic.'

"Because Tao cannot be measured, defined or described in a definite way, the truly great man does not harm others, yet he does not consider himself charitable or merciful. He is not looking for profit. He does not congratulate himself for letting it alone nor does he belittle those who seek it. He asks help from no one. He does not credit himself for his self-reliance nor despise those who seek position through the help of others. His behavior differs from that of the majority of people, yet he criticizes no one. He does not set himself above others or consider himself exceptional.

"Worldly titles and wages are not the source of joy for him, just as punishment and shame are not cause for disgrace. He knows that positive and negative do not differ. What is positive in one circumstance will be negative in another. Great and small cannot be defined because they are infinite.

"It is taught that the man of Tao wins no fame, perfect virtue acquires nothing, and that the truly great man has no self. This is the height of self-cultivation."

The Spirit of the River asked, "Then how are value and worthlessness, greatness and smallness, right and wrong to be determined when there is no standard of measurement either internally or externally?"

"From the viewpoint of Tao, the eternal path," replied the Spirit of the Ocean, "there are no such extremes.   From the point of view of man, however, each individual regards himself as valuable and others as less worthy.   Most people do not really determine this for themselves, but only follow the opinion of the latest fashion.

"If we say that something is big or small because of its size in comparison to something else, then there is nothing in all of creation which is not gigantic and nothing which is not small.   Everything is relative: the universe is like a seed, and the tip of a single hair is like a mountain.

"If we say that something exists or does not exist in regard to its function, then everything exists and everything does not exist.   We must understand that east and west exist only in relation to each other; they oppose, yet cannot be separated from one another. Opposites work against each other and at the same time accomplish, complete and define the other.   By understanding this truth, we can know the value, the use and the function of the existence of a thing and the nature of its opposite.   These attributes are not decided by a human mind; they are naturally so.   If we look into the deeper sphere of nature, no mind should be bothered by what exists naturally so.   Even then, what is naturally so cannot be separated from the totality of all life.

"From the point of view of personal preference, if we look on something as right, then all things in our lives must be right.   If we look at something as wrong, then all things in our lives must be wrong.   This is demonstrated by Yao, the wise emperor, and Chieh, the cruel tyrant, who were each right in their own point of view and who were each wrong in terms of understanding the point of view of the other.

"In ancient times, Yao gave the throne to Shun, who ruled virtuously.   Kuai, the prince of Yen, imitating the example of Yao, abdicated the throne in favor of his prime minister, Tzu-Tzi.   But this man failed miserably because the people did not accept him.   Within three years, internal conflict had torn the state apart making it ripe for invasion from external sources. T'ang and Wu each obtained the throne by fighting for it. Yet from these examples, one may see that whether one chooses to abdicate or fight, whether the time is ripe to succeed virtuously or fail miserably is determined by the particular opportunity that nature presents in the moment rather than by following any fixed code of ethics or behavior.

"A beam or a pillar can be used to knock down a city wall, but it is of no use in plugging up a small hole. This illustrates rightness in function.

"A fast steed can travel a thousand li in one day, but it is no match for a wild cat when it comes to catching rats. This illustrates difference in skill.

"An owl can catch mice at night and see the tip of a hair clearly, but its eyes are so dazzled by daylight that it cannot even see a mountain. This illustrates following one's nature.

"It has been said that those who would have right without wrong, order without disorder, do not apprehend the great principles of the universe nor the conditions to which all creation is subject. One might as well talk of the existence of Heaven without that of Earth or of Yin without Yang, which is clearly absurd. Those who hold tightly to this view must be either fools or liars.

"Rulers come to the throne by different means and under different conditions, and rulers leave the throne in different ways. If the time was favorable and they were in accordance with the age, a ruler would be called a patriot; but if the times were inopportune and they did not harmonize with their age, a ruler would be called an idiotic sovereign or a reactionary. Thus things are not always as they appear. My river friend, do you really think you know something about value and worthlessness, great and small?"

"It seems I know less than I thought," replied the Spirit of the River. "So in that case, what should I do and what should I not do? How am I to know what to accept and what to reject, what to live by and what to disregard?"

"From the viewpoint of Tao," said the Spirit of the Ocean, "what we decide as valuable or worthless is only a temporary conclusion of the moment. Do not limit your perception or cause your thinking to oppose the truth of the constant changeability in nature. Do not cling to your own opinion or you will lose the harmony in your life. What is fewer and what is more are interchangeable; in endless alternation, back and forth, they replace one another. If one rigidly holds onto one way, it will soon be in opposition with the natural changeability of nature. Insisting on one viewpoint will lead to discordance with the entire natural metabolism. There must not be acceptance of this and rejection of that, or there will be great confusion in your life.

"One should maintain his mind, the true lord, as if he were a king who must supervise all his subjects equally, without favor or partiality. One should also maintain one's mind as if he were the deity of the Earth, equally blessing all without preference for any particular quality. This is how one embraces all of creation; this is how to develop an unconditioned mind. Don't follow any standard of behavior that is not in accord with the justness and fairness of divine nature.

"Tao is without beginning or end. Things, however, have a birth and death, so put no trust in them; they are impermanent, first better, then worse, their form and condition endlessly changing. Time continues to move forward, one cannot return to the past nor keep the future from arriving. The succession of life and death, prosperity and decline, fullness and emptiness continue infinitely; every end is followed by a new beginning. Whoever knows the truth of this can understand what I say about the great truth of nature and the principle of all lives and things.

"The life of man and of all creatures passes by as swiftly as a galloping horse, with change occurring at every turn or jump. What can man do, other than allow the changes to take place?"

"If that is true, then why should anyone bother to learn about Tao?" wondered the Spirit of the River.

"The person who understands Tao," answered the Spirit of the Ocean, "lives his life by a set of guiding principles. Such a person knows how to manage himself with regard to events, circumstances and situations. Such a person will not allow anything to harm him.

"The one who lives with Tao, the Integral Way, cannot be harmed by fire, drowned in water, suffer from cold or heat, nor injured by wild animals. He does not take these things lightly; he thoroughly understands what is danger and what is safety. Thus, because he is careful about what he accepts and what he declines, what he avoids and what he pursues, nothing harmful can befall him.

"This is why it has been said, 'The natural exists internally; the artificial exists externally,' and 'The heavenly is on the inside; man is on the outside.' You will find integrity in what is natural. By understanding your own nature, you will be able to discern the natural and the artificial; you will come to live your life with honesty. By living with virtue and honesty, whether you are active or not, you will be flexible and adaptable, and you will always return to what is essential within yourself. These unchanging principles underlie all human interactions, large or small.

"What do you mean," inquired the Spirit of the River, "when you talk about what is natural and what is artificial?"

"It is natural that horses and oxen have four feet," answered the Spirit of the Ocean. "However, when you put a halter on a horse's head or pierce an ox's nose, then you have the artificial. Avoid living with a halter on your head and having your nose pierced by a ring; either way, you are controlled by someone else's rope. This is why it has been said, 'Do not let the artificial destroy the natural. Do not let will block destiny. Do not give up your virtue to seek fame.' If you do not fail to follow these axioms, you will certainly return to the divine."

II

Kung Sun Lung[94] said to Prince Mou[95], "When I was younger, I studied the examples of the ancient kings. Then I learned all about benevolence, social responsibility, the standard of how to distinguish like from unlike and the theory of 'hard and white.' Through the skill of dispute, I have developed in myself the capacity of making what is not-so become so, and making the impossible possible. After learning all this history and philosophy, no one could win a debate against me, and I believed I knew everything, but now that I have listened to Chuang Tzu, I know it is not so. Is it that his powers of debate are stronger or that he knows something that I do not? Do you know his secret?"

Prince Mou settled back in his chair and smiled. "Have you ever heard about the frog who lived in the abandoned well?" he asked. "He was having a conversation with a turtle who was visiting from the Great Eastern Ocean, and told him, 'This is the finest place, and I am very content here. I can hop on the rim or rest inside the hollow of a broken brick. When I dive into the water, I keep my legs together and my chin up. When I jump in the mud, my toes sink down deep! None of the tadpoles or crabs around here can do what I do. To be the Master over all the creatures in the well, this is the greatest happiness! I would like to invite you to come in and see.'

"However, before the turtle even got his left foot in the well, his right foot had become stuck by its narrow edge. He stepped back out and said to the frog, 'I live in the Great Eastern Ocean. The distances between its

<hr />

[94]The philosopher who developed the treatise on the 'hard and white,' which is splitting the mind in abstraction from the essence of a thing or splitting the mind from the substance of a thing.

[95]Heir to the throne of the Wei state who was a disciple of Chuang Tzu.

shores cannot be measured, they are so far apart. The depth of the water cannot be imagined, it is so deep. During the time of Yu, there were nine years of flood, but the ocean did not increase. During the time of T'ang, there were seven years of drought, but the ocean did not decrease. The ocean is completely unaffected by time or space, and this is its great happiness and mine too.' The frog became silent, pondering what the turtle had said.

"Your kind of knowledge, Kung Sung, cannot even understand what is right and what is wrong. So how can you expect to use it as a basis for understanding Chuang Tzu? This is like a mosquito trying to carry a mountain or an ant trying to swim a river; it cannot be accomplished. One who is only looking for temporary gain is like the frog in the well; he cannot understand the depth of the words of the other.

"They call him Master for a reason; he is one who soars above to the heights and moves below to the depths. To him, the divisions of north and south are not necessary because he dissolves himself in the infinite. To him, the divisions of east and west are not necessary because he returns to Tao. But I don't know how you could understand that; you are restricted by the rigid ways of logic and reasoning. You are trying to understand the vastness of the sky by looking through a tube; it is though you were using a ruler to determine the depth of the earth! Your way of proceeding is too limited.

"You had best be on your way. Have you ever heard about the young boy of Shou-ling who went to learn how Han-tan people walked? But he forgot his own way of walking before he had learned what the Han-tan people had to teach him, and so he had to crawl all the way back home. If you find you don't know what you are doing, you might have forgotten what you knew before and realize that you do not remember your means of earning a living!"[96]

Kung Sun's mouth fell open and he stood there, gaping. Then, he backed out of the room slowly, and after reaching the door, turned and walked off, heavily and slowly, deeply pondering what had been said.

In the above chapter, the "Spirit of the River watching the sea" and "the vision of a frog in the bottom of a well" have become idioms in the Chinese language.

Kung Sun Lung was a famous scholar in early China. He was a master of logic and a philosopher of ideology; he possessed analytical power. His work still exists, but as with all the old Chinese classics, it is difficult to read. He worked through a conceptual framework, so he cannot be compared to Chuang Tzu, whose mind freely roamed the spheres of concept as well as the spheres where conceptual function loses its capability.

However, in the first section of this chapter, by the understanding of the Spirit of the River that his perception of the universe was indeed small when the universe is truly vast, we understand clearly why Chuang Tzu's dear friend Hui Tzu said to him, "your talk is too big and useless." He was correct, in the sense that no ruler could use the teaching of Chuang Tzu to support his ambition of power over others. Thus, his writing was considered useless. The teaching of Confucius, which functioned on a different level, was considered useful and was received and appreciated by the monarchs in all generations. This is why Confucius is worshipped in a temple built by the rulers of different times; Chuang Tzu had no temples built to him, but his spirit enlivens the hearts of students of Tao everywhere. This is how 2,300 years later, a great person through subtle spiritual development can happily

---

[96]The story of the boy of Shou-ling also became a Chinese idiom that makes fun of people who learn the prevalent fashion and forget the real way.

assimilate the light and the spirit of a very highly developed one who has been through a human form and the difficulty of time. With his inspiration, one can break through the heavy, conventional conceptual structures to reach universal eternal life.

CHAPTER FORTY-TWO

THE MASTERY OF LIFE

I

One who understands the truth of life will not pursue things that are useless to life. One who understands the reality of destiny will not engage in the pursuit of what is beyond his nature.

To maintain the body, it is necessary to give it certain things; yet, often there are cases where the things are provided and the body is not preserved. In having a life, there is a body; yet there are cases where there is a body being maintained but there is no life.

The coming of life cannot be avoided nor its departure stopped. It is pitiful when people think that simply nourishing the body is enough to preserve life! If this is not enough to preserve life, is it worth doing at all? It may not be, but it cannot be left undone; this is necessary and cannot be avoided.

Life comes, and cannot be refused; life goes, and cannot be stopped. It is absurd that people think that life is maintained solely by providing it with things. Providing it with things is unavoidable, but when that does not do it, what can men do about it? Although they can do nothing, they cannot help but do things for it.

If a person is wise enough to avoid over-extending himself merely for his body, the next thing to do is to withdraw from unimportant worldly relationships. By abandoning the complicated social contacts of the world, one sheds unnecessary cares and burdens. The result is a return to a natural rhythm within and without, instead of the negative pattern that follows from being driven by the tensions of the world; this is equivalent to rebirth. He who is reborn into original simplicity returns to Tao, the unity of integral life.

Why, you may ask with hesitation, is it worthwhile to renounce the complexities of worldly life and become indifferent to the external ornaments of life? You can also find the answer easily. First, the physical body will experience a decrease of tension, toil, wear and tear, and secondly, one's vitality will increase. A person whose health is perfect on all levels and who maintains the original purity of his life is one with the organic condition of the macrocosm. We know that all of nature itself is one life, while the human body is a small life and a part of that life.

Heaven and Earth are the parents of all things. They join together as one body. When they part, it is the beginning of all troubles. If in one's life all three spheres - body, mind and spirit - are in perfect balance, one is able to join in the larger flow of universal life. The subtle essence found in this state of perfection originates in the essence of universal life itself.

II

Lieh Tzu confirmed his knowledge with Kuan Yueng.[97] He said, "I have heard that the perfect man can live in society and meet with no obstructions in his life. He can go through fire without being burned, and climb the towering heights without feeling fear. How does he do that?"

To which Kuan Yueng replied, "It is not cunning, skill, knowledge or courage which enables him to dare such feats; he carefully guards his personal spiritual energy in a condition of absolute wholeness. Sit down, and I will tell you more about it.

"Whatever has a face, form, voice or color is a mere thing. How can any thing be very different in nature from another thing? How can any one among all others be worth considering as a leader, a king or

---

[97]Kuan Yueng was a being of natural achievement who was the official of the Han Ku Pass. After meeting Lao Tzu, he became one of Lao Tzu's important spiritual heirs and a great teacher of the period.

somebody with the kind of authority to impose his will over others? They are merely forms and colors, nothing more.

"However, all things have their origin and their return in that which does not change and is without form. If a man can grasp this and understand it fully, then what could possibly stand in his way? Such a man knows the vastness of nonexistence and lives in limitlessness. Such a man expands his breath and unifies the three aspects of his being. Such a man strengthens his virtue. He becomes one with Tao. What Heaven has given him he guards carefully. Nothing can harm him because his spirit is perfect.

"A drunken man that falls out of a traveling carriage may get banged up a bit, but he won't die. There is nothing different about his physical constitution; his spirit or consciousness, though, is in a state of temporary security, temporarily protected. He is not aware of either the cart or the fall. Thoughts of life or death do not arise for him and he feels no fear, so he is not suffering. If such a sense of security is found in a drunken state, how about the true security that is found by being one with the natural subtle essence? A person of true achievement preserves his life in the potency of the subtle essence; in this way he is free from harm.

"A man seeking revenge does not smash the murderer's weapon, nor does an angry man resent the roofing tile that may have accidentally fallen and hit him on the head, because it is not the weapons or the tiles which create war, it is the people who use them.

"Do not increase your artificial intelligence; develop natural knowledge and wisdom. From nature comes virtue, from intelligence only trickery. Those who do not reject what is natural or neglect what is human are near perfection and close to attaining the truth of natural life."

III

A teacher who was traveling with a group of students on his way to the state of Chu was traveling through a forest. There, they saw a hunchback using a pole that was sticky on one end to catch cicadas, performing this task just as easily as if he were picking them up with no tool at all.

"Your skill is amazing!" exclaimed the teacher. "Is there a special trick to this?"

"Well, I do have a special way," replied the hunchback. "For five or six months I practiced balancing two balls, one on top of the other, on the end of my pole. If they didn't fall off, I knew I would not miss many cicadas. When I could balance three balls, I only missed one cicada out of ten. When I could balance five balls, catching cicadas was as easy as picking up stones with my hand. I simply hold my body as stiff as a tree trunk, with my arms like old, dry branches. Although there may be many things or lots of people around me, if I am only aware of the cicada I am trying to catch, how can I not succeed?"

The teacher looked around at his disciples and said, "When one is single-minded, his total being becomes concentrated on that one thing. The success of this hunchback has come from keeping an undivided will and concentrating his spirit. This is how a student learns to maintain and develop his life essence."

IV

A student once asked his teacher, "When I crossed the gulf of Shang-shan Lake, the ferryman controlled the boat with extraordinary skill. I asked him if it were possible to learn how to handle a boat the way he did, and he replied, "Certainly! A good swimmer, for example, will pick up the skill in no time, because he knows the water so well that he has forgotten it. If somebody knows how to dive and swim underwater, he may never have seen a boat before, but he will know how to handle it because water to him is like dry land is to the rest of us. Even if his boat were to capsize, it wouldn't affect him; it would be like an overturned cart is to people on land. The person who can easily deal with upsets, overturns and capsizings will find that there is no place in the water he could go that he wouldn't feel at ease."

His teacher said, "When a person is practicing archery at home, they do really well. When a person makes a wager with another on their shooting, he worries about how good his aim is. And when a person enters a contest with many other skilled archers, he becomes nervous. The person is the same, his skill in archery is the same; but he has lost his sense of ease because he has let outside considerations enter his mind. Outside considerations must be to the archer like water is to the ferryman."

V

T'ien K'ai Chih went to see Duke Wei of Chou. The Duke asked him, "I have heard that Chu Hsien is studying the art of living. You are his friend and spend some time with him. What has he told you about it?"

T'ien K'ai Chih replied, "I only sweep and take care of his garden. How should I know about my Master's research?"

"You are being modest," said the Duke. "Come, tell me about it."

"Well," replied T'ien, "I have heard my Master say that keeping life is like herding a flock of sheep; you watch for strays and round them up."

"I don't understand," said the Duke.

"In the state of Lu there was a man named Shan Pao who lived in the mountains. He only drank water and did not rush around trying to make lots of money like most people do. He had no worldly interests, and lived this way until he was in his seventies. He still had a youthful appearance, like that of a child. Unfortunately, one day he met up with a tiger who devoured him.

"In that state also lived a man named Chang I; he was a great socialite. He attended all the special occasions put on by rich families and indulged in all kinds of luxury and vanity. Chang I lived this way until the age of forty; he was then troubled by internal poisoning of the heart which burst into cancer and quickly killed him.

"Shan Pao took care of his inner self, but lost his external self to a tiger. Chang I took care of himself externally, but disease attacked him from the inside. These two neglected to watch after the strays or to keep a happy medium.

"My master has commented, 'Do not deliberately hide and do not deliberately show yourself. The Way to live is to maintain yourself poised and in the middle of those two. Whoever attains this will enjoy high achievement indeed.

"'When people are traveling in a dangerous place where murder by bandits is frequent, their families urge them to travel with many companions. This is wisdom. However, in matters where there is really great danger to a person - in bed and at the dinner table[98] - it is a grave mistake not to practice constant caution.'"

VI

One day Chuang Tzu was fishing in the P'u River when the King of Ch'u sent two envoys to call him in to take charge of the entire state administration. They found him and conveyed the king's message. Chuang Tzu went right on with his fishing and, without even turning his head, said, "I have heard that in Ch'u there is a sacred tortoise that died after living about three thousand years. It is kept in a box on the altar of the ancestral temple. Do you think this tortoise would rather be dead, with its bones locked up and worshipped, or alive and walking through the mud?"

"It would rather be alive, walking in the mud," replied the two officials without hesitation.

"Then go away!" cried Chuang Tzu. "I too prefer to walk in the mud."

---

[98]This refers to excessive sex and overeating.

A person of Tao can live and work with a good leader and can even be a good leader himself, depending on the maturity of the individual. At that time, Chuang Tzu might have been the director of the state's lacquer tree plantation or he may have been out of a job. His choice was to be content with work and a position which provided only the necessities of life and allowed him his spiritual pursuits. He would not accept any official offer that was against his principle, even though his material circumstances were not overly abundant.

VII

When Hui Tzu was Prime Minister of Liang, Chuang Tzu traveled to Liang to visit him. One of his advisers said, "Chuang Tzu is coming on his way to Liang, probably to replace you as Prime Minister. His name has been admired by our king for a long time." When he heard that, Hui Tzu became somewhat anxious and let his men search the entire state for three days and nights to try to see him right away. Finally, Chuang Tzu arrived and said to him, "In the south there is a bird called the phoenix. Have you ever heard of it? It rises up from the Southern Sea and flies to the Northern Sea. It will rest on nothing but the Wu-t'ung tree,[99] eat nothing but bamboo seeds and drink only from springs with sweet-tasting water.

"Once there was an owl that had gotten a half–rotten rat for its meal. As the phoenix passed by, the owl raised its head, looked up at it and making itself look threatening, said, 'Shoo! Go away!'

"Now you, Hui Tzu, have gotten the state of Liang for yourself. Do you think you need to shoo me away?"

VIII

When Confucius was passing through K'uang, the men of Sung surrounded him with several battalions,

---

[99]The kolanut tree, which has magnificent shade.

but he continued playing his lute and singing.[100] His student Tzu Lu went up to him and said, "Master, how can you be so untroubled?"

His teacher answered, "See if you can understand what I have to say. For a long time I have tried to avoid trouble in my life; but it is fate that I cannot. For a long time I have tried to be successful; but it is the times we live in that makes it impossible. When people live in the time of righteous and wise government, under leaders like Yao and Shun, then nobody in the world experiences trouble, but not because the people themselves are so wise. When people live in the time of cruel tyranny under leaders like Chieh or Chou, then nobody in the world is successful, but not because the people's wisdom is lacking. It is time and circumstance that makes a person what he is.

"A fisherman's courage is from continuing to fish even though he knows of the presence of the crocodile or serpent. A hunter's courage comes from hunting even with the awareness of the dangers of tiger and rhinoceros. A warrior's courage is his facing the possibility of death by the sword. A sage's courage is his knowing that trouble in life is dependent upon fate and success in life is dependent upon circumstance. No matter what the result, the outcome is already determined. So why not just be content?"

Shortly afterwards, the leader of the battalions came forward and apologized. "We thought you were Yang Hu and that was why we surrounded you. Now that we know our error, we will leave you to go on your way."

IX

Chi Sheng-tzu was training a fighting cock for the king. After ten days the king asked him if it was ready yet and he replied, "Not yet. He is still too self-assured and ready to pick a fight." Ten days later, the

---

[100]The people of the state had mistaken him for an enemy named Yang Hu.

king asked again and Chi Sheng-tzu replied, "Not yet. The noise or movement of the other cocks still startle him." Ten more days passed and he said, "Not yet. At the sight of another cock he is still enraged." In another ten days, "Almost! The other cocks may crow to pick a fight, but he is not bothered. He stands as firm and tall as wood. His virtue is complete. The others won't face him; they back off or run away."

X

A teacher had traveled with his students to see the sights at Lu-liang[101] where there is a waterfall about two hundred feet high, after which the water races along in rapids for about twelve miles so swiftly that no fish or other living creature can swim in it. The teacher saw a man dive into the water there. Not knowing if he was in danger or committing suicide, but wishing to save him, he ordered his disciples to stand along the banks to be ready to pull him out. But the man climbed out of the water a hundred yards down the way, took out a comb and straightened his hair and began to walk off, singing a song. The teacher ran after him and said, "At first I thought you might be a ghost-like creature, but now I see that you're a man. How is it that you can swim in water like that and stay alive?"

"There is no special way that I follow," replied the man. "What was mine in the beginning was allowed to develop and was matured by fate. I follow along with the current, going up when it goes up and down when it goes down, doing what the water does. I rest in the swirls and pause with the eddies. That is how I swim in moving water."

The teacher asked, "What do you mean when you say, 'What was mine in the beginning was allowed to develop and was matured by fate'?"

"I grew up on land with water nearby, that is how I began. Moving on both of them was taught to me

---

[101]In Shan Si province.

and allowed to develop. I am at home in both places; I do not know why I do what I do, that is how fate has matured me. Do you know that by becoming one with one's living environment, one can become achieved? Scholars may think I had to attend a special school for that."

XI

Ch'ing, the Chief Carpenter in the state of Lu, was carving a musical instrument out of wood. When he finished, the work appeared to be of divine beauty, and the prince of Lu asked him, "What is the secret of your art?"

"There is no secret, Your Majesty," replied Ch'ing, "Although there is a way that I accomplish it. When I am getting ready to sculpt an instrument, I allow my mind to become quiet so that my vital essence does not decrease. After three days, I forget about the profits I will make. After five days, I forget about people's delight or disapproval at seeing the instrument. After seven days, I am unconscious of myself. Thus, after removing all thoughts about the Royal Court, eliminating external and internal disturbances, my skill becomes concentrated. Then I go to the mountains and look for the right tree. I find one that already is like the instrument I wish to make, and I just carve it out. I picture the instrument in my mind and then begin to carve. It is a joining of my natural capacity with that of the wood. Whatever you might consider special in my work is only this."

XII

Tung Yeh Chi was displaying his skill in driving a chariot before Duke Chuang. Back and forth he drove, in lines as straight as if they were drawn with a ruler, sweeping round at each end in curves as neat as if he had used a compass.

The Duke commented, "I have never seen such skill in driving as that which you display," and he ordered him to drive around a hundred more times. Then he re-entered the palace.

Yen Ho, a wise and virtuous person who was the teacher of the heir of Weh, went in and told the Duke, "Chi's horses are going to break down."

The Duke made no reply, but a short time later he was told that the horses had broken down.

"How did you know this?" he asked Yen Ho.

"Because," said Yen Ho, "Chi was trying to make the horses perform a task to which they were unequal. Their strength was already gone, and he demanded still more of them. Thus, I knew they would break down.

"The same will occur in human life, if we strain ourselves in the pursuit of external fantasies overly taxing our bodies and minds and other people, looking for something truly unworthy."

XIII

The skillful artisan can draw circles with his hand that are better than those drawn by a compass. His fingers seem to accommodate themselves so naturally to whatever he is working on that he doesn't need any special effort. There is no mental obstruction blocking his attention on the object of his work.

To be unaware of one's feet means that one's shoes fit comfortably. To be unaware of one's waist means that one's belt fits comfortably. For the mind to be unaware of positive and negative, right or wrong, means that the heart is at ease. Ease under all conditions comes from making no internal changes nor external adaptations. One who lives in such ease, never knowing its opposite, even becomes unaware of the ease of ease. Such ease is essential to the development of the natural potency of life.

CHAPTER FORTY-THREE

LIFE AND PRESSURE, COMPETITION AND TROUBLE

I
The True Use of Life

Chuang Tzu, a tree lover, was traveling one time through a mountain village with a few of his students where he saw a beautiful large tree with abundant foliage. There, a woodcutter was sitting beside the tree with his axe, but he was obviously uninterested in it. Chuang Tzu asked him why, and was told that the tree was worthless.

"Because of its worthlessness," said Chuang Tzu, "this tree is able to spare its life from human hands."

When Chuang Tzu left the mountain village, he continued on his way and went to stay in the house of an old friend. His friend was so pleased at his visit that he instructed his attendant to kill a goose and roast it.

"Which one shall I kill?" asked the young man. "the one that cackles or the one that doesn't?"

His master told him to kill the one which did not cackle.

The next day, a disciple asked Chuang Tzu, "Yesterday, that tree on the mountain was able to live out its natural life because it was worthless, but now our host's goose had to die because it cannot be of use. What can be learned by this, Master?"

"One would like to take a position between what is useful and what is not useful," replied Chuang Tzu with a smile. "Nevertheless, such a position is still not free from trouble; there is no place that is a middle point between useful and useless, worthy and worthless, having the wisdom of life and not having the wisdom of life.

"However, a person who has attained mastery in following the subtle truth has evolved to the highest stage of natural life. It is beyond the reach of most moral systems that sit in judgement or apply their standards to your life. Use or no use, worthy or worthless; because such a master has achieved spiritual independence, he is not bothered by either praise or criticism. When he reaches out, he can be like a dragon; when he rests, he can be like a hiding snake. He enjoys complete freedom. He changes along with the times, not being fixed in any circumstance or in any direction. He is flexible; he can stretch or bend himself in harmony with nature. His understanding comes from the principle of balance. He fills his heart with the subtle essence which exists prior to form. He recognizes objective reality, but is not limited by it. How could he be troubled by external forms? This is the way of life shown to us by Shen Nung and the Yellow Emperor, who had attained their spiritual independence. With this achievement, they maintained their spiritual wholeness without being damaged in worldly life.

"The worldly person is chained by his attachment to human society, and is not like the master I have just described. For the worldly person, where there is union, there is separation. Where there is success, there is failure. Where there is righteousness, there is injury. Where there is a respectful position, there is prejudicial criticism. Where there is virtue, there is subversion. Where there is lack of virtue, there is attack. How can such a one be free from the trouble of externals? My friends, if you wish to secure your life free from trouble, the only way is to attain Tao! The one who has attained Tao embraces the integral truth and is undisturbed. Ordinary people live with their spirit under the weight of the relative and dualistic perception of life, while a person who attains Tao has lifted his spirit above the dualistic plane. He becomes absolutely spiritual.

"Anyone who makes the purpose of his life the avoidance of trouble has chosen a negative purpose, and has no chance to attain growth. It is impossible to avoid trouble or problems in any creative life. It is important to keep your focus on two thing: first, not creating any trouble by yourself, and secondly, avoiding any negative influences from others in your environment. It is a loss to the world that many talented and creative people are unable to contribute because they must put their time and energy into fighting negative forces in themselves and their environment. Sometimes, the influence of practical life is too overwhelming. Students of a healthy life of Tao should learn to adapt to any situation, and thus avoid the destructive influence that society has created for the natural healthy life."

Chuang Tzu's teaching concentrates on the path of creating a natural life during times when negative social forces are very strong. Students of Tao prefer to maintain the quality of their lives and achieve a spiritual independence that can empower them to withstand the destructive tide of the times. They can move away from the negative confrontation of time.

No one can spend his life watching and avoiding the swings of the external world. What one can do is follow the great Way, moving forward to fulfill the purpose of his or her life as a useful and effective individual.

II
Riding Above the Pressure,
Not being Chased by Pressure

I Liao, the developed civilian of South City, paid a visit to the Prince of Lu. The Prince looked terribly worried, so I Liao asked him why.

"I study the way of former kings and do my best to carry on their achievements. I respect religion and honor good. Never for a moment am I lax in these respects, yet I cannot escape misfortune. This greatly troubles me."

"The manner in which your highness attempts to avoid misfortune," said I Liao, "lacks depth. Sleek

yellow foxes and beautifully spotted leopards make
their homes in mountains and forests. During the day
they do not wander from their caves for any reason;
during the protection of the darkness of the night they
guardedly come out to hunt. They are always alert
and watchful, but even though, they still meet with the
misfortune of traps and snares. What brings their
downfall is the beauty of their coat. The same is true
of you; it is the state of Lu which is your coat. Spiritually, empty your form, forsake the hide and flesh.
Leave all your desire behind you, free yourself of
greed, purify your heart and mind, and make a voyage
into the land where misfortune and mortality do not
reach.

"In the remote Nan-yueh there is a place called the
Kingdom of Building Virtue. Its people are simple and
honest, selfless and without many desires. Having
little interest in owning much property, they know how
to make things grow, but they are not concerned with
how much they take home. When giving, they seek
nothing in return. They do not need to talk about
righteousness or ceremony, yet everyone lives within
the good way. While alive they are happy, not bound
by thought and feeling; when dead, they are buried in
peace. I wish your highness would leave behind your
kingdom and all its concerns and binding customs, and
travel with your trust in Tao."

"That is a long and perilous road for me to embark
upon," replied the prince, with some understanding of
what the developed one was referring to by his philosophical language. "Moreover, I will be blocked in my
journey by the rivers and mountains, and will have no
boat or carriage to cross them. What can I do?"

"Your vehicle can be not depending on high position and not getting stuck in old rules and regulations."

"Whom shall I keep as company? Without pro-
vision of food and drink, how shall I ever be able to
get there?"

"Decrease expenditure of your vital energy and
lessen your desires; then, even if you are without great
quantity of provisions, you will be content. Across

rivers and the sea you will travel into open space and see the boundless nature. Your escort will go only as far as the shore and return, but you will go far beyond.

"What burdens you is the possession of people, wealth and kingdoms. This is what causes you care and concern and enslavement. Great ones like Yao did not own people; neither was he owned by people. I wish you would get rid of your burden and entanglement to leave behind the fetters of your cares and concerns, and wander in the vastness with Tao.

"If a boat is crossing a river and an empty boat drifts in its path, even a cantankerous man would not lose his temper. However, if someone was sitting in the second boat, the helmsman of the first boat would yell at him to clear his path, and if there was no response, then he would yell again. If there was still no response, he would shout a third time with a string of curses and unlovely words. When the boat was empty, there was no anger; when it was occupied, there was indeed anger. It is the same with man: if he could keep himself like an empty boat as he roams in the world of people, no misfortune or trouble would befall him!"

III

On one occasion, an assembly of learned people came together to debate the way the world could be guided back to peace.

One group insisted that the way to restore the social order and morality of the people was to follow the example of the lives of Yao and Shun. The leader of the group holding this opinion said, "Where there is compliance, there will be peace." Their model was of a social order under the rulership of kings in local communities who in turn accepted the direction of one central emperor as the leader of all kings. However, they did not mention why the people should establish others as their kings and emperors, and in so doing subject themselves to the possibility of unreasonable dominance by them.

Another group emphasized that unification and peace could be attained if everyone followed only one religious practice. "There is only one Heaven above all of us," the leader maintained, "And we should love one another since all people are children of Heaven. Then, true peace will be restored." However, he did not recognize and respect differences in spiritual experience, and different conceptions of God that were already established.

The dispute between the two sides became very active, and tempers were beginning to heat up. A man who had been listening from a distance quietly joined the meeting. He stood up before the group and told the following story:

"Once there was an ambitious scholar whose interest was political unification. He believed that all people should listen to their kings, and all kings should obey their emperor. He was convinced that such an established order would assure the peace of the world. This was the convention of his society, and he believed in following it. Once, he and his followers were besieged in the countryside by a small band of people who were mistreated by the administration that was favored by his theory. They were trapped there for many days and were without food or fire.

"The respected elder, Jen the Kindly, went to offer his empathy and said to him, 'It appears that you are near death.'

"'It certainly does,' replied the scholar.

"'Do you want to die?' inquired Jen.

"'No,' said the scholar.

"'Then I will explain to you how not to die,' said Jen. 'Near the eastern ocean live some birds called I-daih or the unambitious. They flutter about, seemingly helpless, as though they had no ability or skill. None act independently. None of them wish to be the first to act nor the last to depart. When eating, none wish to be the first to eat - rather than do that, they would rather eat the leftovers. However, because of their behavior, they are peaceful among themselves and are never harmed by outsiders. Among themselves, there is no king or artificial social order. This is how they avoid misfortune; they follow the natural, undisturbed order.

"Jen continued, 'A straight, strong tree is the first one cut by the carpenter. A well with sweet water is the first one to be drawn dry. You, my friend, show off the strength of your knowledge trying to impress simpletons; you try to bolster the sweetness of your reputation. Do you think you are carrying the sun and the moon[102] on your shoulders? This is why misfortune surrounds you.'

"And so Jen concluded his talk and left. The ambitious scholar and his followers reflected on the words of the kindly man, and understood that they should think over what they had been taught and were soon released from their captivity."

After he finished telling his story, the man paused. Some of the people at the assembly felt rather uncomfortable because it appeared that the man was taking sides with the group who believed in religious practice rather than political dominance. However, the man continued speaking, "There was another ambitious scholar whose interest was to unify all people through a faith in Heaven. He believed that all leaders and people should follow Heavenly will, not human will. His slogan was that Heavenly will is peace, and human will brings separation; thus, all people should unconditionally love one another. He did not mention that separation was often caused by the conflicting perspectives of the one faith, resulting in religious conflicts and war. Once he and his followers were stopped by a group of people whose conception of Heaven was different from theirs. The two sides argued and all insisted that what they believed was right and the other side was wrong. They would not yield to one another. This confrontation went on for seven days, and each side was without food, fire or water.

---

[102]which imply the emperor and the kings.

"At the beginning, each paused on the way to pray for the help of God. God listened to the prayers of each side. Thus, they were all refreshed the second day, and the following day, too. During the fifth day with no food, there was still someone on each side who was confrontive and expressed a strong opinion, insisting on the rightness of his position. Their argument was fueled and refueled by the last ounce of their physical strength.

"Surely, before long God became tired of the argument; he himself had became confused about who was right. Thus, he hid away on the highest cloud. And on the seventh day, there was no more voice that could be heard from the battlefield of these strong soldiers, because they had all become weakened from argument and lack of food.

"The elder man, Jen the kindly, went there and saw each soldier of God laying on the ground, watching him with imploring eyes. Jen said to the leaders of each side, 'I was sent by God, whose name is Kindly, born by his mother who is called Nature, to carry a special message to you. God said: "Heaven or God, as you all call it, is spiritual. Spiritual reality cannot be conceptualized. It especially cannot be conceptualized by human thought which is based on your limited experience." God says: "My glory cannot be conceived of or imagined on the basis of people's experience of being on a throne, owning property, possessing many great works of art, being beautiful, having tremendous strength, having brown skin or olive skin, having brown eyes or blue ones, as obtaining power, as producing magic, as commanding a great number of servants or an army, living with luxury, having a big group of flatterers, listening to wonderful music, etc. Anything that humans can visualize is not me."

"God continued, 'Once the ageless Lao Tzu gave you my message: "Boasting is a sign of failure. When success does come, it faces inevitable decline. Fame brings loss. Behaving in one extreme way arouses another extreme way." These are all associated with the ego of man. Thus, it is the way of man in the world. Then, you might ask, what is the way of the man of God? If you wish to be a man of God, it is best to set your mind free from both the pursuit of success and fame, to live with the naturalness of your own life, so that you can understand.'

"And then God concluded, 'A divine one keeps moving with virtue. He works constantly without seeking the limelight of fame. To see him, you might think he were unachieved, because he leaves no trace of himself. In his purity and constancy, the person of Tao or God may appear no different than the people around him. Not considering himself superior to other people, he cannot blame them for what they do, and he himself is without blame. The man of God maintains his being like that of Tao and Teh. Tao is in all things but you cannot see it. Teh, virtue, moves through all things but does not rest in any of them. Pure and constant, Tao and Teh seem purposeless. This is the line drawn between God and man.'"

When the old man finished his words, he signaled to a group of women and children who carried baskets of food and drink. They all came along to feed the soldiers' physically defeated bodies, but not their stubbornness. Thus, after satisfying the weakened bodies, the old man asked them whether they understood what he had said. Some were clear on some parts only, some were clear about other parts. About the Heavenly message, none had compete knowledge of what they just heard a few minutes ago, even after having fasted for seven days. Then, they started another argument about what they had heard. So then the old man and the group of women and children quietly withdrew from them. It was said that all of them argued to death, because each was unwilling to understand what the other had to say.

"Noble ladies and gentlemen, distinguished scholars, for all of you, I have a secret herbal medicine which is the cure of the worst disease in the world, which is stubbornness. I learned about this secret medicine from my teacher who was taught by his teacher. His teacher obtained it from the greatest teacher of many generations go. This is the medicine which can cure the disease of stubbornness: it is spiritual self-cultivation." After the man finished speaking, he quietly left.

IV

There was a man whose goal was to improve society. After many years of unsuccessful efforts, he went to Sang Hu, a hermit, and said, "I have twice been expelled from important positions in my home state, humiliated in another state and almost lost my life in another. In two other places, a lot of trouble befell me. In addition to all this, my friends drift farther and farther away, and my supporters leave me. Why is this happening?"

"I would like to tell you about a man I knew," replied Sang Hu. "There was an invasion in the state of Kuo, and when the people fled, one man named Lin Hui threw away his gold bullion and took his child with him instead. Why was that? Some people thought that perhaps it was because the value of the child was great, but certainly the gold was worth more. Some people thought that perhaps it was because the gold was too inconvenient to carry, but carrying the child would have been more inconvenient. So why did he discard the gold and take the child? Lin Hui said it was because the gold was only a matter of money; the child, however, was from nature.

"What comes together because of money does not remain together in times of misfortune or danger. But what nature has brought together becomes closer. The huge difference between the two is easily seen.

"Friendship between great people is balanced, like water. Friendship between petty people is falsely sweet like overly rich wine. Great people admire and respect each other, thus the friendship between them passes from the stage of mutual interest to affection. Mean people are brought together by profit, each wishing to take advantage of the other. When the profit is made, the friendship is forsaken. This is the nature of friendship among people of smallness; it passes from being full of flavor to nothing. Those with other specific reasons for joining together[103] will part upon the achievement of their purpose."

The man replied, "I do believe you are right." Then slowly and thoughtfully he returned home. He ended his studies and gave away his books. He no longer required his followers to obey him, but the affection between them became ever greater.

When the man came to see him on another occasion, Sang Hu said, "When Shun was about to die, he carefully instructed the Great Yu as follows: 'Be careful. Concerning the health of the body, there is nothing better than harmony. In all relationships there is nothing better than straightforwardness and uprightness. When there is harmony, there will be no discord within oneself. When there is straightforwardness and uprightness, there will be no strain. When there is neither discord nor strain, there will be no need to ornament your life. If you do not ornament your life, you will not be dependent upon external things!'"

V

When Chuang Tzu was wandering in the countryside of Tiao-ling carrying his crossbow, he saw an unusual bird fly by. Its wings had a span of seven feet. Its eyes were at least an inch across. After brushing against Chuang Tzu's forehead as it flew past, it settled nearby in someone's chestnut grove. Tempted by the bird, Chuang Tzu unconsciously went into the grove to follow it.

"What kind of bird can that be?" he cried. "It has really huge wings but it doesn't fly very well. Its eyes are really big, but it doesn't see very well." Then he tied up the ends of his long coat and went forward, set his crossbow and was ready to aim. As he did this, he noticed a cicada that was so pleased with having found a nice shady spot that it forgot to protect itself from danger. A mantis sprang up and seized it, forgetting in the act to guard itself from danger. Then the

---

[103]For instance, political purposes.

strange bird pounced on the mantis and made off with it, forgetting that it could easily have been preyed upon.

Chuang Tzu stood there stunned. "The injury of it all! Every creature makes another its prey and then in turn becomes the bait. This is the life of the world; loss inevitably follows the pursuit of gain."

Throwing down his crossbow, he turned and hurried out of the grove. Because of his awakening, he was willing to walk away from being one of the conditions in the chain of the hunt in worldly life. As he was leaving, the keeper of the grove ran after him, shouting, because he thought that Chuang Tzu had been poaching chestnuts.

For three months after this, Chuang Tzu did not leave the house. At length, Lin Chu, one of his disciples, asked him, "Master, why have you not been out for so long?"

"I learned from Lao Tzu that when you go into the world you must respect its customs and follow its rules," he replied. "While putting my attention on external things, I lost sight of my real self. After gazing at muddy water for so long, I became deluded into taking it for a clear, refreshing pool.

"When I strolled into that chestnut grove at Tiaoling, I forgot myself because of that strange bird which also forgot about itself. The mantis forgot itself by concentrating on the cicada which had forsaken its safety for the sake of some shade. I put myself in the lower phase of a chain-reaction in the hunt and was taken for a poacher by the keeper of the grove. What does that say about my development? This is why I have not been out."

By clinging to the outer world, people forget and risk their own lives. By staring at muddy water, they neglect to see the clear water, and drown themselves.

VI

When Yang Tzu went to the state of Sung, he stayed overnight at an inn. The innkeeper had two women helpers, one beautiful and the other ugly. He

treated the ugly one like a lady and the beautiful one
like a servant. When Yang Tzu asked why, the inn
keeper told him, "The beautiful one is so conscious of
her beauty that one does not think her beautiful.
Likewise, the ugly one is so conscious of her ugliness
that one does not think her ugly." Yang Tzu was
enlightened by this. He said, "Perform your tasks with
the highest standards, but avoid thinking of yourselves
as being of the highest character. Then where can you
go and not be loved?"

When Chuang Tzu heard this, he told his students,
"You can be unconscious of your beauty, but you cannot be unconscious of entering someone else's chestnut
grove!"

VII

A teacher who promoted rigid moral standards was
traveling with his students. On their voyage, they met
with trouble in a place and had been without food for
a number of days. Holding a piece of dry wood in his
left hand and rubbing it with a dry stick in his right to
make a kind of primitive music, he sang an old song
from the time of Shen Nung. There was no fixed
rhythm to the melody. The sound of wood accompanying the teacher's voice was harsh to the ear, but it
clearly conveyed the reality of that moment.

One of the students who was standing nearby
began to gaze intently at the teacher. Fearing that the
student would form too high an opinion of him, or
that out of his love he might begin to feel sorrow for
the difficulty of the situation, the teacher said, "Dear
friend, it is easy not to suffer from the troubles inflicted by nature. It is also difficult not to accept the
disadvantages conferred by man. Life can hardly be
said to have a beginning or an end. Nature and people are all one. I am myself and am not myself, both.
Therefore, it is not necessarily I who is singing here
today."

The student thought a moment, and then replied, "What do you mean by saying, 'it is easy not to suffer from the trouble inflicted by nature'?"

"The shifts of things," said the teacher, "such as hunger, thirst, heat and cold, barriers and box canyons that will not allow you to go through them are the workings of nature. But, with man's intelligence, we still can overcome the problem. It is through the situations which trouble us in our lives that we can learn how to handle ourselves through an acceptance of the experience of life. This is called traveling with the rhythm of change or rolling with the tides. Thus, I say it is easy not to suffer from the trouble inflicted by nature."

"What did you mean by it being difficult to not accept the disadvantages conferred by man?" asked the student.

"If one adapts to his surroundings" replied the teacher, "position and power follow without cease. Such disadvantages are external; they are not derived from oneself.

"For instance, when a man sets out on a career, he soon advances toward his goal. Title and pay soon come to him, but they are merely material rewards and have nothing to do with the man himself.

"Sometimes it is otherwise, but fate is something we cannot completely control. That is why a gentleman will not pilfer and a worthy man will not steal; they follow their fate and accept what comes to them. This is also why I do not become attached to external things or try to control them.

"It has been said that no bird is as wise as the swallow. Let us look to the wisdom of this bird. The example of its life can give us some guidelines on how to live. If it sees a place unfit to dwell in, it will not give it a second thought. Even if it accidently dropped its food there, it would leave the food and fly away. Swallows know people; they live among them because they are comfortable there. Man should adapt himself to the situation around him in the same way as the swallow.

"My life is more or less dependent upon the internal. Like the swallow, a good way to live one's life is to be more or less dependent upon internal capability. No one can steal it or pilfer it. In that way, one learns to take life as it comes.

"When one clearly understands the importance of flowing with the changes of life, it is unimportant to think about the beginning and the end. It is to say, because all of creation is constantly in a state of transformation, no one knows when the changes end and when the changes begin or what will follow. All one can do is be upright and cultivate one's internal spirit to attain the power of independence and follow the natural flow of changes, like the swallow."

"What did you mean when you said that Heaven and man are one?" asked the student.

"You have become a human, and all humans have nature; man cannot be separated from nature. Nature, however, is just itself. Thus the true sage, calm and placid, becomes part of the natural procession of nature and quietly follows its changes.

"We can learn from the life of Shen Nung who became one of the pre-historical leaders[104] and began the development of agriculture, initiated the collection of the achieved knowledge of herbal medicine and further developed and established this trade during his reign of 140 years. We can learn from the life of the Yellow Emperor.[105] He designed the mortar and pestle, supported the development of astronomy by Yung Sheng, developed natural medicine as described in the Book of Internal Medicine written with Ch'i Po, furthered the development of mathematics with Li Hsu, supported the development of music with Ling Lung, adapted the stems and branches system of time cycles, invented the compass, the boat, the cart and the chariot, constructed houses and public buildings and

---

[104]in 3218 B.C.

[105]who reigned from 2698 to 2358 B.C

assisted the development of writing by Tsung Ch'i. You can see how men like Shen Nung and the Yellow Emperor benefited people's lives with their great creative genius for many generations without forming any particular system of thought or institution. They provide good examples of selfless service for all those who devote their lives life to learning and attaining the Truth, first fulfilling their moral obligations and second, by never leading others in argument and conflict.

"Your life would be very different if you were able to follow the Way and its virtue and go drifting and wandering, neither praised nor damned, first active like a dragon, then inactive and hidden like a snake, shifting with the times, and unwilling to hold to one course. If you lived first coiled up, then stretched out, taking harmony to measure your success, drifting and wandering with what is prior to the beginning of creation, treating things as things and seeing yourself as the offspring of nature, you would have the sense of your spiritual wholeness. Living in such a manner, how could you get into any trouble with this undefeated spirit of life? This was the way of Shen Nung and the Yellow Emperor."

The misunderstanding of some students is that the life of a Taoist is passive. "Inaction" simply means spiritual neutrality. Inaction cannot be interpreted as passivity. Passivity is not life guidance.

A divine being is spiritually achieved and cannot be differentiated by gender, although in human language such a being is usually referred to as "he" or "she."

A divine being is an individual formed of universal spiritual energy: either a human being who has achieved himself through spiritual cultivation or a natural spiritual being that developed itself highly and attained the divine level.

A divine being can only be conceived in the harmonious universal energy that is attained through self-cultivation. Such a being is never born from confusion. The being that manifests from such an energy is called a devil.

In human spiritual education, misconceptions of divinity are harmful, because a person can form an image that will shape their own internal energy, and this conceptual form or divinity that they then believe in is, in essence, their own spirit. One who conceives of and believes in an aggressive god becomes aggressive himself. Being aggressive is not an act against God. It is simply a characteristic one attributes to God. It does not represent the total spiritual reality of a true Divine One.

The understanding of the universal truth developed naturally, before the widespread domination of mental conceptions. It was derived from a pure and uncontaminated spiritual vision that was keen and fresh. Thus, the invaluable guidance for all generations can be used in finding the way out of entrapment in confused conceptual creations. The teaching of Tao explores individual spiritual cultivation in depth, which is the true key to the original divine realm.

CHAPTER FORTY-FOUR

THE EXAMPLE OF A TRUTHFUL MAN

I

T'ien Tzu Fang, a respectful wise man, sat with Prince Wen of Wei at the prince's court. Tzu Fang praised Ch'i Kung, another virtuous person, so much and so often that Prince Wen finally asked him, "Is Ch'i Kung your teacher?"

"No," replied Tzu Fang, "he is only my neighbor, but when we discuss Tao, he seems to know something about it. That is why I praise him so."

"So then, you have no teacher?" inquired the Prince.

"Yes, I have a teacher." replied Tzu Fang.

"Who is it?" asked the Prince.

"Shun Tzu," said Tzu Fang.

"Why don't you ever praise him?" asked the Prince.

"I do not praise him because he is a perfect man," answered Tzu Fang. "Although he looks like a man, he has the qualities of nature itself. He is free from all attachments; he is unconditioned. He maintains patience with the conditioned; in oneness, he embraces all creation. When undeveloped people come to him, his silence enlightens them; they see their mistakes and correct themselves. It is not possible to praise one like this; he is beyond praise!"

When Tzu Fang had gone, the Prince was silent for the rest of the day, pondering what he had said. Then he called one of his close advisers over to him and said, "Such a man of perfect nature lives in a realm beyond our own; he is truly a developed person. I used to believe that benevolence and righteousness, social obligation and duty were perfection itself. But in hearing about Tzu Fang's teacher, I feel a kind of emptiness and stillness; my mouth is closed and I have no desire to speak. All that I have learned about government and the affairs of man is insignificant, like a salt doll that melts in the rain. The state of Wei ties me and is a burden. There really is such a thing as Tao that cannot be reached through superficial ways or by the general population who value only the narrow distinctions of this world."

II

Lieh Yu K'oh, a developed one whose achievement was earlier than that of Chuang Tzu, was exhibiting his skill at archery to Poh Hun Wu Jen, a developed one who taught Tao through archery. When he had drawn his bow as far as it would go, a cup of water was placed on his left elbow, and he let the arrow fly. Before the arrow had even hit the target, he drew another arrow and had it ready on the string, all without spilling a single drop of water from the cup. He was standing as firmly as a statue.

"Your shooting is that of a professional," Poh Hun Wu Jen commented. "But could you shoot with your mind like that of an amateur? Let us climb to the top of a mountain where there is a cliff a thousand feet high. You can stand on the edge, and we can see how well you can shoot!"

So the two men climbed up the mountain and went over to the edge of the precipice. Po Hun Wu Jen turned his back to the edge and moved to where he was standing with his feet partway over the edge. He told Lieh Tzu to come along and do the same, but the latter was lying flat on the ground, trembling and sweating, and would not go any closer.

"The perfect, natural man," said Poh Hun Wu Jen, "wherever he goes, whether entering the blue sky, going down to the yellow springs, or wandering in the eight directions, never changes in his spirit or bearing. You are fearful now; Tao has yet to be found by you!"

This was a result of the achievement Poh Hun Wu Jen had obtained through his spiritual cultivation; it is not like what an ordinary dare-devil does from a crazy and egotistical mind.

III

Chien Wu, a teacher of truth, asked Sun Shu Ao, a famous minister of the Ch'u state, "Sir, three times you have been given the post of minister, and none of those times did you display any pleasure or delight. Three times you left the post, and none of those times did you display any distress or regret. You remained then as you are now, unconcerned, breathing peacefully and deeply. Is there some special way you use your mind to control your emotions?"

At several other times, the same question was asked. His reply was the same in expressing his spiritual detachment. His words are worth repeating a thousand times.

"I am no better or different than any other person," answered Sun Shu. "I could not make the appointments happen, nor could I stop the dismissals; they are not matters of success or failure, but events that happen. Success and failure, profit and loss are not something that I control; it happens outside of myself. Any glory or honor that comes with such a post belongs to the post, not to me; I am no better than anyone else. Therefore, when I am at leisure, I enjoy; when I am called to duty, I work. There is no concern on my part about fame or whether people honor or despise me."

A teacher of attainment, on hearing this, commented, "Sun Shu Ao is like the wise men of ancient times. These men could not be convinced by a false argument, seduced by a beautiful woman, or stolen from by thieves; they were unshakable when it came to accomplishing what needed to be done. Even Fu Hsi and the Yellow Emperor would not have been able to become friends with him if the time was not right. To most people, life and death are most important, but fear of them did not enter the hearts of the ancient ones. High positions, power and salary did not control them. A spirit of this kind can soar to the top of Mount T'ai without any hindrance, or go through deep water without getting wet; he may be in the lowest position on the earth, but still he is not affected or distressed. Containing the fullness of the universe within them, they give to others ceaselessly, never running low themselves."

IV

Wen-po Hsueh-Tzu, a truthful man from the state of Ch'u, was on his way to the state of Ch'i and stopped for a while in the state of Lu. Confucius requested to meet him, but Wen-po Hsueh-tzu said, "No, indeed! I have heard that this man is only external and is well versed on the performance of superficial rituals, but has no inside. I have no wish to see such a person."

He continued on to his destination, but on his way home he stopped again in Lu, and once again Confucius requested to meet him. Wen-po Hsueh-tzu said, "This fellow must have something important to communicate to me," and he went out to receive the man. After the meeting he returned to his rooms with a sigh of astonishment. The next day, he met him again, and once more returned with a sigh. His traveling companion said, "Every time you receive these people, you come back sighing. Why?"

"As I mentioned to you earlier, I heard many times that this man from Lu is external and well versed on the performance of superficial rituals, but fails to reach the depth of heart. However, he is different from what people have said about him. When he came to see me yesterday and today, his coming and going were as precise as if measured by a yardstick; but he conversed with me as humbly as if he were my son and kindly offered me advice, as if he were as close as my father. I discovered that he is honest and sincere. This is why I sighed; because I have been touched deeply at heart and recognize my incorrect preconception."

After Confucius returned from his two interviews with Wen-po Hsueh-tzu, he didn't say anything. One of his students asked him, "You have wanted to see Wen-po Hsueh-tzu for a long time. Since you have had an opportunity to see him, why don't you tell us about it?"

Confucius replied, "With that kind of man, you have received sufficient teaching from his presence; his being tells you that the truth of a great life is embodied in such a person. What room does that leave to define him? Neither pride at having made his acquaintance nor diplomatic manners win his friendship. I will tell you what has so deeply touched and enlightened me; it is his spiritual sincerity."

V

A wise student asked his teacher, "Master, when you walk, I walk; when you speed up, so do I; and when you run, I run. But when you move out of the ordinary realm, I can only stand watching."

"Explain yourself," said the teacher.

"I mean," continued the student, "the way you walk, I walk. The way you speak, I speak. The way you describe Tao, I describe Tao. By 'move out of the ordinary realm,' I mean that without speaking people believe you; without striving people love you; without any ornament people gather around you. I do not understand how you do it."

"This is nothing to admire. The best thing to do is look into our own life," replied the teacher. "There is nothing sadder than the death of the mind; then it can no longer be open to a fresh reality. Even the death of the body is secondary to that."

"What is the fresh reality?" asked the student.

"The sun rises in the east and sets in the west, and all things move with it." The teacher answered, "All creatures with eyes and ears wait for it before doing their tasks. For all creation it is so. They must wait for the natural creative force to depart before they can die, and wait for it to come before they can receive life. By developing and transforming from the natural creative force, we are physically formed and receive life; we continue to join the big transformation of nature. We are here temporarily; the just formed life awaits its gradual dissolution. We move according to nature, day and night without ceasing, but we do not know what the end of all this continual transformation will be.

Even those who understand the natural fate of human
life cannot fathom what preceded or will follow in
their life. This is the way I proceed, cooperating each
day with the new natural flow of universal transformation. I am selfless."

"I have gone through life together with you. It is
like we have just met each other, and soon we will depart. We cannot afford to fail to understand the reality
of life. The reality of life exists only in the right moment. It is impossible for you to know me by the
image you have in your mind. That is like looking for
a horse after the horse fair has ended. That is the
past, and it is impossible for me to know you in that
way, too. Even so, what of it? What is past does not
stay, but there is that which goes beyond the transformation of time. One who learns the truth cannot rely
on the witness of past experience; your immediate
vision is what reads and catches the fresh alive moment. This is the true life."

VI

A man who had achieved himself in a scholarly
way and who had acquired great fame and influence
was inspired by hearing the teaching of Lao Tzu.
Realizing the emptiness of his achievement, he decided
to re-educate himself and learn from Lao Tzu. One
time when he went to see Lao Tzu, the sage had just
washed his hair and it was hanging down his back to
dry. Utterly motionless, he looked like a lifeless body.
The visiting scholar stood there for a while, waiting for
him. Then he approached and said, "Are my eyes
seeing correctly? You were just standing there alone
and still with your body as stiff as a dead tree."

"I was letting my heart and mind dwell in the
unborn," replied Lao Tzu.

"What do you mean?" asked the student.

"The mind may become tired, but will never understand it," replied Lao Tzu. "The mouth may talk endlessly, but can never explain it. But I will try to give
you an approximation of the truth of nature.

"Yin energy is a magnificently receptive energy that comes from Earth. Yang energy is a powerfully creative force that emanates from Heaven. The interaction of the two result in the harmony by which all things are produced. There is a subtle law at work, but you will never find any trace of it. Things rise and fall, prosper and decline, fill and empty. Days and nights come and go, work is constantly performed, yet we never witness its performance. Life brings us into being and death carries us out. Beginning and end follow ceaselessly upon each other, and we cannot say when they will be exhausted. Is this not governed by the subtle law? If it is not Tao, where else could it be from?"

"What does it mean to dwell in the unborn?" asked the visiting scholar.

"To attain the essence of all beauty and happiness," answered Lao Tzu, "one must reach beyond all concepts of beauty and happiness. He who attains the perfect essence of all beauty can be called a complete one."

"How can this be done?" inquired the scholar.

"Grazing animals accept a change of grasslands," replied Lao Tzu. "Ducks are known to move from pond to pond. As long as the basic element remains the same, it is all right to make some changes.

"If you can accept the changes, then joy, anger, sorrow and happiness will not arise in you. In this world, all creation is One. Because all things are joined in oneness, he who can realize it will find that his body becomes like earth, life and death will become like night and day, and peace is constant. Loss or gain, fortune or misfortune, will be like mere trifles.

"A person of this stature rejects the limitation of externals as though they were unnecessary, for he knows that life itself is more important than any circumstance; its essence cannot be lost or exhausted by any modification of existence. A person's worth is intrinsic in his or her nature; it cannot be lost because of external things. None of the myriad transformations is final, so what can cause the heart and mind anxiety? Those who practice Tao understand the secret of this."

"Respectful Master," said the scholar, "Your great life being is the very substance of Heaven and Earth, yet even you use these perfect teachings in order to cultivate your mind. All the great ones of the past must certainly have known this!"

"Not so," answered Lao Tzu. "Water flows not by its own effort, but as its natural property commands. It cannot separate from this property. Heaven is clear, earth is characterized by gravity; the sun and moon are light. They do not need to cultivate these characteristics. They are natural; they are of nature. To be an achieved one is to be nature."

After learning that, the scholar went away and told his own students, "As far as Tao is concerned, I am like a firefly in a glass jar. It is good that my Master removed the lid, or I would not have rejoined the great unity of Heaven and Earth.

"One should clearly understand that the creative nature of the universe is interconnected with the natural creative energy of our lives. Discussions and teachings about spiritual self-cultivation should not be mistaken for the main elements in the teaching of Tao."

CHAPTER FORTY-FIVE

THE WISDOM OF LIFE

I

Mr. Intellectual Knowledge, who was searching for profound wisdom, traveled north across the Black River and climbed the Mountain of Hidden Heights where he met the One of Nothing That Can Be Presented by Words. He asked him, "Through what kind of thinking, contemplation, reflecting and pondering does one come to know Tao as the integral truth? Where and in what guise does one feel secure in Tao? What sort of practices and what path does one follow to reach Tao?"

To these questions the One of Nothing That Can Be Presented by Words made no reply. It was not that he would not answer, he just didn't know how to answer verbally.

When the seeker got no reply he left and went across the South River and climbed Mount Certainty. There he met the One of Abandoning All Extremes and asked him the same questions.

"Oh yes," said the One of Abandoning All Extremes, whose nickname is the One of Mad Abandon, "I know and I will tell you." But just as he was about to speak, he forgot what he was going to say.

The seeker, having failed twice to get an answer, went to the Imperial Palace where he was received by the Yellow Emperor himself. The seeker posed his questions to the Emperor and the Emperor said, "Thought and reflection may begin one on a path to Tao, but only when there is neither thought nor pondering will you truly come to know Tao as the integral truth. Only when there is no practice, no path, no seeking and no procedure can a person attain Tao."

Then the seeker said to the Yellow Emperor, "You and I know about this, but when I asked the other two, they did not know. Of all of us, who is right?" The Emperor replied, "The One of Nothing That Can be Presented by Words is the one who is correct. The One of Abandoning all Extremes is close. You and I are not even close at all. True knowledge of the integral truth does not speak, because it is unspeakable and thus avoids any speech that would separate one from the integral truth. That is the reason why the truly wise ones instruct their students non-verbally. To use words would be to divorce the individual's own spirit from the oneness of the universal spiritual nature.

"One cannot attain natural action, virtue or Tao by forcing it. Practicing benevolence is equal to participating in calculated, artificial action. Practicing moral performance and particular good deeds demonstrates approval for what is defective. Ceremony is only an empty shell. That is why it is said: 'When Tao was lost, then virtue was established; when virtue was lost, benevolence was established; when benevolence was lost, moral performance and particular good deeds were established; when moral performance and good deeds were lost, ceremony was established. Ceremonies are nothing more than ornaments, and they court disaster.' It is also said: 'The man concerned with the integral truth eliminates his artificialities and disguises more and more each day until there is no more external creation to confuse the natural truth. This one receives true freedom.'

"When these artificialities have been reduced, one attains perfect freedom in action. At this stage, everything gets done naturally and not as the result of using force. Those who practice Tao simplify their life. If that simplification proceeds until inaction or spontaneous action occurs, then there is nothing which cannot be done.

"We are already conditioned beings; things, as it were. If you wanted to return to perfect freedom, it would be difficult. If such a change could be made in a person's life, such a person must be one of the greatest among us!

"Life and death are truly companions one to the other, because life continues evolving. Who understands the true order of life and death? Which comes first? The birth of a human being is an amassing of natural energy. While this amassment continues, there is life; when it ceases, there is death. Since life and death are companions, then what is there to be worried about?

"All creation is really one. We like what is growing and dislike what is decaying. But it is from what has decayed that new growth comes. So it is said, 'You have only to understand the entire world as one natural energy.' Thus, the wise person values the oneness of all things."

The seeker said to the Yellow Emperor, "I asked One of Nothing That Can Be Presented by Words and he didn't reply to me because he didn't know how to put it in words. I asked the One of Abandoning All Extremes and he was about to explain it to me, but he didn't explain anything in words. It wasn't that he wouldn't, he just forgot. Was it because the One of Abandoning All Extremes knows the difference between deep enlightenment and simply drawing close to the truth through abandonment? Now I have asked you and you know the answer. Why, then, do you say that you are not even close?"

The Yellow Emperor said, "The One of Nothing That Can Be Presented by Words is the one who is truly right, because he doesn't know how. The One of Mad Abandon appears to be right because he forgets the center and sees the edges. But you and I, in the end, are not close at all because we have an answer. We are not close because we comment on the integral flow of universal natural life, rather than completely joining in with the natural vitality. We live by the activity of intellectual movement rather than by total union. Thus Tao is not attained by knowledge, but by the absence of partializing concepts and expressions of words. Intellect is not direct experience, joining nor uniting; it is only the derivative activity of knowledge." When the One of Abandoning All Extremes heard of this incident, he felt that the Yellow Emperor had described it very well.

II

Heaven and Earth have great beauty and goodness, and the four seasons have their clearly seen regular changes. All lives have principles of growth. Yet they do not speak of themselves, their beauty, regularity or growth. One of natural wisdom seeks out and comes to understand the beauty and order inherent in all creation; thus he is an observer of nature in its entirety and master of the principles of all creation. Yet the one of complete and integral virtue does not need to do anything to make his own life like that of the universe; the highest form of life is natural in itself, thus there is nothing that needs to be done. The wise become achieved by observation and thus reach integrity. The integral one, who is naturally so, is the teacher of the wise.

To understand intellectually that Tao is the unity of universal life is not difficult. To be it, meaning to achieve and maintain union with universal being, requires unimaginable effort for people of intellectual habits. They must give up their deviation from what is natural; each moment they must move back from their deviation of creating different centers of life and in projecting a different focus of life so that they can become aware of it. This is the practice on the spiritual level.

On the practical level, I have interpreted the integral way of life as being like a developed person who is able to live a healthy, normal life without looking for extraordinary achievement which would cause an imbalance. The problem is that people can no longer recognize what is a healthy, normal way of life. Lao Tzu, therefore, used about five thousand characters to illustrate it for people. Chuang Tzu and his students used a volume about ten times the size of Lao Tzu's work in a further attempt to convey it. I myself have produced fourteen books, each from a different angle, to introduce the natural, moral life to all my fellow people with spiritual awareness. All these issue a warning against further unnatural development of human culture; yet the condition of human society continues to deteriorate. It suggests making a timely adjustment.

III

Yeh Ch'ueh asked P'i[106] about Tao. P'i answered, "Straighten your body, concentrate on oneness and the harmonious energy of nature will descend upon you. Restrain intellectual thought and concentrate on oneness, keep your body upright, and the integral nature of the universe will abide with you in all its clarity; virtue will beautify you; Tao will shelter you. You will be like a new-born calf which knows nothing and does not pursue knowledge but only true life."

While P'i was still speaking, Yeh Ch'ueh fell asleep, at which P'i greatly rejoiced and departed singing:

"His body is like a dry bone,
His mind is like dead ashes.
Body and mind block the most truthful knowledge.
He is not proud of the attainment of truth.
He does not strive for more reasons
　　　for living a complete life.
In darkness and obscurity his mind dwells;
　　　you cannot get any ideas from him!
What kind of person is that?
Well might you wonder!"

IV

Shun asked his teacher, Ch'eng, "Is it possible to possess Tao?"

"How could you possibly possess Tao? You do not even possess your own body," answered Ch'eng.

---

[106]Both men were developed ones.

"Really? If I don't possess it, then to whom does it belong?" said Shun.
"Your body is a form that has been given to you by nature," replied Ch'eng. "It is the same with your life. It is an acquiescence, a contingency conferred by nature. Your children and grandchildren do not belong to you either. They are like cast-off skins conferred by the natural subtle substance of life. That is why you are journeying through life without knowing your destination, you live but do not know what truly keeps you alive, and you eat yet do not know what you taste. All this is the strong, creative yang energy of nature in action. How then could you think you could possess Tao only for your self?"[107]

V

There was once a scholar of exceptional academic achievement who was accepted by Lao Tzu as a student. On one occasion he asked Lao Tzu, "Since there is time today, please tell me about Tao."
"Cleanse your heart by fasting and cultivation," answered Lao Tzu. "Purify your inner spirit, destroy and do away with your knowledge. Tao is subtle and not easily put into words, but I will try to give you a sense of it.
"Light comes out of darkness. What is ordered comes out of the formless. Souls and spirits are from Tao, and bodies and forms are from sperm or vital essence. Things give form to one another, each to its own kind; this is called birth. Those with nine channels (orifices) of communication come from the womb; those with eight come from the egg.
"Tao, however, leaves no trace when it comes and goes. It is as expansive as the four directions. He who lives with Tao will be strong in body, sharp and

---

[107]This is to illustrate the potency of the deathless universal life and the attainment of nothingness as the integral truth. This is the reality of the attainment of integral life.

clear in mind, acute in vision and hearing, and universal in his response to things. Heaven is always high, earth is always broad; the sun and the moon always turn; all of the projected thrives. All this because of Tao.

"Being highly educated does not mean that one knows the truth. Being a polished speaker does not necessarily mean that one is wise. This is why the person who lives with natural wisdom does not concern himself deeply with those things. The wise ones safeguard that which increases without being seen and that which diminishes without being lost.

"Deep and immeasurable as the sea, tall and splendid as the mountains, Tao supports all things at all times.

"There are some people in the Middle Land who are attached to neither yin nor yang and who live between Heaven and Earth. For a brief time they are temporarily here as human beings, and then they return to their root. Looking at them from the standpoint of the source, their lives are a mere gathering of energy, and whether they die young or old, the two fates scarcely differ - a difference of a few moments, you might say. What reason, then, have we to say that the benevolent Yao is good and the tyrant Chieh is bad?

"The trees and vines and grasses all have their own patterns and cycles of growth. Human relationships, in all their complexity, also have their orderliness.[108] When a sage is involved in such relationships, he respects them. When he gets beyond them, he does not hold tightly to them because he always adapts to his environment. Harmonizing with people is a virtue. Responding to them with universal love is Tao. When emperors and kings have correctly raised themselves to

---

[108]The classifications of human relationships are: ruler and subject; husband and wife; parent and child; elder sibling and younger sibling; friend and friend.

power, it has been a result of the harmony of all people, not a false victory that utilizes force.

"Man passes through this earthly life like a sunbeam passes through a crack in the wall; first here, then gone, quick as can be. Each man is equally subject to the coming and going of life. Those who remain behind may grieve over it. The umbrella falls to the ground, the knapsack tumbles down, the body drops to the ground, and the soul takes flight on the great journey home.

"Those without bodies try to attain them, and those with them try to attain bodylessness. This is understood by all, but not through the intellect. Men may argue over how to do it, but those who know do not argue. Those who argue do not know how. Staring will not help you see it. Listening cannot help you hear it. Plugging up your ears might work better, because Tao cannot be heard. To know this is a great achievement."

VI

Tung Kuo Tzu, a searcher of truth, asked Chuang Tzu, "Where is Tao?"

"Well," replied Chuang Tzu, "there is nowhere that it is not."

"Alright," said Kuo Tzu, "then tell me just one place where it is."

"It is in an ant," answered Chuang Tzu.

"So lowly?" exclaimed Kuo Tzu.

"Alright, then, it is in the weeds," said Chuang Tzu.

"As low as that?" cried Kuo Tzu.

"It is in broken tiles and rubble," said Chuang Tzu.

"I can't believe it!" moaned Kuo Tzu.

"It is in excrement!" said Chuang Tzu, and Kuo Tzu did not reply.

Then Chuang Tzu said, "Noble friend, your question does not hit the mark. Whenever Huo, the woman assistant of the Inspector, went to the overseer of the market place, she customarily checked out with him the higher priced merchandise first, then continued down to the lower priced things like shoes and pork. The

further along she got in her questioning, the lower
down she went. Your question is similar to her way
of asking. The more you ask, the farther away you are
from your destination. The deeper you search, the
wider the distance from your goal.

"Do not look for Tao in only one single item; it is
the entirety of all things. There is nothing beyond Tao.
Tao is just that. The great word which can present the
truth is just that. The entirety of the universe cannot
be beyond "Tao", "it" and the "word." All these sound
different, but they all point to the single reality of
nature.

"Try to enjoy the place of non-individualized existence where the universe is as one integral reality.
Identity and accord are of the same foundation there,
and we will never come to an end, never reach exhaustion. This means the man of Tao does not hold onto a
single ideological invention, discovery or creation as
truth. By doing so, we will not be trapped in the
painted glass room of our thoughts and preconceptions
as we observe the outside world. Let us not be the
intellectually inquisitive, but let us rest in an undisturbed mental state. The high practice of spiritual non-
effort or inactivity leads a person to an inner stillness
which in turn produces a mind of crystal clearness. It
brings the vision of purity, harmony, and balance. It is
a place where your will becomes empty and your spirit
unites with the integral truth, in independence. There
is nowhere to go. There is no awareness of the goings
and comings. With no goal, there is also no other
destination. There is movement and repose where
infinity exists, where intellect cannot be applied. Only
the great mind of the sages can wholly know this
truth. There, no borders of vast space or length of
time exists. There, all things come to exist without
extending preference or applying judgement. There,
things come to life and go to their finish according to
their own internal truth. The internal truth of every
life contains its innate limit. By extending their truth
of limits, life and existence are given a positive
function and benefit to the world. The sages break

their own limits. Ordinary people hold onto their limits and work to actualize their limits and to extend them over all others. Thus, they live with a destructive reality.

"That which allows forms to be what they are is not limited to the forms themselves. This is Tao. Individually however, a form is limited. Tao has no limits, yet it joins in the limits of all forms. Thus, in limited experience, there is still the limitless Tao.[109]

"To experience limits in the limitless is the nature of life. Limitlessness in the limited is Tao. Tao can let things be full and less full, although it is neither full nor empty itself. It can let things increase or decrease, although it neither increases nor decreases itself. It can allow renewal or decay, beginning and end, accumulation and dispersion, but it is none of these itself.

"Everything in itself is complete in terms of the completeness of Tao. Is it not what you inquire into?"

VII

Ah Ho Kan and Shen Nung were both students of Lung Chi. Shen Nung was taking a nap with the door shut, leaning on the armrest of his chair, holding his walking staff in his hand. At noon, Ah Ho-Kan opened the door and said, "Our teacher has died!"

Shen Nung arose from the chair, threw down his staff on the ground noisily and laughed, "Our master went off and died without speaking the words to open my mind! He knew how egotistical and inferior, how inglorious I am!"

When Yen Kang Tiao, a man of Tao, went to pay his condolences, he commented, "The man who embodies Tao is sought by all men. If he, who had not been of the greatest achievement, had sufficient wisdom to keep it unspoken, how much more those who are

---

[109]Put more simply, Tao allows things be what they are but is not limited by them. It joins in their limits, but is not confined by their limits.

highly achieved. Tao cannot be seen; Tao cannot be heard. When it is discussed, it seems obscure, but that is because when Tao is discussed, it is not Tao."

VIII

Light Giver asked Non-Existence, "Sir, do you exist or not?"

Receiving no reply, all day long Light Giver stared at Non-Existence, but could see nothing. He listened intently, but heard nothing. He reached out, but touched nothing.

"You are perfection itself!" exclaimed Light Giver. "I have known about the existence of non-existence, but now I realize the non-existence of non-existence. How could this height of perfection have been attained?"

IX

The swordmaker for the Minister of War was eighty years old and had never made the slightest mistake in his work. One day the Minister of War said to him, "Is your ability due to skill or have you special achievement?"

"It is simply a matter of concentration," replied the old man. "I was twenty years old when I first began making swords; that was all I cared about. I paid no attention to anything that was not a sword. Whatever energy was not used to support the bare necessities of my life I turned toward my craft."

By deliberate single-mindedness, the old sword-maker was able, over the years, to master the subject of his concentration. How much greater would a man be if, by the same method, he reached the point where there was nothing that escaped his attention. All things would come to share the peace and safety from his influence.[110]

---

[110]This is a great illustration of pure spiritual cultivation.

X

A student asked his teacher, "Master, I have heard you say that a person should not chase anything away, nor welcome anything to him. How is this done?"

The teacher said, "The developed ones of ancient times changed their egos to meet the situation they were in but maintained internal peace as a constant state. They allowed themselves to change in relationship to externals; they also allowed themselves to change internally.

"Today's people, however, would like to change the world to suit themselves. They do not like to change themselves. Or they change their mood and mind internally all the time. How and what shall you change, and how and what shall you not change? How do you adapt to an external situation? How do you reconcile a dispute or adapt to a needed change? In making changes, never allow yourself to treat others with arrogance, if so, you should change yourself, not the others. If by quietly observing, you know you are treated with arrogance, you leave the others without needing to change yourself.

"Hsi-Wei[111] had his country estate, the Yellow Emperor kept to his garden, Shun stayed in his palace, T'ang and Wu did not leave their halls. That is to say, when one becomes inconsiderate and rough, one should withdraw and become one's own teacher in the quiet hours. Among good men there were those like the Confucians, who practiced humanitarianism in personal and social relationships, and Mohists, who practiced humanitarianism on a worldwide basis and became teachers of their own specific guidance for all other people. As a result of the teaching of these good men, their ideas of right and wrong became a stiff standard in society. People learn to depend on the external standard rather than refining their own personality to attain inner strength. How can a person know what and how to change?

---

[111]A kind leader before the time of Fu Hsi.

"One of Integral Wisdom lives with external things and does not harm them; he who does not harm external things is not harmed by them in return. Only he who receives no harm is able to be among others without chasing or welcoming anything. He lets whatever happens happen, never pushing anything away, but letting it go by itself.

"Mountains, forests, hills and meadows all fill us with delight, but before the joy is gone, grief comes following quickly behind. There is no way to prevent grief or joy from coming and no way to prevent their departure; one cannot either chase nor welcome them. Living a human life is like stopping at an inn for a short time. And rushing everywhere is not how to build the strength of upright characteristics.

"People can know about the things they see in their daily life, but not that with which they do not have contact with. They know how to do the things they can do, but not the things that they cannot do. To not know something and to not be able to do something are the two great realities that mankind can never escape, yet there are those who would try to escape the inescapable by rushing around everywhere. The limits of our knowledge and capability are two realities one cannot escape, and it is a pity that people try to escape the acceptance of their own limits.

"Perfect speech is to be silent. Perfect action is inaction. To be limited to understanding intellectual knowledge is to have a shallow understanding."

Lacking in quiet reflection, world leaders wish to make all people equal without allowing the existence of individual differences and growth. People are thus kept within the bounds of conventional thought. This is shallow. This has been the darkness of human society throughout history, especially in times of political and religious dominance. It is a shame to see this system of external control established and extended to all aspects of modern life.

XI

Maintaining Purity asked Limitlessness, "Do you know Tao?"

"No, I don't," replied Limitlessness.

Then, Maintaining Purity went to ask the same question to Doing Nothing Extra.

"Yes I do," replied Doing Nothing Extra.

"Is there any special way that brought you to know Tao?" asked Maintaining Purity.

"There is," replied Doing Nothing Extra.

"What is it?" asked Maintaining Purity.

"I understand," said Doing Nothing Extra, "that Tao is in the most exalted things as well as in the most humble; it causes them to be born and to die. That is how I know Tao."

Maintaining Purity repeated these words to Trace-lessness and asked him who was right: the "ignorant" Limitlessness or the "knowledgeable" Doing Nothing Extra.

"He who admits that he does not know," replied Tracelessness, "is profound. He who claims to know is shallow. He who admits to not knowing is, in reality, within Tao. He who claims to know is, in reality, outside of Tao because he splits it in two. Knowing requires the duality of subject and object."

Maintaining Purity pondered, "Then ignorance is knowledge, and knowledge is ignorance! How can we understand what one can know through ignorance?"

Tracelessness said, "There is no name that fits Tao. Can you understand that?

"Tao cannot be heard. What can be heard is not Tao.

"Tao cannot be seen. What can be seen is not Tao.

"Tao cannot be described. What can be described is not Tao.

"That which gives form to the formed is itself formless.

"That is why to reply to something to which there is no reply reveals the absence of Tao in the one who answers. Such a person does not understand the plain source of all wonders and the great beginning of all things, and will never reach the height of the K'un-lun Mountains nor soar in the enjoyment of the supreme mystery."

XII

A student asked a teacher of Tao, "Can we know about the time before the universe existed?"

"Yes," replied the teacher, "time was then exactly what it is now."

At this the student said, "Oh, yes," and withdrew. The next day he visited the teacher again and asked, "When I asked you about time yesterday, I understood your answer clearly, but now I am confused. Why is this?"

"Your clarity yesterday," answered the teacher, "came because your spirit experienced it through my words. If it seems obscure today, it is because you are trying to understand it with something other than direct spiritual experience. Look within yourself to see if this is true.

"There is no past, no present, no beginning, no end. Is it possible for sons and grandsons to exist before there have been any sons and grandsons?"

Before the student could answer he continued, "Please, do not answer. With the birth of life comes the inevitability of death. The two arise at the same time; they cannot be independent, one of the other. Yet, that which ends life does not die; that which gives life does not live.

"Did anything exist before the birth of Heaven and Earth? We may say that what causes a life to take shape is not the life itself; something exists before the creation of life. Because there is life, there is no end to reproduction and creation; it is a path of endless development. What makes formed items what they are is not itself formed, so for things to come forth, no preceding form is needed. Objects are around by virtue of the 'something' that never ends. Tao is the model for the endless love of the sages for mankind.

"Tao, the great flow of nature, brews the birth of all creatures of material existence, yet no one knows where it resides itself. It continually brings forth all things, but its beginning and end, origin and result cannot be found. It is the great channel from which all smaller channels derive life, yet the precise location of its existence cannot be known. Thus it clearly reveals itself in the six directions and in boundless space. Without finding its origin in life and death, we know it exists in the past, present and future, without beginning or end. Movement is its existence, creating time and space and all necessary manifestation.

"The six cardinal points[112] which extend into infinity are one dimension of Tao. An autumn leaf, however small, can carry Tao within itself. All things on earth have a beginning and an end, but life itself does not perish. Tao is not only the path of the great nature, it is also the subtle law and the name for the universal vitality of nature itself.

"Yin and yang follow one another; the four seasons have their sequence. They maintain their order and follow the rules of nature. All lives naturally spring forth and grow. Change is the greatest power, but it is unformed. All things are raised by it, though they do not know it is the root and source. The one who understands the subtle root of all lives can discover the existence of the path of the integral truth.

"Tao, the flow of nature, gives birth to all things without showing any source and root. All things eventually disappear and return to the great flow of nature, but nobody can find any trace of them or the direction in which they went.

"Among all things some come forth, some die, some appear and some disappear. The immeasurable changes of life and death, of coming and going leave no trace behind them. This is the Great Gate of natural creation which unifies all things and which changes nothingness into form. All things are produced through the interchange of nothingness and form. Anything of name and form cannot rely on permanence

---

[112]The four directions, up and down.

in its existence.   It will in turn shift back to the nothingness from which it came.

"The unnameable origin penetrates and assimilates
the changes of life and death, the development from
nothing to something and of something to nothing
again.

"Vast as the universe is, its movement and change
all arise from nature.   Although its contents and phenomena are without number, there are laws which
regulate the growth and development of each life."

CHAPTER FORTY-SIX

NAN YUNG CH'U

I

Among the students of Lao Tzu was one named Keng Sang Ch'u. He was one of the students of his master who attained Tao. So after having learned everything that Lao Tzu had to teach him, he went north and lived in the Wei-lei mountains. People flocked there to follow and serve him, but he accepted very few. Of his students and attendants, he did not keep those who displayed any special cleverness, who verbally exalted charity or restricted themselves to intellectual knowledge only, and kept at a distance those who were only interested in leading a narrow religious life. He let those of a simple nature stay with him and only accepted the ones who knew how to work very hard and be happy. Within a few years the entire district of Wei-lei benefited and began to enjoy prosperity.

The people of Wei-lei discussed him among themselves. "When Keng Sang first came here, we did not know what kind of person he was. Now we are amazed by him. It is not the everyday things he does, but the general view that we have of him. He must be a man of great wisdom. Day by day we seem to slowly improve. Year by year we enjoy more prosperity. We love him! We should make him our king and build a temple in which to worship him."

Upon hearing this, Keng Sang turned his face to the south, toward the abode of Lao Tzu, displeased with what the people wanted to do. His disciples were astonished at his response, but he said, "What surprises you? Do you think this is my achievement? When spring arrives, the grass begins to grow. Later, when autumn comes, the grain becomes ripe and is ready to harvest. It is Tao that accomplishes all things. It is not the person who simply appears to be performing the task. How could it be otherwise? The way of Heaven sets things in motion; it is nature in operation. This is Tao. No man deserves to be a king. It is unvirtuous to put oneself above others.

"I have heard that the person of integral nature and virtue dwells in quietude and stillness, attending only to matters which pertain to him. He is like a fish who enjoys its life in a quiet mountain lake. He lets others follow their coarse and heedless ways, rushing madly here and there without knowing where they are going. Now, the unthinking people of Wei-lei wish to exalt me as wise and good, holding me up as a model for man. That is why, remembering the teaching of Lao Tzu, I am displeased."

His students said, "Do not feel that way. In a small stream, a big fish barely has room to move, but minnows and tadpoles dart about easily. On a small hill, a water buffalo cannot hide, but a fox can.

"For worthy men to be duly honored and for people of ability to be promoted has been a custom from the days of Shun and Yao, the benevolent emperors. So, why not let the people of Wei-lei honor you if they wish?"

Keng Sang said, "Even a large, powerful animal like a water buffalo, when it leaves its proper habitat, cannot escape the dangers of net and snare. Even the largest and most graceful of fishes, if caught in a storm and lifted onto the land by the large waves, will become the prey of ants. This is why birds fly high, beasts stay in the deep forest and fishes swim near the bottom of the lake. Similarly, even the greatest of men protects himself, no matter how secluded or remote he must go. His habitat is the deep mountain and his companions the pure springs; he goes where he can be away from the crowds of people.

"The worldly leaders deserve no praise; they establish and promote unnatural standards of living. People follow their false fashions, and the result is that without realizing it, they also turn out to be false themselves; in the pursuit of what is false they become competitive and end up behaving unnaturally. They struggle to maintain an artificial 'good' life of combing one hair at a time and counting the number of grains to go in the rice pudding, or purposely knocking a hole in a wall so that they can seal it up. So how do you think that the worldly leaders have helped the world? They should have left things alone!

"When you begin to honor people, other people, wishing to be so honored themselves, will do anything. When men of intellect are advanced, the moral nature of the community begins its downfall, and people begin to steal from one another. Policies of honor and advancement are, in the end, unhelpful; they cause people to become crafty and ingenious as they pursue their gains, until they go to the extremes of trampling on one another, sons killing their fathers, people stealing in broad daylight, government officials overthrowing one another, and knocking holes in walls so they can be filled up. The cause of all this is the honor and advancement promoted by the world's leaders. The result of this will be, that in the generations that follow, people will kill each other for ideas or conceptual creations that they don't even understand!"

Nan Yung Ch'u, one of his disciples, was so startled by what was said that he straightened himself up quickly in his seat and said, "For one who has matured in understanding through experience in life, how would you advise me to discipline myself to become a man like yourself?"

"Preserve your body and health," replied Keng Sang. "Maintain your vitality. Do not allow the fluctuations of your mind to pull you into elaborate plans for profits or honors. Do not allow the mind to pull you into worries and troubles. If you can do this for three years, you will become attained."

"All eyes have a certain form, yet blind men cannot see. Ears have a certain form, yet deaf men cannot hear," replied Nan Yung. "The head is the seat of the intellect, yet fools cannot use theirs to accomplish anything very beneficial. Thus, forms, minds and bodies are alike, but yet there is something different between one person and another. One succeeds while another does not. You are telling me to preserve my body and health, maintain my vitality and keep my mind calm, but I do not think that I truly hear what it is you mean."

"This is all that I can say," replied Keng Sang Ch'u. "An eagle cannot be hatched from a hummingbird's egg, but from a great eagle nest atop a high mountain. A beautiful and trusty horse cannot be born from a wasp's nest, but only from a mother of its own kind. Each has the power of reproduction, but the capability of some is of large proportion and the capability of others is of a smaller proportion. My abilities would seem to be of the second kind, as there has been no transformation in you. Perhaps you would benefit from a visit with Lao Tzu."

II

Nan Yung packed up some food for his trip, and because at that time walking was the means of travel, after seven days he arrived at the home of Lao Tzu.

"So you have come from the place of Keng Sang Ch'u?" asked Lao Tzu.

"Yes," replied Nan Yung.

"Why did you bring such a crowd with you?" asked Lao Tzu.[113]

Nan Yung, startled, looked around and behind him for the crowd.

"Don't you understand what I mean?" said Lao Tzu.

Nan Yung, embarrassed, bent his head. He looked up and sighed, and said to the master, "I do not know how to reply to that, and I have also forgotten all the questions I was going to ask you."

"What do you mean?" said Lao Tzu. "Tell me about yourself."

---

[113]He was referring to all the questions Nan Yung was going to ask.

"If I don't know things, people call me stupid," replied Nan Yung. "If I say I do know, or tell them, I either bring harm to others or start to worry. "If I am not kind to other people, it seems they are harmed by it. But if I am kind, I either harm myself or end up causing trouble in some way. "If I do not perform my social obligations, others are injured. If I do accomplish my duty, I injure myself or cause myself distress. I cannot see how to escape these three dilemmas. On the suggestion of Keng Sang Ch'u, I have come to request your advice."

"The moment I saw you I could tell what kind of person you were," said Lao Tzu. "Your reply also gives it away. You are confused, as though you were a child who had lost its mother and father. Having lost the basics, you seek them as if you were trying to fathom the sea with a pole. You are hesitant and unsure; a lost soul. You want to return to your inborn nature, but don't know how to do it. You are quite pitiful."

Nan Yung, crestfallen, begged to be allowed to stay so that he might work to cultivate the good in himself and eliminate the darkness. After he spent ten days making himself miserable, he returned to Lao Tzu for another meeting.

Lao Tzu said, "You have been relentless in your cleansing and purifying, but there is still something distressing you; it seems that there is some negativity remaining within you.

"When external things disturb you, and you cannot control yourself, your mind becomes set; it locks the inside gate. When internal things disturb you and you can't dissolve them, it blocks the outside gate. If external and internal both disturb you, then even the Tao and its virtue can't keep you safe, much less the one who is simply a follower of Tao in his actions."[114]

---

[114]What Lao Tzu means is that the one whose senses are controlled by outside things, has lost control of himself. Therefore, he must work internally to purify the desire that forms those attach-

Nan Yung said, "When a villager gets sick and his neighbor asks him how he feels, if he can describe the sickness, then he truly isn't very sick, because he can still recognize that he is ill. If I were to ask about the Great Way, any answer would be like a medicine that would only make me sicker. What I wish to know is simply how to preserve life, that is all."

Lao Tzu said, "Ah! Preserving life consists of embracing unity, losing nothing, foretelling good fortune and misfortune without using any system of divination, knowing how much is enough and when to stop, forgetting about what is over and done, not interfering with others and attending to your own nature. You keep to what is true and give up what is false. You maintain what is innate without losing it. You comply with so-called destiny. You are peaceful and content with what you have and with what you can do. You are not greedy once you are supported. You are gentle in blaming others and strict in disciplining yourself. You take it easy and feel free in any circumstance. You keep your mind off things you really do not need to know. You maintain your desire at the level of a baby.

"A baby cries all day, but its voice does not become hoarse; this is constitutional harmony. A baby makes fists all day long, but its hand holds nothing; this is perfect, natural behavior. A baby gazes all day without blinking; it is not distracted by external things.

"Like a baby, to move about without knowing where you are going, to sit without knowing where you are, to unconsciously accept the way things are and adapt to the environment; this is the art of preserving life."

"Is this, then, the virtue of one who has attained perfection?" asked Nan Yung.

---

ments. The one whose mind is attached to things cannot control himself and he must work externally to be able to see clearly and avoid temptation. If one is bound to internal and external things, then it is hard for even a person of high achievement to help him.

"No," replied Lao Tzu, "this is just an illustration of how to disperse the stagnancy of your mind like thawing a block of frozen ice. Can you do it? Man in his highest expression dines and shares joys with what nature can provide. He is not disturbed by the mundaneness of his life, the external gains or losses. He does not join others in plotting and erecting strange standards to live by. He does not take part in schemes nor in the performance of what is titillating.

"It is to say that one who has attained perfection eats the food from the earth and takes his happiness from Heaven. He does not become involved in establishing a monument to his ego, with excessive profits or by performing outrageous acts. Leaving with complete freedom and arriving without preconception is the way of spiritual health."

"Is this what describes perfection?" asked Nan Yung.

"No," replied Lao Tzu. "Just a moment ago I asked you if you could be like a baby. When a baby acts, it does not know what it is doing.[115] Its body is like the new branch from a withered tree, its mind like a new spark from the dead ashes. Such a wonderful new life, neither bad fortune nor good fortune has ever touched it. Its integral spirit is free from the taint of good and bad fortune alike, suffering can find no place in it."

III

Lao Tzu continued, "Those whose inner being is calm shine with a heavenly radiance, by which light they can see themselves as they are. Only by training oneself to such calmness, peace and repose can one achieve constancy.

---

[115]It is the original model of our natural, integral being. As an adult, we have experienced all the divergences of good and bad, enjoyable and troublesome, yet we can still restore the original unity of our being on both an internal and external level. This is the way of life and the law of life. It is innate to us but extends outward.

"Those who possess constancy are relied upon by people and assisted by nature. Those who are trusted by people are beings of Heaven. Those who are assisted by Heaven are true masters.

"To learn this is to learn what cannot be studied; to practice this is to accomplish what cannot be practiced; to speak this is to describe what cannot be spoken. True knowledge stops at what cannot be known. That is perfection; those who do not follow this are handicapped by their own blocks and fail to unite with nature.

"Utilize what comes to you from the abundance of nature to nourish your body (1). Withdraw into thoughtlessness to give energy to your spiritual nature (2). Be respectful toward what is within you and extend the same respect to others (3). If you do these things and calamities occur, they are calamities of circumstance, not of your creation. Do not allow them to disturb the composure you have achieved (4). Do not let them stay with you (5).

Natural spiritual energy is supported through the achievement of composure. Inner and outer equilibrium is not formed by knowledge, nor can you use your knowledge to maintain it. It is traditional practice to not let any trouble enter the "Tower of Spirit", mount your "Spiritual Platform" or step onto the "Terrace of the Soul". The "Tower of Spirit" refers to the mind which is always guarded. When you apply what you have attained spiritually to the understanding of problems and worries, it consumes the spiritual energy that has gathered in your peaceful mind. Following this guidance is thus important in each individual's cultivation.

"Whatever is said without complete sincerity is untrue. If you try to move forward without sincerity, each step will miss its correct pace. If outer concerns enter and are not eliminated, each step you take will only add failure to failure. If desires are not removed as they arise, loss will increase with each recurring desire. Whoever openly commits a crime will be punished by men, but whoever does it secretly will be punished internally by one's own conscience, which can bring about ill health or bad fortune by causing internal conflict, or the attack of evil spirits. Doing harm and wrong can diminish one's spiritual reserves.[116]

"One who concentrates upon the internal does not attempt to gain a good reputation for himself (1). One who concentrates upon the external thinks about the acquiring and hoarding of goods and money (2). One who does deeds without thoughts of reputation is forever a source of light, while he who sets his mind on gain is no more than a greedy merchant; to discerning eyes, he acts only out of greed, yet he surely thinks well of himself (3).

"If a man gets along well with others, then people will come to him, but if he sets up barriers between himself and others, then he will not find enough room even for himself, much less for other people. He who is not friendly to others will find that no one is friendly to him. If he likes no one, then no one likes to be close to him and he finds all men to be strangers. Whoever cannot accept differences among other human beings will have no one to accept his differences and no one who is close to him. This is the balance of all relationships.

"There is no weapon more deadly than prejudice. Even the famous sword Mo-yeh is not as powerful.

---

[116]Human life is on the bright side of the spectrum of life, while all kinds of undeveloped spiritual beings are at the darker end. It is easy for the darker sphere to trouble the bright, but the bright side does not know what is causing the trouble or how to correctly respond to it. Being righteous in one's mind and behavior is one's greatest protection. The high spiritual realm of nature is the birthright of all people, but people weaken their spirit through improper behavior and improper thoughts. Understanding the power of spiritual retribution is one important principle in the learning of Tao. The great sage Mo Tzu included this in his doctrine. This truth is evidenced in the lives of ambitious world leaders and groups who have fallen from power; it is something that should not be ignored.

There are no enemies greater than yin and yang,[117] because there is nowhere between Heaven and Earth that a person can escape from them. It is not that yin and yang deliberately become destructive, but your own mind makes them act in such a way.[118]

IV

Lao Tzu said, "Now let us speak of attainment and Tao.   The spiritual development of the ancients extended as far as pre-creation, the time before anything existed, which was earlier than what can be conceived. The highest achieved ones never experienced the subtle origin of universal life as a separate entity from their own lives.

"Other spiritually developed ones clearly understood the interplay of yin and yang in the physical sphere of nature, but they viewed formed life as a departure from the integral truth.   For them, death and the dissolution of form was a return to the integral truth. There was already separation for them.

"Later developed ones regarded Nothing as the head, Life as the trunk and Death as the rear.   They claimed as friends those who knew that existence and non-existence, life and death were one unified and indispensable entity.

"Although the above three views of developed ones differ, they are one big flow of truth.

"Tao, the great flow of one universal life, unifies the differences in all things.   It forms things and destroys all forms.   An integral being does not emphasize discrimination, because such emphasis leads to the search for external, individual perfection (1).   An integral being does not seek external perfection, because once it is pursued and attained, there is a still higher perfection to reach for (2).   External effort only makes one's

---

[117]i.e., the interaction between positive and negative principles which produces the visible universe.

[118]The workings of the mind will upset the balance of yin and yang within the body and automatically cause illness.

spiritual essence run outward and not return to the original oneness, thus causing the dispersion of one's form and spiritual essence. The person who pursues an externally perfect life single-mindedly can sometimes make things happen the way he wishes, but in reality he is pushing himself down the road of death and extinction. One whose spiritual essence has left him lives through his form only and is a harmful, destructive person. One who applies integral vision to his life will treat his physical form as well as he treats his true, invisible form. He will have no conflict; only peace and security will come to him.

"The integral one unites his spirit with the traceless core of universal nature within change, and does not become extinct through change (3).

"The integral one exits through the trunk that is perfect freedom and enters through the channel that is perfect freedom (4). The integral one is real life, but without attachment to any fixed dwelling (5). The integral one endures, but has no trunk or branches.[119] (6). The integral one has exits, but no channels.[120] (7). The integral one is real life. What is real but cannot be housed is nature itself. What endures but has no trunk or branches is the great flow of universal life (8)."

In this chapter, Chuang Tzu has changed his usual metaphorical way, straightforwardly concentrating the essence and practice of Tao. Readers who find difficulty in understanding his parables, can receive the clear message if they work with this chapter.

---

[119]This refers to the unification of all as one complete being without further division or splitting.

[120]Or openings - it still expresses the total spiritual envelopment and spiritual all-encompassment.

CHAPTER FORTY-SEVEN

KENG SANG CH'U

I

Nan Yung Ch'u went back to Keng Sang Ch'u to become his assistant and learn the practice with his help and guidance. One day, Nan Yung Ch'u asked how Keng Sang Ch'u was instructed by Lao Tzu. Here is the teaching that Lao Tzu gave to him.

Keng Sang Ch'u said, "I was Lao Tzu's attendant. When I went to him, I was young, the age of only twenty-one. Lao Tzu was old; nobody really knew how old he was, because it seemed that he was always the same age. I offered my personal service to him and thus spent most of my lifetime learning from him. He finally sent me away when he thought I had been there long enough and could be independent, at the new year celebration of my hundred and third year. At that time, I was sent to live independently.

"Many people believed, wrongly so, that I was the only person who attained Tao and learned Lao Tzu's art among his many students. When I first came to Wei Lei to live, many people flocked to me with the expectation of learning Tao. I do not think I attained anything; it only seems that I have become older than the other people. I suppose that because I came from the home of Lao Tzu, people mistakenly believed that I was a divine power and a sage. Truthfully, I was still an ordinary man; at most, a student of Tao.

"Lao Tzu's formal work was to maintain the historical records of all the major events that happened through the generations. He was one of the few who could understand the meaning of the different knots tied up in the thick ropes. This is how history was recorded before words were written down. By the knowledge he obtained from his work, his mind became deeply familiar with the events and changes in the lives of many humans. He trained us to learn the way of quiet observation, which is not to become emotionally involved in any situation. He himself mostly remained quiet. He did not participate in social movements or activities of any kind, yet I would say that he participated in the social movement and activity of all time. This was how he could remain himself and be independent from the world.

"As a person, he did not extend himself in anything extreme in his speech or actions, because he did not want any of his many students to misunderstand him. Personal interpretations of his actions would differ so from the intention of his achieved depth. Certainly none of us have attained that level of achievement. Each student, as he stands in his own viewpoint, looks to him as one who gazes up at a majestic mountain. Each sees from a different perspective, and each sees a reflection of himself. Thus, to some his teaching was an elucidation in the art of leadership, while some saw instruction in the skill of political competition. From his teaching, some received the guidelines of eminent military action. There are many other ways he was seen and interpreted.

"Personally, I do not perceive his teaching in any of the above mentioned ways. I stay at the root of his teaching in ageless way of Tao. Tao should perhaps be practically interpreted as the moral duty of life; certainly we could see the example of moral duty in Lao Tzu's regard for life. The duty of life is to protect one's life morally, and not run into anything that would be overly troublesome, harmful or burdensome to the nature of your life. Most people, however, in taking care of their life, over-extend themselves in negative pursuits; they waste their energy or squander it away fruitlessly. That is not what he suggests. By his example, he demonstrates personal moral realization. It requires great patience, when others accuse you falsely, not to become rough and violent in relation to your own life. When you treat other people and your living environment violently, you treat your own life with roughness and violence. Such action not only endangers your life, but it is immoral. As basic a matter as this is, it is neglected by many people, so there is no need to mention any kind of higher spiritual attainment to them. When one does not even know how to live, nothing else can be really useful in serving them.

"In spirituality, there is only one subtle law that operates within and without. This is why he does not approve of people promoting something external without first attaining an internal realization. Only one who can take care of his life with great tenderness the way one takes care of a newborn baby is qualified to take care of the world. The world has many obstacles that can upset you, but if you learn to respond gently, you can be the real king, even if you are not a socially established king or queen. If you would like to be a king or a queen of the world, learn to be gentle first. And if you would like to be your own king or queen, treat yourself with gentleness. There is only one ultimate law, inside and outside of life. The ultimate law is the subtle law. It governs all people and all things. The subtle is Tao. Do you follow Tao in your life or have you lost Tao?

"From what I have learned by the example of Lao Tzu's life, the morning hours are jade and cannot be wasted. The hours before noon are gold and cannot be wasted. The hours of the afternoon and before night are silver and cannot be thrown away. He was always doing things, and by his kindness he taught us and shared his jade, gold and silver with us. His teaching was straight and direct. If you search for his teaching, he will not try to please you with his response. Those who do not respect the time he gives cannot learn from him. Some just come to fool around; to those, he offers them anything as guidance. He is not a god to them. He is, however, a god to gods.

"This was my personal experience of Lao Tzu. I was a student and an attendant to our teacher, and by the opportunity of serving our teacher, I learned to do things and learned to live. I have learned the general practice and his common teaching given all his students, and in particular received the precious instruction of his response to my own questions or to the problems of my personality in my young life at that time. Once, because I was the most argumentative of the students, the great master instructed me. His language is simple and direct, so here is my own interpretation. I expect that it will be understood as I go along.

"All lives were brought forth from a darkness that was like the soot on the bottom of a kettle. Once a life comes into being, it displays itself among many other lives, creates its own standard and judges this to be right and that to be wrong. This is what we call the subjective point of view. Right and wrong, however, are not absolutes that not subject to change; they are inter-related and interchanging.

"Let us consider the fact of the interchangeability of right and wrong. Even though it is not a profound issue, most people are unaware of it. As we already know, the human mind is as dark as soot on a kettle. Men speak of a subjective point of view, but such a mental view does not hold up under testing. The experience of one's subjective mind as inactive is an achievement that undeveloped people do not know about.[121] Spiritual comprehension of a matter is direct and immediate, but a person often doubts their own direct experience in favor of what they have learned intellectually. What they learn intellectually from someone else is indirect. Thus, spiritual capability is recognized only after repeated mistakes and is attained from one's own thorough achievement.

"Different viewpoints emanate from different mentalities. Some are partial, others are complete. A partial perspective will always differ with others. A complete vision involves the integration of both the

---

[121]An example of the subjective mind is the response of a sixteen year old girl who's parents refuse to allow her to go out at night. She might say, "But this will ruin the rest of my life!" The girl cannot take the whole situation into consideration nor understand that she will have other opportunities in her life.

mental and spiritual dimensions of life.   When one
achieves complete vision, one achieves Tao.   Human
beings are students of Tao, but no one can claim, "I am
the Truth, I am the Tao."   If "I" can be established
here, it would mean all people and all life, not a single
isolated existence.   Whoever establishes an "I" will
experience duality with the subsequent establishment of
right and wrong.   In disputable matters, a good mind
sees that what is subjective from one point of view is
objective from another.   This leads to a higher level of
mind.

"Right and wrong are not fixed conditions.   They
only exist in relation to the other elements of a situation.   For example, at the winter sacrifice, all parts of
the sacrificial cow are separated and displayed.   Each
still carries the characteristics of the whole.   A similar
illustration is a painting; no one part can be isolated
for one to consider the beauty of the painting, because
all elements join in creating the whole.   In looking at a
house where the ancestors lived, for example, one
checks out everything from the sacrificial halls or guest
chambers to the living room and the bathrooms.   All
the parts are characteristics of the whole, whereas a
fixed point of view defines certain parts of a house as
holy or unholy.   All rooms are needed by the inhabitants and guests.   For instance, after you have
enjoyed a royal feast, it is not in the most elegant part
of the building where you can go to release your
internal physical tension. Applying a dualistic standard
to a general life by rigidly defining what part is holy
and what part is unholy, what is right and what is
wrong, is also merely a segmented vision.

"People are in the habit of projecting a higher
standard on others when they have expectations or
when they judge others; in this way, prejudice and
discrimination are established.   If they could learn not
to be overly idealistic in their expectations of others or
in their judgments, then nothing would be singled out
as more important than anything else.

"Out of the indistinguishable oneness, things, events
and people come into life.   Through experiencing the

circumstances and events, one is impressed by life. Some of the momentary impressions are named or described. There is, of course, a great distance between what is real and the name that is applied to it by a person.

"The analytic mind processes past impressions of circumstances and this forms the basis of its knowledge. From there, his mind proceeds to establish right and wrong. This is called having a subjective point of view or the establishment of ego. It is a great mistake to formulate a subjective point of view. We say this because when there is an issue and one uses his knowledge in the situation, the difference between what is named and what is real in the new situation has become confused.

"What happens is that one's own standard of right becomes 'The Standard' to which all others must adapt. You see, all individuals consider themselves as the most important in the world's existence and would like to have others accept their life as the standard for living their lives. In attempting to make other men recognize him as the model of perfection, some individuals will go as far as death to prove their devotion or invite their followers to accept death to prove the model of their creation. We are, of course, talking about spiritually undeveloped individuals.

"They regard only what is useful in the moment as wisdom and whatever is useless in the moment as foolish or stupid. They see success as honorable and failure as dishonorable; thus, one who is successful and shows off is considered wise to them and he who runs into trouble but is self-contained is considered stupid. They do not know that success can be built on failure and do not realize that what they consider to be useless at one time is not useless at another.

"To them, winning arguments brings fame, and losing them brings disgrace. 'I need to set others straight' is the attitude of most undeveloped people. This type of subjectivity, which is often held by the younger generation, is similar to the view of the cicada and the young dove who see things only from their own perspective. Like the cicada and the little dove, they take their little part to be the truth for all life, but do not know that their limited experience cannot match the vastness of the totality. They have strong faith in their own shallow, mistaken point of view.

"If a person does not work toward spiritual development, his life becomes a deposit of soot and darkness. There is no spiritual evolution. In a given situation a person may act like a bug. Only a bug abides by bug nature. This one is the victim of one's own darkness or lower nature. He might then offer his darkness to the public. Like the winter sacrifice in which the life of a cow is taken to invite blessings, people have made a habit of sacrificing the lives of others as a means of obtaining blessings and calling it a spiritual practice. They create a God who can be pleased by money. This God then becomes the very source of their darkness and keeps them at the level of animal intelligence.

"The world is like a house: one should make proper use of it and keep it in good order. A house can be used for a good purpose or a bad one. Responsibility for its use does not lie with the house, but with the user - the mind. Right and wrong are products of the mind, not of life."

II

"On another occasion, I was asking about how to regulate my mind. I was instructed by the great master to watch the artificial and unnatural rituals that humans build for themselves. He said, 'There are too many rigid institutions and ceremonies in the world, and they only separate people from each other and from their own nature. For example, if you were to step on a stranger's foot while out shopping, you would apologize greatly for your carelessness. If you were to step on your brother's foot, you might pat him on the back. But if you step on your parent's foot, you already know that it is excused. That is why it is said that ceremony, in its highest form, admits that ceremony is not always necessary. Duty, in its highest form, requires no recognition from others. Wisdom, in its highest form, is not planned. Benevolence, in its highest form, is without affection or partiality. Perfect trust requires no pledge or contract.

"'Therefore, consider honor, wealth, recognition, authority, fame and profit; it is these six which are the delusions of the will and the source of all ambition.

"'Consider appearance, behavior, beauty, temperament, attitude and thoughts; it is these six which are the disturbances of the mind.

"'Consider hate, ambition, joy, anger, sorrow and pleasure; it is these six which are the entanglements that block one's nature.

"'Give up the stimuli of ambition and the delusions of will; free your mind from all conceptual disturbances; loosen the entanglements that block one's nature; break through all obstructions to Tao.

"'Thus, giving away or including; accepting or rejecting; to be or not to be; to keep testing one's own wisdom and capability without looking for growth through practical living; these are obstructions to Tao. In other words, high ability and too much intellectual knowledge separates one from others, accepting and rejecting from an egotistical point of view rather than from spiritual inaction or non-effort, and giving and taking improperly are the six delusions which obstruct Tao.

"'When all of these are tamed or mastered, then one's mind is in good order and will be at rest. When the mind is at rest and unconditioned, one can see clearly. The unconditioned mind reposes in a state of inaction in which there is natural growth. With such a mind, there is nothing that cannot be accomplished.

"'When all of these do not rage within us, we are calm. If we are calm and composed, we are sensitive. With sensitivity, we can maintain ourselves as neutral. When we are neutral, we can act in perfect freedom, and everything proceeds rightly.

"'When the emotions no longer experience these, we achieve righteousness. Being righteous, one is silent. Being silent, one becomes enlightened. Enlightened,

one becomes empty or clear. Empty, one does nothing,
and yet there is nothing that remains undone.'"

III

"At another time, I asked to know what is the right
way to live in such a confused world. He answered
me, 'Let Tao and Teh be your supports when you live
in a confused world without the knowledge of how to
guide yourself. Tao, as natural life within the Subtle
Law, governs Teh. Teh is the natural instinct of life,
which is harmony and spontaneity. Teh is seen in the
movement of life. Life embodies the code of nature.
Life is the very essence of nature.

"'Tao is the light of virtue. Life is its channel.
One's innate nature is the substance of life, and that
innate nature in motion is called virtue.

"'Movement on behalf of life is natural action.
Nature operating smoothly is action. Anything active
that goes against nature is loss. Action which deviates
from natural virtue is artificial and is called loss.

"'Movement that is inevitable is perfect, natural
action. Movement, when it does not oppose our selves,
is considered to be in perfect order.

"'Action which is accomplished from one's true
nature because one cannot do otherwise is called virtue.
Action in which there is nothing other than self-nature
expressing itself is orderly and harmonious.

"'Spontaneous or involuntary emotion is called
receptive virtue. Emotion which is not caused by
anything external is called active virtue.

"'These pairs may seem different or opposing, but
in reality they are essentially the same. All virtue
should proceed from the real self as an expression of
harmony within and without.

"'In contrast to perfect, natural motion, there is the
motion that comes from intellectual knowledge.
Knowledge is forming connections. Knowledge is
planning. Because the nature of intellectual knowledge
is incomplete, if you once accept the incomplete nature
of intellectual knowledge, your personal view is
formed. By that, your vision is incomplete, thus it is

not safe. It can be compared to a side glance that does not see the complete picture of a situation.

"'If he who does something out of anger is not really angry, then his outburst is foolishness. If he who plunges into action does not act from internal motivations, then his action is self-entrapping. He who wishes to be still and quiet must calm his energies and emotions. He who wishes to be spiritual must cultivate the well-being of his mind. He who wishes his actions to hit the right mark must go along with the understanding that what he does impulsively is done negatively. Such things are corrected by the sage who untangles the childish misdoings.

"'Most people have learned how to exert their physical power and mental effort; this is called plotting or scheming. Few people have learned how to develop themselves spiritually. Concentration of pure spiritual energy is a training and cultivation which becomes as effortless as a child's stare; but concentration of pure mind is not the same as a child's stare. It is what we call the eye that sees without looking and the hand that accomplishes without working.'

"'Yi was a skilled archer who could hit the smallest target, but he was inept in keeping people from praising him. Sages are skilled with regards to what is of Heaven and Nature, and are awkward with human matters. To have great ability in Heavenly matters as well as human ones as well can only be achieved by one of integral nature.[122]

"'Any sparrow that came within the range of Archer Yi was sure to be killed. This is truly great skill, and it is not dangerous to all birds because there is only one killed at a time. But it is dangerous when someone tries to make a big net, because then sparrows have nowhere to flee. It is worst when the whole world is made into a cage. None can escape it. This

---

[122]One of integral nature has nothing to do with the artificial nature of human creation. He is far from those who comply with their personal interests and artificial concepts.

is so true of people who have been caged by false cultural and conceptual creations: they have come within the range of somebody else's bow, so they can be easily captured or killed.

"'If you hope to persuade a man of talent to work for you, you cage him with what he likes, such as fame, position, payment or other support.   That was what happened when Emperor T'ang caged Yi Yien, a very talented minister, by raising him from the position of cook to prime minister.   Duke Mu of Ch'in caged Pai-li Hsi, another very talented man, by ransoming him from captivity for the price of five ram's skins and then making him run the country.   They did not only fulfill the kings' desire for trust; they also used the opportunity provided them to serve the people with selfless sincerity.   They could exercise their talent to the maximum service of their given position.   Others become the hounds and falcons of an undeveloped dictator and subjected all other people to his cruelty.'"

"I received the above instruction in the first decade that I served him.   By guiding me to practice quiet observation of myself and other people, I began to forget language.   My mind, then, became united with my own being, internally and externally.   I enjoy being that way.   The great master said, 'Tao cannot be reached by talking.   Tao also cannot be reached by limiting one's self to not talking.   One who learns from nature would tend to attain Tao by not talking, while one who learns Tao from serving the world would tend to attain Tao by talking and communicating.

"'However, people cannot unite their mind by talking all the time.   Neither can they unite the mind by never talking.   The united mind itself is a great achievement for any student of Tao.'"

IV

Keng Sang Ch'u continued, "The following is what I offer to you: The big, worldly cage was built by leaders of 'handicraft' who specialized in external institutions.   They too were caged in, along with people of general intelligence.   Their descendants are caged.   It has become more and more difficult for people to escape the different kinds of unnatural social pressures that have established authority over one's life. One's life is treated like a sacrificial cow to be cut any way the evil ruler wishes. Who has given others this authority over your life? Are you aware that we are also joining them in building the cage of the world?

"This is the last thing I would like to share with you today. I was certainly an ambitious young man. I thought I had a lot of talent and I could be of use in the right direction. That is why he reformed me with his vision of great depth. He said, 'When most people view their life, they forget whether the source of the trouble is man or nature. They compete against others to become superior authorities in different fields of life, but all within unnatural cultural and religious confines. They forget their true life nature and accept the cage. They do not know that they can break out by not helping build the cage.

"'Now you wish to be out of the cage, but you cannot find a way. You will watch the world continue toward total destruction until a new world is built by people who have a new intelligence and destiny. The vicious cycle we are in will not end unless there is a spiritual awakening among all people. Spiritual development is therefore of utmost importance to the world and to individuals, because it cannot be confined by a cage.

"'The health of the world has been destroyed by its leaders. The well-being of your own mind is destroyed by the unnatural, poisonous fodder you feed it. Trouble comes from too much artificiality at all levels. Nature has one concern for all things: to return to nature and to be natural. You can find health and well-being in nature itself. Stop what you are doing and quietly join the flow of universal natural vitality. Here is where you receive and refresh your life. Conceptual creations destroy the unity of the universal, great and endless life!

"'A man who has had his feet cut off as punishment rejects ornament and accepts simplicity because externally he is not worthy of praise or adornment. A condemned criminal can climb the highest peak without fear because there is no more concern of life and death. These two were submitted to artificial authorities that were established by the circumstances of their lives. They cannot serve as models for your learning. But the one who discards the artificial, worldly moral concepts no longer pays attention to his own interest; by no longer being conscious of himself, he becomes a person of Heaven. He rests with the consciousness of nature. Such persons can attain balance because they are no longer bothered by receiving either praise or anger for their contribution to the world. They do not help to build the cage stronger.[123] After you understand that it is not you who have built the world the way it is, what in your life is there to blame yourself for or feel badly about? Do not be discouraged by the worldly situation.

"'I would like to ask whether you would like to be in or out of the cage. Surely, you would like to be out of the cage. But how could it be done? Is it at all possible?

"'If you stay in, people cause you lots of trouble. If you go out, you will feel troubled within your own life being which needs to be supported. This is a dilemma. The false sages offer solutions that increase the strength of the caging or increase the difficulty of the dilemma, or teach a negative solution of giving up. These approaches are not truthful. The truthful teaching of the true sage, one of integral wisdom, is to strengthen your individual natural moral character. For example, if you are troubled by your own life, you can broaden your sense of life. The entire universe is your life. You can change your idea of what your life is to be more than just a limited person; you can transfer your life to the sun, the moon, a star, the ocean, a river, a mountain or a tree. If you feel troubled by your family, you can broaden your sense of family to include all people in

---

[123]The institution of human society is the cage.

that one family; all men are your brothers and all women are your sisters. If you feel troubled by your society, you can broaden the sense of society; all human race is one society.

"'By broadening your individual consciousness to merge with universal consciousness and by broadening your material limitations to be your spiritual awakening, you can save yourself from the dilemma. By the attainment of broadness, you save yourself from the narrowness of concepts that wither your life force. The problem of the world cannot be cured by treating the world. The only cure is to improve the individual. We all know that monarchy is unfair and dictators are violent, but if you turn out to be a person in that kind of role, what kind of leader will you be? Yao and Shun lived during a time of virtuousness and natural mindedness, and their virtuous leadership was sufficient. Today however, our generation has developed their minds in imbalanced ways; it appears that even if Yao and Shun were to be the leaders of our time, they would not be able to help the situation much.

"'Fortunately, anyone with sincerity in learning Tao, can find his or her own way back to a true life. Once you are saved, the world is saved. Then, the practical improvements can be put in the world to undo the extreme ones.'"

CHAPTER FORTY-EIGHT

THE WORLD REACHING FOR ITS NATURAL HEALTH

It is generally believed that the first nine chapters of Part Two were Chuang Tzu's own writing. The rest of the book was the record of Chuang Tzu's teaching on different occasions by his students, gathered from their direct as well as indirect experiences with him. In most Chinese classics, only the direct work of the teacher is given; however, because Taoists accept differences, Chuang Tzu as a book is an exception, and different teachings were discussed. Following the tradition of broadness and openness, the effort of different teachers in the Period of Spring and Autumn and the Period of the Warring Kingdoms were included in the following chapter as the conclusion of the entire teaching of Chuang Tzu. During times of evil power struggles and the expansion of small kingdoms through ruthless force and schemes, this chapter focuses on the unity of the various teachings. Thus, they can nurture human nature and the development of a natural life. Can you see the new light in this? At this time, what we can do to reform the world is to focus on ourselves as an individual person. It is us who make this work possible or impossible.

I
General Comment and Direction

This is practical guidance from all great sages of Tao. It is gathered here in the next discussion like the cream is gathered from the top of the milk pail. After careful study, you might be able to find some very useful teachings or help for your spiritual evolution and progress. Let us review some thought here before we start our exploration.

There are many in the world who believe that they have reached the highest truth and seek no further improvement, and there are also many who continue to study and search for the truth. If we were to ask an achieved person where the truth can be found, he might reply, "Everywhere." If we were to inquire further and ask how the highest spirituality expresses itself and what a true master achieves, the answer might be something like this: "First of all there must be a reason for a high spiritual being to manifest, and then there must be specific circumstances that allow him to fulfill his mission." This would certainly be the most objective statement one could make. True achievement brings about practical improvement in one's life and in the world itself. This is the truth of life.

A person of great natural truth is one who remains united with the root of truth. A person of pure spirituality is one who maintains the purity of spiritual truth within himself. A person of Great Life is one who maintains his connection with the truth of one universal life.

A sage of all time is one who makes the high sphere of nature his master and the fulfillment of natural virtue his root of life. He makes learning the integral truth the gateway. He can see the trends of the world and set a true course.

A person of self-cultivation treats people with kindness, is righteous in all relationships, disciplines his own behavior properly, nurtures his emotions with good music and dance, and has a gentle nature and attitude.

A person who is a leader of others can consider different names as descriptions for the different functions of things, and can observe, compare and analyze things in order to judge them fairly. He can unravel the complication of public affairs with these four categories: 1) right principle; 2) correct definitions and

names applied to reality; 3) reliable reference and re-
source; and 4) demonstrable proof or results of actions.

All people, whatever their position or profession,
have a positive function to fulfill in life.   Their good
lives and dedication is what determines the direction
the world takes.   The correct nutrition of life includes
good education, sufficient material support, and general
security, especially for the weak and elderly, orphans
and widows, who need more protection than others.

An individual who does not depart from the truth
of the universal essence is a person of natural spiritual
virtue.   He who makes great nature the guiding principle of his life has a virtuous foundation that is non-
cosmetic, follows the subtle law as his own nature, and
is able to impartially observe the growth and decline of
the world.   Such a person is a developed individual.

The ancient ones developed integrally, thus they
functioned integrally.   They were able to keep the same
pace with universal nature.   They learned spiritually
from nature, with creative and nourishing energy,
without needing to organize their minds specifically for
themselves or for others.   Thus all people were benefited.   Not only did they understand the big principles
and procedures, but they also understood the details
contained within the bigger picture.   Things did not
become stagnant; the small and the large, the fine and
the coarse, everything everywhere expressed the great
harmony of nature itself.   This is how far-reaching Tao
was among the ancients.   In the modern world, the
artificial pressures of social and family life have damaged the integral nature of people so much that universal natural life is cut off by conceptual walls that are
called nations, parties, families, individuality, etc.

As for the specific methods the ancient enlightened
ones devised, many of them are still preserved in ac-
counts that have been passed from generation to generation and can still be understood by the wise ones of
each country and each generation.   Their poems are
useful in directing our emotion; their writings for
guiding our thoughts; their ceremonies for conducting
our behavior; their music for teaching us harmony.

The *Book of Changes* explains yin and yang, *The Annuals*[124] directs us in matters of duty and decision. Spread throughout the world, this ancient establishment was concentrated and developed in the Middle Land and all traditions render constant homage to this source of integral truth.

At the time the world began to enter the age of conceptual confusion, the good direction and healthy development of life[125] were ruined. Wisdom and natural inspiration were no longer respected. Human desire, emotion and action became separated and lost their unity. When such natural unity is gone, so is the integrity of nature. The world then seizes upon one aspect of nature, extends it to its utmost extreme and pronounces it "good." In the case of the ears, eyes, nose and mouth, each has its own function, and they are all mutually supportive of one another. Thus it is with religion, politics, economics and philosophy. Individually they are incomplete, yet today they have become the life-work of narrow specialists who splinter the beauty of nature's integrity with their analytical approach to the natural unity that was recognized by the ancient developed ones.

Everyone in the world today follows his own desires and makes them his "doctrine," regarding his personal preference as an infallible course. Various schools of thought diverge and never meet. The future generations are robbed of the original purity of the universe and the grand achievement of the ancients. The great path of oneness now lies in scattered fragments over the face of the earth.

----

[124]An almanac of stems and branches.

[125]In its six aspects: 1) poetry and song; 2) the natural relationship between Heaven and Mankind — i.e. natural political principles and a natural environment; 3) public ceremony and personal manners; 4) the universally common rules of public and private behavior; 5) sports; and 6) mathematics and philosophy.

II - 1
Various Approaches and Their Unification

It was taught that the way to realize Tao was to avoid indulging in luxury or wasting useful materials. We were taught to practice strict spiritual self-discipline yet be forgiving toward the faults of others. This was the guidance which the ancient developed ones learned from universal life.

Two men of Tao, Mo Tzu[126] and Jein Wah Li, his important disciple, learned this, and took great joy in it. They promoted it among mankind. They were straight in their views and unyieldingly practiced these principles in their own lives. One of them did not even allow the enjoyment of music because it would bring scatteredness to his spiritual concentration in life, and this he proclaimed in his writing, "The Disapproval of Music." The other one emphasized the practice of temperance in the material sphere of life; thus he exalted the so-called "Moderation in Expenditure." This moderation was extended to general life activity; it was suggested even to stop singing in life and end mourning for death because they considered them to be wasteful expenditures of good energy. They acted out of motivations of their boundless love and a great desire for the increased benefit of the world. However, they condemned warfare for themselves and disallowed anger by themselves. They had a fondness for learning and each had acquired great knowledge, but in deep spirituality, it seems that one who teaches this approach to other people truly has great love for them although few people happily accepted this asceticism. They and their followers followed these doctrines themselves, and were greatly respected, but not accepted by the others.

It is my intention to credit their teachings. They tell people who want to sing, "No singing!" and people who wish to mourn, "No weeping!" However, general people do not develop enough spiritually, thus, also

---

[126]501-416 B.C.

their universal love is hardly understood. To have a life that is all toil and no pleasure as in their recommended ascetic practices, and when a relative dies, to have no feeling of loss; these express their attained spiritual qualities. They observed strict observations in order to achieve such a high purpose of helping the troubled world and the undeveloped majority with no rest for themselves. They should be regarded as true guides to self-development because they move far away from general undeveloped sentimentality. Mo Tzu himself was capable of such strictness, but we cannot expect the rest of the world to be able to do the same. One whose goal differs so much from the reality of the world cannot expect the establishment of his ideal to take root in the world. But his spirit is forever identified with the later spiritually developed leaders of the same great goal in promoting harmony and cooperation of the entire human society.

Mo Tzu says about his teachings, "In ancient times, the Great Yu[127] drained off the flood waters and brought the hundreds of rivers and thousands of streams to flow through the divisions of the empire. He himself went out, using bucket and shovel to organize the rivers, until there was no hair left on his legs. He worked through wind and rain, but through it all he accomplished the establishment of the states. Thus, he was known as a great sage for his work performed for the good of the world."

In later times, followers of his teaching, called Mohists, dressed themselves in skins and coarse cloth, wooden or straw sandals, as the great Yu did in his time. They never rested day or night. They drove and exerted themselves constantly, saying, "If we do

---

[127]2205 - 2197 B.C.

not follow the way of the Great Yu, we cannot call
ourselves Mohists."[128]

They meant well and some were even geniuses;
they were true sages who held firm to their ideas
despite the diminishing effect of failure.

Most of these examples and ideas are based on the
ancient heritage of individual life in a natural society.
This should be accepted as the good guidance of all
human society, even today. The guidance of creative
and diligent life is the correct guidance for all of
human society. Mo Tzu primarily responded to the
conditions of the society in which he lived, under the
pressure of the worst moral corruption to be experienced. Many generations later, these practices, with
some rectification, can still be very useful guidelines to
a healthy life. Both the Great Yu[129] and Mo Tzu[130] were
examples of devotion to worldwide humanistic virtue.
It is our respect to accept his work spirit as our model
and practice community spirit under the principle of
balance.

II - 2

It was taught that this is the way to realize Tao: to
be involved in the mundane but not make a proud
display of material things, not to be indifferent to
others or antagonistic toward the public, but desire
peace in the world and long life for all. Seeking no
more than is sufficient for one's own or others' needs
without ulterior motives and thus purifying the heart is
the path of a natural, good life that was followed by
the ancient ones who realized Tao.

---

[128]Yu worked most of the time outdoors in the sun, and as a
result became very tan. He wore black when he worked. The
Mohists respected Yu, thus they liked to become tan and dress in
black as a spiritual symbol.

[129]2205-2197 B.C.

[130]501-416 B.C.

Two men of Tao, Sung Ben and I Wen, active in the time of Spring and Autumn, learned this and took great joy in it; they carried it to the top. They made caps in the shape of Mount Hua which they wore so that they could be easily recognized. They carried themselves with a manner of kindness and tolerance toward all things and called it "heartfelt giving." Their purpose was to bring about cooperation, which would thus establish harmony and joy in the world. To accomplish this, they took the principle of kindness and tolerance for their guide. They wished to end conflict and discord, abolish aggression and arms, and save the world from war. These were the doctrines they circulated, expounded and taught throughout the world. When the world refused to listen, they would not give up; instead, they increased their efforts. Although the people were tired of listening to them, those in high positions as well as those in low, they did not stop speaking. They took much thought for others and little for themselves.

"Five cups of grain will be enough for us to eat," they said, although with that small amount they did not eat fully. Their focus was on the world. They were determined and set their goal in seeing that all men could live. Their goal was high. Scorning material benefit for themselves, they did not judge others who pursued it.

They worked very diligently in the daytime and at night, they did not wish to rest. They said, "We live to help." We are afraid to see how they lived with so few provisions, however, they were truly respectful and had great enthusiasm in saving the world. They taught that a person of development does not think it is of utmost importance how he is treated, when he has a great goal that he is pursuing. He is not enslaved by his personal desires in making meticulous demands in his personal life.

Their external goals were to do away with aggression and use of arms. Their internal goals were to lessen desire and decrease the effect of the emotions.

In all matters, great or small, they followed these principles.

I Wen and Sung Ben were people of great heart, but their way is hard to learn. If worldly leaders could learn only half of what they taught, the world would be a much more beautiful place. Thus, students of Tao should accept them in their lives.

II - 3

It was taught that this is the way to realize Tao: to have the spirit of public service yet not belong to any political party, to be even-minded and not succumb to favoritism; to be free from desire, having no rigid doctrine, to move spiritually without being bound to a given course, to take what comes, choosing neither this nor that but going along with all things, having no regret for the past and no worry about the future, and holding good will toward all men. They expressed these principles of universal life discovered by the ancient developed ones. There were masters in ancient times who believed that Tao could be realized not by preconception, but by harmonizing oneself with all things, not by turning things over and over in the mind or by looking for advantages, but by treating all things and people without personal preference. This describes the way to live in the world.

Some men of Tao like Hsan Dau, active in the period of Spring and Autumn, and his teacher and followers learned of this and took joy in it. They took the equality of all creation as a whole as their main theme, and they expressed it thus: "Heaven covers us, but cannot hold us up. Earth can hold us up, but cannot cover us. Tao embraces us, but we cannot make it clear. Thus all things are equal in incompleteness at some level. By viewing things so, they considered that all things have positive and negative aspects in their single existence, therefore, being mentally discerning is not a trustworthy solution. If we think education can save the world, we must realize that education can also strengthen ambition and aggression. So education is unable to help. Hsan Dau, his teacher and followers thought that by following unified laws and regulations, which were based on the natural universal subtle law, it would be possible to put the world in good order.

They also concluded that, "Preference shows partiality. Comparison causes deviation from the goal. When we follow the Great Path of Oneness, however, all is embraced." This is why they stopped accumulating fragmented intellectual knowledge, disregarded self-interest, and followed the path that was before them with compliancy and steadfastness. This they believed was following Tao.

"To know is not to know," said Hsan Dau. He despised incomplete knowledge and worked to destroy and be rid of it. He accepted no commitment; indifferent and casual, he did not admire the worthy men whom the world so greatly honor. He did nothing to establish himself, but belittled the big names. Without struggle, he went along with the flow of life, taking a neutral position.

In this way, he was never guilty of any fault. He stayed where he was, not participating in plotting or scheming. He made no attempt to understand what is special, but following the principle of harmony, he moved when pushed, budged when pulled. Going round and round with things, he was free from blame. This was because a person without the narrow consciousness of self does not face the difficulty and entanglements of establishing oneself. Thus he incurs neither blame nor praise.

He and his followers therefore believed, "By being without the narrow knowledge of self, we can find the way. One without the narrow knowledge of self has no need for salvation from somebody else. He who has no preference never deviates from Tao." The men of his day laughed at him, but he said, "The principles the world accepts are fit for the dead; mine are for the living!"

This is the same as Dien Pien, who learned from Pong Mong.[131] Their teacher also used to say, "People who attain Tao have reached the point where they regard nothing as either right nor wrong. He insists nothing is necessarily right and nothing is necessarily wrong. Things are at changes like a gust of wind, no trace is left behind. What is there worth talking about?" They sounded contrary to other people's understanding. Somebody gave them support, however, so they still kept teaching people to be simple minded and give up self-interest and be compliant with the law and regulations. You need to understand which law they were talking about, the subtle law or the human artificial law. If it is the subtle law, you need first to develop yourself to know it. If it is the man-made law and regulations, each law or rule carries its own defect. When a law or set of regulations is postulated as right, it also brings forth wrong. At the same time, it encourages people to depend on man-made laws and regulations, and one cannot reach the subtle law behind all the man-made laws and reach their independence, which means able to make independent and objective judgments. To attain Tao means to live a life, naturally and harmoniously, without depending on artificial restraint to make you moral and decent, if you do not understand the subtle law. It would guide one to misconceptions. We think that they did really attain Tao, although they had not made things too distinctly clear.

The teaching of this group and Han Dsau did contain some essence of the ancient, naturally inspired ones. Thus, we should accept the essence that he does have to offer but not the ambitious mind.

II - 4

It was taught that this is the way to realize Tao: to attain the learning of greatness by knowing the virtue of human life, to help each other and to reach natural,

---

[131]Both were active in the time of Spring and Autumn.

moral perfection. What is innate is spiritual nature; to follow one's innate nature is Tao; to cultivate Tao is the most important teaching.

When Confucius learned of this, he took great joy in it and wished that each individual of the world could realize it. He traveled around to all the kingdoms, hoping to be put in an important post of government so that he might be able to realize his moral ideas as passed down by Yao and Shun. They were the Five Great Relationships: 1) the relationship between the emperor and the people, 2) the relationship between parents and their sons and daughters, 3) the relationship between brothers and sisters, 4) the relationship between a husband and wife, and 5) the relationship between friends. Shun set up the guidelines: one must be loyal to one's king in a broad sense (meaning job or boss), dutiful to one's parents, helpful to one's brothers and sisters, close and loving to one's spouse, and faithful to one's friend. These are correct and natural.

Those teachings should be accepted as internal guidance, so they cannot be turned into rigid external demands rather than a description of personal awareness. If they are external rather than internal, they turned out to be more like: One must be loyal to one's king without questioning what kind of king he is, etc. The guidelines must be practiced by taking the situation into consideration. It would be the fault of the people if they were practiced rigidly. Confucius taught that if something is not done in the context of a rite or ceremony, you should not speak about it, listen to it, look at it, or touch it. Rite and ceremony are something external; though rite and ceremony can be well intentioned. His teaching would be then interpreted as: If it is not right, don't say it. If it is not right, don't listen to it. If it is not right, don't look at it, and if it is not right, do not have contact with it. This is a grand self-discipline in building an upright personality. The first important thing is obtaining the knowledge of what is right. How does one go about

that?   In Tao, what is natural and beneficial is right.
What is artificial and harmful is wrong.   Confucius'
intention was to promote the existing conceptual structure of morality.   In his work, *The Book of Spring and
Autumn*, he made strong comments about kings who
were not the way kings should be, ministers who were
not the way ministers should be and sons who were
not the way a son should be.   Therefore, he concluded,
society is disordered.   His strong advice, however, was
that disloyal ministers and undutiful kings (he used the
word sons instead of kings) should be punished and
killed by anyone with the call of a righteous conscience.   However, those who Confucius named disloyal ministers and disobeyed sons were the very ones
who, out of a call of righteous conscience, killed their
kings and their fathers to take the throne.   Confucius
expected that the righteous strength of people could
discipline the government; he was not aware that the
disloyal and the disobeyed ones were the most powerful and dangerous among people.   The kings themselves used the social structure outlined in his teaching as
a support so that they could enjoy the throne in safety.

Since that time and continuing up to the present,
science in China was suffocated by a rigid social structure and the thought of a personalized Heaven.   The
emperor was considered the Son of a Heaven in which
things were already ordered; thus no new invention
was encouraged.   This was a very suffocating religion.
However, it was not Confucius' expectation or fault
that such a society was built.   His work was misused
with the purpose of controlling people.   He taught that
one's loyal heart can be applied to one's job and boss.
He taught that one should be considerate to others.
Confucius' famous saying was, "Do not do to others
what you would not like them to do to you."[132]

---

[132]This is different from the religious approach of "doing,"
which can be a habitual nuisance, pushing sons to have the ambition to become doctors and daughters to seek good fortune by
marrying them, and pushing much immature knowledge upon one
another.   The "doing" approach causes a lot of psychological
problems in youngsters.

However, we can see that the control point of Confucius' teaching is the application of moral discipline of a society.[133] Only when it is one's personal awareness that brings one to practice this kind of moral discipline is it a true expression of one's personality. Confucius' teaching is incomplete, along with that of many other sages, when it comes to reforming worldly trends to have a new destiny for the world. If all sages could work together, the walls of the incomplete individual schools of thought might be broken down and unity be achieved. In that way, the future generations would enjoy securing the true value of the ancient teaching. Otherwise they would be defeated and die by displaying the wisdom in a rat's hole. It is not a problem of whether ancient sages had enough openness; it is the people of modern generations who are not open enough to receive the light of the different ancient great attainment which came from the actual experience of solving social and individual difficulties.

II - 5
It was taught that this is the way to realize Tao: to regard the source as pure and the things that emerge from it as coarse, to look upon accumulation of only material possession as a defect and to dwell in utter calmness with godly clarity. It was believed that therein lay the principle of universal life. These lines were trusted by some masters in ancient times.[134]

---

[133]It is too external and has caused the antipathy of the young generation of Chinese heritage.

[134]Individual vision and interpretation of the one absolute way differs in breadth and depth. Spiritually, no one can realize the absolute by treating it as a separate object or by taking an attitude toward it or adding another belief about it to one's mind. One's vision and understanding can be expressed in a personal way, but not the absolute itself. Thus different teachings developed out of different understanding of the truth.

When this was taught, the respectful Kuan Yein[135] and Lao Tzu took great joy in it. This occurred during Lao Tzu's trip to the west in his 160th year as recorded by Hsi Ma Chiang,[136] the great Chinese historian of the Han Dynasty.[137]   They became enthusiastic followers of Tao.   They spoke in terms of constancy and unity. Their teaching was of gentleness and humility, empty mindedness and non-injury to others.

Kuan Yein said, "When one does not take a personal point of view, then things will, of themselves, reveal themselves to him.   Their movement is like water; his stillness is like a mirror that reflects their true likeness.   His responses are like those of an echo that dies away into quietude once the sound has gone. He lets all things disappear by themselves.   He keeps nothing in his mind.   His heart is pure and quiet and harbors no personal, extravagant desires.   He becomes one among all others and follows the flow of universal nature.   It can be lost when he allows his mind to be caught up with something.   He does not place himself above others, but cheerfully brings up the rear.

"What is shared with others is harmony.   What is obtained from them is a loss.   When one is one with anyone or anything, he achieves harmony.   When he reaches for something or someone, he loses it."

Lao Tzu said, "He who is conscious of being strong but is content to be weak is like a ravine into which the world can flow.   He who is conscious of purity yet can bear disgrace is like a valley in which the world can rest.   When others strive to be first, he is content

---

[135]The official at the Han Gu Pass who was a supporter and student of Lao Tzu.

[136]145-86 B.C.

[137]206 B.C.-219 A.D.

with the lowest place. Contenting himself with the formless while others pursue the formed, he stores nothing up and thus enjoys abundance without effort. His mind is without cunning and he laughs at those who scheme against others.

"To have tolerance and sympathy towards others, without causing others pain is the mark of perfection."

Others seek good fortune, but Lao Tzu alone kept himself whole by being elastic. He said, "Let us try to avoid causing any damage." He regarded the profundity of the subtle path as the root of his life and simplicity as his teacher.

Lao Tzu is a teacher of universal life. He himself is one with universal life. Kuan Yein and Chuang Tzu join this one great being of eternal truth, to be the learners who identify themselves with universal life as the great master does with himself.

These are the two that who had truly attained Tao.

II - 6

It was taught that this was the way to realize Tao: maintain your spirit being as vast, formless and unlimited, transforming at where life cannot be defined in a fossilized way as life and death cannot be defined definitely as death. Be with heaven and earth. Be with gods. Elusively, where does it go? Evasively, where does it stay? All things and all lives are encompassed by it, yet it shows no beginning and no ending and no belonging. It is Tao.

In ancient times, these were believed to be the way to realize Tao. By attaining these qualities, the principles of universal life were discovered by the ancient developed ones.

Chuang Tzu learned this and took joy in it and became an enthusiastic follower of Tao. Without holding to any particular school, he used bold words and expressive phrases to give life to his thoughts.

He believed that Tao is crystal clear as the truth of all, yet people's vision is blocked; they are unable to see it. He also was aware that the world had become so confused and twisted that one could not speak to it directly. This is why he spoke with parables, quoted the ancient developed ones and greatly used his imagination while writing. Yet, he maintains himself in accordance with nature, and honors the forms of creation. By not judging his fellows, he lived harmoniously with his time. Though his writing is most unusual, it is not harmful to others; it shows ingenuity. A great thinker, he fills his work with the truths of life.

He soars above in the heavens and makes friends with those on earth who deny life and death, existence and non-existence. Yet he responds to the changes and exigencies of his day. His work is ever useful. He is mysterious and ingenious, but boundless. He is the teacher all of us follow.

This announcement came from Chuang Tzu's students in. the end of the book. It shows the independence of Chuang Tzu's teaching, the correct understanding of his followers and the formation of the fellowship of Tao which gradually became stronger after Chuang Tzu. This fellowship accepts Chuang Tzu's guidance in their life and organized all good teaching in one unity.

We recognize that Lao Tzu elucidated the spiritual achievement of the countless masters before the Yellow Emperor. Confucius elucidated the early cultural accomplishments of the Great Yao and Shun, and his work is still valuable and useful for delineating basic human roles. Then Mo-tzu elucidated the example and guidance of the Great Yu. All of these different teachings were derived from early great minds which were inspired by universal nature. Their single purpose is to serve and guide natural life. Confucius alone was a student of ancient customs and rituals that were not all useful and which are no longer applicable to modern society. His spiritual and ethical contribution, however, does offer fundamental guidelines for human social behavior. Lao Tzu and Chuang Tzu's work, on the other hand, preserved the essence of human spiritual development and enlightenment that took at least one or two million years to achieve. It would be foolish to throw away this fruit of human evolution and depend only on our own undeveloped mind and spirit.

Mo Tzu continued the work of Yu, but Yu was not only a great student of the early culture of Tao, he faced the problem of the Great Deluge when water covered the face of the earth. With his great engineering mind and leadership, he successfully channeled the water into the ocean. At that time, bare hands and the human mind were not adequate to accomplish such a feat. Yu, therefore, naturally looked for spiritual power to help him overcome the difficulty of human life. He received the help of genuine achievement of spiritual power performance and practice in the aspect related to fully mobilized individual spiritual energy and natural spiritual beings on earth. After he used those precious spiritual practices and methods of spiritual fortification, he was able to solve the mechanical calamity of physical nature. Those valuable methods were passed down from generation to generation until the time of Mo Tzu.

Mo Tzu was not merely an intellectual scholar. His practice supported him to face a new world situation of wars that touched his mind. Thus he offered the things he had learned, including the spiritual practice of Yu. He recorded this practice in his book, "The Record That Is Hidden In Pillows." He organized his followers well, but because of overly strict discipline, the fellowship became a small group of activists who sought to put an end to any wrong-doing or unrighteousness around them. They practiced what would be called "chivalry" by Westerners. Unfortunately, Mo Tzu's "Record That Is Hidden in Pillows" was lost. If it had endured, modern physics could not dominate the field of pure science as it now does includes the incomplete knowledge of human life. All in all, Mo Tzu's school was an active one of special discipline and power.

At last, we classify Lao Tzu's work as integral and natural, as the big fundamental principle of all.

Confucius' work is humanistic and socialistic principles while the work of Mo Tzu is religious in respecting the Impersonal Heaven. It expresses the general common spiritual background of all people. It is the natural creative spirits that are the source of all beneficial human spirits. Thus, they can work together to serve a positive human life, to guide the world back to a harmonious nature.

Unification
The Integral Guidance of All the Great Achieved Ones in this section:

1. Befriend ones of spiritual independence
2. Practice self-cultivation
3. Respect good standards
4. Observe moderation
5. Exalt virtue
6. Identify with ancient spiritually developed ones
7. Practice universal love
8. Practice non-aggression
9. Be economic in expenditures
10. Observe simplicity in funerals
11. Respect nature and the natural spiritual order
12. Cultivate objective understanding and recognition of the spiritual sphere of nature
13. Correctly use and maintain the good quality of music
14. Do not be fatalistic
15. Hold righteousness in esteem
16. Do not value rituals
17. Be aware that all people can be morally uplifted and socially respected and that this should be included in your own personal spiritual cultivation and achievement
18. Give total support, devotion and positive involvement to one who regards the rise or fall of all people's morality and security as his or her personal responsibility without concern for his or her own life and death.

CONCLUSION

Q: Master Ni, I greatly appreciate your guidance for my personal cultivation and the explanation of the essential teaching of your tradition.

Master Ni: The important teaching of my tradition has been introduced through my writings in different books. At this time, I have introduced the teaching of Chuang Tzu, one of the most important teachers, second to Lao Tzu. In accomplishing this work, I have needed great patience to straighten out the linguistic and organizational problems of the original book. It was written in a metaphoric or symbolic style to protect it from destruction at the hands of hostile rulers in different generations of human history. Fortunately, it was preserved because of this language. There are still many Taoist books that are disguised by an outward appearance that makes them look unimportant and which has served to preserve them for future developed ones.

Another fifty percent of the mistakes in the book of Chuang Tzu are due to the fact that the ancient book was made from bamboo or wood strips and bound by a leather strap. The book was not kept very well, and once the strap had broken, the book was disordered and hard to restore to its original state.

The book of Chuang Tzu, however, cannot be completely understood through the intellectual mind of a scholar unless he or she has received direct spiritual teaching or has achieved the same spiritual level of Chuang Tzu or his students. Now, the time of political dictatorship is over, at least in this country, so this book can be presented in a clear and direct way. It is like a guidepost on the roadside for both the healthy individual and society to find its way.

Chuang Tzu was endowed with a great mind and lived around 2,300 years ago. His work is a great treasure. His writing is for those of you who possess the same great mind. Before we begin to discuss his writing, let us review the teaching of Tao.

The great ones believe that the offspring of nature reflect that nature. And nature exists as a result of the harmony of two forces, yin and yang. No life can be beyond this and no world is beyond this. The integral truth is a higher learning for all beings.

Even a spiritual being has gender, size, color and other characteristics when the conceptual mind describes it. Although what is describable cannot reach the level of spiritual reality, spiritual reality must still be described in human terms. Once it takes a form such as someone's artistic creation, it falls into a range of describability.

Therefore, it is always important to check the balance between each side of an individual's existence: the unformed subtle source and the formed nature of external reality. What is the deep nature of an individual life? It springs from the same nature as the greater sphere of the universe. One seeks balance between yin and yang: the subtle life force and the apparent or concrete achievement. Do they assist and complement each other or do they conflict and separate from each other? At any time, in any successful practical situation, the harmonization of yin and yang can be seen.

Each individual life has three spheres: spiritual, physical and their harmonization in the mind. Harmonization is the integration of the Heavenly and the Earthly manifesting as Life, especially human life, which is complete with Heaven, Earth and Man. If we talk about yin and yang energies, spiritual energy and physical energy, they can go together or they can separate without ever mingling. The best model of the integration of these energies is a fully developed human life. A developed human life is complete with its universal energies: a small model of the universe, with the mind in between the physical and spiritual energy.

Chuang Tzu emphasized the specific ability of how to resolve the problems of worldly life. He suggested that one seek to establish harmony and cooperation between the two seemingly contradictory forces of world and self; and also that each individual develop spiritual self-worth as the balancing center of being. He observed that a human life does not have an isolated or separate existence in the universe but rather is interconnected in the vast energy network of the universe. Human life is not a shallow phenomenon like the simple life of grass or trees which can only exist at certain locations on this earth. A natural life cannot be separated from its environment; nothing can live by itself in a vacuum or test tube. Human beings can develop their spiritual sensitivity to feel the pulsation of nature within themselves and merge with the palpitation of the entire universe. This is what the student of Tao practices. No one can set his individual life apart from the natural universe through a conceptual discrimination; this only creates the separation between nations, races and even genders. If you can go back spiritually to the origin of life itself, you can dissolve conceptual differentiation and live with others while appreciating their differences.

All conflict between the two levels, material and conceptual, are unnecessary. The mutual source of life is profound; it is possible for an individual to reconnect himself with universal nature and enjoy the completeness of his own life-being, rather than die in the conflicts over small life matters. One who achieves this can also extend his positive virtue to lives other than his own. This is an important principle in Chuang Tzu, although he words it differently.

Q: Master Ni, how do we apply the true gold of Chuang Tzu's teaching in our life?

Master Ni: I have adopted this teaching for modern people because of my personal appreciation for Chuang Tzu. The answer you look for can be discovered in the discussion of different chapters. To set our focus in studying him, we need to review the background of the teaching.

During the undeveloped stages of human society, there are two forces that need to be observed. One is the external conquering force of aggressive neighboring countries and the other is the internal interference of political regimes. Natural lives have always suffered from these forces at different stages of human evolution. Unnatural forces, or forces that interfere and conquer, were what Chuang Tzu strongly opposed.

We can see the many social and cultural mistakes that have caused human suffering throughout history. Chuang Tzu pointed out the repercussions of actions by immature and ambitious leaders of different times and asked those leaders to allow people to be free to develop naturally. As Lao Tzu warned, people are like water and strong leaders are like fish. Once the water is drained, the fish cannot live. In order to maintain the life of the fish, it is wise to protect the water, not to disturb or drain it. This is a universal principle: one should do nothing to disturb the natural growth of others. The question is whether people have the spiritual awareness necessary to know the value of natural development in individual life as well as in society as a whole.

There have been many social leaders at different places and different times who poisoned the nature of human society. Chuang Tzu therefore spoke out against those who interfere with what nature offers us. He taught that conquering force of any kind - religious, political, economic, personal, etc. - is evil. Ambitious leaders use their political, religious, social and economic systems to bend people to accept their unnatural creations. If you understand what underlies the voice of Chuang Tzu, you will appreciate what this sage of 2,300 years ago has done for us. He especially pointed out the value of attaining spiritual freedom and taught people that furthering spiritual development is the goal of all natural life.

As I have mentioned, human problems, whether in society at large or in the family or in the relationship between a husband and wife, are all due to spiritual undevelopment and unconsciousness. The major contribution of Chuang Tzu is to point out the value of continual spiritual development.

Some people have wondered if Chuang Tzu has a an open, receptive spirit with people. I feel that he loved all people. His work is dedicated to assist individuals in outgrowing their childishness. In human life, you share what you have achieved with others, whether it is on a small or a large scale. This is a very important quality. Chuang Tzu shared his vision of a healthy life with all of us, without participating in the foolish games people play with each other every day. Because of this, people tend to view him differently.

Does Chuang Tzu mind that people view him differently? No, not at all, because his values are eternal. Whenever and wherever one is in life on earth, the righteous way of life remains the same and does not depend on the form of cultural or social custom. Basic human nature recognizes the existence of others.

The simplest expression of Chuang Tzu's teaching is the respect for natural life. You respect your life and that of others. You do not think yourself superior and try to put anyone under your control. Growth is an individual process. A father's growth cannot be transferred to his sons. The wisdom gained from the mistakes of our ancestors cannot really make the descendants wise. It is the responsibility of each individual and each generation to strive for spiritual growth. The process of continual spiritual development must always continue.

I myself am dedicated to this work, because I think Chuang Tzu's teaching is valuable, even if it is hard to understand. It is worth preserving for future generations.

In a word, whatever your achievement happens to be - social, political, artistic, or spiritual - do not turn it into a conquering force or use it to interfere with the lives of others. The problems of the world are created by a few people who are too enthusiastic and push their ideas on the world. This was the problem in Chuang Tzu's day as well. Let people appreciate the

value of your contribution and absorb the value of
your wisdom, but do not force it on them. True spiritual achievement cannot be externalized as dogma.
Once dogmatized, spiritual achievement becomes destructive.

In many places throughout Chuang Tzu's writing,
we see that he is against any religious or organized
social system that offers the security of an equal dis-
tribution of wealth as an allurement that disguises an
external suppressing force. Human problems arise from
spiritual underdevelopment. Religions are psychologi-
cally oriented. They do not support internal spiritual
growth, but rather pull people down and mold them to
a collective social value that wraps itself in the banner
of a conceptual God. True spiritual unfoldment and
development, therefore, shuns religious organizations as
if they were poison because they utilize force rather
than the promotion of individual internal growth.

I wish worldly leaders of all fields would not force
anyone to follow them, but strengthen themselves
instead and set good examples by the virtue of their
good lives, allowing people to develop their own appreciation, understanding and acceptance.

*Q: Master Ni, as an everyday person, how do you suggest I
put the good teaching of Chuang Tzu in practice?*

Master Ni: I cannot concretize or fossilize the teaching
of Chuang Tzu in a scholastic way. Chuang Tzu's
work is a living ocean. It has been continued by the
practitioners of the Zahn tradition. Please refer to my
work, *Enlightenment: Mother of Spiritual Independence*,
which is the teaching of Hui Neng, the sixth patriarch
of the Zahn tradition, and *The Way of Integral Life*,
which is my learning from the tradition of the integral
way. I combine these three works under one title:
The Wisdom of Three Masters.

As to your question of how to apply Chuang Tzu's
teaching in our everyday life as an ordinary or an
important person, the following are the most important
principles of the ancient great masters' teachings which

nurtured and enriched every one of us spiritually. I hope that they may produce some benefit in your life.

I
Six Grand Guidelines for Realizing Tao in your Life
These guidelines were derived from the source of spiritual development before Lao Tzu and Chuang Tzu, the great masters. They are valued as the fundamental guidance of the tradition of Tao. This is a summary of the last chapter.

To realize Tao: one does not indulge in luxury or waste useful materials. One adopts a strict spiritual self-discipline and does not discriminate between people, yet is forgiving toward the faults of others.

To realize Tao: one is involved in the mundane but does not make a proud display of material things. He or she seeks no more than is sufficient for one's own and related others' needs and functions without ulterior motives, and in this way, purifies the heart. A person of Tao desires peace in the world and long life for all. He or she works not to be indifferent to others or antagonistic toward the public.

To realize Tao is to be public-spirited yet not belong to any political party, to be even-minded and not succumb to favoritism; to be free from desire, having no rigid doctrine, to move spiritually without being bound to a given course, to take things as they come, choosing neither this nor that but going along with all things, have no remorse for the past and no anxiety for the future, and be on good terms with all people.

To realize Tao: one attains the learning of greatness by knowing the virtue of human life. A person of Tao helps others to reach natural, moral perfection. What is innate is spiritual nature and to follow one's innate nature is Tao. To cultivate Tao is the most important teaching.

To realize Tao: one regards the source as pure and
the things that emerge from it as coarse.   A person
looks upon accumulation of only material possessions
as a defect and dwells in utter calmness with godly
clarity.

To realize Tao: maintain your spirit-being as vast,
formless and unlimited, transforming at where life
cannot be defined as life, and death cannot be defined
definitely as death. Be with heaven and earth. Be
with gods. Elusively, where does it go? Evasively,
where does it stay? All things and all lives are encompassed by it, yet it shows no beginning and no ending
and no belonging. It is Tao.

In ancient times, these were believed to be the way
to realize Tao. By attaining these qualities, the principles of universal life were discovered by the ancient
developed ones.

II
Review of the Great Examples of Passing Tao

*Q: Master Ni, you have introduced different schools of
Taoist teachings appearing at the same time with Chuang
Tzu. Each of them, though, seems to respond to the worldly
situation from a different angle. I am still not sure about
exactly what should be followed. Would you go over them
once again so that we understand the importance of the
different sages for our own goal of spiritual realization?*

Master Ni: I would simply like to repeat the description of the teachings of the different ancient great
teachers from the previous chapter; they are the shortest summary of numerous teachings of these sages'
whole life of devotion and work. Unfortunately, most
of their own writings were lost. I think it is most
valuable to repeat these lines in order to replant the
spiritual seeds in the productive soil of the healthy
mind of the students of later generations.

This is a review of the active teachers of the previous chapter. In the original book of Chuang Tzu, the last chapter was written by a student or follower of Chuang Tzu who's name was not given. He introduced the different schools of teaching Tao that existed in his time. From his comments about each of the schools, it is apparent that he chose Chuang Tzu's teaching as the most essential teaching of Tao. Practically, in this tradition, all were accepted along with the teaching of Chuang Tzu; they were integrated into the whole through moderate practice. In other words, all useful teachings were continued. The whole of the teaching, therefore, is the integration of adopted, enriching elements of many teachers with different focuses. Therefore, these good teachings are presented to the students of Tao in all coming generations.

The book of Chuang Tzu is the work of several of his students or followers. From the original writing style, it is apparent that at least five of them worked on different chapters. There was only a small portion of Chuang Tzu's own writing; this fact has been recognized by many scholars of different generations. Chapter Twenty-Five to Chapter Thirty-Four of Part II were Chuang Tzu's own work; the rest of this big, invaluable book is the work of these uncredited students and their adoption of the work of other teachers of Tao. When it comes to my hand, I wash the face of the writing, a face covered with 2,000 years of dust.

The following section of repetition describes the teachings of other teachers are not my reproduction, but are simply a translation. After reviewing the following, I do not think that we, the people of modern times, have made any advancement in consciousness and morality. Those teachers were sincere and achieved, and the common people were broad and receptive. The teachers were not corrupt, and the people cared for their teachers. No teachers were persecuted. Thus, how can we be so proud as to not devotedly and humbly become the students of those great teachers and their great minds and hearts? They are still the light of the entirety of the human world.

Through these last 2,000 years, in the arena of the human world of spiritual undevelopment, the ambition of leaders of different generations brought personal glory for themselves but also turmoil and disaster to the world at the same time. King, Queen and Emperors were the title given to people of evil ambition and greed. What true good have those individuals brought to the world? The spiritual leaders of that time were none the better. In the East, spiritual teachers withdrew from society because they rejected the pressure of what they viewed as the disgusting worldly life. In the West, external religions became expanded in the play for dominance over people's beliefs. When external religion grows, people's internal spiritual growth suffocates and shrinks. Also, as we witness the creation of bigger and stronger governmental systems, they also further the intensification of competition and contention in international society. A higher concentration of power in government by the crazy leaders is sure to turn into higher central control played by a government; which would harm or make it harder to maintain the natural, organic lives of people. The more complicated a government becomes, the less effective it is. This erroneous game has been repeated again and again by the egotistic impulse of the leaders.

In such a world situation, can we still not share the understanding of the spiritual awakening from the attainment and realization of these few everlasting examples of true sages?

Let us not blindly worship the conventionally socially promoted images we really do not know anything about, but have habitually followed out of custom. Let us choose our own truthful examples for our life from those who did not take advantage of conventional worship to base their teaching upon. True sages are the ones who teach one's own awakening. The true students of sages are the ones who share the understanding of the awakening of those true sages. Let us recognize that the truly meritorious political leaders are those who express a good spiritual quality in their political leadership. They can truly bring about progress in the world. The example set by the true spiritual leaders are of a person who serves the world but does not attract people away from their own balanced lives.

Let us clearly recognize what is the correct spiritual work. Correct spiritual work shares the personal awakening derived from the inspiration and enlightenment of many masters and the entire spiritual realm. The correct spiritual work is not to erect a brute faith to fight another faith. Cannibals also have faith. Because they believe that eating human life is right, therefore they will do anything to get a human life to eat. How much difference is there between this and the faith of the modern popular religions which is associated with the worship of war and slaughter under any beautiful name? The teaching of Tao is the teaching of spiritual awakening; it does not promote arrogant faith. Faith can be opinionated; it is provocative, it can be the source of wars as exemplified by the conventional international society. Let us clearly know that faith is a function of mind, yet it is not the spiritual achievement. Let us have the understanding to not make personal faith as personal spiritual achievement. Also, let us be students of the great spiritual awakening of Tao and exercise our own faith with the growing understanding of our own. Let us not make any faith as our spiritual banner for war. A religious faith can be the disguise for arrogance or roughness of an individual or society.

A religious faith can be the excuse of lower mentality to reject other people of different faith; it expresses the inability to see other faiths and ideas while it remains fixed upon one thought. It obstructs a person from being able to reach different light or filter the different lights to refresh the life of its own spirits. A good, healthy mind is a mind related to one understanding that can still progress with inspiration from different sources.   A healthy, natural mind is a mind that defossilizes itself from its customary beliefs to reach for new light.   A healthy mind is a mind which can apply personal spiritual examination to itself and the material it reaches.   Therefore, people of spiritual achievement have reached spiritual broadmindedness and objectivity.   They put the simple integral truth above all limited spiritual attainment and the establishments of the world.   They are not assertive in whatever people call faith, which has only been a banner in the world for war games.   Numerous lives have been wasted under the leadership of those war banners of faith which made people into tools to be sacrificed for an ideology which, realistically speaking, only served the spiritual ego of the initiators.   What real benefit have the initiators' egos brought to the world?   Their creation brought more problems than benefit.   Yet, people still do not awaken from their own misguided thinking or faith.   Is it not the time for all people to wake up to see their own obstruction, to see their own spiritual barrier before the total wasteful destruction of the entire world is reached?   Many generations have been burdened down by so much mischief and unhealthy establishment from the spiritually undeveloped world.

After you have studied Chuang Tzu, I believe that your mind has been expanded and your spiritual vision has been purified.   By the enjoyment of your personal spiritual attainment, you can decide what stage of life you have reached.   You also should look at what is your new reached life expression and the spiritual standpoint in the world; it should not be the conventional spiritual undevelopment that you are going to continue, but it must be the attainment of the learning from the spiritual awakening of those great sages, when you have reached Heaven while most other people still cover their innocent vision by the false heaven of conventional religious mischief.

Now is the time to return to your original nature; it is your nature before you were dyed by the underdeveloped human culture.   Now you might have the unobstructable clear vision that enables you to see through the things that have pulled you back from making progress in your life. Now is the time to renew your life and spirit to reach out for the great path of one universal natural life. After we enjoy the exploration of the vastness and profundity of Chuang Tzu's spiritual reality, after we deepen our understanding of universal nature, we must return to the modern reality. When we shift our focus from our communication with the sages to the world and local news on television or in the papers, we come right up to the kind of world we live in. Thus, we must question what kind of spiritual attitude we need to hold in order to live in the world. For the importance in answering, I have endeavored to present this great teaching which comes from the source of the awakening Tao.

Now, I beg your tolerance for the repetition of those great examples of true spiritual awakening. I am not attempting to motivate you to combine your physical strength with mine to build a physical monument for them. My clear intention is the wish to preserve their teaching so that it is still available as the everlasting spring from which all of us may drink and receive nutrition and inspiration.

It is always worthy to remember them to enliven our spiritual vitality in carrying out our daily life and moral mission.

1. Let us learn the spirit of Mo Tzu and Jein Wah Li.

Two men of Tao, Mo Tzu and Jein Wah Li, his important disciple, took great joy in practicing Tao. They acted out of a motivation of boundless love and a great desire for the increased benefit of the world. They condemned their own personal warfare and disallowed their own anger. They had a fondness for learning and each had acquired great knowledge.

They expressed living a life that was all toil and no pleasure but still had universal love toward all fellow lives. Mo Tzu himself was capable of such strictness because his spiritual awareness was so deep, and he expected the rest of the world to have a better life.

Mo Tzu took the example of Yu in his teaching, "The Great Yu drained off the flood waters and brought the hundreds of rivers and thousands of streams to flow through the divisions of the empire. He himself went out, using bucket and shovel to organize the rivers, until there was no hair left on his legs. He worked through wind and rain, but through it all he accomplished the recovery and prosperity of the big undiscriminative society. Thus, he was a great sage; his work was performed for the good of the world."

The followers of his teaching, the Mohists, dressed themselves in skins and coarse cloth, wooden or straw sandals, as the great Yu did in his time, and they never rested day or night. They drove and exerted themselves constantly, saying, "If we do not follow the way of the Great Yu, we cannot call ourselves the students of Tao." Mo Tzu was also a great organizer. His followers were people of action. He could have been a king if he had liked, because he had five hundred of his students trained as an army among many. It was a most excellent army at that time, but only for the purpose of righteousness. It was used only in demonstration to persuade others to stop aggressive wars. The army was very well versed in defence and attack. It was not his purpose to establish another monarchy; he offered strict moral discipline and remained a good citizen.

His guidance of creative and diligent life in particular can be accepted as the correct guidance for all of human society. Many generations later, these practices are still very useful guidelines for a healthy life. Both the Great Yu and Mo Tzu were examples of devotion to worldwide humanistic virtue. We respect the spirit of hard work as our model, practicing a community spirit under the principle of balance.

2. Let us learn from the spirit of Sung Ben and I Wen.

Two men of Tao, Sung Ben and I Wen, active in the time of Spring and Autumn, took great joy in practicing Tao. They carried themselves with a manner of kindness and tolerance toward all things and called it "heartfelt giving." Their wish and purpose was to attract joy through cooperation and to bring the entire world into harmony with the principle of kindness and tolerance as their guide. They wished to end conflict, abolish aggression and arms, and save the world from war. These were the doctrines they circulated, expounded and taught throughout the world. When the world refused to listen, they would not give up; instead, they increased their efforts. Although the people were tired of listening to them, those in high positions as well as those in low, they did not stop. They took too much thought for others and too little for themselves.

"Five cups of grain will be enough for us to eat," they said, although with that small amount they did not eat fully. Their focus was on the world, never mind that their own lives were well-provided. They never asked those who learned from them to give everything to them as some imposters of later generations would do. They were determined and set their goal to seeing that all men could live. Their goal was high. Scorning material benefit for themselves, they did not judge others who pursued it.

They worked very diligently in the daytime and at night they did not wish to rest. They said, "we live to help." We are afraid to see how they can live and help with insufficient provisions. However, they were truly respectful and had great enthusiasm for saving the world. They taught that a person of development does not think it is of great importance how he is treated when he has a great goal that he is pursuing. He is not enslaved by his personal desires from making meticulous demands on his personal life.

Their external goals were to do away with aggression and the use of arms. Their internal goals were to lessen desire and decrease the effect of the emotions.

In all matters, great or small, they followed these principles.

I Wen Tzu and Sung Ben were people of great heart, but their way is hard to learn. If worldly leaders could learn only half of what they taught, the world would be a much more beautiful place. Thus, students of Tao should accept them in their lives.

3. Let us learn the spirit of Hsan Dau, his teacher and followers.

People of Tao like Hsan Dau, active in the period of Spring and Autumn, and his teacher and followers took joy in practicing Tao. They took the equality of all creation as a whole as their main theme, and they expressed it thus: "Heaven covers us, but cannot hold us up. Earth can hold us up, but cannot cover us. Tao embraces us, but we cannot make it clear. Thus all things are equal in incompleteness on some level." By viewing things so, they considered that all things in existence have a positive and negative aspect, therefore keeping one's mind selective is not always a solution. For example, if we think intellectual education can save the world, we must also realize there is something intellectual education will be unable to help; unfortunately, merely intellectual education can cause people to become more ambitious and aggressive. Hsan Dau, the teacher and followers thought that by following unified laws and regulations which were based on the natural universal subtle law, it would be possible to put the world in good order.

They also concluded that, "Preference shows partiality. Comparison causes deviation from the goal. When we follow the Great Path of Oneness, however, all is embraced." This is why they stopped accumulating incomplete intellectual knowledge, disregarded self-interest; followed the path that was before them with compliancy and steadfastness. This they believed was following Tao.

"To know is not to know," said Hsan Dau. So he despised fragmented knowledge and worked to be rid of it. He accepted no commitment; indifferent or casual, he did not admire the worthy men whom the world so greatly honors. He did nothing to establish himself. Without creating any struggle, he followed the natural flow of life and took a neutral position.

In this way, he was never guilty of any fault. He stayed where he was, not participating in plotting or scheming. He made no attempt to worship what is special, but following the principle of harmony, he moved when pushed, budged when pulled. Going round and round with things, he was free from blame. This was because a person without the narrow consciousness of self does not face the difficulty and entanglements of establishing oneself. Thus he does not incur blame or praise.

He and his followers therefore believed, "By being without the narrow knowledge of self, we find the way. One without the narrow knowledge of self has no need for salvation by someone else. He who has no preference never deviates from Tao."

This is the same as Dien Pien, who learned from Pong Mong. Their teacher also used to say, "People who attain Tao have reached the point where they regard nothing as either right nor wrong. They do not insist on what is right and what is wrong. They deny the direction of becoming opinionated. They recognized that conceptual disputes, like a gust of wind, leave no trace behind. Why is it worth emphasizing one's view?" They kept teaching people to be simple and give up personal narrow knowledge while being compliant with the universal law. The teaching of this group and Hsan Dau did contain some of the essence of the ancient, naturally inspired ones. Thus, we should accept the essence what he has to offer.

4. Let us learn the spirit of Confucius.

Confucius took great joy in practicing Tao and wished that each individual of the world could realize it. He traveled around to all the kingdoms, hoping to be put in an important post of government so that he might be able to realize his moral ideas as passed down by Yao and Shun. They were the Five Great Relationships: 1) the relationship between the ruler and the people, 2) the relationship between parents and their sons and daughters, 3) the relationship between brothers and sisters, 4) the relationship between a husband and wife, and 5) the relationship between friends. Shun set up the guidelines: one must be loyal to one's king in a broad sense (one's job or boss), dutiful to one's parents, helpful to one's brothers and sisters, close and loving to one's spouse, and faithful to one's friend. These are correct and natural.

The guidelines must be practiced considering the situation, otherwise it is the fault of the people who practice them rigidly. He taught that if something is not right, don't say it. If it is not right, don't listen to it. If it is not right, don't look at it, and if it is not right, do not have contact with it. This is a grand self-discipline in building a good, upright personality. The first important thing is obtaining the knowledge of what is right. In Tao, what is natural and beneficial is right. What is artificial and harmful is wrong.

He taught that one's loyal heart can be applied to one's duty. He taught that one should be considerate to others. Confucius' famous saying was, "Do not do to others what you would not like them to do to you." However, we can see that the control point of Confucius' teaching is the application of moral discipline to a society. Only when it is one's personal awareness that brings one to practice this kind of moral discipline, is it a true expression of one's personality.

Let all sages work together for the future generations which would enjoy securing the true value of the ancient teaching.

It is not a question of whether ancient sages had enough openness; the problem is that the people of modern generations are not open enough to receive the light of the great attainments which came from the actual experience of the sages in solving social and individual difficulties.

5. Let us learn the spirit of Lao Tzu and Kuan Yien.

The respectful Lao Tzu and Kuan Yien took great joy in practicing Tao. They became enthusiastic followers of Tao. They spoke in terms of constancy and unity. Their teaching was of gentleness and humility, empty mindedness and non-injury to others.

Kuan Yien said, "When one does not take a personal point of view, then things will, of themselves, be revealed. Their movement is like water; their stillness is like a mirror that reflects their true likeness. His responses are like those of an echo that dies away into quietude once the sound has gone. He lets all things disappear by themselves. He keeps nothing in his mind. His heart is pure and quiet and harbors no personal desires. He becomes one among all others and follows the flow of universal nature. It can be lost when he allows his mind to be caught up with something. He does not place himself above others, but cheerfully brings up the rear.

"What is shared with others is harmony. What is obtained from them is a loss. When one is one with anyone or anything, he achieves harmony. When he reaches for something or someone, he loses it."

Lao Tzu said, "He who is conscious of being strong but is content to be weak is like a ravine into which the world can flow. He who is conscious of purity yet can bear disgrace is like a valley in which the world can rest. When others strive to be first, he is content with the lowest place. Contenting himself with the unsubstantial while others strive for the substantial, he stores nothing up and therefore has abundance without effort. His mind is without cunning and he laughs at those who scheme against others.

"To have tolerance and sympathy towards others, without causing others pain is the mark of perfection."

Others seek good fortune, but Lao Tzu alone kept himself whole by being elastic. He said, "Let us try to avoid causing any damage." He regarded the profundity of the subtle path as the root of his life and simplicity as his teacher.

Lao Tzu is a teacher of universal life. He himself is one with universal life. Kuan Yien and Chuang Tzu join with this great being of eternal truth, to be the learners who identify themselves with universal life as the great master does himself.

These are two who had truly attained Tao.

6. Let us learn the spirit of Chuang Tzu.

Chuang Tzu took joy in practicing Tao and became an enthusiastic follower of Tao.   Without holding to any particular school, he used bold words and expressive phrases to give life to his thoughts.

He believed that Tao is crystal clear as the truth of all, but that people's vision is blocked.   They are unable to see it and also do not easily understand it, though it is so lucid all the time and in all places. Also, since the world had become confused and twisted, one could not speak to it directly.   This is why he spoke in parables, quoted the ancient developed ones and used his imagination while writing.   Yet, he maintains himself in accordance with nature, and honors the forms of creation.   By not judging his fellows, he lived harmoniously with his time.   Though his writing is most unusual, it is not harmful to others; it shows ingenuity.   A great thinker, he fills his work with the truths of life.

He soars above in the heavens and makes friends with those on earth who deny life and death, existence and non-existence.   Yet he responds to the changes and exigencies of his day.   His work is ever useful.   He is mysterious and ingenious, but boundless.   He is the teacher all of us follow.

Q: The lives of the above mentioned Great Ones are truly marvelous examples of worthy human lives. However, in my own case, I know that I could never do those great things in my life. The situation is so different and I am not a highly talented person, but just an ordinary working person. After reading about the Great Ones, I am disillusioned. Do you think I still have a chance of making any spiritual progress?

Master Ni: What I try to show people by giving them the examples of the Great Ones is not that everybody has to be just like them.   There are different goals for different individuals.   These great models are for people who were born with leader energy and those who were leaders in other life experiences.   Because of their grand spiritual quality, they do not need to hide somewhere to do their individual self-cultivation, but through personal moral realization, render service with great moral leadership.   With their selfless achievement, they do not need to turn their heads back, for their souls are already much ahead of their consciousness of bodily life.   This means that they do not need to cultivate themselves, for they are already achieved.

In the tradition of Tao, we honor people's differences; what we promote is that each one bring forth his or her own talents and make a positive contribution to the world.   On a different level, one does not have to be as illustrious as the Great Yu or as perfect as Hsan Dau.   What is important is to hold them as your ideals as you put forth your best, most positive effort in your own life, in whatever situations you find before you.   If you are a cook, see how you can make each meal just a little better.   If you are a carpenter, see how you can best serve others with your work.   If you are a father, see what you can do to improve your fathering.   If you are a cashier, see if you can keep your thoughts positive even if you are having a day filled with difficult customers.

Making spiritual progress is, at best, done slowly. It is not something that can happen overnight.   The Great Ones that you read about in the books took their entire lifetimes to become what they were; you should not expect that it will be any different for you in your search for refinement.   It is something that is accomplished a little at a time, and the accumulation of 'littles' turns out to be something great.

Today, perhaps our task in becoming achieved is a little more difficult than back then.   The world is certainly more complicated and there is much, much more unnaturalness, in addition to there being many more people. However, the principles that the Great Ones followed are still the same. In all the books I have written, I say the same things, but in many different ways, to be sure that all of you can hear it in your own way. Apply yourself positively to your work and in your life; avoid hurting other people through conflict or aggression; control your impulses and do the spiritual practices. This is as great a human achievement as many of the external things that have been accomplished by others!

There was a young man I am acquainted with, and when he was 16 years old, having had more study than most other children his age, he was an ambitious young man. He was born into a family with a deep spiritual background, so his father and mother let him freely exercise his interests in any areas and develop himself. He was very interested in spiritual subjects and thought he could receive enlightenment overnight. Because he had read many stories of people who had become enlightened and learned about what they did and the things they said, he copied them in his actions and speech.

Generally, when you live with a family, you have certain duties like watering the garden, sweeping the floors, etc. But because he believed himself to be a highly enlightened person, he thought that he should not do those things. He was not interested in doing trivial things, because he was achieved, so instead, everyday he put more time into those things that he believed fit for his level. He rejected those things that he believed were too low for him. His family usually ate their meals together with everybody at the table, but because he had become such a VIP, he began meditating at mealtime and did not show up to eat until the food was cold. His mother was not happy with him, especially when he repeated this VIP attitude and behavior over time. His thoughts were full of being a spiritually achieved person, so he talked about high subjects. He made his friends become his students and had them sit in a group and listen to him. He read the sacred books. He believed those things were what would express his special enlightened energy. But his behavior was exactly the opposite of that level! One day, his mother became really mad about his not taking care of his duties and talking so loftily. One day she scolded him. She said, "You think that you are enlightened because you keep reading sacred books and keep talking about spiritual loftiness. Do you think that doing that is Tao? You know, before I gave birth to you, I was also a spiritual student. I also thought I was achieved, but finally, I gave that up and went to live a different way of life. I became the wife of your father, gave birth to you, your sisters and your brothers. I took ten months to conceive each of you, to nurse you and raise you. Do you remember? I changed your diapers; don't you think that is Tao? I feed you; don't you think that is Tao? I wash you, don't you think that is Tao? Every day, I do the family chores from the morning to the evening time. No minute do I rest; I always do things. From your head to your feet, everything you wear is made by my hand; because I think it is Tao, I do it. If I don't think it is Tao, I do not do it. One who is falsely enlightened only reads sacred books, and sits there and gives lofty talks. But true enlightenment will recognize that everything, whether big or small, needs to be done it earnestly. Put your best quality into it, put your sweetness into it, put your kindness into it. This is what I call Tao. Do you understand now what is Tao?"

This was his mother's gift. As spiritual students, we sometimes overemphasize reading, studying and sitting in meditation; this is only one aspect of many. All learners should not neglect the value of their daily life as a true cultivation. It is not when people live in a monastery or a nunnery; that is not enlightenment. I hope that this information from my personal experience can be helpful to you.

III
A Simple Summary of the Invaluable Teaching
Which Guides Our Life like Permanent Friendly Advice

1. Have trust in the constancy of the natural cyclic movement. In good times, do not be too excited, but foresee the downward slope; in bad times, do not be dismayed, because it will turn around. Nothing is stuck forever. (From Lao Tzu and Chuang Tzu)

2. Attain the knowledge of the subtle law, which can be quietly observed: any trouble has its precondition. Thus, do not build the conditions for trouble, but quietly live with the subtle law. (From Lao Tzu and Chuang Tzu)

3. Unite oneself with the impersonal Heaven, disassociate from the conceptual trap of undeveloped religion. Extend universal love and life without obstruction by personal, racial or cultural background. (From Lao Tzu, Mo Tzu, and Chuang Tzu)

4. Be kind and just to all. (From Lao Tzu, Confucius, Mo Tzu and Chuang Tzu)

5. Promote what is beneficial to the world and do away with what is harmful to the world. This is the goal of a leader and teacher and person of influence. (From Mo Tzu)

6. Do what is beneficial to the world and do not do what is harmful to the world, on the basis of an individual. (From Chuang Tzu)

7. Decrease the burden of the mind. Increase the unity of the body, mind and spirit. (From Lao Tzu)

8. Keep your body and mind moving and your spirit quiet. (From Lao Tzu)

9. Strengthen your physical body, weaken your detrimental ambition. (From Lao Tzu)

10. Be non-impulsive. (From Lao Tzu)

11. Be practical and matter-of-fact, do not be fancy or crazy. (From Lao Tzu)

12. Concentrate on the essential. (From Lao Tzu)

13. Concentrate on the foundation. (From Lao Tzu and Confucius)

14. Apply the golden mean to all levels of life, which means never go to the extreme in anything. (From Lao Tzu and Confucius)

15. Be natural and accept what is natural; do not be artificial and accept what is artificially developed from the natural. (From Chuang Tzu)

16. Be egoless. (From Chuang Tzu)

17. Be objective. (From Chuang Tzu)

18. Do not be argumentative, but look for harmony. (From Chuang Tzu)

19. Do not be judgmental in speech, keep your discernment in the quiet of your mind. (From Chuang Tzu)

20. Look at the balance point between spiritual selflessness and self-responsibility in all aspects of your life. (From the I Ching)

21. Practice moderation in life, such as in food and sex.

BOOKS ON THE INTEGRAL WAY BY THE NI FAMILY

 **Love of Mother Universe**—Imagine a life without artificial goodness, without fear and without social divisions. This work lays the foundation for a global society that honors the natural rhythms, subtle laws and sacred unity of the Mother Universe. It is from this universal perspective that you can make a real and lasting contribution to humanity.

#BLOVE—304 pages, softcover. $19.95

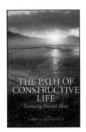 **The Path of Constructive Life: Embracing Heaven's Heart**—Unveils the new vehicle of the Integral Way known as The Path of Constructive Life. It gives fresh direction and effective self-practices to achieve sexual harmony, emotional well-being, protection from harmful influences and a universal soul.

#BHEART—315 pages, softcover. $19.95

 **The Power of the Feminine: Using Feminine Energy to Heal the World's Spiritual Problems**—The feminine approach is the true foundation of human civilization and spiritual growth. When positive feminine virtues are usurped in favor of masculine strength, aggression results. This book touches on how and why this imbalance occurs and encourages women to apply their gentle feminine virtue.

#BFEM—270 pages, softcover. $16.95

 **The New Universal Morality: How to Find God in Modern Times**—An in-depth look at living in accord with universal virtue. Authors Hua-Ching Ni and Maoshing Ni, Ph.D. reveal a natural religion in which universal morality is the essence, the true God that supports our lives and all existence. Included is a discussion on the process of becoming a spiritual coach to serve both our community and ourselves.

#BMOR—280 pages, softcover. $16.95

To order: 800-578-9526 🌿 www.taostar.com:

Second Spring: Dr. Mao's Hundreds of Natural Secrets For Women to Revitalize and Rejunvenate at Any Age —This tip-filled guide for women shows how to enhance energy, sexuality and health, especially during the second half of life. Dr. Maoshing Ni invites women to fulfill their innate potential and be at their most vital, energetic and attractive.

#BSPR—264 pages, softcover. $17.95

The Complete Works of Lao Tzu—The *Tao Teh Ching* is one of the most widely translated and cherished works of literature. Its timeless wisdom provides a bridge to the subtle spiritual truth and assists you to live harmoniously and peacefully. Also included is the *Hua Hu Ching*, a later work by Lao Tzu which has been lost to the general public for a thousand years.

#BCOMP—212 pages, softcover. $13.95

Tao, the Subtle Universal Law—Most people are unaware that their thoughts and behavior evoke responses from the invisible net of universal energy. To lead a good stable life is to be aware of the universal subtle law in every moment of our lives. This book presents practical methods that have been successfully used for centuries to accomplish this.

#BTAOS—208 pages, softcover. $16.95

I Ching, The Book of Changes and the Unchanging Truth—This legendary classic is recognized as the first written book of wisdom. Leaders and sages throughout history have consulted it as a trusted advisor, which reveals the appropriate action in any circumstance. Includes over 200 pages of background material on natural energy cycles, instruction and commentaries.

#BBOOK—669 pages, hardcover. $35.00

Attune Your Body with Dao-In—The ancients discovered that Dao-In exercises solved problems of stagnant energy, increased their health and lengthened their years. The exercises are also used as practical support for cultivation and higher achievements of spiritual immortality.

#BDAOI—144 pages, softcover. $16.95
Also on VHS & DVD. $24.95

Secrets of Longevity: Hundreds of Ways To Live To Be 100— Looking to live a longer, happier, healthier life? Try eating more blueberries, telling the truth, and saying no to undue burdens. Dr. Maoshing Ni brings together simple and unusual ways to live longer.

#BLON—320 pages, softcover. $14.95

Published by Chronicle Books

Secrets of Self-Healing—This landmark book on natural healing combines the wisdom of thousands of years of Eastern tradition with the best of modern medicine. Learn to treat common ailments with foods and herbs, and balance your mind and body to create vitality, wellness, and longevity.

#BSHEAL—576 pages. $24.95

Published by Penguin Group

Dr. Mao's Harmony Tai Chi: Simple Practice for Health and Well-Being—This book focuses on awakening the spirit while strengthening the body. Ideal for both beginners and those looking to deepen their spiritual understanding of t'ai chi practice. Dr. Mao skillfully and clearly outlines the eighteen foundational movements.

#BTAI—124 pages. $19.95 / Published by Chronicle Books

Chinese Herbology Made Easy—This text provides an overview of Oriental Medical theory, in-depth descriptions of each herb category, over 300 black and white photographs, extensive tables of individual herbs for easy reference and an index of pharmaceutical names.

#BHERB—202 pages, softcover. $18.95

The Tao of Fertility: A Healing Chinese Medicine Program to Prepare Body, Mind, and Spirit for New Life—Dr. Daoshing Ni, an esteemed doctor who has helped countless women achieve their dream of having a child, offers his program for enhancing fertility through Traditional Chinese Medicine (TCM) and Taoist principles.

#BFERT—304 pages, softcover. $15.95 / Published by Collins

101 Vegetarian Delights—by Lily Chuang and Cathy McNease. From exotic flavorful feast to nutritious everyday meal, enjoy preparing these easy-to-make recipes. Based on the ancient Chinese tradition of balance and harmony, these dishes were created for the new or seasoned vegetarian. The desserts are truly delightful, and healthy as well.

#B101—176 pages, softcover. $15.95

Power of Natural Healing—Hua-Ching Ni discusses the natural capability of self-healing and presents methods of cultivation–practices that can assist any treatment method– which promote a healthy life, longevity, and spiritual achievement. There is a natural healing process inherent in the very nature of life itself. One's own spirit is the source of health.

#BHEAL—143 pages, softcover. $14.95

The Uncharted Voyage Toward the Subtle Light—This book provides a profound understanding and insight into the underlying heart of all paths of spiritual growth, the subtle origin, and the eternal truth of one universal life. Readers will enter a voyage of discovery, finding a fresh new light toward which to direct their life energy.

#BVOY—424 pages, softcover. $19.95

The Key to Good Fortune: Refining Your Spirit (Revised)—"Straighten your Way" (*Tai Shan Kan Yin Pien*) and "The Silent Way of Blessing" (*Yin Chi Wen*) are the main guidance for a mature, healthy life. Spiritual improvement can be an integral part of realizing a Heavenly life on earth.

#BKEY—153 pages, softcover. $17.95

8,000 Years of Wisdom, Volume I and II—This two-volume set contains a wealth of practical, down-to-earth advice given by Hua-Ching Ni. Drawing on his training in Traditional Chinese Medicine, herbology and acupuncture, Hua-Ching Ni gives candid answers to questions on many topics.
#BWIS1—Vol. I: (Revised edition)
                 Includes dietary guidance. $18.50
#BWIS2—Vol. II: Sex and pregnancy guidance. $18.50

Resources

College of Tao & Integral Health
Distance Learning Courses

Spiritual Self-Development: The Integral Way of Life
Internet study
info@taostudies.com
www.taostar.com

People who have read one or more books on the Integral Way of Life will find support in this study program. Having deepened their understanding and experience of the Way, students will learn how to live a constructive path of life.

Traditional Chinese Medicine Concepts of Chinese Nutrition
Includes DVD and course materials
CEU credit available
800-772-0222
taostar@taostar.com

Achieve a basic understanding of Chinese nutrition theories and its practical applications. In four illustrated manuals, topics covered are food energetics, Zang-Fu syndromes, diagnosis and nutrition counseling, food choices for specific illnesses, and patient education. Please contact us for a brochure.

Traditional Chinese Medicine (TCM) Studies
Includes CD, classroom notes, and all course materials
800-772-0222
taostar@taostar.com
www.collegeoftao.org

Listen to actual classroom lectures by exceptional teachers while having classroom notes for your home study. May include reading and journal assignments, charts, textbooks, or raw herbs. Courses include:

Chinese Herbology
Traditional Chinese Medicine Theory: I, II, III
Chinese Acupuncture Points
Becoming a TCM Healer
The Power of Natural Healing

Please contact us for updates and a brochure.

Yo San University of Traditional Chinese Medicine

13315 W. Washington Boulevard, 2nd floor
Los Angeles, CA 90066
877-967-2648; 310-577-3000
www.yosan.edu

One of the finest and most academically rigorous Traditional Chinese Medical schools in the United States, Yo San University offers a fully accredited Master's degree program in acupuncture, herbology, *tui na* body work, and *chi* movement arts. In this program, students explore their spiritual growth as an integral part of learning the healing arts.

Tao of Wellness, Inc.

1131 Wilshire Boulevard, Suite 300
Santa Monica, CA 90401
310-917-2200
www.taoofwellness.com

The Tao of Wellness center for Traditional Chinese Medicine is the integral way to total well-being and a long life. Each patient is seen as an individual whose health is immediately affected by his or her lifestyle including diet, habits, emotions, attitude, and environment. The center, co-founded by Drs. Daoshing and Maoshing Ni, focuses on acupuncture and Chinese herbs for complete health, longevity, and fertility.

Tao of Wellness Herbs and Books

13315 W. Washington Boulevard, Suite 200
Los Angeles, CA 90066
800-772-0222; 310-302-1207
www.taostar.com
taostar@taostar.com

The 38th-generation Ni family healing tradition brings us nourishing Chinese herbal products, books on Taoist teachings that nurture the spirit, and tools for positive living. Tai chi and chi gong are taught on DVD, and guided meditations for stress, healing a broken heart, and pain management are available on CD. Contact us for further information.

Chi Health Institute
PO Box 2035
Santa Monica, California 90406-2035
www.taostar.com

The Chi Health Institute (CHI) offers professional education and certification in the Ni family *chi* movement arts including *tai chi*, *chi gong*, and Taoist meditation.

Integral Way Society
PO Box 1530
Santa Monica, CA 90406-1530
www.taostar.com

Learn about natural spiritual teachings as transmitted by the Ni family through books, mentoring, and retreats organized by the mentors of the Integral Way. The IWS assists people in achieving physical, mental, spiritual, moral and financial health by nurturing self-respect and by offering methods of self-improvement based on the principles in the classic works of the *I Ching* and Lao Tzu's *Tao Teh Ching*.

InfiniChi Institute International
PO Box 26712
San Jose, CA 95159-6712
408-295-5911
www.taostar.com

Professional training in *chi* healing leads to certification as an InfiniChi practitioner. The program is designed to develop your energetic healing abilities utilizing the Ni family books and texts that relate to Traditional Chinese Medicine, *chi gong*, Chinese bodywork, and natural spirituality. It features a progressive, systematic program that nurtures understanding, facilitates skill development, and promotes self-growth.

Acupuncture.com
www.acupuncture.com

Acupuncture.com is the gateway to Chinese medicine, health, and wellness. From this site you can purchase Tao of Wellness herbal products, choose from a large selection of traditional formulas, and buy acupuncture books and related products.

INDEX